HAYNES **EXTREME** Ford

escort

The definitive guide to **modifying**

by **Bob Jex** and **Em Willmott**

AMPS
R.P.M.

HAYNES **EXTREME** Ford

escort

The definitive guide to **modifying**

by **Bob Jex** and **Em Willmott**

Haynes Publishing

© Haynes Publishing 2007

All rights reserved. No part of this book may be reproduced or transmitted in any form or by any means, electronic or mechanical, including photocopying, recording or by any information storage or retrieval system, without permission in writing from the copyright holder.

ISBN 978 1 84425 628 0

Printed by **J H Haynes & Co Ltd,**
Sparkford, Yeovil, Somerset BA22 7JJ, England.

First published 2003
Reprinted 2004
Reprinted 2007

Tel: 01963 442030 Fax: 01963 440001
Int. tel: +44 1963 442030 Fax: +44 1963 440001
E-mail: sales@haynes.co.uk
Web site: www.haynes.co.uk

Haynes North America, Inc
861 Lawrence Drive, Newbury Park, California 91320, USA

Haynes Publishing Nordiska AB
Box 1504, 751 45 UPPSALA, Sweden

(4055 - 1AL2)

It wasn't my idea guv'nor!

1 Advice on safety procedures and precautions is contained throughout this manual, and more specifically on page 210. You are strongly recommended to note these comments, and to pay close attention to any instructions that may be given by the parts supplier.

2 J H Haynes recommends that vehicle customisation should only be undertaken by individuals with experience of vehicle mechanics; if you are unsure as to how to go about the customisation, advice should be sought from a competent and experienced individual. Any queries regarding customisation should be addressed to the product manufacturer concerned, and not to J H Haynes, nor the vehicle manufacturer.

3 The instructions in this manual are followed at the risk of the reader who remains fully and solely responsible for the safety, roadworthiness and legality of his/her vehicle. Thus J H Haynes are giving only non-specific advice in this respect.

4 When modifying a car it is important to bear in mind the legal responsibilities placed on the owners, driver and modifiers of cars, including, but not limited to, the Road Traffic Act 1988. IN PARTICULAR, IT IS AN OFFENCE TO DRIVE ON A PUBLIC ROAD A VEHICLE WHICH IS NOT INSURED OR WHICH DOES NOT COMPLY WITH THE CONSTRUCTION AND USE REGULATIONS, OR WHICH IS DANGEROUS AND MAY CAUSE INJURY TO ANY PERSON, OR WHICH DOES NOT HOLD A CURRENT MOT CERTIFICATE OR DISPLAY A VALID TAX DISC.

5 The safety of any alteration and its compliance with construction and use regulations should be checked before a modified vehicle is sold as it may be an offence to sell a vehicle which is not roadworthy.

6 Any advice provided is correct to the best of our knowledge at the time of publication, but the reader should pay particular attention to any changes of specification to the vehicles, or parts, which can occur without notice.

7 Alterations to vehicles should be disclosed to insurers and licensing authorities, and legal advice taken from the police, vehicle testing centres, or appropriate regulatory bodies.

8 The vehicle has been chosen for this project as it is one of those most widely customised by its owners, and readers should not assume that the vehicle manufacturers have given their approval to the modifications.

9 Neither J H Haynes nor the manufacturers give any warranty as to the safety of a vehicle after alterations, such as those contained in this book, have been made. J H Haynes will not accept liability for any economic loss, damage to property or death and personal injury arising from use of this manual other than in respect of injury or death resulting directly from J H Haynes' negligence.

Contents

Haynes Extreme

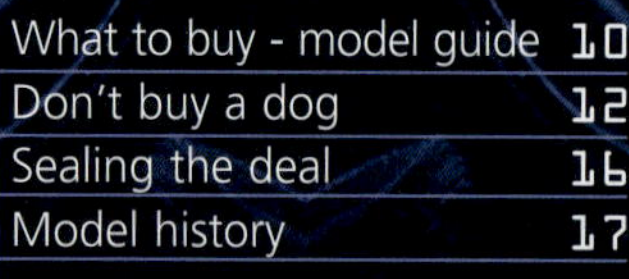

Buyer's guide

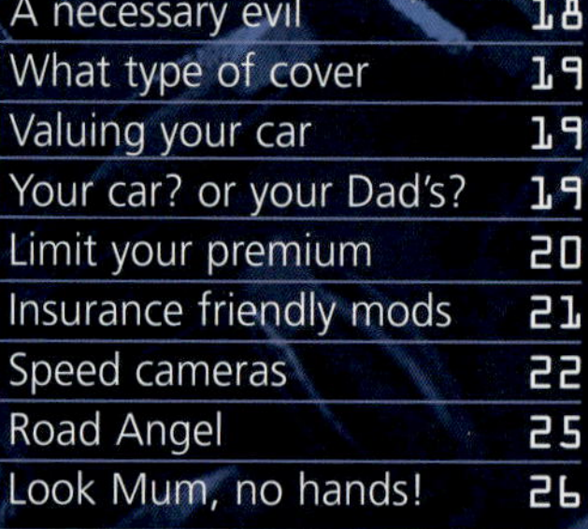

Insurance & The Law

Suspension

Brakes

Interiors

Security

04

Body styling

05

Lights & bulbs

06

Wheels & tyres

07

11

ICE

12

Engines

13

Exhausts

14

Reference

Haynes Extreme

What's that then?

Haynes Publishing have, for the last forty years, been helping people keep their cars on the roads in countries all over the world by publishing maintenance manuals. Chances are you've either got one of them yourself or you know somebody who has.

"Lights & bulbs" includes fitting high-power blue headlight bulbs, coloured rear light clusters, etc.

Before

After

Remember what it feels like on your birthday, or at Christmas, when you're faced by a pile of pressies? So do we, that gnawing feeling in your gut, what's in them? What did I get? Take that feeling and multiply it by twelve, that's how we felt when we started this project. When we decided that it was time to try something new, we couldn't wait. Because the same theories apply to modifying your car as servicing it, we reckoned we'd better get on and do it ourselves. We don't pay other people to do it for us, and we get the same dodgy instructions with kit as everybody else.

So if you've ever wondered how to fit a universal door mirror properly, smooth a tailgate or just bolt a seat in, this book is for you.

We've picked up a skip full of tips along the way, and they're all here for you to use. We haven't tried to set any trends, but we've covered every possible process we think you'll need. So where we've tinted a front door window, the same rules apply to a rear one, job done.

If you look in the magazines and want some of that, join us, 'cos so do we, and we'll show you how to get it.

Keeping it real

Modifying a car is not without its problems in the 'real world', as opposed to the seemingly fantasy world of the glossy mags. For instance, it's pretty silly to spend hours fitting illegal window tints or smoked lights if you get pulled the first time you're out afterwards. Of course, you can get pulled for all sorts of reasons (and just driving a modified car is reason enough sometimes), but keeping the car actually legal is one of the 'hidden' challenges with modifying. Throughout the book, our tips should give all the help you need to at least appear to be on the right side of the law. The annual MOT test is another favourite time for your mods to get panned, and again, we aim to give you all the help necessary to ensure at least that what you've changed doesn't lead to a fail.

Security is another major issue with a tweaked motor, and the perils of insurance cannot be taken lightly, either. We aim to give down-to-earth advice to help you keep the car in the first place, and to help you in not upsetting your insurers too much if the worst happens.

A word about fashion

In producing this book, we're aware that fashions change. What we show being fitted to our car might well be hideously out of date in 6 months time, or might not be your thing in the first place! Also, some of the stuff we've acquired from our various suppliers may no longer be available by the time you read this. We hope that, despite this, our approach of showing you step-by-step how to fit the various parts will mean that, even if the parts change slightly, the procedures we show for fitting will still be valid.

Our main project car was a 1.8 XR3i (105 bhp), 1993 L reg, with some additional work being carried out on other Escorts.

"Wheels & tyres" takes a detailed look at all the options.

"Body styling" shows you how to fit universal mirrors to full body kits.

"Interiors" includes seats, painting trim, gear knobs and loads more.

Escort - dynamite from Dagenham?

It's been dubbed "Britain's favourite". It stayed in production for more than 30 years. It sold over 5 million. It's a household name. Nearly everyone's either owned one, or at least been in one. What are we talking about? The Ford Escort.

Anyone who knows anything about cars has an opinion on the Escort, and it's often not too pleasant. We've all heard the 'Dagenham Dustbin' gags (though the Escort was actually built at the Halewood plant), but the Escort's British through and through, and as good n' honest as fish n' chips. We love it.

The Escort Mk 5 went through a tough time when it was first launched, late in 1990. The Mk 4 that came before it, though pretty outdated by then, was still selling well, and much was expected from the new model. Frankly, it didn't deliver at first, and all sections of the motoring press (even the Sundays) gave it a right slagging. Ford had been caught napping - despite spending vast sums on developing the new Escort, it felt like a cheap makeover of the old car, and with the quality of the soon-to-come opposition, it wasn't good enough. The styling was unadventurous, the seats were cheap, the steering heavy, and the

handling was actually worse than the Mk 4. The new Zetec 16-valve engines were late, so the range kicked off with the old HCS and CVH lumps seen before. Not good.

Ford soon set about putting things right, and within a year, the car was greatly improved. The first of the free-revving 16-valve Zetec motors landed early in 1992, then the range received a huge image boost from the Cosworth's introduction in June. When the facelifted Mk 6 arrived in late 1992, most people felt this was the car the Escort should've been all along - we modifiers reserve judgement on the huge oval grille and equally-massive rear light treatment... The long-awaited XR3i made a welcome comeback, even if it wasn't quite as hard-core as before - at least the RS2000 lived up to its name.

By the time the Mk 7 Escort came along in 1995, Ford had already produced the excellent-handling Mondeo, and they'd learned plenty about how to make their cars ride and handle better. The press loved the Escort's new rear suspension and fresher styling - this was as good as it would get.

Why is the Escort popular with modders? It wasn't called our favourite car for nothing - they sold millions of 'em, so there's plenty to choose from. They're cheap to buy and insure, easy to work on, and there's loads of other Ford bits you can bolt on, straight from the scrapyard, to make things better than standard. Escorts at least have more room for ICE than midgets like the Saxo. There's the Cossie look to aspire to, besides an increasing number of more radical Jap and Euro-look designs. The modifying world seems at last to be waking up to the Escort. Well, it only took 30 years.

02

Buyer's guide

What to buy

With so many different models available, which one would you buy? Here at Haynes we've compiled our own list of models that we believe are the bee's knees, as well as those that aren't!! So sit back, open your beer and read on... we've done all the hard work for you - think of it as our Escort service...

Okay - first, say no to diesels, 5-doors and automatics - not cool (though at least there's some hope for a high-spec 5-door with a decent engine). If you can choose, select a 3-door, even if this might limit your choice of engine. The 3-door Escorts only sold in any great numbers with the smallest, least-Max-friendly engine - the gorgeous 1.3 litre pushrod, known as the HCS or Endura (or 'the rattler' by those in the know). Better to try for a 1.4 CVH, if you can find a 3-door one. Otherwise, the 3-doors were all pretty sporty - XR3is and RSs - which is fine if you can afford Group 15 insurance.

Now we've mentioned insurance, it's a good idea to budget your money and get some insurance quotes done so you know exactly what you can afford. All post-1993 models had Safeguard key immobilisers, which helps. Otherwise, you're going to be stuck with a small engine if you want a sensible premium - but there are exceptions, as we'll see later.

Choosing an Escort is made harder by the fact they came in three facelifts, and each has a major impact on how your finished modded motor will look. The facelifts are so different, some mods aren't available for certain years. The first Escorts (1990 to 1992) were known as the Mark 5s - these are the easiest to 'Cosworth', but avoid the early 90/91 models with orange indicators, as they really were awful. Most common are the Mk 6 models, from 1992 to 1995, with the big oval-mouth grille, and the huge rear lights that extend into the tailgate (unfortunately, this is also the time when 'cats' became standard). The best Escorts in many ways were the Mk 7s, from 1995 to 2000, with the thin, wide grille and roundy headlights (but they can be less easy to work on, and to modify).

Ford are well known for their excessive use of 'limited edition' models - only buy a limited edition when the extras are useful (electric windows, sunroofs etc). There's little point in paying extra for a Ghia for the sports/luxury seats, if you're going to change them to buckets - d'oh! Base models make a good basis for stripping out the dull interior and smartening it to your own taste for the total custom-made look! Power assisted steering (PAS) became standard on most of Escort range in 1994. Always try and buy a car with PAS, or else the combination of phat rims and small trendy steering wheels will have you breaking out into a sweat! Oh, and unless you're a hairdresser, don't buy the Cabriolet versions - they're not very sexy, and you pay stupidly-high insurance costs.

We've chosen the Haynes best-buys from the hundreds of Escort models that Ford made - all these are at least available as 3-doors, and we've listed them in order of engine size.

1.3 litre

1991/2 - 1.3 LX & Quartz. Grp 5 ins, electric windows, tints.

1.4 litre

1993/4 - Duet, Chicane and Mistral limited editions. Grp 5 ins, electric windows, tints, metallic.

1995 - Multi-point injection , boosting power, but ins unchanged.

1.6 litre

1991 - Mk 5 1.6 Si. CVH engine. Electric windows/mirrors, central locking, RS bodykit. Grp 8 ins.

1994 on - Mk 6/7 1.6 Si. Now with 1.6 16-valve Zetec, still Grp 8.

1994/5 - Mexico, Mistral and Chicane limited editions. Sports trim, white dials, Zetec engine, Grp 7 ins.

1.8 litre

1992 - 1.8 LX. 105 bhp 16v Zetec, tints, electric windows. Grp 10 ins.

1994 - 1.8 Si. Slightly sportier 1.8 LX, still Grp 10.

1995 - Mk 7 1.8 Si. Now 115 bhp, but drops to Grp 8 ins!

Money no object

So, what if insurance isn't a problem, and you want an Escort with more than just a bit of oomph? These last few Escorts are the daddies of the entire range...

The new XR3i, one of Ford's longest-awaited cars ever (apart from the new Focus RS!) graced us in 1992. Ford gave us two possible options to choose from - the 105 bhp car (our chosen project vehicle), and a 130 bhp version, which had rear disc brakes. Both ended up in Group 15 for insurance, which seems a bit unfair, but it's obviously all in that XR name tag. There's quite a few mint ones around today, as well as plenty that've been ragged to death. Apart from the extra go, the excellent front seats almost justify the extra expense on their own.

The 1.8 GTI, launched in 1997, replaced the XR3i. Its main claim to fame was the reduced Group 13 insurance - otherwise, it's much the same, with a 115 bhp Zetec motor.

Two litres? Yes please!! In 1991, the Escort RS2000 was launched. Uprated suspension and brakes (front and rear discs) improved the performance of this sporty little 150 bhp number. Insurance group 16 might leave you little money left over to modify it, but it's quite sporty as standard. Available with features like ABS, 4-wheel-drive and traction control, the hot Escort stayed with us until 1996, so you can have one in all three facelift styles. Quite a few of these around, and they tend to have been well looked after. If you're thinking of buying one, the 4-wheel-drive is the best option, and air con was featured on some of the later models too.

Money to burn

We've left the best 'til last. No Escort buyer's guide is complete without the legendary Cosworth. A 227bhp turbo engine and four-wheel-drive traction will blast you from 0-60 in a matter of about 6 seconds. Spon-tastic insurance, in Group 20, means it's a dream car for most of us. If you're gonna splash your cash on one, get some expert advice first.

The Luxury model's well worth seeking out, with leather and air con to help you forget you're still in an Escort. With a Cossie, stock is actually best, but don't be concerned by quad headlight conversions or big brakes - these are very common, quite cheap mods that people do to further enhance the look of the car. Beware of ones with major engine mods (they've probably seen track use).

Apart from sharing the Escort name, the Cosworth had very little to do with the Escort, and more closely resembled the 4x4 Sierra Sapphire underneath. The Cossie is 2.3 inches shorter than the standard Escort, and had a wide body kit fitted, made by German car giants Karmann. Engine-wise, there are two main versions of the car - the first is the T3 big-turbo competition car, while the later T25 (1995 to 1997) has a smaller turbo, yet gives the impression of being faster than the T3, as the turbo spins up quicker.

During 2000 the entire Escort range was discontinued, and Ford said farewell to a model that started life in 1968, and was rightly named 'Britain's favourite car'.

0A 1 1A 2 2A 3

Don't buy a **dog**

In general, the Escort's a decent used buy - and there's so many out there, you're bound to find a good one eventually.

In true Ford tradition, they do rust, but at least it holds off a bit longer than Ford owners are used to. First to go are the rear arches, then random areas under the car, like the rear chassis outriggers and the floorpan near the driver's seat. Check the sills too - they go first on the sill flanges.

Most of the standard Ford alarms will probably have been disconnected by now - they're notorious for playing up. If the alarm's red LED next to the clock stays on, it's a sign of trouble. Other electrical problems are heater panels which don't light up, light switches which don't work (or don't go cleanly from main beam to dipped), and horn buttons which stick on. Scrapyards are very well-informed of the Escort troublespots, so don't expect any bargains. A new set of column switches is over £70 from Ford.

Engines are basically reliable, but the 1.3 HCS fitted to early carb models just gets more and more rattly as it racks up miles - some sound like a diesel. The later 1.3 injection motors are much quieter,

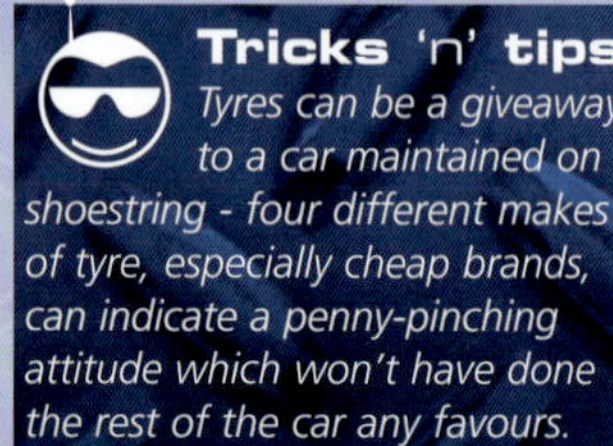

Tricks 'n' tips

Tyres can be a giveaway to a car maintained on a shoestring - four different makes of tyre, especially cheap brands, can indicate a penny-pinching attitude which won't have done the rest of the car any favours.

but check that the CFi unit starts properly from cold, and runs smoothly. The CVH engine's problems are well-known - regular cambelt changes are essential, and lack of oil changes leads to sludging inside, which can block oilways. The oil-fed hydraulic tappets can also pack up after a high mileage, making them rattle and misfire badly. The later Zetec engines aren't as hard on their cambelts, and don't suffer any particular problems (though a well-serviced one is a big plus).

The suspension causes a few problems - rear shocks especially wear out fast, as do the bushes in the front suspension arms (which means replacing both arms, complete). Another point worth checking is the locking fuel filler cap - these seize up for a pastime, which results in a knackered key before long.

Full service history (fsh)

Is there any service history? If so, this is good, but study the service book carefully:

a *Which garage has done the servicing? Is it a proper dealer, or a backstreet bodger? Do you know the garage, and if so, would you use it?*

b *Do the mileages show a nice even progression, or are there huge gaps? Check the dates too.*

c *Does it look as if the stamps are authentic? Do the oldest ones look old, or could this 'service history' have been created last week, to make the car look good?*

d *When was the last service, and what exactly was carried out? When was the cambelt last changed? Has the owner got receipts for any of this servicing work?*

One sign of a genuine car is a good batch of old MOTs, and as many receipts as possible - even if they're for fairly irrelevant things like tyres.

General stuff

Unless you're planning on spending big money on a Cosworth, it's far better to buy your Escort privately, as long as you know what you're doing. Dealers still think they can charge over the odds for Fords, but all you'll get for the extra money is a full valet and some degree of comeback if the car's a dog. Buying privately, you get to meet the owner, and this can tell you plenty about how the car's been treated. Everyone's nervous when buying a car, but don't ignore your 'gut feelings' when you first see the car, or meet its owner. Also, DON'T make the common mistake of deciding to buy the car before you've even seen it - too many people seem to make up their minds before setting out, and blindly ignore all the warning signs. Remember, there are other cars, and you can walk away! Think of a good excuse before you set out.

Take someone who 'knows a bit about cars' along with you - preferably, try and find someone who's either got an Escort, or who's had one in the past.

Never buy a car in the dark, or when it's raining. If you do have to view any car in these conditions, agree not to hand over any money until you've seen it in daylight, and when the paintwork's dry (dull, faded paint, or metallic paint that's lost its lacquer, will appear to be shiny in the rain).

Check that the mileages and dates shown on the receipts and MOTs follow a pattern indicating normal use, with no gaps in the dates, and no sudden drop in the mileage between MOTs (which might suggest the mileage has been 'clocked'). If you are presented with a sheaf of paperwork, it's worth going through it - maybe the car's had a history of problems, or maybe it's just had some nice expensive new parts fitted (like a clutch, starter motor or alternator).

The VIN plate is attached to the bonnet front slam panel . . .

. . . and the VIN is also stamped into the floorpan next to the driver's seat.

Check the chassis number (VIN number) and engine number on the registration document AND on the car. Any sign of welding near one of these numbers should be treated with suspicion - to disguise the real number, a thief will run a line of weld over the old number, grind it flat, then stamp in a new number. Other scams include cutting the section of bodywork with the numbers on from another car, then cutting and welding this section into place. The VIN number appears on a plate at the front of the engine compartment, or under a flap next to the driver's seat. If there's any sign this plate has been tampered with, walk away - the car could be a 'ringer' (a stolen car with a fake I.D.). Later cars also have the VIN on the dashboard, or etched into the windscreen glass - make sure it matches (or has someone covered it with a sticker, to hide it?).

The engine number position varies by model, but it's stamped into the front of the engine block, on a raised section just below the cylinder head - shouldn't be difficult to spot. If the number's been removed, or if there's anything suspicious about it, you could be buying trouble.

Check the registration document very carefully - all the details should match the car. If buying privately, make sure that it's definitely the owner's name and address printed on it - if not, be very careful! If buying from a dealer, note the name and address, and try to contact the previous owner to confirm mileage, etc, before handing over more than a deposit. Unless the car's very old, it shouldn't have had too many previous owners - if it's into double figures, it may mean the car is trouble, so checking its owner history is more important.

While the trim on an Escort is very durable, it should still be obvious whether the car's been abused over a long period, or whether the mileage showing is genuine or not (shiny steering wheels and floppy window winder handles are a good place to start checking if you're suspicious). Okay, so you may be planning to junk most of the interior at some point, but why should you pay over the odds for a tat car which the owner hasn't given a stuff about?

Although you may feel a bit stupid doing it, check simple things too, like making sure the windows and sunroof open and shut, and that all the doors and tailgate can be locked (if a lock's been replaced, ask why). Check all the basic electrical equipment too, as far as possible - lights, front and rear wipers, heated rear window, heater fan; it's amazing how often these things are taken for granted by buyers! If your chosen Escort already has alloys fitted, does it have locking wheel bolts? Where's the key? What about the code and removal tools for the stereo?

One thing to check on later Escorts is that the catalytic converter ('cat') is working - this is a wickedly expensive part to replace, but the best way to ensure at least one year's grace is to only buy a car with a full MOT (the cat is checked during the emissions test).

Many later Escorts will have a driver's airbag fitted - these will have the initials 'SRS' (supplementary restraint system) on the steering wheel centre pad. The orange airbag warning light should come on and go off when the engine's started - if the warning light stays on, this counts as an MOT fail, and curing the fault could be mega-bucks (it might also indicate that the airbag's gone off, in a crash!). If the light never comes on, this could still mean there's a fault with the airbag, but your dishonest seller's just taken out the bulb... nice try.

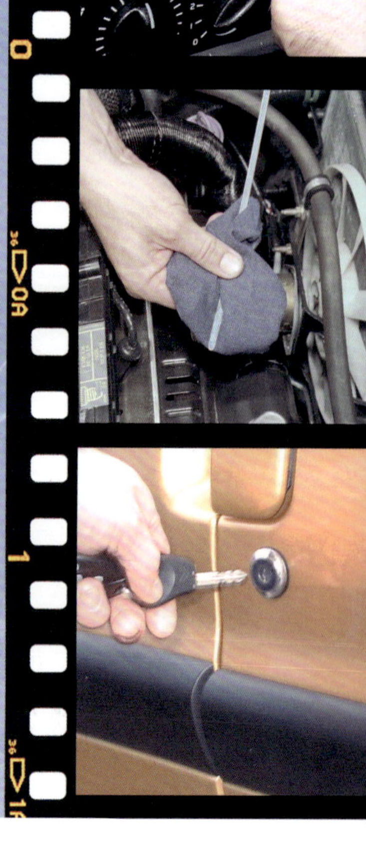

Sports models

Has it been treated well, or thrashed to death? We wouldn't pay top dollar for any XR or RS Escort without seeing evidence of careful maintenance, because any car will stand a good ragging much better if it's been properly serviced. Even a fully-

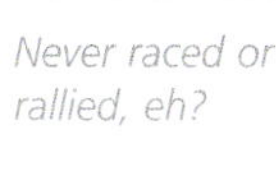

Never raced or rallied, eh?

stamped service book only tells half the story, though. Does the owner look bright enough to even know what a dipstick IS, never mind how to check the oil level between services?

Remember that there's even more to look out for than on a lesser model. If the car's temptingly cheap (and even if it's not), never take anything just at face value - check everything you can about the car yourself. Getting your hands on a really good sporty Escort is not a simple task - dodgy dealers (and owners!) know there's a market for repaired write-offs and stolen cars ('ringers'), and gullible private punters get ripped every day.

More so than any other model, check for signs of accident damage, especially at the front end. Ask if it's ever been in a shunt - if the seller says no, but there's paint overspray under the bonnet, what's going on? Also check for paint overspray on the window rubbers, light units and bumpers/trim. With the bonnet open, check that the headlight rear shells are the same colour - mis-matched or new-looking ones merit an explanation from the seller.

Does the front number plate carry details of the supplying garage, like the back one? If not, why has a new plate been fitted?

Check the glass (and even the head and tail lights) for etched-in registration numbers - are they all the same, and does it match the car's actual registration? A windscreen could've been replaced for any number of innocent reasons, but new side glass indicates a break-in at least - is the car a 'stolen/recovered' (joyridden) example? Find the chassis and engine numbers, as described earlier in this Section, and satisfy yourself that they are genuine - check them against the 'logbook' (registration document). An HPI check (or similar) could be well worthwhile, but even this won't tell you everything. If you're at all suspicious, or if the answers to your questions don't ring true, then walk away. Make any excuse you like.

The sporty models tend to get driven hard, and while they're better able to take this than some cars, hard driving will take its toll somewhere. The suspension should feel quite stiff and taut - any sogginess is usually caused by worn shock absorbers (not a problem, if you're fitting a full lowering kit, but use it to haggle the price down). Any vibration or juddering through the steering when braking indicates serious brake wear (warped brake discs), or possibly, play in the suspension/steering joints (fitting a lowering kit will not cure this kind of play, which also eats front tyres!).

It's still worth a bit of discount if an approved (Thatcham Cat 1 or 2) alarm or immobiliser is fitted, and you might find it's an essential fitment, just to get any kind of quote. Make sure that any alarm actually works, that it looks properly installed, with no stray wires hanging out, and that you get the Thatcham certificate or other paperwork to go with it. If the seller fitted it, it's worth finding out exactly how it's been wired in - if it goes wrong later, you could be stranded with no chance of disabling the system to get you home.

Sealing the deal

Everything as expected and the car's just what you want? It's time to start haggling. Never just agree to hand over the full advertised price for the car, but don't be too ambitious, either (it's best to stay friendly at this point - winding-up the owner is the last thing you need). If the ad says 'o.n.o.', expect at least 10% off - if not, why bother putting it on the ad? Try a low offer to test the owner's reaction (they can only say no!) then reluctantly increase the offer until you're both happy. Haggling can also include other considerations besides cash - will the owner chuck in the nice stereo and wheels, leave the tax on, or put a new MOT ('ticket') on it?

Bagged a bargain? Sorted! Offer to leave a deposit (this shows you're serious), but before parting with any more cash, it may be worth considering the following.

Ask for time to get in touch with the previous owner shown on the 'logbook' (registration document). If you can speak to them, it's a useful exercise in confirming the car's history and mileage.

A wise thing to do is to run a vehicle check on the car with an organisation such as HPI Autodata or the AA. It'll cost you (usually around the 30-quid mark) but could save a lot of hassle in future. They'll need the details of all the identification numbers on the vehicle and documents, as well as the mileage etc. For your money, they'll run the details of the car through their computer database. This database contains the records of all vehicles reported stolen, which have been total losses (ie. have been totalled after a serious accident) or have outstanding finance against them. They can then confirm over the phone the vehicle is straight, and in theory you can proceed with the deal, safe in the knowledge you're not about to purchase a ringer. Not only will you receive a nice certificate through the post with your vehicle details on it, but running the check also gives you financial insurance. The information given is guaranteed (usually to the tune of about ten grand) so if Plod turns up on your doorstep a month later, demanding you return your new vehicle to its rightful owner, you should be able to claim your cash back. No worries.

Tricks 'n' tips

If your understanding of the mechanical workings of the modern automobile is a bit vague and you want a second opinion, it may also be worth considering having the vehicle inspected. The AA and RAC offer this service, but there may be other people in your area too - check in the Yellow Pages. This is a bit pricier than the vehicle check, but will give you peace of mind and some comeback should things not be as expected. If you've got a friendly garage, maybe they could be persuaded to check the car over for a small fee.

Model history

September 1990 (H reg) - Escort Mk 5 range introduced. 1.3 HCS, 1.4 and 1.6 CVH petrol engines, 1.8 diesel. 3/5-door Hatch, 5-door Estate, trim levels from Popular to Ghia. Base 1.3s have 4-speed gearbox.

October 1991 (J reg) - First revisions - improved seats, steering and suspension, several models get rear spoiler, colour-keyed bumpers, all get clear front indicators.

November 1991 (J reg) - RS 2000 launched, with 150 bhp, 'cat', ABS, Recaro interior.

February 1992 (J reg) - 1.8 litre Zetec models introduced - LX and Ghia, and 105/130 bhp XR3i models, including Cabrio. All Zetecs have standard 'cat'.

June 1992 (J reg) - 2.0 litre turbo Cosworth models introduced - 227 bhp, 4-wheel-drive, rear wing and tailgate spoiler. Standard, Motorsport (stripped-out) and Luxury (leather interior) models available.

September 1992 (K reg) - Major changes, later known as 'Mk 6' models. New bonnet with wide oval grille; new rear lights incorporated into tailgate, strengthened shell and side impact bars. All petrol models now have 'cat' and fuel injection. 1.6 Zetec engine replaces 1.6 CVH, while 1.4 CVH continues.

September 1993 (L reg) - RS 2000 4x4 introduced. All models have driver's airbag and Safeguard key immobiliser. Escort Saloon replaces Orion models.

March 1994 (L reg) - 1.6 Si introduced, with 90 bhp Zetec engine and sports interior.

January 1995 (M reg) - Major changes, later known as 'Mk 7' models. New front treatment with thinner grille, rounder headlights. New interior design, with oval Ford clock. New rear suspension. 1.4 CVH engine redesignated PTE. 1.3 and 1.4 models gain SEFi sequential injection.

June 1995 (M reg) - Mexico special edition launched, similar to 1.6 Si.

August 1995 (N reg) - 1.8 Si gains 115 bhp Zetec engine.

April 1997 (P reg) - 1.8 GTI introduced.

August 1997 (R reg) - All models gain tinted glass and high-level brake light.

22nd July 2000 - The last Escort ever built is driven off the production line at Halewood.

Performance figures

	0-60 (sec)	Top speed (mph)
1.3	15.0	95
1.4	12.8	105
1.6 CVH	11.3	111
1.6 Zetec	12.4	108
1.8 Zetec (105 bhp)	9.7	117
1.8 Zetec (130 bhp)	8.9	122
RS2000	8.3	133
RS Cosworth	6.2	137

Insurance & The Law

A necessary evil

Ah, insurance - loads of money, and all you get is a piece of paper you're not really supposed to use! Of course, you MUST have insurance - you're illegal on the road without it, and you won't be able to get the car taxed, either. If you drive without insurance and are caught, you may have great trouble ever getting an insurance quote again - the insurance companies seem to regard this offence nearly as seriously as drink-driving on your record, so don't do it.

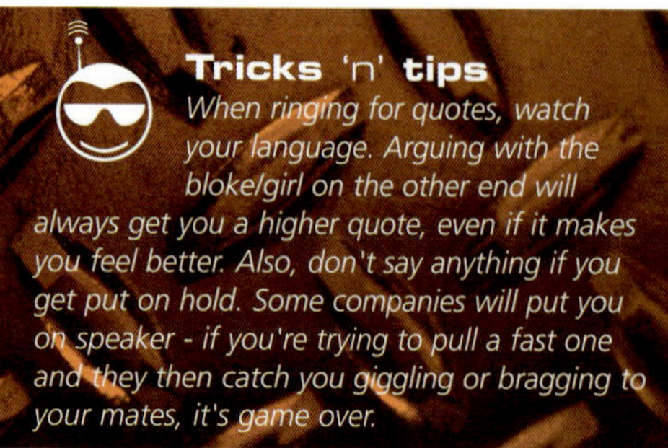

Tricks 'n' tips
When ringing for quotes, watch your language. Arguing with the bloke/girl on the other end will always get you a higher quote, even if it makes you feel better. Also, don't say anything if you get put on hold. Some companies will put you on speaker - if you're trying to pull a fast one and they then catch you giggling or bragging to your mates, it's game over.

The way the insurance companies work out premiums and assess risks is a mystery to most of us. In general, the smaller the engine you have in your Escort, the less you'll pay for insurance, so hopefully, a Escort 1.3 Encore will be lots less to insure than an RS/XR. However, it's possible that, if one company has had a lot of claims on Escorts in the past, the RS2000/XR3i factor might 'unfairly' influence the premiums of lesser Escorts, too (this is why it's important to shop around). An 'insurance-friendly' 1.6 Si should be a good bet for a sensible premium, but remember that insurance companies aren't stupid - if you turn your Si into a Cossie-lookalike, they may well 'load' the premium to nearly Cossie level (and that's Group 20), because the potential car-thief might not spot it's not a real one.

If your annual premium seems like the national debt of a small African country (and whose isn't!), always ring as many brokers and get as many quotes as you possibly can. Yes, there's loads better ways to spend an evening/afternoon than answering the same twenty questions over and over again, but you never know what the next quote will be. A few extra minutes spent on the phone (or on the 'net) once a year may result in an extra few hundred quid in your back pocket. Well, you live in hope don't you?

With modified cars, insurance becomes even more of a problem. By putting on all the alloys, trick body kits, nice interiors, big ICE, you're making the car much more of a target for thieves (yes, ok, we know you know this). The point is, the insurance companies know this too, and they don't want to be paying out for the car, plus all the money you've spent on it, should it go missing. There is a temptation 'not to tell the insurance' about the mods you've made. Let's deal with this right now. Our experience has been that, while it can be painful, honesty is best. Generally, the insurance company line is: "...thanks for telling us - we won't put the car 'up a group' (ie charge you more), but we also won't cover the extra cost of your alloy wheels/body kit/tasty seats in the event of any claim...". This is fair enough - in other words, if your car goes missing, you get paid out, based on a standard car, minus all the goodies. If you particularly want all the extras covered, you might have a long hard search - most companies (if they'll offer you cover at all) will only offer "modified for standard" policies. There are specialist insurers who are more friendly towards fully-loaded cars, but even they won't actually cover the cost of replacement goodies.

What type of cover, Sir?

For most of us, cost means there's only one option - TPF&T (third party, fire and theft). Fully-comp insurance is an unattainable dream for most people until they reach the "magic" age of 25, but what's the real story?

Third Party only

The most basic cover you can get. Basically covers you for damage to other people's cars or property, and for personal injury claims. Virtually no cover for your own stuff, beyond what you get if you take the optional "legal protection" cover.

Third Party, Fire and Theft

As above, with cover for fire and theft, of course! Better, but not much better. This is really only cover in the event of a "total loss", if your car goes missing or goes up in smoke. Still no cover for your car if you stack it into a tree, or if someone breaks in and pinches your stereo (check your policy small-print).

Fully-comprehensive

In theory at least, covers you for any loss or damage. Will cover the cost of repairing or replacing your car, often with discounted windscreen cover and other benefits. If you lose control of the car on an icy road (arguably, not your fault) you get paid. If someone pinches your wheels and drops the car on the floor, you get paid - at least for the damage done to the underside, and for standard wheels and tyres. Most policies include provision of a hire car after a shunt, which is pretty useful. Some offer cheap breakdown cover packages in with the main policy. With a fully-comp policy, you can "protect" your no-claims bonus for a small fee so you don't automatically lose all those hard-earned years' worth of discount if you prang it (generally, you can only do this on fully-comp).

All this extra cover costs, obviously, but how much? You might be surprised what the actual difference is (if they'll quote you). Think about it, anyway - it's got to be worth a couple of hundred quid more to go fully-comp, if your car's worth into four figures, surely?

Valuing your car

When your insurance pays out in the event of a total loss or write-off, they base their offer on the current market value of an identical standard model to yours (less your excess). The only way you'll get more than the average amount is to prove your Escort is in above-average nick (with photos?) or that the mileage was especially low for the year.

With this in mind, don't bother over-valuing your Escort in the hope you'll get more in the event of a claim - you won't! The only way to do this is to seek out an "agreed-value" deal, which you can usually only get on classic-car policies (with these, the car's value is agreed in advance between you, not worked out later by the company with you having no say in it). By over-valuing your Escort, you could be increasing your premium without gaining any benefit - sound smart to you?

Equally though, don't under-value, in the hope you'll get a reduction in premium. You won't, and if there's a total loss claim, you won't get any more than your under-valued amount, no matter how loudly you complain.

Work on what you paid for the car, backed up with the sort of prices you see for similar cars in the ads (or use a secondhand car price guide). Add no more than 10% for the sake of optimism, and that's it.

Your car? Or your Dad's?

Insurance really costs when you're the wrong side of twenty-five. Ever been tempted to tell your insurance that your full-on sorted Escort belongs to your Dad (old insurance-friendly person), then get him to insure it, with you as a named driver? Oh dear. This idea (known as "fronting") is so old, it's grown a long white beard. And it sucks, too. First of all, insurance companies aren't stupid. They know your Dad (or your Mum, or old Uncle Bert) isn't likely to be running around in a kid's pocket-rocket, and they treat any "named driver" application with great suspicion. Even if they do take your money, don't imagine they've been suckered. In the event of a claim, they'll look into everything very carefully, and will ask lots of awkward questions. If you get caught out in the lie, they've taken your money, and you've got no insurance - who's been suckered now?

This dubious practice also does you no favours in future years. All the time you're living the lie, you're not building up any no-claims bonus of your own - you're just delaying the pain 'til later, and without having real cover in the meantime.

"Legit" ways to limit your premium

If you do enough ringing around for quotes, you'll soon learn what the "right answers" to some of the questions are - even if you can't actually give them (but, as we've already said, don't tell lies to your insurance company). Mind you, with a little thought, you can start to play their game and win - try these:

Limit your mileage. Most companies offer a small discount if you only cover a small annual mileage. To get any meaningful reduction, the mileage has to be a lot less than 10,000 per year. Few companies, though, ever ask what the car's current mileage is - so how are they gonna know if you've gone over your self-imposed limit?

Volunteer to increase your excess. The "excess" is put there to stop people claiming for piddling little amounts - when they pay out, it's always the repair/replacement cost minus whatever the "excess" is. So, for instance, if you've got a £200 theft excess, it means you'll automatically get £200 less than the agreed value of your car, should it be stolen. Most policies have "compulsory" excess amounts, which you can do nothing about. By increasing excesses voluntarily, you're limiting the amount you'll get still further. Insurance companies like this, and should reduce your premium in return - but this only goes so far, so ask what the effect of different voluntary excesses will be. Don't increase your excess too far, or you'll get paid nowt if you claim!

Make yourself the only driver. Pretty self-explanatory. The more people who drive your car, the greater the risk to the company, and a car's owner will always drive more carefully (it's their money that bought it) than any named driver. If you've built up 2 years' worth of no-claims, but your partner hasn't, putting them on your insurance will bump it up, due to their relative inexperience

Get a garage - and use it. Where you park can have a big effect on your premium. Parking it on the street is the worst. Park off the road (on a driveway) when you're at home. The best thing is to have a garage of your own (don't pretend you use your Dad's garage) - see if you can rent one locally, even if it means walking a few hundred yards. If you're a student living away from home, tell your company where the car will be parked during term-time - if you're at Uni in London, this is a bigger risk than living at home "in the country", and *vice-versa*.

Fit an approved alarm or immobiliser. See if you can get a list from your company of all their approved security devices, and fit whatever you can afford. Not all companies approve the same kit, so it might even be worth contacting more than one company for advice. Any device with a Thatcham or Sold Secure rating should be recognised. In some cases, the discounts offered are not that great any more - but an alarm is still a nice way to get peace of mind. Most Escorts from mid-1993 had a Ford immobiliser as standard.

Build up your no-claims bonus. You'll only do this by owning and insuring a car in your own name, and then not making any claims. Simple really. One dodge is to buy an old banger, insure it cheap, then never drive it. You'll need to keep it fully road-legal (with tax, MOT) if you park it on the road. For every year you do this, you'll build up another year of NCB.

Hang onto your no-claims bonus. Obviously, the less you claim, the less your insurance will cost. If something happens to your car, don't be in too big a hurry to make a claim before you've thought it all through. How much will it cost to fix? How much is your excess? How much will your renewal premium be, next year? If you have a big enough accident which you're sure isn't your fault, ring your company, but make it quite clear you're not claiming yet - just informing them of the accident. It should be down to the other driver's insurance to pay. You don't always lose all your no-claims, either, even if it was your fault - depends how many years you've built up. Once you've got a few years, ask whether you can "protect" your no-claims.

Avoid speed cameras and The Law. Yes, okay, easier said than done! But anything less than a clean licence is not good from the insurance perspective. One SP30 won't hurt much, but the second strike will, so take it easy. Don't get caught on traffic-light cameras, either - just one is a major no-no.

Insurance-friendly mods?

Insurers don't like any changes from standard, but some things you'll do are worse from their viewpoint than others. The guidelines below are just that - for guidance. No two companies will have the same outlook, and your own circumstances will play a big part too.

Golden Rule Number One: *Before you spend huge money modifying the car, ring your insurance, and ask them how it will affect things.*

Golden Rule Number Two: *If in doubt, declare everything. Insurance companies are legally entitled to dispute any claim if the car is found to be non-standard in any way.*

Body mods - Even a tiny rear spoiler could be classed as a "bodykit" (yes, it's daft, but that's how it is). Anything which alters the exterior appearance should be declared. As long as the mods don't include a radical full-on bodykit, the jump in premium should be fairly small.

Brakes - The companies view brake mods as tampering with safety-related kit, and modifying the brakes implies that you drive fast and hard. You might get away will standard-sized grooved/drilled discs and pads, but fitting bigger discs and replacement calipers will prove expensive.

Engine mods - "Mild" mods, such as induction kits and exhausts don't give much more power, so don't generally hurt. But "chipping" your Escort will lead to drastic rises in premiums, or a complete refusal of cover. With complete engine transplants, you'll be required to give an engineer's report, and to get your wad out.

Interior mods - Don't assume that tarting up the inside won't interest the insurance company. By making any part of the car more attractive, you're also attracting the crims. Cars get trashed for parts, as often as not - and your racing seats and sexy steering wheel could be worth major money. Still, the effect on premiums shouldn't be too great, especially if you've got an alarm/immobiliser.

Lights - Change the car's appearance, and are safety-related. You'll probably get asked for lots of details, but as long as you've kept it sensible (and legal, as far as possible), the effect on your wallet shouldn't be too harsh.

Security - Make sure you mention all security stuff - alarms, immobilisers (including mechanical devices), locking wheel nuts, large Alsatian in the back seat... But - don't over-sell the car. Tell the truth, in other words. If you've got a steering wheel lock, do you always fit it? If you didn't when your car went missing, you're in trouble. Don't say you've got a Cat 1 alarm if it really came from Argos, and don't tell them you garage the car at night if it's stuck out in the road.

Suspension - Changes the car's appearance, and is safety-related. Some enlightened companies once took the view that modded suspension helps the car corner better, so it's safer. Drops of only 30 to 40 mm shouldn't mean bigger premiums.

Wheels - Very appearance-altering, and very nickable. At least show some responsibility by fitting some locking nuts/bolts and an approved alarm/immobiliser. Quite likely to attract a low-to-moderate rise in premium, which still won't cover your wheels properly - you could arrange separate cover for your wheels, then at least you'll get paid. Some companies ask for a photo of the car with the wheels on.

And finally - a new nightmare

Not telling the insurance the whole truth gets a little tricky when you make a claim. If the insurance assessor comes to check your bent/burnt/stolen-and-recovered "standard" Escort, and finds he's looking at a vehicle fitted with trick alloys/bodykit/radical interior, he's not going to turn a blind eye. Has the car got an MOT? Oh, and did you declare those points on your licence? No? You're then very much at the mercy of your insurer, especially if they can prove any mods contributed to the claim. At best, you'll have a long-drawn-out battle with your insurer to get a part-payout, and at worst they'll just refuse to get involved at all.

One more thing - *be careful what you hit.* If your insurance is declared void, they won't pay out for the repairs to the other car you smacked into, or for the lamp-post you knock down (several hundred quid, actually). And then there's the personal injury claims - if your insurance company disowns you, it'll be you who has to foot the bill. Even sprains and bruises can warrant claims, and more serious injuries can result in claims running into lots of zeroes! Without insurance cover, **you'll** have to pay. Probably for a long, long time. Think about it, and we won't see you in court.

Big Brother in a Box

Speed cameras have to be one of the most unpopular things ever. We're talking worse than exams, dentists, alcohol-free beer, and the Budget. Does anyone actually like them? Well, the makers do - they should all be living it up on a beach in the Bahamas. The people making speed camera signs are obviously lovin' it. And the Chancellor? Nuff said.

Speed, of course, is fun. The sensation of speed is the main reason we enjoy driving, and it's one of the best ways to show off your motor. There's nothing like giving your ride a good caning, being pushed back in the seat, exhaust snarling, engine singing. Sounds like fun to me - so these things are really fun cameras, then?

Like it or not, we live in a world obsessed with limiting speed. Excess speed, we're told, causes accidents and costs lives. As most of us have realised by now, excess speed really means more money for the Government. What causes accidents is driving like a tw*t. But they don't have cameras for that.

Before we get ourselves in too much trouble, we have to admit the cameras might save lives in built-up areas with lots of peds, kids and old folk about. Driving like a hooligan in those situations probably should get you a slap on the wrist for 'endangering lives'. But at night, on a dead-straight road with no traffic? We think not.

Pay attention

The best you can say about cameras is that they're a necessary evil which we all have to live with. So what's the best way of avoiding the 'bad news' letter in the post?

There is one 100% foolproof method, which is totally legal, and it's dead simple - don't ever speed. That should do the trick. Yeah, right. Back in the real world, everyone speeds some time, even if it's only by a few mph. Add a few more miles-per because you weren't really watching your speed, and then do it somewhere there's a camera (or a sneaky mobile trap you'd never spotted before), and you're nicked. Is it any wonder that clean licences are getting as rare as rocking-horse leftovers?

Even on roads you know well, the do-gooders are forever lowering the limits, so if you don't watch it, you'll be sailing through more than 10 mph over today's new limit. And that's definitely worth a few points! You've gotta concentrate, to stay clean.

Know your enemy

First of all, you've got to know what you're up against. It's the only way (short of the fantasy world of never, ever speeding) that you stand a chance. And the first thing to know is - not all cameras are the same. Some can even be beaten.

Gatso (and PEEK)

The first, the best-known, the most common, and probably the most-hated. Invented by the winner of the 1953 Monte Carlo Rally, Gatsos are the familiar large, square box in stealth grey or high-viz yellow, with a square lens and flash unit (the later, less-common PEEK cameras have two round items, set one above the other). These are radar-operated (type 24) and can only 'get' you from behind, because they use a flash to take the photo, and this would blind you if it went off with you coming towards it. These cameras, therefore, cannot in theory catch you speeding towards them (don't quote us on that). As a result of this limitation, some authorities will turn the cameras round from time to time, to catch you out.

RLCs are also Gatso-based, but they work through sensors in the road, which are active when the lights are on red. If your car passes over them in this condition, it's gotcha. Some RLCs use radar too, so if you speed through on red, you'll also get a speeding fine. Gee, thanks.

Gatsos have 35 mm film inside, with about 400 shots possible before the film runs out. It's obviously vital that the film is recovered from the camera, or a prosecution can't be made - these cameras get vandalised for all sorts of reasons. Some cameras are rumoured not to contain any film, so they flash without recording any evidence (that bloke down the pub could be wrong, though).

If the radar detects excess speed, the flash is triggered twice as you pass over the measured line markings on the road. From the distance you travel between the set flashes, your speed can be proved. It's anyone's guess where the trigger speed for a camera will be set, but it's almost bound to be quite a few mph over the posted limit - if it wasn't, the camera would quickly catch dozens of speeders, and run out of film. Be more wary of inner-city Gatsos, as they're probably 'emptied' more often, allowing a lower speed tolerance.

tricks 'n' tips

In a thirty limit, you're less likely to speed if you hook a lower gear than normal. Most cars will comfortably cruise through a thirty in 4th gear, but it's too easy to add speed in 4th. Try using 3rd, and the natural engine braking (and extra engine/exhaust noise) will help you keep a lid on your speed. It's not foolproof, but give it a try anyway.

Truvelo

Oooh, nasty. The forward-facing 'gatso' is particularly unpleasant, but luckily for us, it's also more expensive than the rear-facing Gatso, so not as common. Yet. The Truvelo camera can be recognised by two round lenses side by side in the centre of its box, and one of these is a pinky-red colour (hence the 'pinkeye' nickname). The unusual pink 'lens' is actually a flash unit, fitted with a red filter to avoid blinding the driver. Because the photo's taken from the front, it's hard for the driver to claim someone else was driving, or that they 'don't know'

who was driving (a common ploy to try and 'get off' Gatso offences). The less-visible flash gives less warning to following motorists, too. Not that we're suggesting they're out to get us. Oh no.

These babies are triggered by the car passing over piezo sensors set into the road, not radar. If you see three stripes across your path, slow the heck down.

Red Light Cameras

Intended to catch people who go through traffic lights on red. Which, you have to say, is pretty dodgy. And have you ever risked it on a single amber? If you remember your Highway Code, this means stop, the same as a red light. 'Amber-gamblers' should also beware the traffic-light cams, 'cos they'll get you one day. Unlike (a few) points for speeding, points for traffic light offences will really hurt your insurance premiums, so watch it.

SPECS

Yikes - this really is Big Bro stuff. This system uses digital cameras (no film needed), mounted high on special gantries - these are a set distance apart, and create a speed monitoring zone. When you 'enter the zone', your number plate is recorded digitally, with a date and time stamp (regardless of whether you're speeding). When you leave the zone, another camera does the same thing. Because you've travelled a known distance between the two cameras, it's possible to calculate your average speed - if you're over the limit for the stretch of road, the computer spits out a fine in your direction.

What's really worrying about this technology is that it can be used to cross-check you and your car for other offences (whether your car's taxed and MoT'd, for instance). Anything dodgy, and the next time you pass by those cameras at that time of day, you could be in for a jam-sandwich surprise. Still, it could also catch the crims making off with your motor...

Mobile or temporary speed traps

These are either Gatso, Mini-Gatso, or laser type.

The potential Gatso sites are easy enough to spot - look for three shiny strips across the road, with a sturdy grey metal post alongside, on the pavement. Mr Plod comes along, sets up his camera (which uses sensors in the road strips not radar to detect your speed), catches his daily quota of speeders, and moves on. Don't give him a short day by being one of his victims.

Mini-Gatsos are just smaller, mobile versions of the UK's least-favourite roadside 'furniture', operated out of cop-cars and anonymous white vans - to get you, you have to be driving away from them.

More sinister (and much on the increase) are the laser cameras, which are aimed at your number plate (usually the front one) and record your speed on video. Often seen mounted on tripods, on bridges overlooking busy roads, or hidden inside those white 'safety camera partnership' vans. Lasers have quite a range (1000 metres, or over half a mile), so by the time you've spotted them, they've spotted you speeding. It's up to the operator to target likely speeding vehicles - so will they pick on your maxed motor? You bet!

Achtung!

Do you live in, or regularly drive through, Northamptonshire or North Wales? We've got two words for you. Oh, dear. Northamptonshire is the area with the most cameras, and where new camera technology is often first tried out, while North Wales has one of the most active safety cam partnerships, with many roaming vans. But don't feel too bad, guys - the way it's going, the rest of us will soon catch you up.

Beating the system

No-one's condoning regular speeding, but these days, it's just too easy to get 'done' for a fairly minor speed infringement. Which hardly seems fair. There must be some way of fighting back, surely?

Cheap and legal

Don't. Ever. Speed. Simple, but not easy in the real world. Next!

Neither cheap nor legal

The James Bond option

One of 007's older cars had self-changing number plates - this may have been the inspiration for a highly-illegal speed camera dodge. Since all the detection systems rely heavily on your number plate, some skankers drive round with false plates - they might even have copied yours. Worth remembering if you ever get accused of speeding in the Outer Hebrides. Getting caught on false plates could be a £1000 fine, so is it worth the risk?

For ages now, companies have been advertising 'photo-reflective' plates (they're not illegal, but the dibble take a dim view). Most are a rip-off, but some do appear to work – on traps which flash. Speed cameras take very high-res pictures, however - even if your plates don't give you away, the coppers might i.d. your motor from its non-standard features. Money wasted, then.

Cloaking device?

The mobile laser speed trap is one of the most common, and most hated, in the UK. It sends out a laser beam which targets your front number plate. Wouldn't it be great if you could buy something to mess up its signal, so it couldn't 'lock on' ? You can - it's called a laser diffuser (sometimes marketed under the guise of a remote garage door-opener). And yes, they do work - but careful fitting is needed, and the lenses need regular cleaning. If you're caught using it for speed trap evasion, you can be done for obstruction, or perverting the course of justice - it pays to have a well-placed 'off' switch.

Gatso-beating radar 'scramblers' are said not to work, while radar jammers are an illegal transmitter - using one could see you inside for much longer than a speeding conviction.

A sound investment?

Radar detectors

These have been around for ages, and started life in the US. They're good for detecting radar-based speed cameras (most Gatsos), and any old police radar guns still in use, but that's all. Don't buy an old one (you'll get lots of false alerts if it's not meant for Euro/UK use), or a cheap one (it might not have enough range to give you a chance). ***Stop press: Looks like radar detectors are finally going to be made illegal later this year (2004) — only GPS systems will be legal after this.***

GPS systems

Using Global Positioning Satellite technology, these devices are really speed camera site locators, not detectors. Using an onboard database of camera locations, they constantly monitor your car's position, and warn when you're approaching a 'danger area'. Providing you keep your dash-mounted podule updated (by downloading the latest camera/blackspot info from the maker's website), these will warn you of virtually every potential camera in the country, including Truvelo and SPECS. The only limitations are a lack of laser detection, and it won't get all the mobile sites.

You must download new info regularly, and this costs (you buy a subscription to the website). Also, if your system hasn't been in use for a while, it can take quite a few minutes for the pod to pick up the satellites it needs - during this time, you're unprotected. Don't buy secondhand units with no subscription left, as the makers sometimes can't (won't?) re-activate them.

Laser detectors

The makers say this is essential kit to combat the roaming camera van threat, but be careful. We said earlier that laser cams have a range of up to 1000 metres, but most operators don't trigger theirs until you're much, much closer than that. Which means you have far less time to react. As long as you're not the first car along, your laser detector may pick up laser 'scatter' from cars in front, but there isn't much scatter with a laser. It's said that some laser detectors will only go off if your car's already been targeted - and of course, it's too late by then.

A final word

Don't rely too heavily on even the best anti-camera technology - try and drive within the spirit, if not the letter, of the Law, with a detector as backup.

Road **Angel**

The most effective way to 'detect' a camera is to know where it is. Yeah – obviously! But with cameras still being hidden behind road signs and bridges, and increasing numbers of camera-kitted white vans, knowing where the cams are ain't easy.

A GPS locator monitors your car's position relative to known camera sites, and warns you when you're getting close. The latest offerings also warn when you're approaching schools and other areas where extra care is needed. These devices are definitely not illegal. They increase road safety, by telling you where 'accident blackspots' are – not when to brake...

tricks 'n' tips

Don't leave the mounting cradle fitted when you leave the car – it's all the clue a thief needs that there's some serious money's worth hidden in your glovebox. Even if it's not there (because you've sensibly taken it with you) you're still making it too tempting.

This latest Road Angel offers two main mounting options – a sticky-backed magnetic mount directly on the dash, or this rather neat screen-mounted cradle (also with a mag mount).

01 Either way, make sure the wipers don't obscure the unit's 'view', or the laser detection function won't stand a chance.

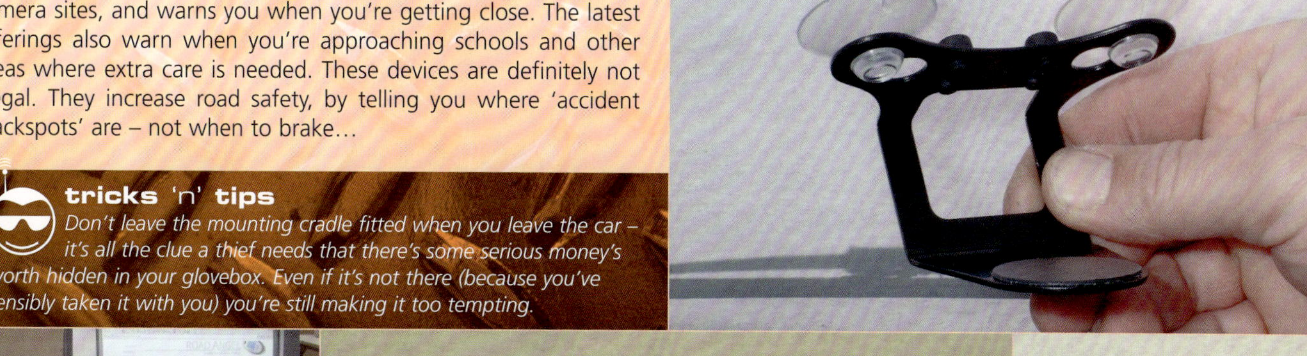

02 A GPS unit like this is only as good as the info it's working from – update it regularly by downloading the latest camera locations, or it's worse than useless. If you can use a PC well enough to download stuff from the Internet, you've got no worries.

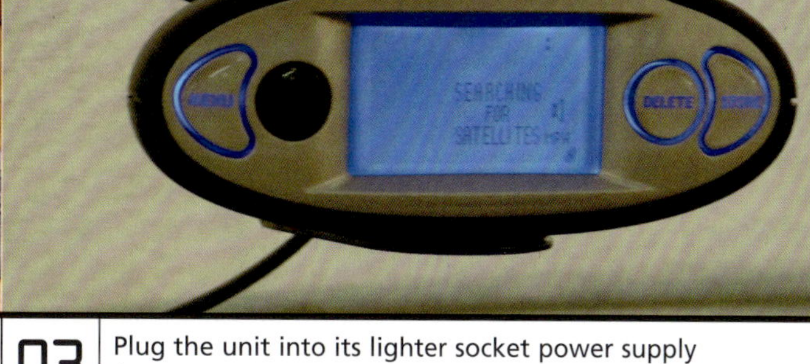

03 Plug the unit into its lighter socket power supply (assuming it's not already taken by your phone charger or hands-free kit), then fit the unit to its bracket. First, you're greeted by a friendly message, then the unit starts searching for its satellites. While this is going on, remember that you're not protected.

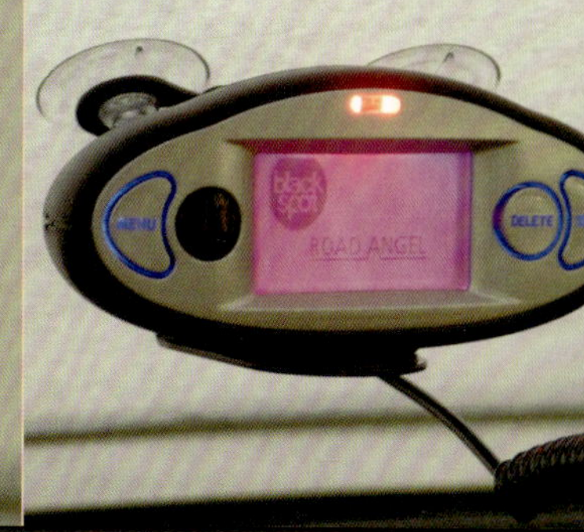

04 Depending which system you've got, when you're getting near a camera site (sorry – accident blackspot), you'll get a warning beep or message, and the display will flash. If you miss all that lot, you probably need to downgrade your ICE install.

Look Mum, **no hands!**

As of December 2003 (okay, March 2004 really) it became illegal to hold your mobile while driving. Well, brilliant - something new to get done for. Like we were really getting short of that kind of thing. But you have to say, yipping and driving always was a pretty dodgy pastime, with driving coming off worse - if only all the UK's traffic legislation made this much sense.

Of course, the people who really benefit are the ones making hands-free car phone kits - you're looking at upwards of £50 (for a conventional kit) to get anything worth fitting. Which one do I go for? Will I have to make holes in my dash? Good questions. But we're jumping ahead - let's deal first with what the new law means in the real world.

Points of law

First, fitting a hands-free kit is merely a way of getting round part of the new legislation. They're not 'fully-legal', they're just 'not prohibited'. Even using a hands-free set-up is a distraction while you're piloting your machine, and if you start weaving about, carve up a cyclist, or run a red light, you're still likely to face a 'driving without due care' charge, or worse. The best solution for making a call is to stop where it's safe - have voicemail enabled if you get called while you're driving.

Answering a call, even with hands-free, might not be safe in all circumstances. Let it ring. As for what you're allowed to do with the phone itself - it's just pressing the buttons (and no, this doesn't mean it's ok 2 txt). Holding the phone in any way is not permitted. Even if you're stuck in traffic, completely stationary, the engine would have to be off before you can use your mobile normally - only then could you really say you weren't 'driving'.

At the moment, getting caught using a phone on the move only carries a fixed fine. But it looks like this hasn't worked, because it's soon going to be a bigger fine, and points on the licence. Use your moby sensibly (better still, don't use it, in the car at least), or it could mean re-sitting your driving test. Paying attention now, aren'tcha?

Achtung!

Don't just pull over and screech to a stop when the phone rings. If you do this somewhere stupid, you're just as likely to get fined as you would for using the phone on the move.

tricks 'n' tips

If you've got a passenger in the car, it's perfectly legal for them to use a mobile, so if yours rings, let them answer it, and relay the message to you - can't be done for that.

What's available?

Conventional kits

The new law has brought a whole range of new product to the market, so there's no need to settle for the old-style in-car kits, which leave holes all over your dash. Most of the latest kits have adhesive pads, and just plug into your fag lighter. The most essential item, to comply with the rules, is a phone holder or 'cradle' (holding phone bad - cradle good).

As no-one keeps the same phone for very long, it's worth looking for a kit which you can convert from one make of phone to another - by buying a different adapter lead, for instance.

Look for kits offering 'full duplex' operation - this means you can talk and listen at the same time. Just like real life. What it really means is conversations are easier and more natural - to understand fully why you need this feature, try one without it. Non-duplex kits cut out the speaker when they pick up any sound - this could be you talking (as intended), or it could just be noise inside the car. Very irritating, especially in an area where you've already got poor reception to deal with.

Some kits feature 'infra-red technology', which means you can answer/end calls by waving your hand in front of the phone. Proper hands-free operation, and great for impressing your passengers. Maybe not so good if you make lots of hand gestures while driving?

Car stereo kits

One of the newest ideas, and catching on fast. Uses a radio transmitter clipped over the phone speaker to transmit calls over a radio channel on your car stereo. When the phone rings, flick on the radio to the preset channel, speak into the phone's mike as normal, and hear your caller through your car speakers (since it's your stereo, you have easy control over call volume). They're cheap, and they appear to work, though there are potential problems with interference. Remember, this is a developing technology - it pays to buy the latest model you can find.

Bluetooth headsets

Bluetooth offers wireless operation, so get yourself a headset with mike, and you can chat away without having the phone up to your ear. Most modern handsets are Bluetooth-capable, and really new ones also have voice-activated dialling, which offers true hands-free operation in the car. Downsides? Some doubts over sound quality, and do you really want to wear a headset all the time you're driving?

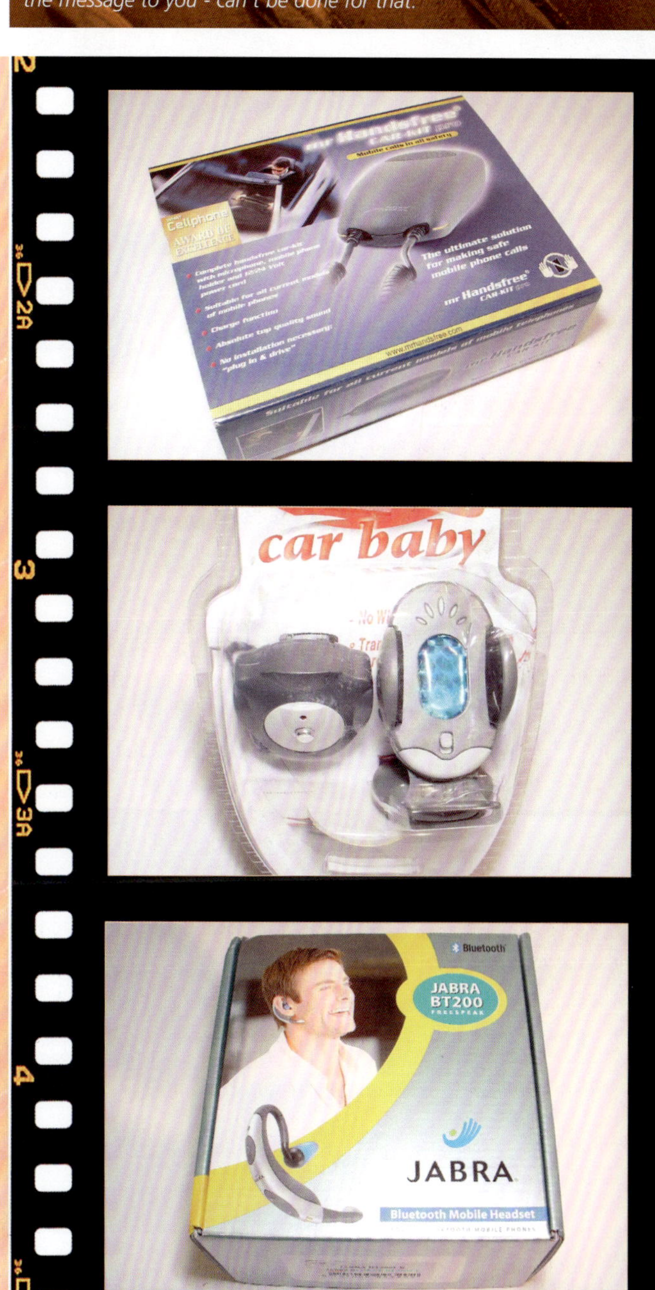

Kit fitting

Fitting details are obviously going to vary, depending on what you've bought – the main trick is to get one which doesn't require you to go drilling holes in your dash. Luckily, this is now so unpopular that most modern kits don't even offer hole-drilling as an option.

Mr Handsfree

01 All these kits (apart from the Bluetooth headset) need power, usually conveniently taken from the fag lighter socket.

02 If you're not going to drill holes, you'll be sticking stuff on. If you want things to stay stuck (and you usually only get one shot at this) a little cleaning is in order first.

03 Mostly, it's Velcro pads you get for sticking the various kit bits in place (so they can be easily ripped off and stashed when you leave the car). Leave the two 'halves' of Velcro stuck together while fitting. With the mounting area clean, it's peel . . .

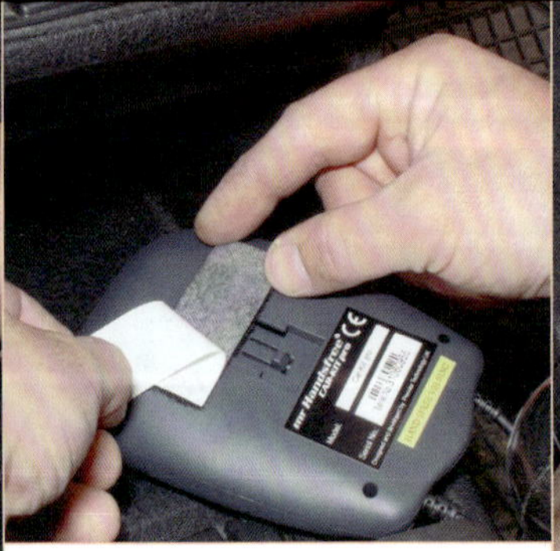

04 . . . and press firmly. This is the main unit, which contains the speaker. We thought the centre console was too good a spot to ignore. You only have to ensure the two curly-cords will reach the lighter socket and the phone.

05 Not all fitting is quite this simple, though. With a little clever thinking, you can do a much neater fitting job than one which leaves all the wires hanging out. Take this little mike which comes with the Mr Handsfree kit – by prising out one of the Escort's blank switches, we hid the wire inside the dash and stuck the mike to the switch, right where it's needed. Result.

06 For mounting the phone itself, we have a magnetic bracket, again stuck with sticky pads. It's only an old Nokia, but we'd still better make sure it doesn't hit the deck, by making sure it's firmly attached.

07 And there it is – the phone's nice and handy, the mike's discreetly mounted, and the speaker unit's tucked in the console. And this is the first one of these we've fitted!

Pama Plug n Go

This is one neat unit – no dangling wires, a well-designed mounting bracket with a huge sucker for sticking to the windscreen, and a built-in speaker which faces the glass, so sound is 'reflected' back. The unit is self-contained, with a built-in battery (car charger supplied), so it can be used anywhere, not just in-car. Looks sweet, works a treat.

01

Jabra Bluetooth headset

Only any good to you if your phone's got Bluetooth, but like the Pama unit we fitted earlier, there's no mess. The headset needs charging before use, but after that, you just 'pair' your phone and headset together, and start jabbering. If your phone's trendy enough to have voice-activated dialling, this is about as hands-free as you'll get. You don't even need a cradle for your mobile with this one!

01

Security

Lock me or lose me

It's a sad fact, but making your car attractive to the opposite sex also tends to attract attention of a less-welcome kind, from less-than-human pond life.

Avoiding trouble

Now come on - you're modifying your car to look cool and to be seen in. Not a problem - but be careful where you choose to show your car off, and who to. Be especially discreet, the nearer you get to home - turn your system down before you turn into your road, for instance, or you'll draw unwelcome attention to where that car with the loud stereo's parked at night.

Without being too paranoid, watch for anyone following you home. At night, if the car behind switches its lights off, be worried. If you suspect this is happening, do not drive home - choose well-lit public places until they give up. Believe us - it happens.

If you're going out, think about where you're parking - well-lit and well-populated is good.

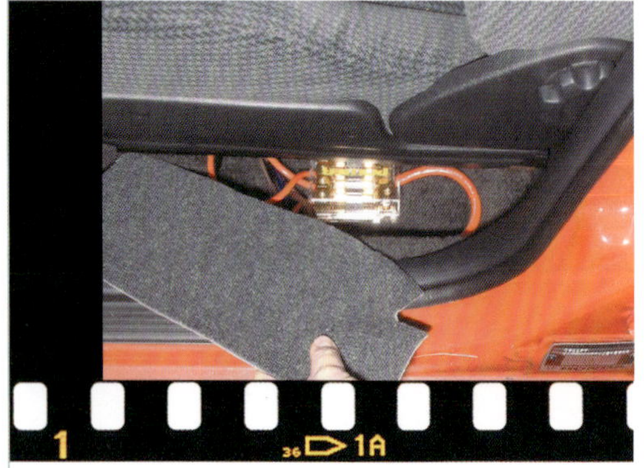

Thieves hate light being on them, so don't make it easy by parking somewhere dark - think about this if you park up in daylight, knowing you won't be back 'til late.

Hands up, who doesn't lock their car when they get petrol?. Your insurance company has a term for this, and it's "contributory negligence". In English, this means you won't get a penny if your car goes missing when you haven't locked it.

If you're lucky enough to have a garage, use it. On up-and-over garage doors, fit extra security like a padlock and ground anchor.

A clever thief will watch your movements and habits over several days before trying your car. Has it got an alarm, and do you always set it? Do you only fit your steering wheel lock when you feel like it? Do you always park in the same place, and is the car hidden from the house or from the road? Don't make his life easier. Ask yourself how YOU'D nick your car...

A word about your stereo

From the moment you bolt on those nice alloys, it's taken as read that you've also got stereo gear that's worth nicking - and the thieves know it. All the discreet installation in the world isn't going to deter them from finding out what's inside that nice motor.

Please don't advertise your love of ICE around your car. Your nice stereo gear will fit other cars too, and can be ripped out in nothing flat. You may be very proud of your ICE install, but nothing is more of an "invite" than a huge ICE sticker or sunstrip. If you've fitted one just to look cool, replace it now with something less provocative - seriously. Your set might not actually be very expensive, but you could still lose a side window for advertising something better.

You'll have got a CD player, obviously, but don't leave discs or empty CD cases lying around inside the car. A nice pair of 6x9s in full view on the back shelf is an invite to having your rear window smashed - stealth shelf, anyone? When you're fitting your system, give some thought to the clues you could accidentally leave in plain view. Oxygen-free speaker cable is great stuff, but it's also a bit bright against dark carpets, and is all the clue necessary that you're serious about your speakers. Hide amps and CD changers under your front seats.

Most modern sets are face-off or MASK, so if they've got security features like this, use them - take your faceplate off when you leave the car, and take it with you rather than leaving it in the door pocket or glovebox (the first places a thief will look).

Things that go beep in the night

Unless your insurance company demands it up front, fitting an alarm is something generally done as an after-thought. We know alarms aren't exactly sexy, but don't skimp - an alarm may never be put to the test, but if it is, you'll be glad you spent wisely…

The simplest first step to car security is to fake it. Tacky "This car is fitted with an alarm" stickers won't fool anyone, but if you want cheap, just fit a flashing LED. We know it's not the real thing, but everyone else will think you've got a posh alarm. An LED is cheap to buy and easy to fit, and can be rigged to a discreet switch inside the car.

Don't overlook the value of so-called "manual" immobilisers, such as steering wheel locking bars and gear-to-handbrake lever locks. These can be a worthwhile deterrent - a thief not specifically after your car may move on to an easier target. Some of the items offered may be "Sold Secure" or Thatcham Cat 3, accolades well worth checking out, since it means they've withstood a full-on brute force attack for a useful length of time.

The only way to combat the more determined thief is to go for a well-specified and intelligently-installed alarm. Immobilisers alone have their place, but sadly, even a pro-fitted immobiliser on its own won't stop someone pinching your wheels, or having it away with the stereo gear. Neither, incidentally, will a cheap alarm - you have to know how the thieves operate to stand any chance defeating them. Any alarm you fit yourself probably won't gain you any insurance discount, but it will give you peace of mind, and DIY means you can do a real trick installation, to make it very hard work for the gyppos.

Finally, one other scam which you might fall victim to. If you find your alarm is suddenly going off a lot at night, when previously it had been well-behaved, don't ignore the problem. It's an old trick for a thief to deliberately set off your alarm several times, each time hiding round the corner when you come out to investigate, then to wait until the fifth or sixth time when you don't reset it (in disgust), leaving him a clear run. If your alarm does keep false-alarming without outside assistance, find out the cause quickly, or your neighbours will quickly become "deaf" to it.

Thatcham categories and meanings:

1. **Cat 1.** For alarms and electronic immobilisers.
2. **Cat 2.** For electronic immobilisers only.
3. **Cat 2-1.** Electronic immobilisers which can be upgraded to Cat 1 alarms later.
4. **Cat 3**. Mechanical immobilisers, eg snap-off steering wheels, locking wheel bolts, window film, steering wheel locks/covers.
5. **Q-class.** Tracking devices.

Other alarm features

Two-stage anti-shock - means that the alarm shouldn't go off, just because the neighbour's cat jumps on your car roof, or because Little Johnny punts his football into your car. Alarm will only sound after a major shock, or after repeated shocks are detected.

Anti-tilt - detects any attempt to lift or jack up the car, preventing any attempt to pinch alloys. Very unpopular with thieves, as it makes the alarm very sensitive (much more so than anti-shock). Alarm may sound if car is parked outside in stormy conditions (but not if your suspension's rock-hard!).

Anti-hijack - immobiliser with built-in delay. If your motor gets hi-jacked, the neanderthals responsible will only get so far down the road before the engine cuts out.

Rolling code - reduces the chance of your alarm remote control signal from being "grabbed" by special electronic equipment.

Total closure - module which connects to electric windows/sunroof and central locking, which closes all items when alarm is set. Alarms like this often have other nifty features such as remote boot opening.

Pager control - yes, really - your alarm can be set to send a message to your pager (why not your mobile?) if your car gets tampered with.

Current-sensing disable - very useful feature on some cars which have a cooling fan which can cut in after the ignition is switched off. Without this feature, your alarm will be triggered every time you leave it parked after a long run - very annoying.

Volumetric-sensing disable - basically allows you to manually disable the interior ultrasonics, leaving the rest of the alarm features active. Useful if you want to leave the sunroof open in hot weather - if a fly gets in the car, the alarm would otherwise be going off constantly.

Talking alarms - no, please, please no. Very annoying, and all that'll happen is you'll attract crowds of kids daring each other to set it off again. Unfortunately, these are becoming more popular, with some offering the facility to record your own message!

The knowledge

What people often fail to realise (at least, until it happens to them) is the level of violence and destruction which thieves will employ to get your stuff - this goes way beyond breaking a window.

It comes as a major shock to most people when they discover the serious kinds of tools (weapons) at many professional thieves' disposal, and how brutally your lovingly-polished car will be attacked. Many people think, for instance, that it's their whole car they're after, whereas it's really only the parts they want, and they don't care how they get them (this means that these parts are still attractive, even when fitted to a basic car which has yet to be fully modded). Obviously, taking the whole car then gives the option of hiding it to strip at leisure, but it won't always be the option chosen, and you could wake up one morning to a well-mangled wreck outside.

Attack 1 The first option to any thief is to smash glass - typically, the toughened-glass side windows, which will shatter, unlike the windscreen. Unfortunately for the thief, this makes a loud noise (not good), but is a quick and easy way in. The reason for taking this approach is that a basic car alarm will only go off if the doors are opened (voltage-drop alarm) - provided the doors aren't opened, the alarm won't go off.

Response 1 A more sophisticated alarm will feature shock sensing (which will be set off by the impact on the glass), and better still, ultrasonic sensing, which will be triggered by the brick coming in through the broken window.

Response 2 This kind of attack can also be stopped by applying security film to the inside of the glass, which holds it all together and prevents easy entry.

Attack 2 An alternative to smashing the glass is to pry open the door using a crowbar - this attack involves literally folding open the door's window frame by prising from the top corner. The glass will still shatter, but as long as the door stays shut, a voltage-drop alarm won't be triggered.

Response This method might not be defeated by a shock-sensing alarm, but an ultrasonic unit would pick it up. Incidentally, another bonus with ultrasonic alarms is that the sensors are visible from outside - and act as a deterrent.

Attack 3 The next line of attack is to disable the alarm. The commonest way to kill the alarm is either to cut the wiring to the alarm itself, or to disconnect the battery, "safely" hidden away under the bonnet. And just how strong is a bonnet? Not strong enough to resist being crowbarred open, which is exactly what happens.

Response 1 If your alarm has extra pin-switches, be sure to fit one to the bonnet, and fit it in the bonnet channel next to the battery, so that it'll set off the alarm if the bonnet is prised up. Also make sure that the wire to the pin-switch cannot be cut easily though a partly-open bonnet.

Response 2 Make sure that the alarm module is well-hidden, and cannot be got at from underneath the car.

Response 3 Make the alarm power supply connection somewhere less obvious than directly at the battery terminal - any thief who knows his stuff will immediately cut any "spare" red wires at the battery. Try taking power from the fusebox, or if you must source it under the bonnet, trace the large red battery lead to the starter motor connections, and tap into the power there.

Response 4 Always disguise the new alarm wiring, by using black insulating tape to wrap it to the existing wiring loom. Tidying up in this way also helps to ensure the wires can't get trapped, cut, melted, or accidentally ripped out - any of which could leave you with an alarm siren which won't switch off, or an immobiliser you can't disable.

Response 5 An alarm which has a "battery back-up" facility is a real kiss of death to the average thief's chances. Even if he's successfully crow-barred your bonnet and snipped the battery connections, the alarm will still go off, powered by a separate battery of its own. A Cat 1 alarm has to have battery back-up.

Fitting a basic **LED**

All you need for this is a permanent live feed, an earth, a switch if you want to be able to turn it on/off, and the flashing LED itself (very cheap, from any car accessory shop).

An LED draws very little current, so you'll be quite safe tapping into almost any live feed you fancy. If you've wired in your ICE, take a live feed from the permanent (radio memory supply) wire at the back of your head unit, or have a delve into the back of the fusebox with your test light (as featured in the full alarm fitting procedure, further on). An earth can easily be tapped again from your head unit, or you can make one almost anywhere on the metal body of the car, by drilling a small hole, fitting a self-tapping screw, then wrapping the bared end of wire around and tightening it.

The best and easiest place to mount an LED is into one of the many blank switches the makers seem to love fitting. The blank switch is easily pried out, and a hole can then be drilled to take the LED (which usually comes in a separate little holder). Feed the LED wiring down behind the dashboard to where you've tapped your live and earth, taking care not to trap it anywhere, nor to accidentally wrap it around any moving parts.

Connect your live to the LED red wire, then rig your earth to one side of the switch, and connect the LED black wire to the other switch terminal. You should now have a switchable LED! Tidy up the wiring, and mount the switch somewhere discreet, but where you can still get at it. Switch on when you leave the car, and it looks as if you've got some sort of alarm - better than nothing!

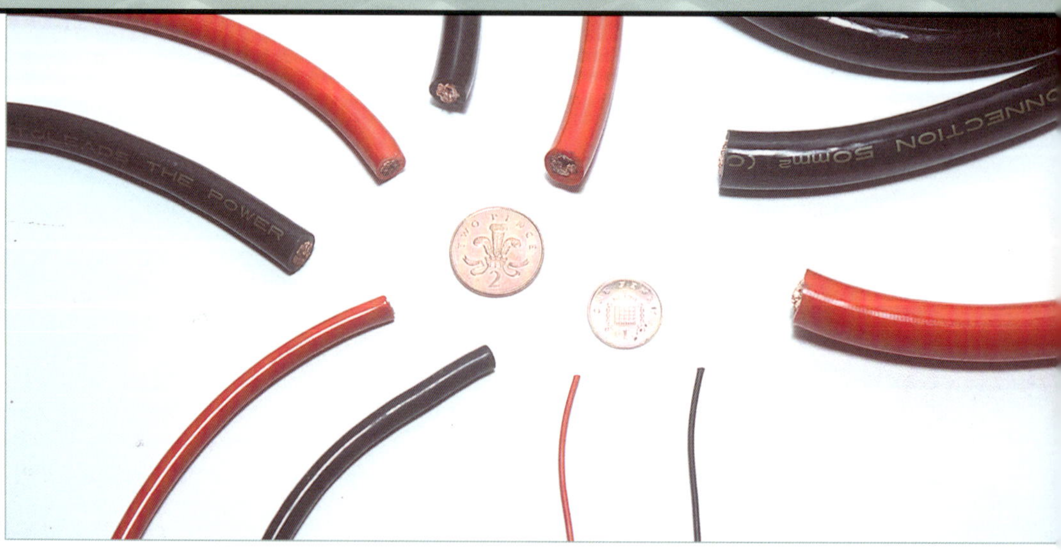

Wiring basics

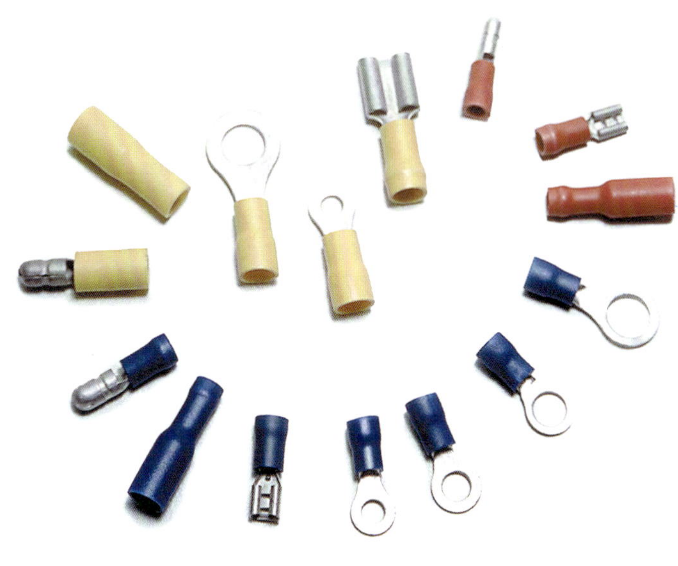

With your wires identified, how to tap into them? Before we even get that far, is that wire you're planning on playing with live?

Switch off the ignition at least - and ideally disconnect the battery before you do anything else. On cars with airbags, don't go tapping into any of the airbag wiring, which is usually bright yellow. With that cleared up, how were you planning on joining the old and new wires together?

The best options are:

Soldering - avoids cutting through your chosen wire - strip away a short section of insulation, wrap your new wire around the bared section, then apply solder to secure it. If you're a bit new to soldering, practice on a few offcuts of wire first - it ain't rocket science! Re-insulate the soldered connection afterwards, with tape or heatshrink tube.

Bullet connectors - cut and strip the end of your chosen wire, wrap your new one to it, push both into one half of the bullet. Connect the other end of your victim wire to the other bullet, and connect together. Always use the "female" half on any live feed - it'll be safer if you disconnect it than a male bullet, which could touch bare metal and send your motor up in smoke.

Block connectors - so easy to use. Just remember that the wires can come adrift if the screws aren't really tight, and don't get too ambitious about how many wires you can stuff in one hole (block connectors, like bullets, are available in several sizes). Steer clear of connectors like the one below - they're convenient, but they can give rise to problems.

With any of these options, always insulate around your connection - especially when soldering, or you'll be leaving bare metal exposed. Remember that you'll probably be shoving all the wires up into the dark recesses of the under-dash area - by the time the wires are nice and kinked/squashed together, that tiny bit of protruding wire might just touch that bit of metal bodywork, and that'll be a fire...

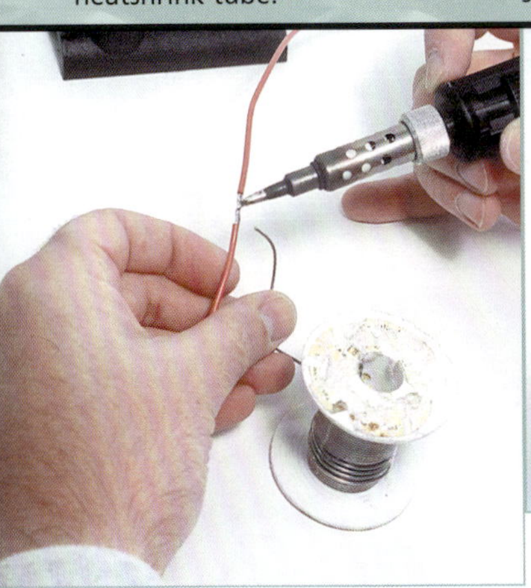

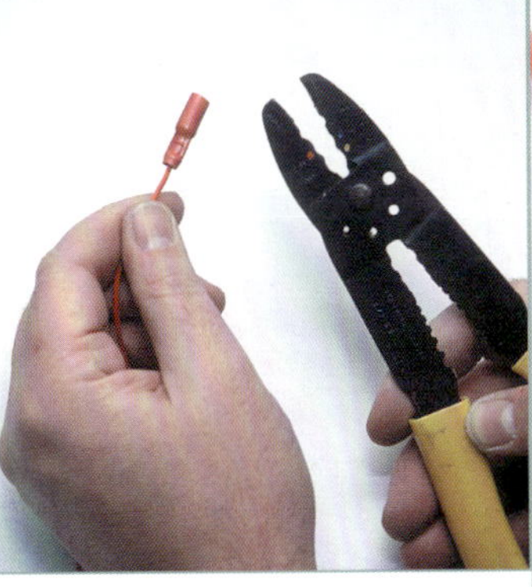

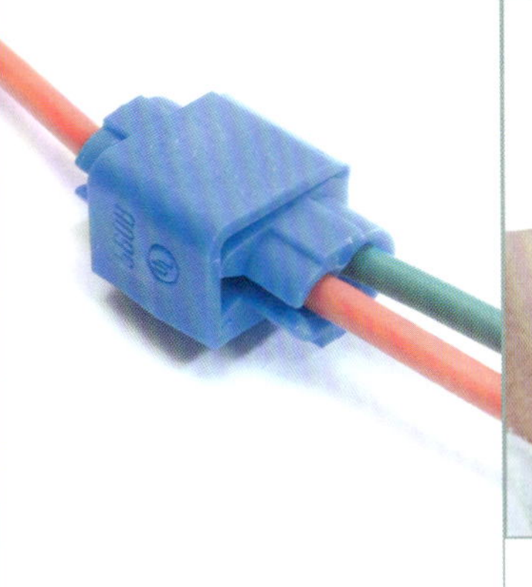

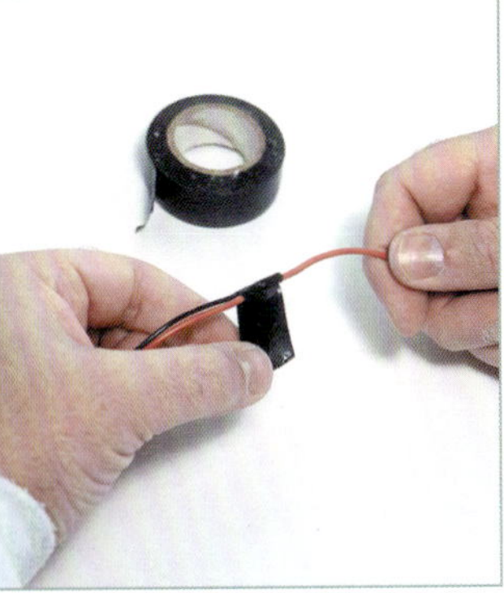

Fitting an **auxiliary fusebox**

You'll need plenty of fused live feeds from the battery during the modifying process, for stereo gear, neons, starter buttons - and alarms, and it's always a pain working out where to tap into one. If you make up your own little fusebox, mounted somewhere easy to get at, you'll never have this problem again - and it's easy enough to do.

The first job is to run a main supply cable from the battery positive terminal, to inside the car - but don't connect the wire up to the battery terminal just yet. Make sure that the main cable is man enough for all the loads you're likely to put on it - starting with four-gauge wire (available from all good ICE suppliers) will mean you're never short of current. As for where to feed the cable through, see the section on fitting an alarm (next in this chapter) or the ICE chapter for some good spots for a hole.

Make a note of which fuse is for which circuit, and carry the paper around in the glovebox (along with some spare fuses). If a fuse ever blows, you won't end up with your head stuck under the dash, trying to remember where you tapped in, and where the fuse is. You'll just pull the cover off, and replace the fuse. Who would've thought electrical safety could be so cool?

01 Okay, so you've got your large live wire into the car - what's next? Our fusebox (bought from our local branch of Lucas) came in two parts - a junction box (which takes the live feed, and splits it into several small ones) and the fusebox itself. Wiring the junction box is simple - live feed on one terminal, all the small feeds on the other (with wire long enough to reach your new fusebox, of course).

02 The junction box can be hidden almost anywhere, but just above where the fusebox will go seems logical. Captain.

03 Attach all the live feeds to one side of the fusebox (using insulated spade terminals, please), and she's ready to mount. In position, that is.

04 Our fusebox is going to sit neatly inside a hole (which we'll cut out later) in the driver's footwell kick panel, so it can be got at easily if a fuse blows. For now though, if we need a live feed for anything, all we do is attach a wire to the other side of the fusebox, and pop in an appropriate-size fuse. Simple.

Alarm fitting

The alarm we've chosen to fit is a MicroScan, which, whilst it isn't a Clifford, still offers a decent level of protection, and a useful array of features for a sensible price. When it goes off, it actually sounds like a Clifford - result!

As with everything else in this book, remember that we're showing you just how this particular alarm is fitted. All the same, whatever alarm you fit, it'll still be useful to pick out the fitting principles and tips. Always refer to the instructions which come with your alarm, and don't go joining the red wire to the yellow wire, just because WE say so...

01 Disconnect the battery negative lead, and move the lead away from the battery, or you'll be blowing fuses and your new alarm will go mental the minute it's rigged up.

02 Decide where you're going to mount the alarm/siren. Choose somewhere not easily reached from underneath, for a start, and if you can, pick a location away from where you'll be topping up washers, oil or coolant - fluids and alarm modules don't mix. The most suitable spot on our Escort was on the chassis leg, above the gearbox, so we tried the alarm module and its bracket first for fit . . .

03 . . . before taking off the bracket and drilling us some mounting holes.

04 Refit the alarm module, and we're on our way. Mind you, that's probably the easiest part over...

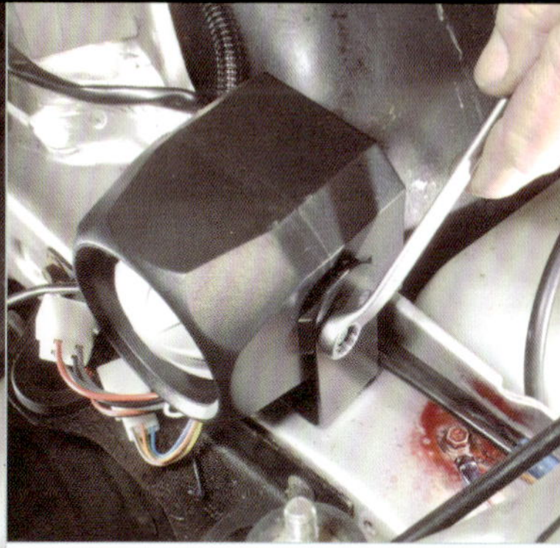

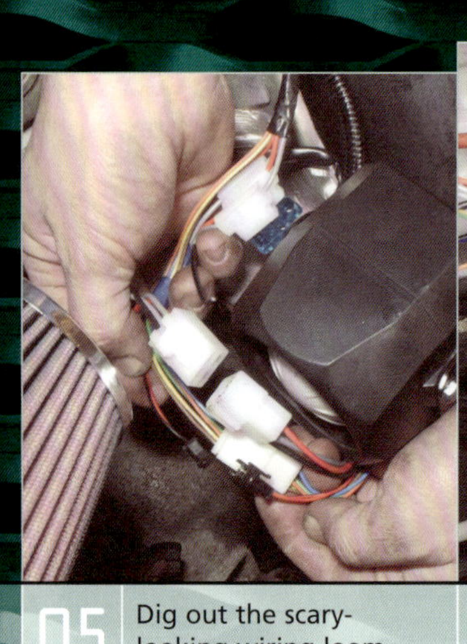

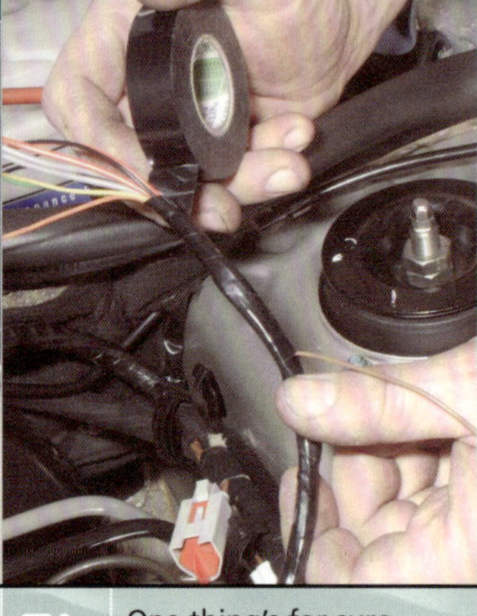

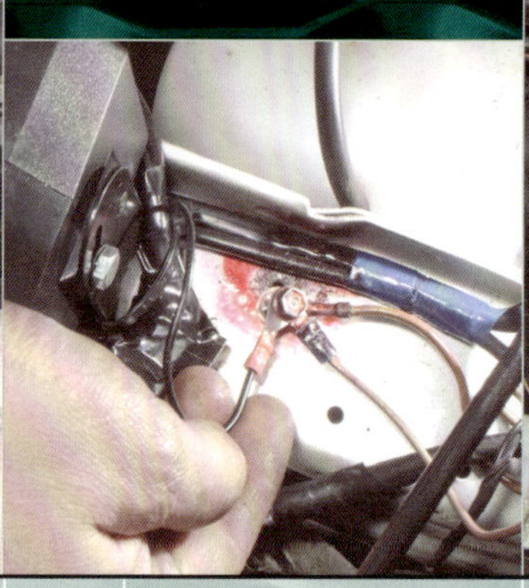

05 Dig out the scary-looking wiring loom from the box. Now would be a good time to start reading your alarm's instructions, and try to work out which wires go through into the car, and which stay under the bonnet.

06 One thing's for sure - you can certainly connect up all the wiring plugs now (as long as that battery stays off). Typically, the only alarm wires not going into the car will be the earth, and the one for the bonnet pin switch - all the rest can be neatly 'loomed' with insulating tape (makes it much easier to poke them all through into the car).

07 The Escort's blessed with several good ready-made earth points under its bonnet, so adding another wire (with a ring terminal attached, please) to the browns already there is no problem. Do your chosen bolt up tight, and squirt on some WD-40 to keep it free of rust.

08 Those other wires you loomed together now have to start their journey into the car. Drill yourself a decent hole through the 'bulkhead' in front of the battery . . .

13 The pin switch has to be mounted on its own little bracket (not supplied, so a bit of fabrication is needed). A simple strip of bent metal will do - but it's got to be strong, to resist further bending when the bonnet shuts. Notice our crafty bracket has two slotted holes, and one larger hole for the switch? The slotted holes mean that the bracket's adjustable for height, which is great for setting the switch nice and sensitive.

14 Fit the switch into the bracket, and tighten its mounting screw. With a spade terminal fitted to the alarm's pin switch wire (brown in our case), we're ready to test its operation.

15 Testing's a lot easier with a posh multi-meter, set to read continuity (resistance), and with an audible signal. Connect one terminal to the pin switch spade, and the other to a good earth. Shut the bonnet, and when the beep stops is the point your alarm would go off. You can duplicate this test with a simple test light, but instead of a good earth, connect one test light wire to the battery positive (+) terminal.

16 If the bonnet opens much before the switch works, you'll be giving access which the crims can exploit. With our slotted mounting plate, adjusting the pin switch height was easy. If your switch is mounted in a non-adjustable stylee, just trim off some of the plastic switch plunger until all's well - trimming the pin switch down will make it 'go off' sooner, but only take off a little plastic at a time, then re-test.

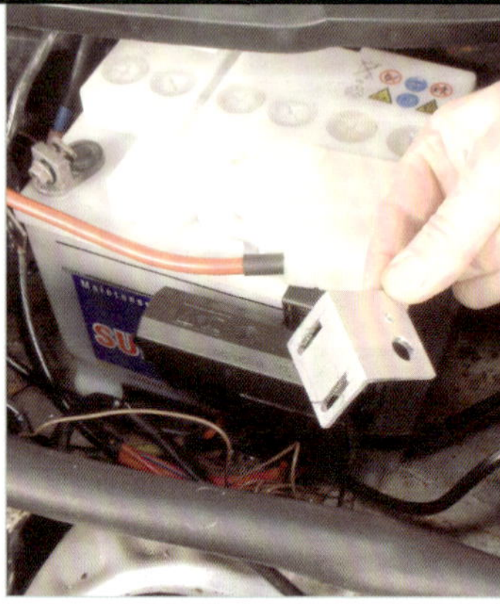

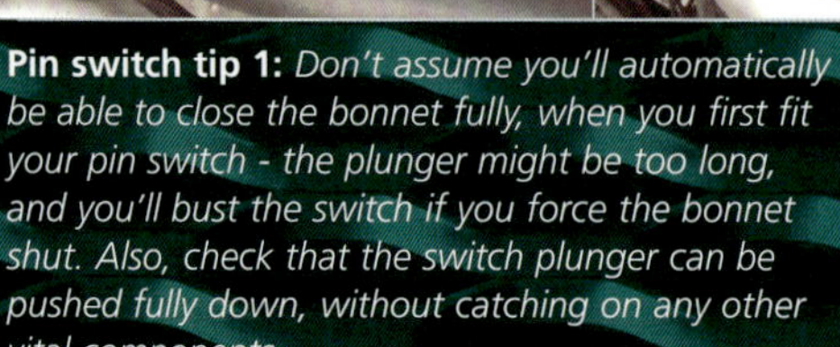

Pin switch tip 1: *Don't assume you'll automatically be able to close the bonnet fully, when you first fit your pin switch - the plunger might be too long, and you'll bust the switch if you force the bonnet shut. Also, check that the switch plunger can be pushed fully down, without catching on any other vital components.*

Pin switch tip 2: *If you go too far when trimming down a pin switch, you can sometimes rescue the situation by screwing a little self-tapping screw into the top of the plunger. You can then 'adjust' the length of the plunger at will. The proper answer, though, is to buy a new switch.*

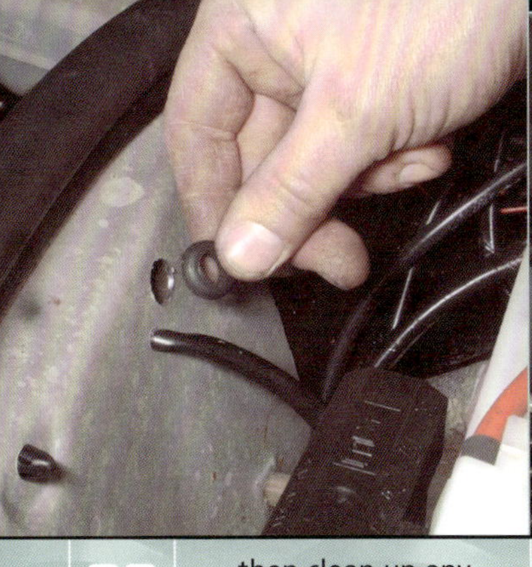

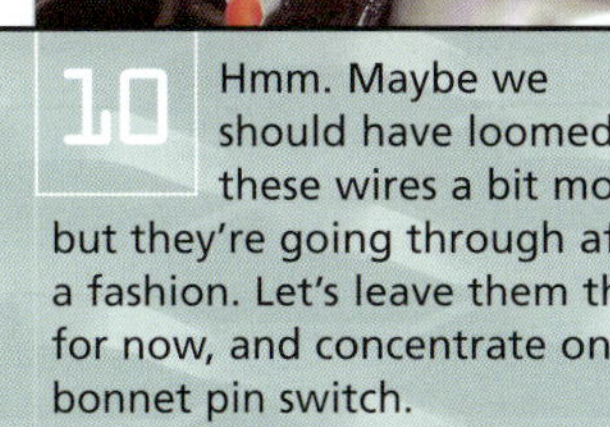

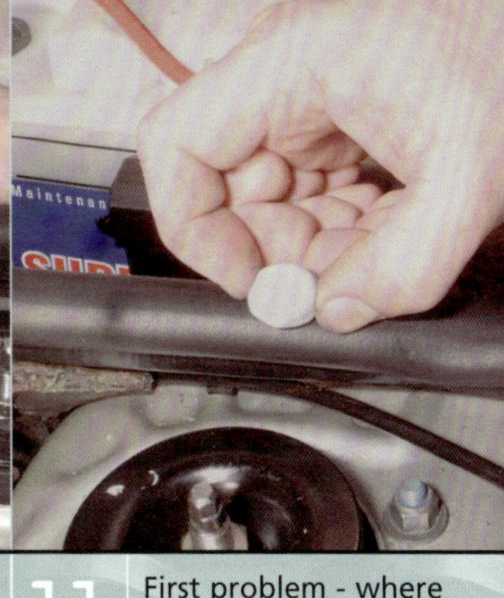

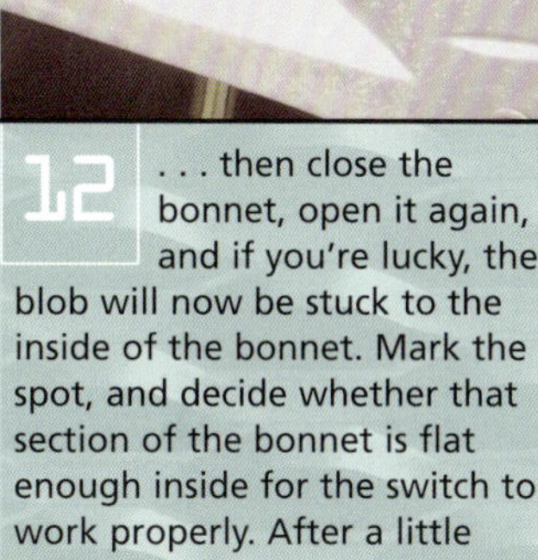

09 . . . then clean up any rough edges from the hole, and please fit a grommet. If you don't, there's a good chance those wires will chafe through on the metal edges of the hole, and then your alarm will do all sorts of daft stuff, including setting your car on fire.

10 Hmm. Maybe we should have loomed these wires a bit more, but they're going through after a fashion. Let's leave them there for now, and concentrate on the bonnet pin switch.

11 First problem - where does the switch need to be? Well, as close to the battery as poss, but where can we mount it, and will the switch hit a 'good' spot on the bonnet? To find the answer (and to avoid squinting through a just-cracked-open bonnet), get yourself a blob of Blu-tac, and place it roughly where you'd like your pin switch to be . . .

12 . . . then close the bonnet, open it again, and if you're lucky, the blob will now be stuck to the inside of the bonnet. Mark the spot, and decide whether that section of the bonnet is flat enough inside for the switch to work properly. After a little fiddling about and measuring, you'll hit on the ideal spot.

17 Back to all those other wires, which we're still trying to get into the car. First, we fed them across to the driver's side, behind that 'bulkhead', and down through the gap at the corner, into the wheelarch.

18 With the right-hand front wheel off, and the arch liner removed, you can see where we're going. There's a huge rubber grommet under there, which already has loads of wiring going through. We'll make our own hole, and poke the alarm wires through too. Some careful work with the knife is called for - we don't want to chop any of those other wires, do we?

19 To help push the wires through, try taping them to the shaft of a screwdriver, or to a slim socket extension bar . . .

20 . . . you'll find the extra shoving power this gives will be very useful - that grommet's no pushover.

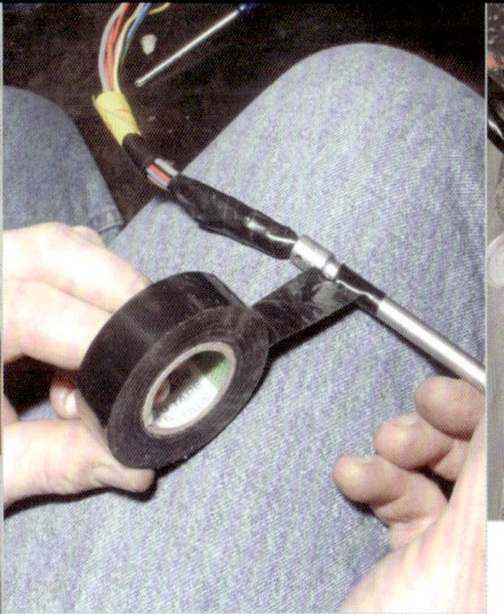

>>

21 With luck, your wires should now be arriving just behind the fusebox, ready to be connected up. Fortunately, access to the Escort fusebox isn't bad - remove the dash trim panel (five screws) for a better view. No, removing the carpets is not essential - just something we did for our 'race-look' machine.

22 The fusebox situation gets even better, though. Above the two rows of fuses, there's an over-centre catch - flip it up to release it, then lift the fusebox and unhook the clip. Fusebox drops down at the front.

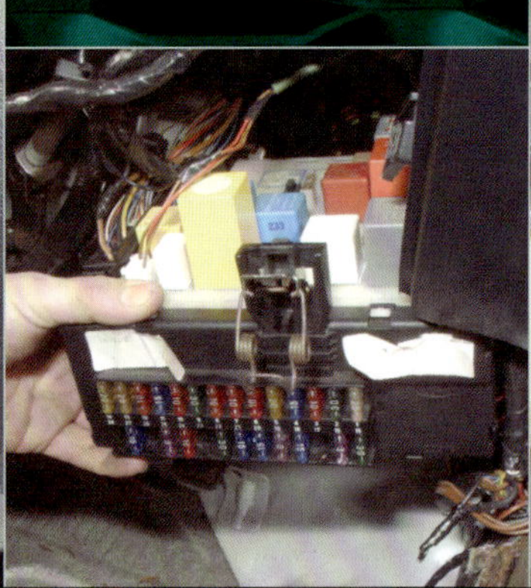

23 The fusebox is further held in by a spring clip on the left side - pull the fusebox forward to hear it go 'twang' . . .

24 . . . but getting the right side released is trickier - there's a peg on the fusebox which clips into a long slot. To release it, lift the box up, then pull forwards, which slides the peg along the slot to a hole. With a bit of wiggling, the box will be freed.

29 . . . and finally, wrap round the bare joint with insulating tape (or heatshrink if you're feeling clever). One neat, reliable job of wire splicing. Unlike chopping wires, there's no danger with this method that your original wiring circuit might stop working - no wires have been cut.

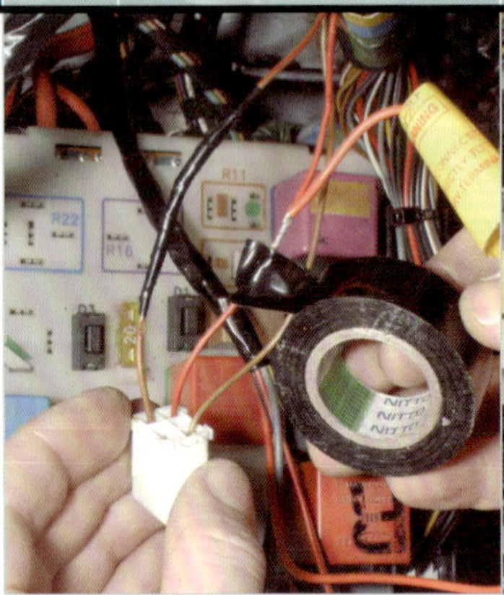

30 According to our Haynes manual wiring diagram, the indicator wires (which we need next) are black/white and black/green in colour. Trouble is, there's more than one set of wires this colour, so after temporarily reconnecting the battery and switching on the indicators, we test with our meter, and find they're together in the big wiring plug on the right-hand side of the fusebox. Strip and solder on your alarm wires, not forgetting to insulate afterwards.

31 All that remains is the oh-so-important LED, to show the world you've got an alarm, and to be afraid. The LED should have been fed through with the rest of the wiring, and now has to be poked up behind your chosen location in the dash. Our XR3i had so many immobilisers previously fitted, there was at least one pre-drilled hole for us - you might have to get the drill out. Fit LED to holder, holder to dash.

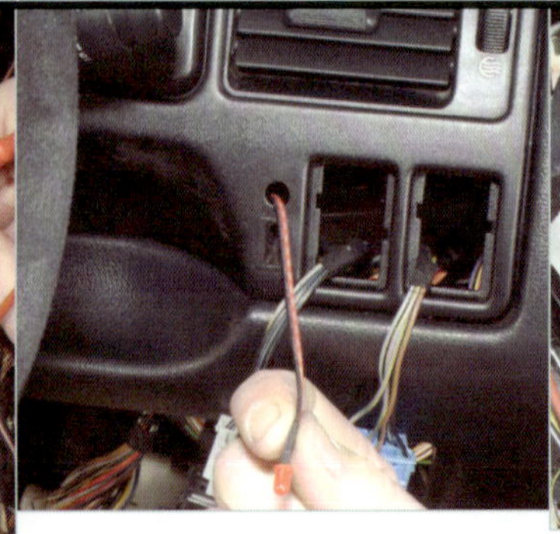

32 At this point, we should've been ready to just connect up our central locking wires, and test the alarm. Sadly, the Escort has what's called 'positive-pulse' central locking, so we needed the optional Microscan locking interface. Before we get to the wiring, we need a place to stash this little black box. Cover the back in double-sided tape, and stuff it up above the fusebox.

Tricks 'n' tips

When you're wiring up anything to do with central locking, it might pay to leave a window open, to avoid accidentally being locked out. It happens, and boy, it's embarrassing.

25 You'll find that the fusebox is now hanging on one particular section of wire - luckily, this is for the interior light, which we need next. The plug just unclips from the fusebox . . .

26 . . . and it's the red interior light live feed we're after. Our rather basic alarm takes its main power from the car's interior light circuit. We're going to do all the wiring joins properly, with solder, so the first job is to strip off about 10 mm of insulation from our target red wire.

27 Now bare the end of the alarm interior light supply wire (also red), and wrap it round the section you just stripped . . .

28 . . . apply heat, apply solder, watch it flow into the wires (excellent to watch) . . .

33 The black box requires its own earth (there's a ready-made beauty, right next to where we're working) and several live feeds (three altogether - count 'em), which we took from our auxiliary fusebox. Knew there was a reason why we fitted that. There's also an alarm trigger wire to join to the interface - just follow the instructions in the box.

34 All that's left now is finding the central locking 'lock' and 'unlock' trigger wires. The most likely place to find them is in the driver's door loom (and it comes into the car right next to the fusebox - oh yes). The Haynes wiring diagrams show us it's a yellow wire (lock) and a white (unlock). More stripping and soldering had these wires joined to the relevant ones on the central locking black box, and we're hot.

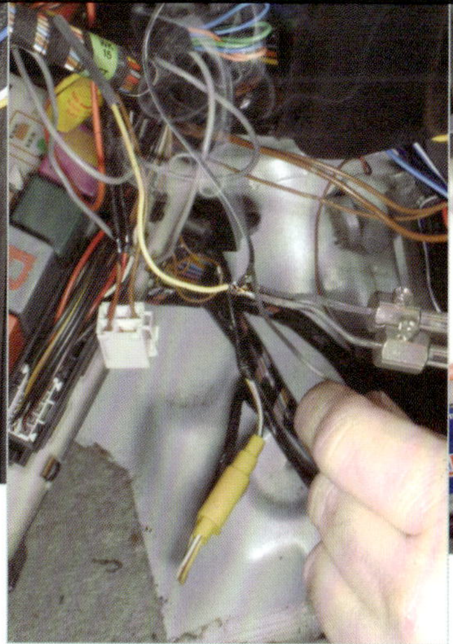

35 So come on - does it work? Most alarms require you to "programme in" the remotes before they'll work. Test all the alarm features in turn, remembering to allow enough time for the alarm to arm itself (usually about 30 seconds). When you test it for the first time, don't forget to either shut the bonnet completely, or do like us, and hold the bonnet pin switch down. Our way, you can pull out the alarm fuses and shut it up, if something goes wrong!

36 Set the anti-shock sensitivity with a thought to where you live and park - will it be set off every night by the neighbour's cat, or by kids playing football? Finally, and most important of all - next time you park up, remember to set it!

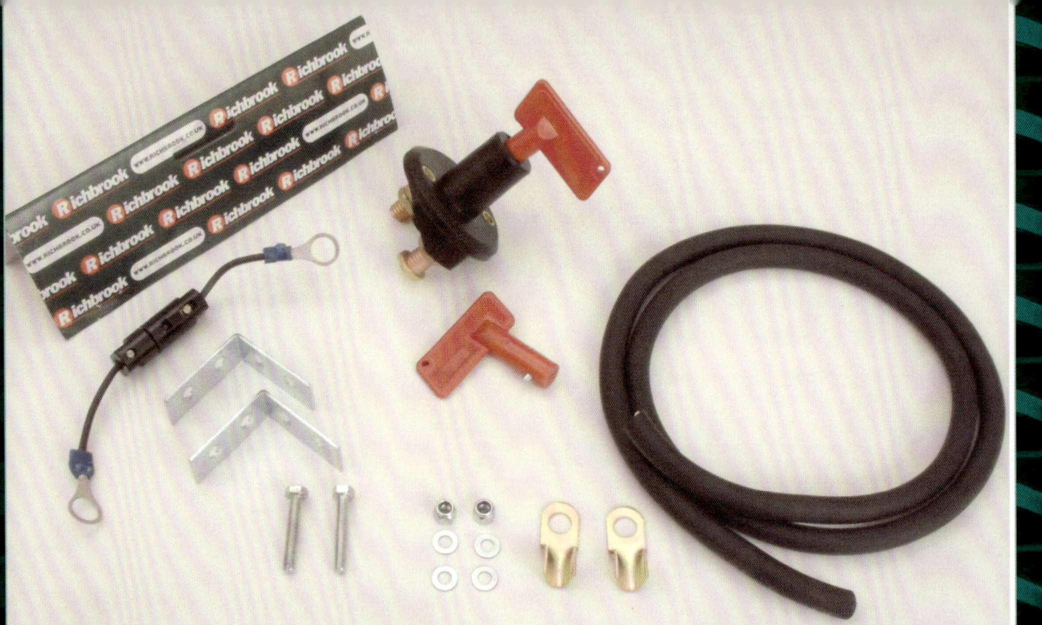

Power cut

It's always a bonus when you come back to find your modded motor just where you left it. If you've ever experienced the gut-wrenching sick feeling of staring at the patch of tarmac once occupied by your trick car, you won't need any encouragement to beef up your security. And for once, security can be fun - ladeez an' gennelmen, we bring you the battery master switch, from our friends at Richbrook (famous, among other things, for starter buttons).

Two uses for this switch, both of which give you an immobiliser after taking out the red master key. Fit it in line with the battery negative lead, and the switch either cuts off all the earth function (car stone-dead, electrically), or you fit the (supplied) fuseholder, which lets a small current pass, to keep alarm, radio and clock settings active. This fuse will blow if anyone tries using the starter motor, however. Neat. The other way to use this switch (without the fuse) is to locate the ignition coil supply, and use the switch to break that. Escorts have a DIS coil pack (sometimes hidden on the back of the engine - follow the HT leads), which has an earth supply (black wire on early models, purple/blue on later ones).

01 So here's what you'll need - okay, so you don't actually get the two (DIY store) brackets, or the nuts and bolts (also DIY store), or the four-gauge wiring, or the big ring terminals, in the kit. But you do get everything else.

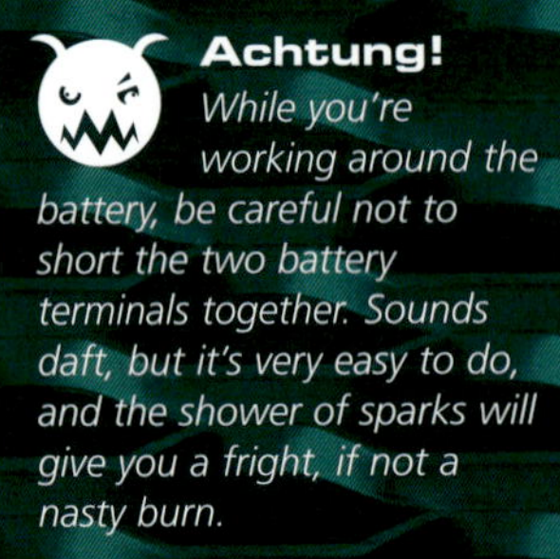

Achtung!

While you're working around the battery, be careful not to short the two battery terminals together. Sounds daft, but it's very easy to do, and the shower of sparks will give you a fright, if not a nasty burn.

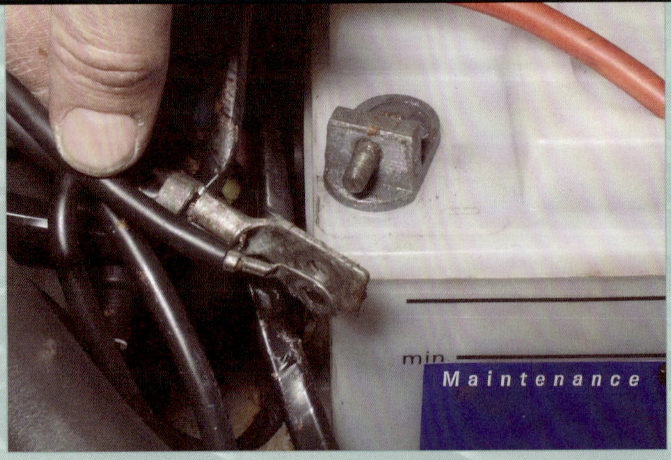

02 We're so keen to get this baby on the car, we've already picked out a spot for it, next to the battery (you might want to choose somewhere more discreet - are you fitting this to work, or as a pose?). The first thing we did was to drill the switch sides, and mount on those DIY-store brackets which you don't get with the kit.

03 If you're breaking into the battery negative lead, you'll be wanting some wire that's just as heavy (any downsizing in the wire department will be very dangerous). So we're talking four-gauge wire from your local ICE shop, and some decent ring terminals, too (you'll need four in total). Preferably, use solder as well as the crimping to hold the terminals on.

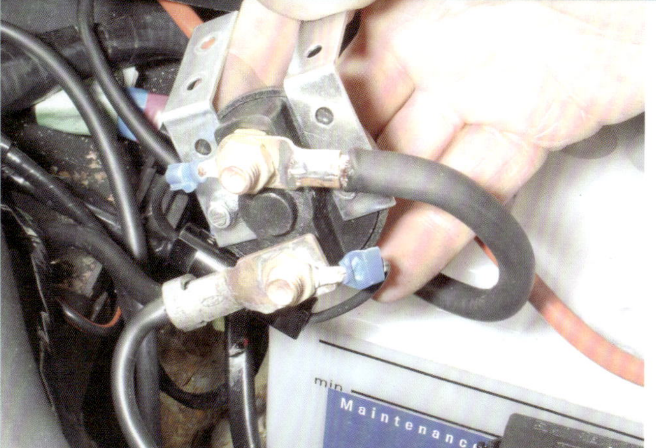

04 Woah - the 'scary' wiring. Disconnect the battery negative lead, and connect to one side of your switch, together with one blue ring terminal for the fuseholder. Fit the other fuseholder blue ring to the other terminal on the switch, and re-join the battery with the heavy wire you made up earlier. Not scary at all.

05 All downhill now - mount your switch in your chosen spot (not much room for a drill in here, with that battery in the way) . . .

06 . . . then separate the fuseholder, and fit the fuse.

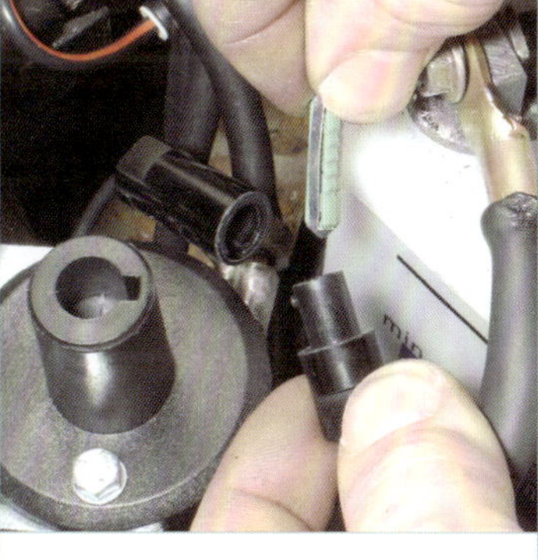

07 All you have to do now, to ensure no-one starts your beloved machine in your absence, is to take out the red key. And then don't put it in the glovebox, with your stereo faceplate. Or lose it, of course. D'oh!

05

Body styling

Body styling

If you're planning a major body job, you've probably already got some good ideas about how you want your Escort to look, from *Max Power* or *Revs*, or maybe from a friend's car. While it can be good to have a target car to aim for, if you're just starting out on the road towards a fully-loaded car, you probably don't want (or can't quite afford) to go 'all the way' all at once.

If you're new to the world of modifying, it's a good idea to start with smaller jobs, and work up to the full body kit gradually, as your skills increase; spending loads on a body kit is a pretty lame idea if you then make a mess of fitting it! There's plenty of small ways to improve the look of your Escort, which don't cost much, and which are simple enough to fit; start with some of these before you go too mad!

One golden rule with any body mods is to plan what you're going to do, and don't rush it. It's better that the car looks a bit stupid for a week (because you couldn't get something finished) than to rush a job and have the car look stupid forever. Do half the job properly than all of it badly. Try and think the jobs through - plan each stage. Have you got all the tools, screws or whatever before you start, or will you have to break off halfway through? If you get stuck, is there someone you can get to help, or have they gone off for the weekend? Above all, if something goes wrong - don't panic - a calm approach will prove to be a huge bonus (that job doesn't have to be done today, does it?).

If a piece of trim won't come off, don't force it. If something feels like it's going to break, it probably will - stop and consider whether to go on and break it, or try another approach. Especially on an older car, things never come off as easily as you think, or else have already been off so many times that they either break or won't fit back on properly. While we'd all like to do a perfect job every time, working on an older car will, sooner or later, teach you the fine art of 'bodging' (finding valid alternative ways of fixing things!). Don't assume that you'll have to bodge something back on, every time - if a trim clip breaks when you take something off, it might be easier and cheaper than you think to simply go to your Ford dealer, and buy a new clip (remember, even Ford mechanics break things from time to time, so they will keep these things in stock!).

Mirror, mirror

Mirrors are simple to fit, must-have accessory. The DTM or M3-style door mirrors are well established on the modified car circuit, but there are lots of variations of mirror styles and finishes, so finding some you like won't be hard.

The nice people at Demon Tweeks supplied our tasty California mirrors. As we decided on a rally theme for our car, these puppies certainly fitted the look. Unfortunately, they're 'universal' items, which means we're in for some work, to make them fit. But we're not scared.

Tricks 'n' tips

Some mirrors aren't supplied with a mirror base - check before you buy. You might be able to buy the bases separately - if not, you're making your own, like us. You can use either Perspex or metal plate, but whatever you choose must be durable.

Fitting California mirrors

01 Firstly remove the door trim panel, as described in 'Interiors'. There's just one screw holding the black triangle of plastic behind the mirror, so that won't tax your brain too much.

02 Behind this trim are three screws that hold the mirror in place. Even without the screws, the mirror is still attached by two plastic plugs, so carefully pull the unit away from the car to dislodge them. If you've got electric mirrors, there's also a wiring plug inside the door to disconnect at this point. Try not to break the mirrors – you may want to sell or use them again. Or perhaps not.

03 To make a base for the new mirrors, we need a template. Fold some paper to mark the mirror area (paper is less rigid than card, and will fit the awkward areas better). Allow 15 to 20 mm extra at the bottom, to create a bent-over flanged edge where the mirror base meets the window. Bending kind-of rules out plastic as a suitable material for the base, doesn't it?

>>

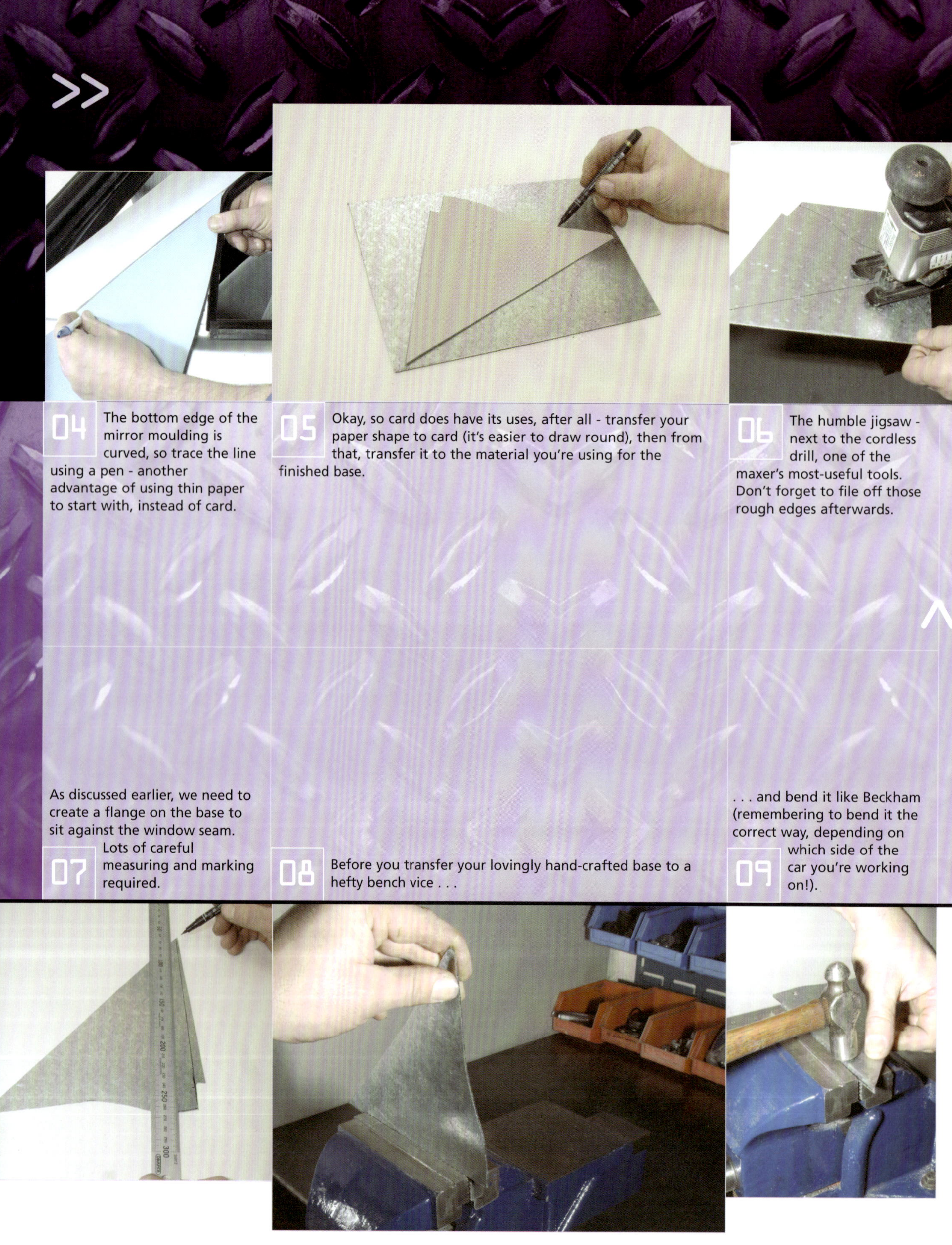

04 The bottom edge of the mirror moulding is curved, so trace the line using a pen - another advantage of using thin paper to start with, instead of card.

05 Okay, so card does have its uses, after all - transfer your paper shape to card (it's easier to draw round), then from that, transfer it to the material you're using for the finished base.

06 The humble jigsaw - next to the cordless drill, one of the maxer's most-useful tools. Don't forget to file off those rough edges afterwards.

07 As discussed earlier, we need to create a flange on the base to sit against the window seam. Lots of careful measuring and marking required.

08 Before you transfer your lovingly hand-crafted base to a hefty bench vice . . .

09 . . . and bend it like Beckham (remembering to bend it the correct way, depending on which side of the car you're working on!).

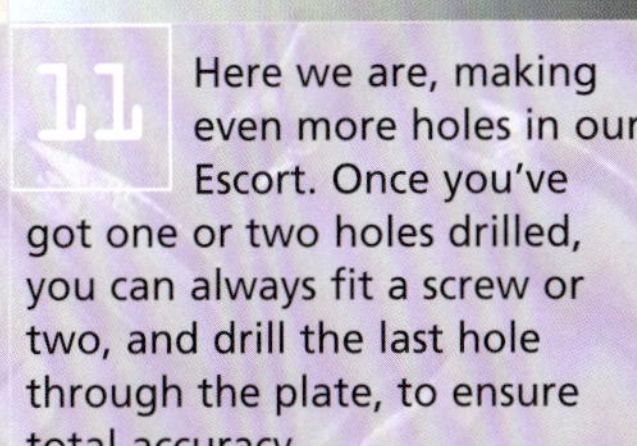

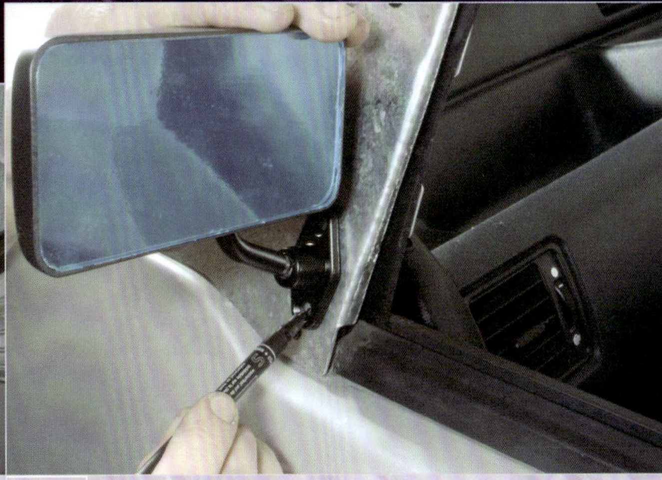

10 Now we want three holes to secure the base to the car. You can use either your card template, or the real thing for this bit - mark the holes, but lift the plate away from the car and check there's actually some metal behind, to drill into. Once you've drilled your three holes in the plate, use the plate to mark through for drilling the door itself.

11 Here we are, making even more holes in our Escort. Once you've got one or two holes drilled, you can always fit a screw or two, and drill the last hole through the plate, to ensure total accuracy.

12 Screw the base to the car, then work out where you want the mirrors to fit. There is some adjustment on these mirrors, but it's best to check from the driving seat, with another helpful bod positioning the mirror for you. Mark the positions of the holes . . .

. . . then take off the bases, and drill them through. The mirrors are held on by two Allen screws, with nuts on the inside. 13

At this point we encountered a problem. If you ever wanted to remove just the mirror, it would mean that the whole base would have to be removed, which is a lengthy process. This can be resolved by using Araldite (or any other wicked-strength adhesive) and gluing the nuts to the back of the base. 14

The alloy plate we used looked a little dull against the car, so we decided to cover the plate in carbon-fibre-look film. Cut round the shape, leaving at least a 10mm edge so that the film can be folded over the edges. The film we were using needed a heat gun to mould and stick the film to the base - check your film's instructions. If all this is too much hassle, get the paint cans out instead. 15

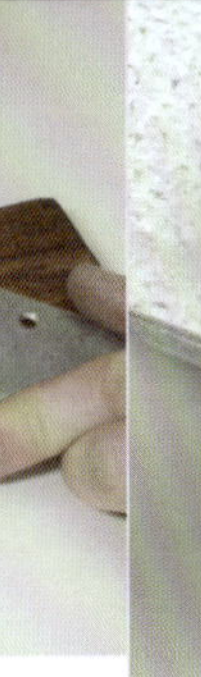

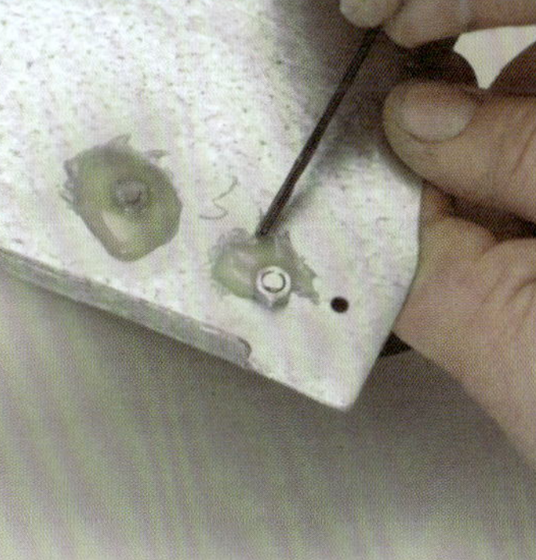

Smoothly **does it**

If you've bought a basic Escort, it's understandable that you might not want to declare this fact loudly from the rear end of your car. Badges also clutter up the otherwise clean lines, and besides, you're trying to make your Escort look different, so why give them obvious clues like a badge? Most Escorts also come with admittedly-useful but actually quite ugly side rubbing strips of some sort (most of which give away the size of your engine, too) - lose these, or at least colour-code, if you're at all serious about raising your game.

General bodywork smoothing (including de-seaming) takes time and skill, and is probably best done on a car which is then getting the full bodykit and wicked respray treatment. There's no doubt, however, that it really looks the business to have a fully-smoothed tailgate, or even to have those rather ugly roof gutters smoothed over. Probably best to put the pros at a bodyshop to work on this. De-badging you can definitely do at home, so get to it.

De-stripping

01 Side rubbing strips. Good - they save your paint if someone opens his rusty Metro door into your car. Bad - they look hideous. If looks are important, removal is easy. Carefully prise the strip at one end, using a bit of card to stop paint damage . . .

02 . . . then give it some heat (or choose a hot day) and it simply peels off. If you don't use heat (or don't use enough), the glue won't soften, and you'll have a long job getting it off the paintwork.

03 Clean any glue off with meths (non-metallic/unlacquered paint might also need T-Cutting), and your Escort is one step less 'sensible' than it was before. Speaking of sensible, you haven't still got mudflaps on, have you? Granddad?

De-badging

01 The tailgate badges are easy to dispose of, and leave no holes behind afterwards - bonus! First, soften the glue with a heatgun, remembering you're not trying to melt the badges - okay?

02 Any wide-bladed tool will do to prise the badge off, but it might be wise to wrap the blade with some tape, to avoid wrecking your paint.

03 A touch of meths later, and you're one step nearer a smoothed tailgate.

04 You might be a devoted Ford fan, but there's really no excuse for leaving the blue oval behind. Get it gone.

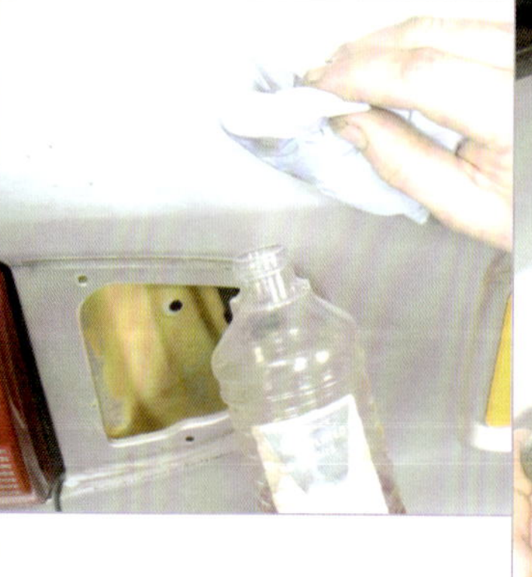

Filling holes - a cunning plan

When it comes to car bodywork, every hole is not a goal. At least small holes can be filled without stretching your talent envelope too far. First, cover the area around your chosen hole (two holes, in this case) with masking

01 tape - make sure you get a decent working area around the hole.

02 Now neatly cut out your holes in the tape.

Here's where we start to see the true cunning of this plan - mix up some Araldite (or similar glue for bonding metals), and apply a blob of it to a washer large enough to cover the hole,

03 on the inside. Rich types among you may prefer to use a coin.

Stick the washer or coin on from inside, then stand around

04 looking stupid, holding it in place while the glue dries.

05 Mix up some filler, and apply to your hole - the masking tape prevents any getting on the paintwork. Apply more than one layer, and build the filler up evenly.

06 We found that the filler could be trimmed flat using a sharp Stanley blade, used at a very shallow angle. The filler doesn't really 'take' to the masking tape, making it easier to trim away the excess.

07 Peel away the masking tape, and your hole is filled - all it needs is paint.

08 If you haven't done such a great job, remember that you can improve things by applying layer after layer of paint (wait for each one to dry). When you've built the paint up proud of the hole, T-Cut it back smooth.

Fitting a **sunstrip**

The modern sunstrip, first seen as a lovely green shadeband on Cortinas and Capris back in the 70s, usually bearing imaginative slogans such as 'DAVE AND SHARON'. Just goes to show that some things improve with age.

There are two options to make your car look (and maybe even feel) cooler:

a The sunvisor, a screen tint band inside the screen, which is usually a graduated-tint strip. As this fits inside, there's a problem straight away - the interior mirror. The Escort mirror is bonded to the screen, and it seriously gets in the way when trying to fit a wet and sticky (nice!) strip of plastic around it. Go for a sunstrip instead.

b The sunstrip, which is opaque vinyl, colour-matched to the car, fits to the outside of the screen. Much more Sir.

A really wide sunstrip imitates the 'roof chop' look seen on American hot rods, and colour-coded, they can look very effective from the front - plus, of course, you can use the space to advertise your preferred brand of ICE (no, no, NO! Not a good idea!). As it's fitted to the outside of the screen, the sunstrip has a good chance of seriously interfering with your wipers (or wiper, if you've been converted). If this happens to the point where the wipers can't clean the screen, Mr MOT might have a point if he fails your car... The wiper blades may need replacing more often, and the sunstrip itself might start peeling off - still want one? Well, you've got to, really.

Legal eagle

The rule for tinting or otherwise modifying the windscreen is that there must be no more than a 25% light reduction from standard. In theory, this means you can have a sunstrip which covers up to 25% of the screen area, but some MOT testers may see it differently. A sunstrip's got to come down the screen a fair way, to look any sense (otherwise, why bother?). You could argue that accurately measuring and calculating the windscreen area isn't actually that easy, if you get stopped, and anyway, a sunstrip also cuts out harmful glare! If you go so far down the screen that you can't see out, though - well, that's just stupid.

01 This is only stuck to the outside, so only the outside of the screen needs cleaning - excellent! Do a good job of cleaning, though - any dirt stuck under the strip will ruin the effect.

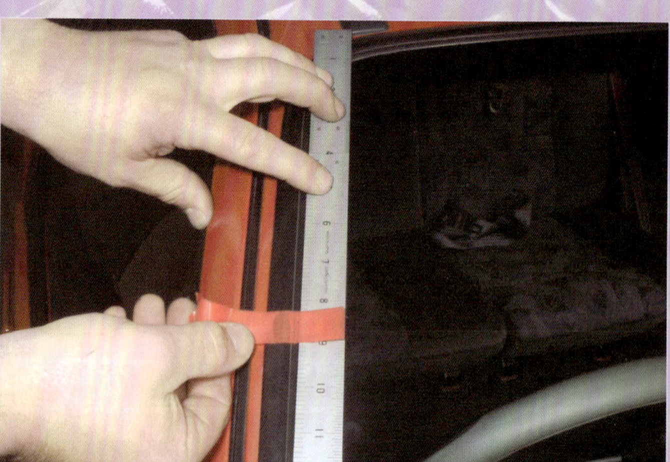

02 With the help of an assistant (if you have one handy), lay the strip onto the car, and decide how far down the screen you're going to go. Legally-speaking, you shouldn't be lower than the wiper swept area - so how much of a 'badboy' are you? If you measure and mark the bottom of the strip with tape, you'll be sure to get it level, even if it's not legal.

Trim off the excess strip at this stage - means you'll have less flapping about when you start trying to stick it down.

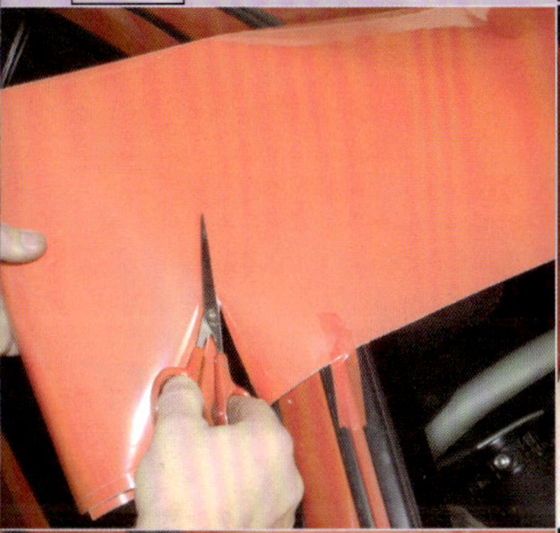

03

04 Spray the screen with water (mixed with a drop of washing-up liquid) . . .

05 . . . then peel off the backing, spraying that as well, and wake up your assistant.

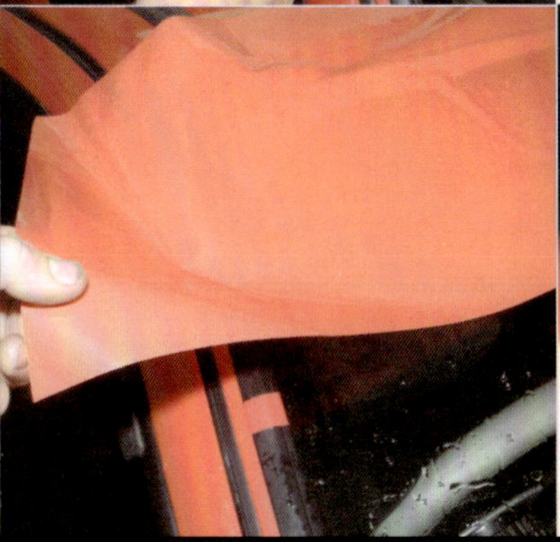

06 With one of you either side of the car, stick the strip on to the masking-tape marks.

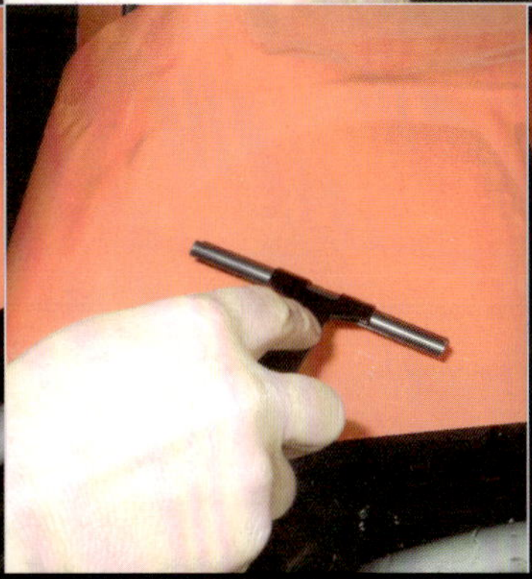

07 Using a squeegee and some more spray, get the worst of the air bubbles out now - keep the squeegee wet while you do this, or your new strip will get well-scuffed (worst-case, you'll peel it off at the edges). Getting rid of all the tiny air bubbles is time-consuming and pretty boring, honestly, but essential for a decent job.

08 Trimming-up isn't as scary as it might seem. Make sure you've got a really sharp blade and a steady hand, and cut with firm, decisive strokes rather than lots of little nicks - this is especially true when you get to the corners. Using an old plastic store card helps no end tucking-in the edges. Don't let the excess strip stick to the roof or A-pillars while you're trimming - keep peeling it off.

Tricks 'n' tips

If you have trouble getting things trimmed up neatly, remember that you can lift the windscreen rubber slightly (using a small screwdriver), and tuck the edge of the strip underneath, for a really neat fit.

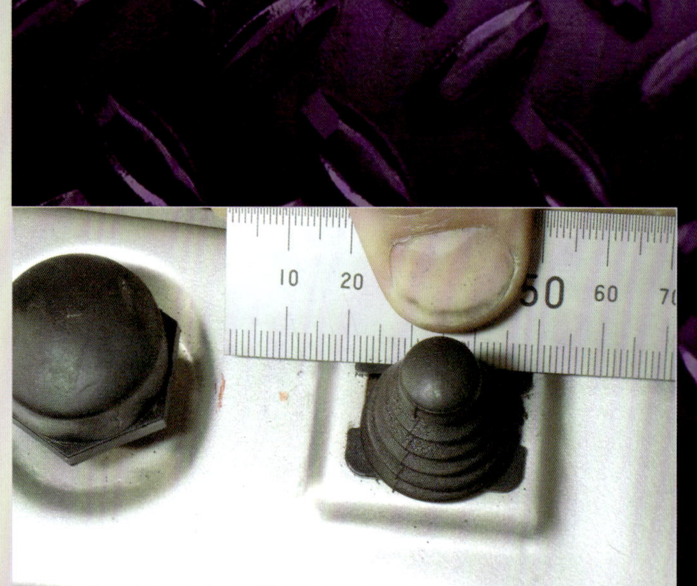

Bonnet pins

Bonnet pins are a trick mod, even if you don't have the engine power to really need them - looks are just as important! Try to steer clear of the stick-on ones – they look pants.

A heavy-duty set of pins will set you back about a tenner, fitting is easy and the results are great. The Cosmic Racing kit we used, supplied to us by Autopoint Car Care, includes everything you need to create the ultimate race/rally look. If you're unsure where to fit the pins, check out some motorsport pictures to see where the pros have them (proper racers have a pin at each corner).

01 Bonnet pins should be placed at the corners of the bonnet (not too far in) - and they're most easily fitted to the front crossmember. On the driver's side, you've got a bump stop and the Ford alarm pin switch in the way, and we wanted our pin in-between. Tricky. A big hole is needed - mark the position to avoid the bump stop recess, or you'll have problems when you fit the nut underneath.

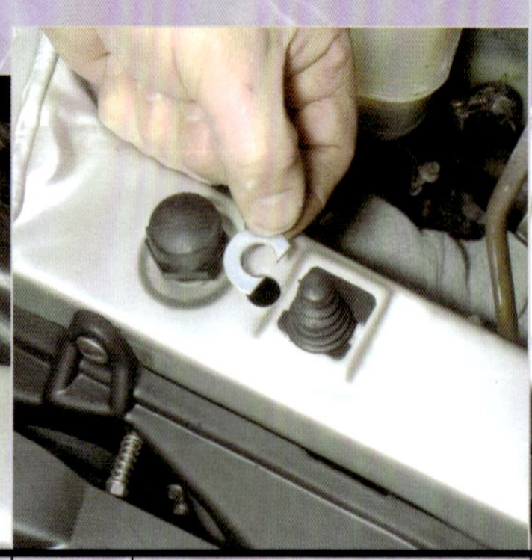

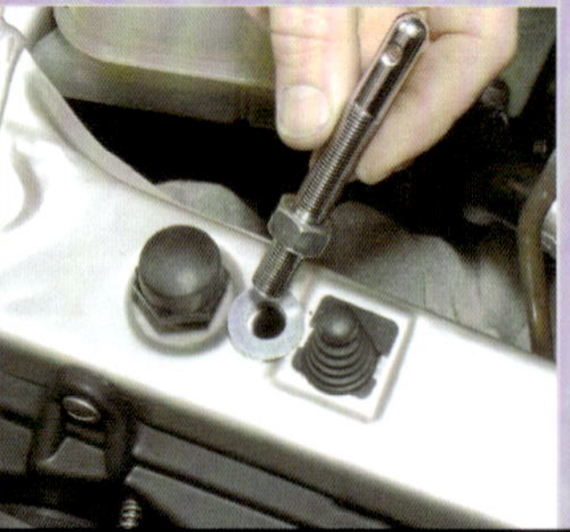

02 Using a centre-punch if you have one, mark the centre point - it just makes drilling the hole easier. Start with a small pilot hole, before working up to the monster needed for the pin - in our case it was a 12mm hole needed, but measure the width of your pin first to be sure.

03 A spacer is needed to allow the upper retaining nut to sit flush against that pin switch raised platform. We used a large normal washer and cut it with tin snips to create this spacer . . .

04 . . . then add another unmolested new washer, and place the pin and upper retaining nut into the hole. Secure it loosely with another washer below, and the lower retaining nut.

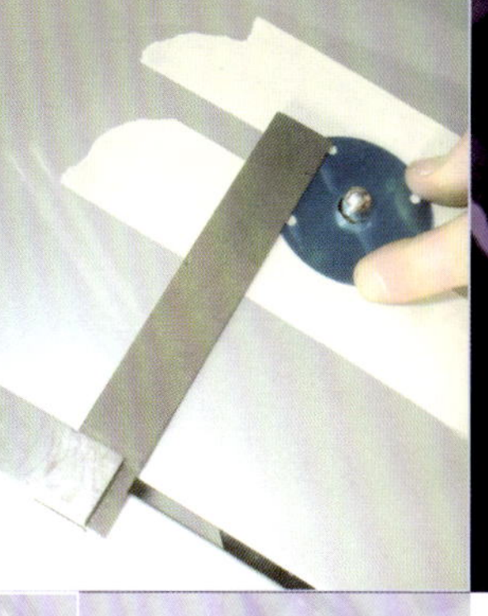

05 Here's the fiddly bit – finding out where on the bonnet you need to drill the hole. We smeared some copper grease onto the top of the bonnet pin we just fitted, and closed the bonnet down until the grease had marked the spot. Here's our midget's-eye-view of this process in action. You can use whatever you have that leaves a mark!

06 Taking your trusty centre-punch, mark the spot left by the grease . . .

07 . . . and drill away (it's only your bonnet, after all) until you get the size of the hole you need. Drill a small hole at first, then lower the bonnet to see where the pin is catching. Keep drilling or filing the hole until the pin fits. Drill your later holes from outside the bonnet - you may find this easier than drilling up from below. Don't worry if you end up with a huge hole - the pin plates will cover this.

08 On both sides of the hole in the bonnet, apply masking tape and place a plate on the pin. For perfectionists, use a set square to make sure the holes that will hold the plate down are in alignment with the edge of the bonnet. You can never do too good a job, after all.

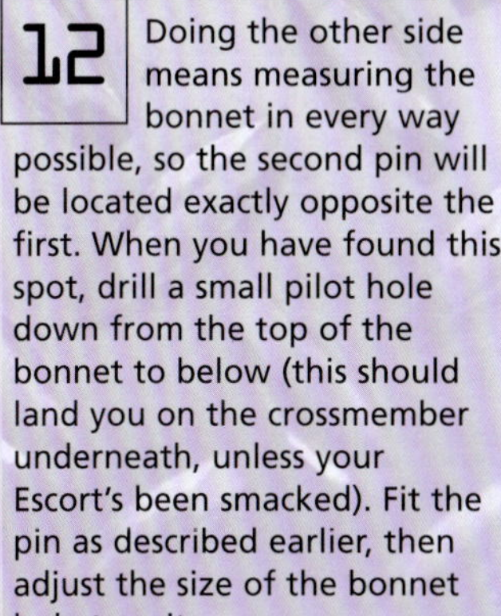

09 Mark the holes through the plates with a pen, remove the plate and drill these holes. Well, what's four more holes in your bonnet, after the monster you did earlier? No fear.

10 Using the self-tapping screws supplied, fix the plate to the bonnet.

11 The final step is to adjust the pin so it sits high enough up through the bonnet to allow the slide-in key to secure it. Adjust the pin by loosening the upper and lower retaining nuts on the crossmember. The key should be a firm fit with the bonnet fully shut. When you're happy, use two spanners to tighten the upper and lower pin nuts.

12 Doing the other side means measuring the bonnet in every way possible, so the second pin will be located exactly opposite the first. When you have found this spot, drill a small pilot hole down from the top of the bonnet to below (this should land you on the crossmember underneath, unless your Escort's been smacked). Fit the pin as described earlier, then adjust the size of the bonnet hole to suit.

Race window **surround**

Okay, so you might want to tint your windows - but everyone knows it's a fiddly pain-in-the-a job, only to be attempted when you're totally mellowed-out. Man. So if you're not into tinting, are there any other options to tart up your glasswork, apart from loads of ICE stickers (which are just an invite to having your glass smashed, after all)?

We know it won't be everyone's cup of java, but we're creating a race/rally-look Escort here, so we thought we'd try something new - Folia Tec race window surround, which (it says on the box) creates the rally/touring car look of bolted-in perspex side glass. Let's see.

01 As with window tinting, the first step is to get your glass clean. Makes sense, if you want anything to stick to anything else, really. Looks suspiciously like gaffer tape to us, but we'll carry on. Trim yourself off a length . . .

02 . . . and stick it on. Only - it's not that simple. This stuff loves to trap air bubbles underneath, and once they're there, they're hell to shift. So - the trick is to keep the tape stretched, and to apply it slowly, using the spreader-type tool they give you in the box. This way, no air gets in from the start, and your stress level stays normal.

03 To do the corners, they give you a wider strip of tape, which you lay on at an angle, like this . . .

04 . . . then (after you trim off the excess over the window rubbers) you take a suitably-round object, and trim a neat curve around it. Folia Tec suggest using french curves, but who's likely to have a set of those lying about?

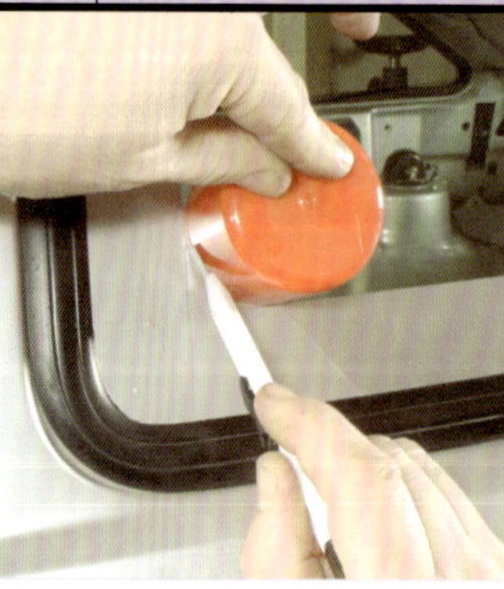

05 The 'bolt heads' are stick-on imitations, obviously. To get any sort of cred from this, those 'bolts' have to be stuck on an equal distance apart, so get measuring and marking.

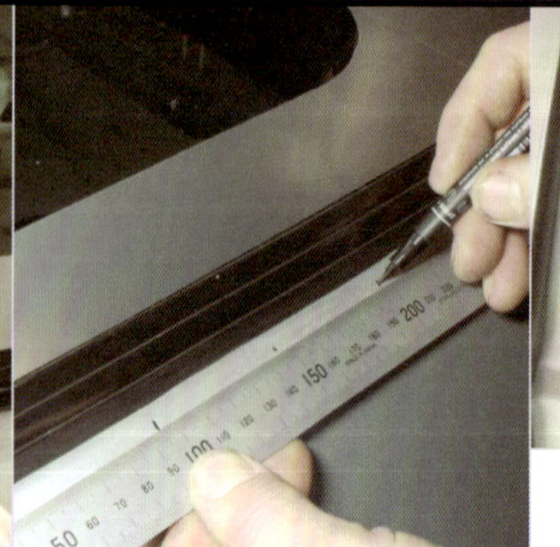

06 A word of warning - once these 'bolts' are applied, they're on for good. Nothing will shift them. So take your steadiest hand, and get them on in the right spot, and in a straight line. We think the end result looks okay, but best seen from a distance (rather than up close, where you can see the joins and overlaps in the tape).

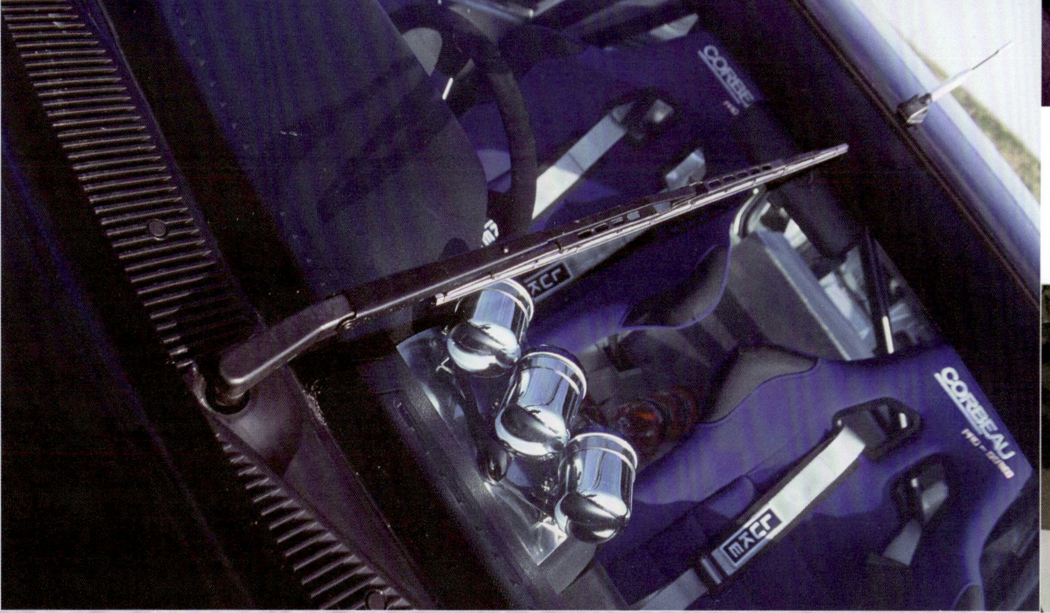

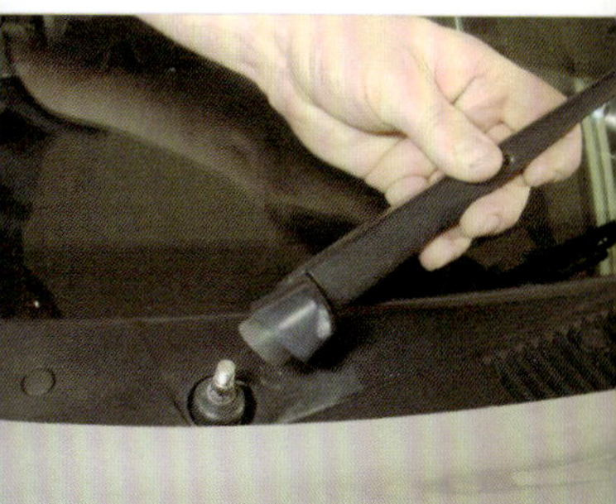

Single **wiper conversion**

Another saloon-car racing-inspired item, the single wiper conversion is a really smart way to make your Escort stand out from the crowd. Presumably, the saloon racers fit single wipers to enhance the view forward (one less wiper arm obscuring the view could make all the difference), improve the aerodynamics, and maybe even to save weight! Many Escort owners want the single wiper because it helps to remove clutter - put two Escorts side by side, and the one with one less wiper looks way better. It's a fairly 'neutral' mod, too - unlike some, it works as well on a 'sport-Escort' as on a 'luxury-Escort'. Our Mono Style kit came from Demon Tweeks.

01 Unsurprisingly, the first job is to remove your old wiper arms. Make sure that the wipers are in their 'parked' position, if necessary by flicking the wipers on, then quickly off. Flip up the cap at the base of each arm, unscrew the nut, and pull the arms off their splined fittings. Hopefully, yours will come off as easy as ours.

02 The windscreen trim panel's a bit of a joker to remove - and don't rush it, 'cos you'll be refitting it later. Seems easy at first - prise off all six plastic caps . . .

03 . . . and undo the screw underneath. Then try removing the panel, only to find you can't.

04 Those screws you just undid are screwed into plastic push-in plugs (a bit like Rawlplugs, if you're into home DIY), and the panel's going nowhere with the plugs in place. Refit the screw by just a thread or two, and use the screw to lever the plugs out. Use a scrap of wood so you're not bearing directly on the fragile plastic below.

05 The trim panel won't come out with the bonnet fully-open or shut, so have a handy assistant to hold the bonnet halfway while you wiggle the panel out.

06 Now we can see the wiper assembly - so stop looking, and start removing. There's four bolts altogether - one next to each wiper spindle . . .

07 . . . and two more on the mounting bracket.

08 Though the four bolts have now gone, getting the wiper frame out isn't easy. The main problem is the great mass of wiring loom which runs along the back of the 'bulkhead'. The only way round is to pull the wiring with one hand, and tip the wiper mounting bracket upwards past the wires.

09 When the whole assembly's almost out, turn it over and disconnect the large wiring plug underneath.

10 The first thing to work out when you've got your wiper assembly on the bench (or the floor) is - which wiper spindle is the centre one? This is the one you'll be doing all the work on, and the only one that'll have a wiper attached when you're finished. Get a small pot to keep all the bits in, as you take them off - first to go is the plastic cap . . .

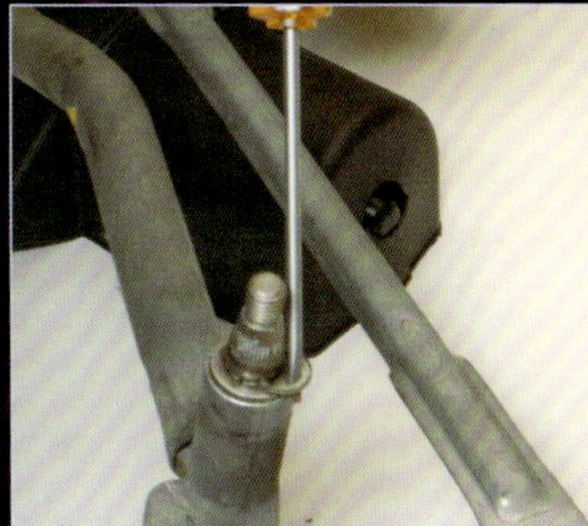

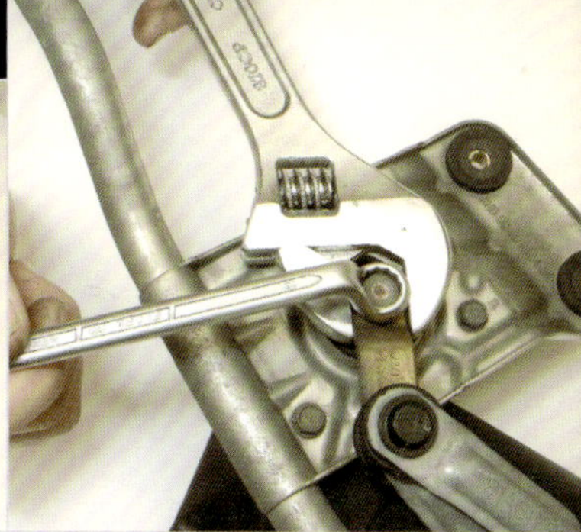

11 . . . then prise out the circlip underneath (this is one of those parts which will fly off - and go anywhere - so watch it).

12 Finally, take off the large plain washer. Repeat this process on the driver's-side spindle . . .

13 . . . then both spindles will slide down, out of the wiper frame. When the spindles are removed, you'll find there are various washers and O-rings - don't throw any away, as we'll want them later.

14 Now the wiper motor arm nut has to be undone. Grab the square end of the arm with an adjustable spanner (or big pair of pliers), and unscrew the nut with another spanner. It's pretty important that the motor arm doesn't turn as you undo the nut - if it does, you'll have lost the 'parked' position for the motor, and things will get tricky later on. You could always quickly plug the motor back in, and work the wipers on and off.

15 Again without turning the motor, prise off the motor arm . . .

16 . . . and remove the old wiper linkage. That's one bit we shouldn't need again.

17 While we're ditching bits, remove all the parts from the mounting hole next to the centre spindle - there's a large flat washer, metal sleeve, and a rubber mounting.

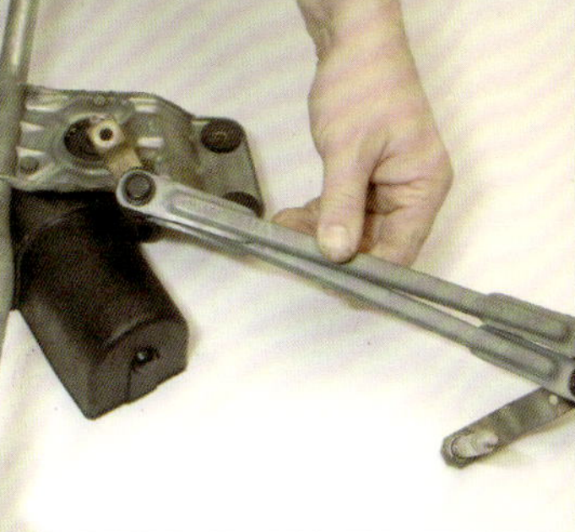

18 Before we start assembling the new stuff, a bit of lube works wonders. Only the centre spindle needs greasing.

19 Ah-ha - the first sighting of our new linkage. Pop one of the old flat washers onto the new spindle . . .

20 . . . then grease it up, and slip it in the hole. Gorgeous.

21 First onto the new spindle is the O-ring (to seal in the grease) . . .

22 . . . followed by enough of the old washers to bring the level just up to the spindle's circlip groove. Then - guess what - the new circlip goes in.

23 Apply a drop of lube onto all the moving joints on the new linkage - the last thing we need is an unwanted stiffy. Now set the new linkage so it's laid out like the photo, and fit it to the wiper motor arm . . .

24 . . . using the same method as before, to ensure the motor arm doesn't turn.

25 The wiper assembly's now ready to go back in the car. After refitting the wiring plug underneath, the first hurdle is getting the mounting bracket back past all that wiring again.

26 Three of the original mounting bolts get re-used, but the one next to the centre spindle has a new arrangement. Remember we took out the mounting rubber from the wiper frame? Here's why. Use the bolt together with the large flat 'nut', which fits underneath, across the big hole in the end of the wiper frame . . .

27 . . . and when tightening this nut, push the frame up towards the windscreen as far as poss.

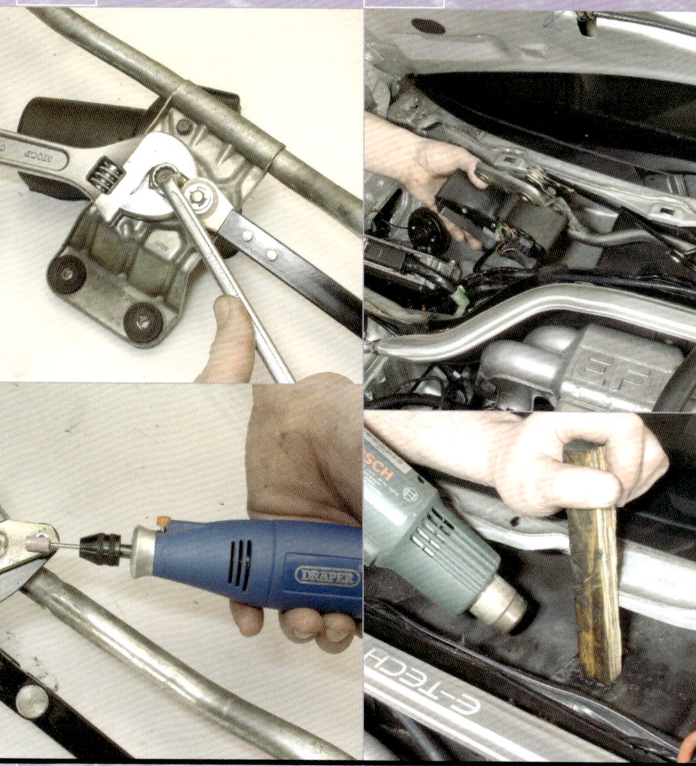

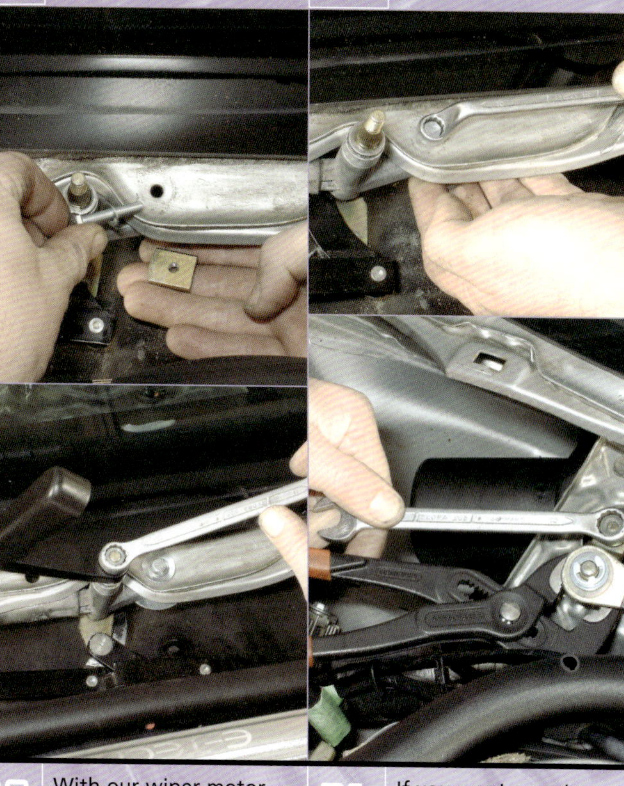

28 Keeping your fingers (and other bodily parts) clear of the linkage, it's time for a trial switching-on of the wipers. Yes, we know the wiper blade's not on yet - this is to see where the new linkage hits. Don't think it'll touch anything? Believe us, it will - we've done a few before, remember. Our linkage was actually touching itself (oo-er), and needed grinding on the spindle lower weld, and the rivet next to it.

29 Things didn't improve when we tried a second time - now the linkage was gouging holes in the blower fan's plastic cover. If you cut holes in this, you'll get water on the blower fan (fan goes bang) or into the car. So - we heated ours carefully with a heat gun, and kind-of re-moulded it. Worked a treat.

30 With our wiper motor arm and linkage set as it is, the instructions say the wiper blade will park on the driver's side. So we fitted our new wiper arm/blade over on the driver's side, and switched the wipers on for a test. Guess what? They weren't lying, and the wiper swept the screen fully.

31 If you want a centre-parking blade (potentially an MOT fail), loosen the motor arm nut (making sure the motor doesn't move from the park position), then prise the motor arm off the splines, and turn it through 90° before re-tightening. If you want passenger-side parking (legal), turn the motor arm 180°. The final touch is a neat plastic plug which (almost) fits into the trim panel, to disguise the now-redundant driver's-side wiper spindle. Time for a beer.

Painting by **numbers**

This is not the section where we tell you how to respray your entire Escort in a weekend, using only spray cans, okay? Mission Impossible, we ain't. This bit's all about how to spray up your various plasticky bits before final fitting - bits such as door mirrors, light brows, spoilers, splitters - hell, even bumpers if you like. As we've no doubt said elsewhere, with anything new, fit your unpainted bits first. Make sure everything fits properly (shape and tidy up all parts as necessary), that all holes have been drilled, and all screws etc are doing their job. Then, and only when you're totally, completely happy with the fit - take them off, and get busy with the spray cans.

01 The first job is to mask off any areas you don't want painted. Do this right at the start, or you could be sorry; on these door mirrors, we decided to mask off just at the lip before the glass, to leave a black unpainted edge - if we hadn't masked it as the very first job, we would've roughed up all the shiny black plastic next, and wrecked the edge finish.

02 Remove any unwanted 'seams' in the plastic, using fine sandpaper or wet-and-dry. Some of these seams look pretty cool, others don't - you decide. Also worth tidying up any other areas you're not happy with, fit-wise, while you're at it.

03 Especially with 'shiny' plastic, you must rough-up the surface before spray will 'bite' to it, or - it'll flippin' flake off. Just take off the shine, no more. You can use fine wet-and-dry for this (used dry), but we prefer Scotchbrite. This stuff, which looks much like a scouring pad, is available from motor factors and bodyshops, in several grades - we used ultra-fine, which is grey. One advantage of Scotchbrite is that it's a bit easier to work into awkward corners than paper.

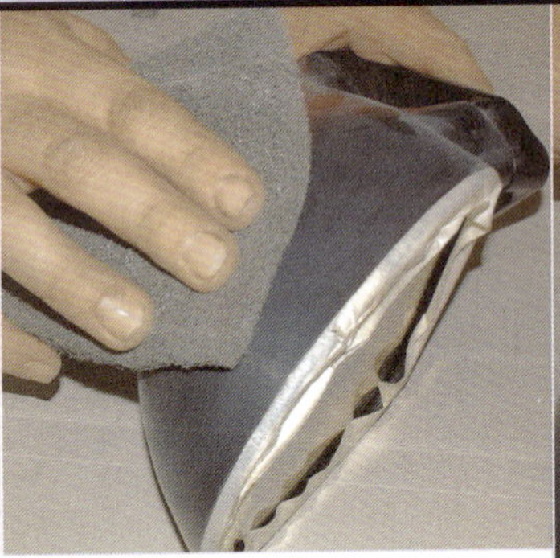

04 Once the surface has been nicely 'roughened', clean up the surface using a suitable degreaser ('suitable' means a type which won't dissolve plastic!). Generally, it's ok to use methylated spirit or cellulose thinners (just don't inhale!), but test it on a not-so-visible bit first, so you don't have a disaster.

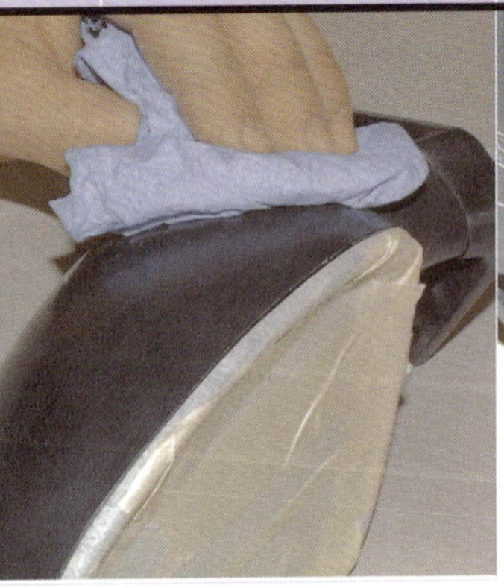

05 Before you start spraying (if it's something smaller than a bumper) it's a good idea to try a work a screw into one of the mounting holes, to use as a 'handle', so you can turn the item to spray all sides.

06 Another good trick is to use the screw to hang the item up on a piece of string or wire - then you can spin the item round to get the spray into awkward areas.

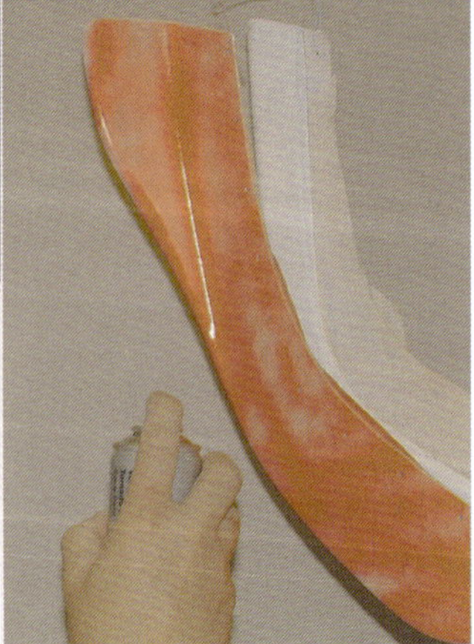

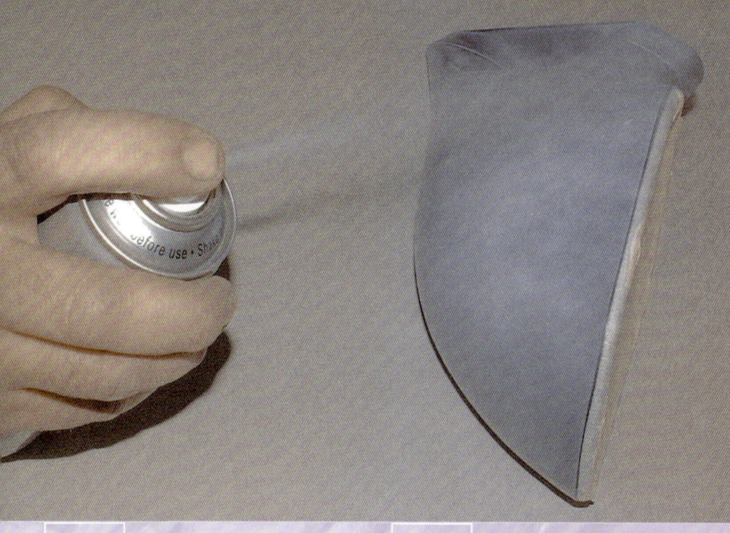

07 If you like a bit of wildlife in your paint, you can't beat the great outdoors. If it's at all windy, you'll end up with a really awful finish and overspray on everything (which can be a real pain to get off). Even indoors, if it's damp weather, you'll have real problems trying to get a shine - some kind of heater is essential if it's cold and wet (but not one with a fan - stirring up the dust is the last thing you want).

08 If you're a bit new at spraying, or if you simply don't want to mess it up, practice your technique first (steady!). Working left-right, then right-left, press the nozzle so you start spraying just before you pass the item, and follow through just past it the other side. Keep the nozzle a constant distance from the item - not in a curved arc. Don't blast the paint on too thick, or you'll have a nasty case of the runs - hold the can about 6 inches away - you're not trying to paint the whole thing in one sweep.

09 Once you've got a patchy 'mist coat' on (which might not even cover the whole thing) - stop, and let it dry (primer dries pretty quickly). Continue building up thin coats until you've got full coverage, then let it dry for half an hour or more.

10 Using 1000- or 1200-grade wet-and-dry paper (used wet), very lightly sand the whole primered surface, to take out any minor imperfections (blobs, where the nozzle was spitting) in the primer. Try not to go through the primer to the plastic, but this doesn't matter too much in small areas.

11 Rinse off thoroughly, then dry the surfaces - let it stand for a while to make sure it's *completely* dry, before starting on the top coat.

12 Make sure once again that the surfaces are clean, with no bits left behind from the drying operations. As with the primer, work up from an initial thin mist coat, allowing time for each pass to dry. As you spray, you'll soon learn how to build a nice shine without runs - any 'dry' (dull) patches are usually due to overspray landing on still-wet shiny paint. Don't worry if you can't eliminate all of these - a light cutting polish will sort it out once the paint's hardened (after several hours).

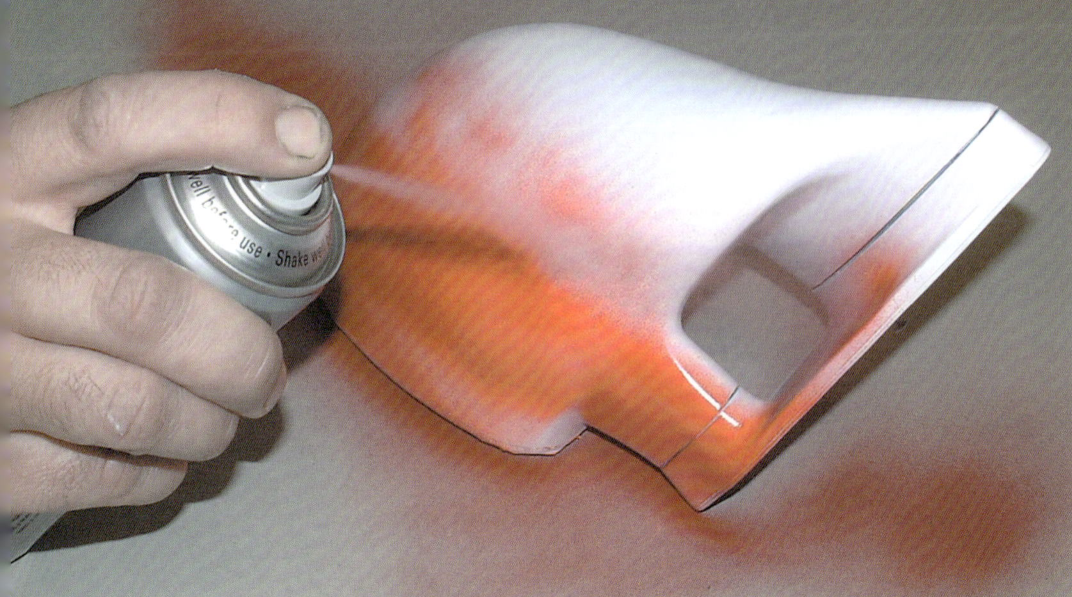

13 Especially with a colour like red (which is notorious for fading easily), it's a good idea to blow on a coat or two of clear lacquer over the top - this will also give you your shine, if you're stuck with a very 'dry' finish. It's best to apply lacquer before the final top coat is fully hardened. The spraying technique is identical, although pro sprayers say that lacquer should be applied pretty thick - just watch those runs! Lacquer also takes a good long while to dry - pick up your item too soon for that unique fingerprint effect!

There's no way in

One very popular way to tidy up the Escort lines is to do away with the door locks, and even the door handles - but be careful. Flushing the rear door handles (on 5-door models) is okay, legally/MOT-speaking, but removing the front door handles will land you in trouble, come MOT time.

There's something in the Construction & Use regs which requires an independent mechanical means of door opening from outside, probably so fire-fighters can get you out, if you stick your Cosworth-lookalike on its roof, or in a ditch... So - don't spend loads of time (or money, at a bodyshop) having cool and trendy mods done, which you then have to spend more money undoing!

Door lock barrels

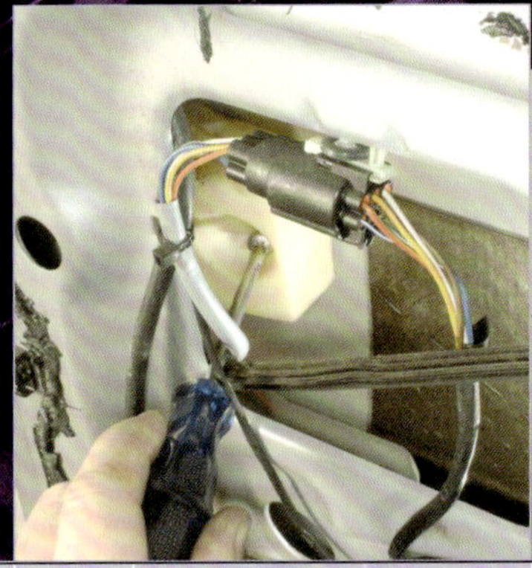

01 See 'Interiors' for door trim panel removal - the foam membrane has to come off too (don't just rip it). In an effort to save your Ford from the TWOCers, Ford have fitted a plastic shield over the inside of the lock, held on by one screw inside . . .

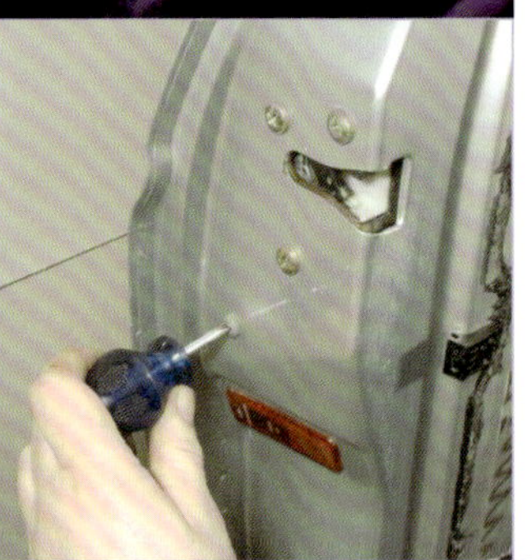

02 . . . another one on the door edge . . .

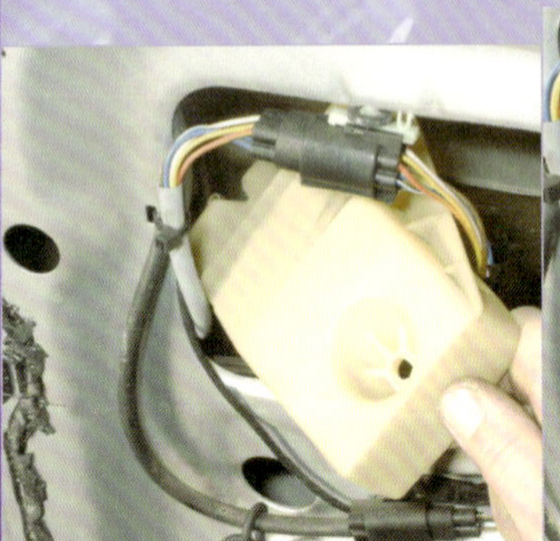

03 . . . and then it's a case of working the shield out through the door.

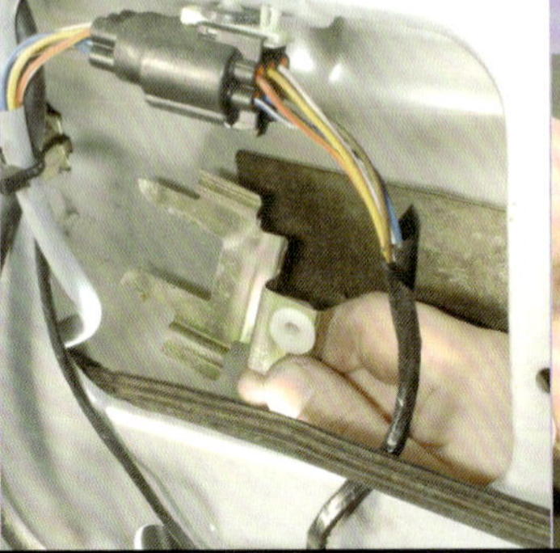

04 The only thing really holding the lock barrel to the door is this horseshoe clip, which you pull off to the side . . .

05 . . . and the lock barrel emerges from the door panel. Now just unhook the operating rod from it, and the ugly lock barrel is history. If you don't want the lock barrel rod rattling around inside the door, trace it down to the door lock inside, and unhook it there as well.

Removing the evidence

Filler alone won't do for sorting the hole left by the absent lock barrel. It's a case of welding a plate behind, and a skim of filler (and paint) to finish. One for the bodyshop?

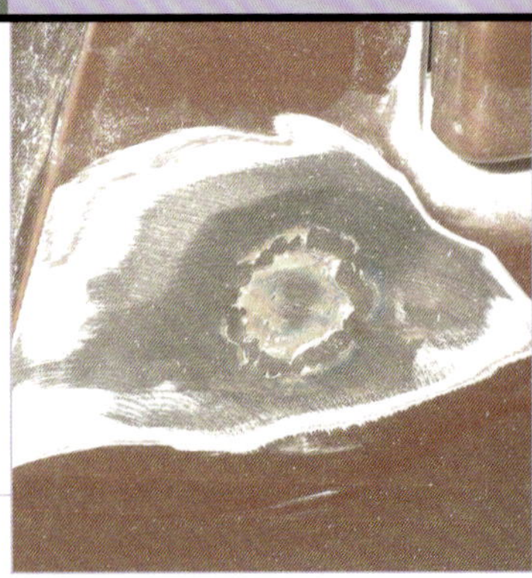

Door handles

Removing your door handles for colour-coding is easy. There's just two screws holding the handle on, accessed from inside the door (so the trim panel and the foam membrane have to come off) Once the handle's loose, you'll just have to unhook the operating rod from one end, and they're ready to spray. Told you it was easy.

Remote **locking**

So you can lock and unlock your freshly de-locked doors, you'll need to buy and fit a remote central locking kit, which you can get from several Max Power-advertised suppliers (our Microscan kit is really an extension kit for our chosen alarm, but is pretty typical of what you'll get). If your Escort already has central locking, you're in luck - buy yourself a cheap car alarm, and a central locking interface (see 'Security' for how we fitted ours).

Tricks 'n' tips

If your battery goes flat, you'll be locked out. We ran two thin wires from the battery terminals (with a 10-amp fuse in the live, and the ends insulated), and tucked them away for access from below in an emergency. By connecting a slave battery to these wires (do not try jump-starting), you'll put enough juice into the system to operate the locks, saving you a red face. Think it over.

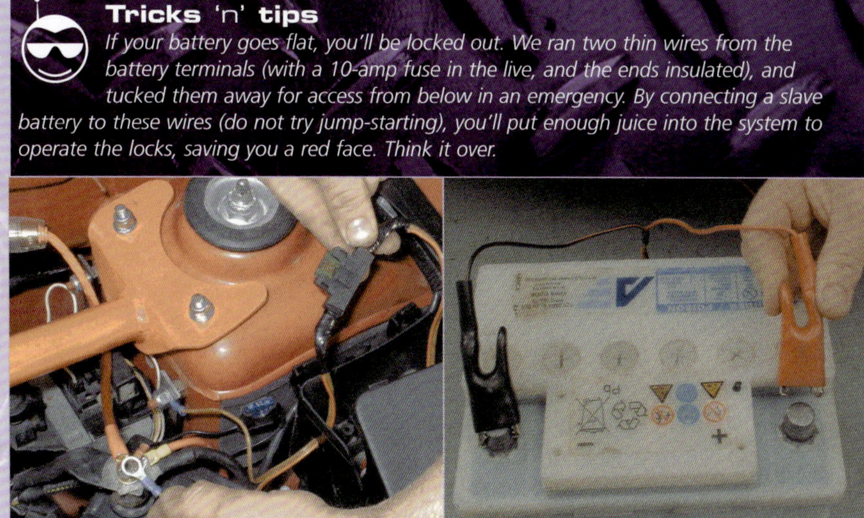

Central locking **kit**

If your Escort doesn't have central locking as standard, don't despair - there's several kits out there to help you towards your goal.

Our project Escort already had central locking, so regrettably there are no Escort-specific photos to show you, but hopefully, the details below, together with your kit's instructions, will help you out.

Before you start fitting your new lock solenoids, it makes sense to test them. Connect them all together as described in your kit's instructions - with power connected to all the solenoids, pull up on the operating plunger of one, and all the rest should pop up too - clever, eh?

Decide where you're going to mount the lock control unit, then identify the various looms, and feed them out to the doors.

The new lock solenoids must be mounted so they work in the same *plane* as the door lock buttons. What this means is it's no good having the lock solenoid plungers moving horizontally, to work a button and rod which operates vertically! Make up the mounting brackets from the metal bits provided in the kit, and fit the solenoids loosely to the brackets, and to the doors.

The kit contains several items which look uncannily like bike spokes - these are your new lock operating rods, which have to be cut to length, then joined onto the old rods using screw clamps. It's best to join the old and new rods at a straight piece of the old rod, so feed the new rod in, and mark it for cutting.

Cut the new rod to the marked length, fit the cut rod to the solenoid, then slip the clamp onto it. Fit the solenoid onto its bracket, and offer the rod into place, to connect to the old rod. Join the new rod and old rod together, and fasten the clamp screws tight. If the clamp screws come loose, you're basically going to be locked out.

Now you can connect up the wires - the easy bit is joining up inside the door. Hopefully, your kit's instructions should be sufficient, but if not, you'll have to resort to the Haynes manual wiring diagrams.

Bumpers 'n' bodykits

Disappointingly, the Mk 5/6/7 Escort sometimes seems like a bit of a forgotten vehicle in the modding world - there's certainly not much choice in bodykits at present.

The main options are various bumpers n' bits which are supposed to make your Escort look more like a Cossie, or bolt-on versions of the RS/XR bodywork. Not terribly inspiring stuff.

Fortunately, bodykit makers are starting to realise the huge potential the later Escort has to offer, and one to watch is ESP Design (excellent website - www.espdesign.co.uk), who specialise in cool-looking stuff for Fords of all sizes. Not wanting to go the Cosworth route, we chose the Evotech front bumper, RS 2000 skirts and ST24 rear bumper.

Rear bumper

01 Taking off the back bumper's as easy as the front - in fact, it's nearly an identical method. Two screws each side hold the bumper ends to the wheelarch (okay, so there's a number plate light to prise out and disconnect), but then it's four nuts (two each side), inside the boot, and she's off to the scrapyard in the sky.

02 Now, unless you want to be very illegal (bad boy), you'll be needing a number plate light in your new bumper. Though it won't be true for every Escort bodykit out there, our bumper has a neatly-moulded recess at the top, designed for our old light. A recess is good, but a hole would be better. Measure the old hole . . .

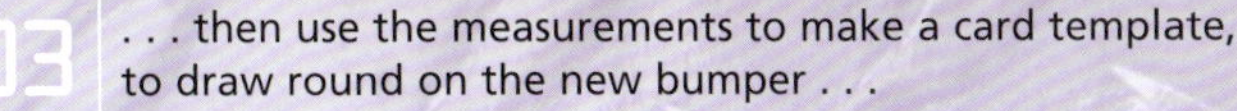

03 . . . then use the measurements to make a card template, to draw round on the new bumper . . .

04 . . . and after drilling a few pilot holes, get to work with a hacksaw blade (this job's a bit much for a Stanley knife, no matter how sharp your blade is). You might also need another small hole drilling, to run the light wiring through.

05 Oh yes - it fits. By the way, though we're pretty sure glassfibre dust isn't a health hazard, it flamin' well ought to be... Why else did we fit our rear foglight into the bumper mesh, instead of cutting another hole in the bumper itself?

06 Time for a trial fitting. Actually, you should do this earlier, before cutting any holes for number plate lights and stuff. If it really doesn't fit, you're stuck with it, if you've holed it. And if you've got more than a few inches in the exhaust department, watch how you fit the bumper over your pipe (the exhaust mountings might have to be loosened or unhooked for a while).

07 Luckily, our bumper was a pretty good fit. We could see it was touching in a couple of spots, so we marked them up for a session with the file. Don't get mad with your bumper, and don't think you can just tighten the mounting nuts to 'improve' the fit. Glassfibre's easy to crack, especially at the corners.

08 When the bumper's looking fit, hang it on using the four mounting nuts inside the boot, and sort out the ends where they fit to the arches. Some ready-made holes would be a bonus, but you're not scared of a little drilling by now.

Front bumper

01 Full marks to Uncle Henry - Escort bumpers might not look much, but at least they're dead easy to get rid of. First up, there's two screws on the bumper ends, inside the wheelarches.

02 While you're in there, if your 'scort has front fogs or other bumper-mounted lights, don't forget to unplug the wiring before going much further.

03 The next bit's easy - but not to photograph. There's four nuts holding the bumper on now - two pairs of them, quite easy to reach from behind . . .

04 . . . and after the ends have been unclipped from the wheelarches, the bumper literally falls off.

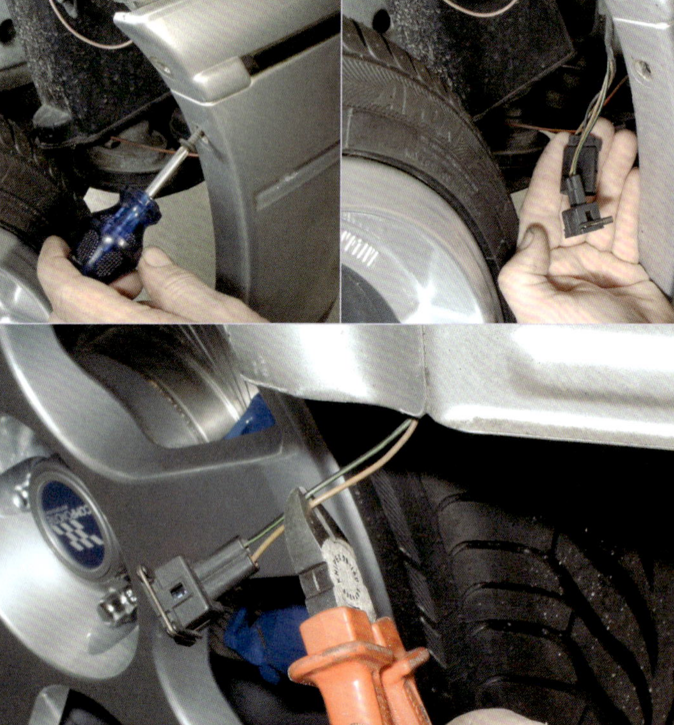

08 So that our new lights (and this includes the front fogs) will work, some surgery is needed on the old wiring plugs - or you might be making up new live-and-earth wiring of your own. With the old plugs removed, it's on with some new bullets, on the wiring and the lights. Now the bumper can be fitted.

09 It's pretty unlikely that your new bumper will be an absolutely perfect fit, first-time - a few trial fittings may well be necessary. Mind you, this item's looking good, straight out of the box.

10 We weren't sure if the old front towing eye was interfering with the bumper or not, but since you can't use it with the new bumper on, we chopped it off.

Tricks 'n' tips
Always do a basic trial fitting of your new bumpers, preferably as soon as they arrive, and definitely before you start drilling any holes in them. You won't get your money back if you've tried to mod them yourself. Expect a little 'adjustment' to be needed to make them fit, but bear in mind you might have been sent the wrong ones (especially on an Escort, which had three different stock bumpers from 1990 to 2000).

05 Our bumper has two wannabe holes in it, crying out for some indicators to be fitted. Most Escorts have their indicators next to, or inside, the headlights, so you might not need this feature - our XR wouldn't have any front flashers otherwise, so we've no choice but to drill.

06 The indicators we chose are fully-legal, and have been for a very long time. Why? They're a Lucas design, used on very old Minis (well, you don't actually have to tell anyone). Hot-glue the orange lens in . . .

07 . . . and the bulbholder part will sit on the back.

11 There's some scope to correct a slight misalignment in bumper fit by elongating the four mounting holes in the bumper mounting bracket. Check you're moving in the right direction by refitting the bumper from time to time.

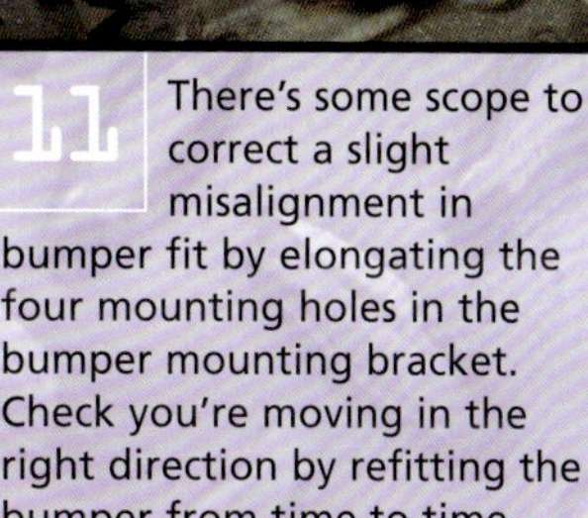

12 With the four main mounting nuts fitted, turn your attention to the bumper ends. Ideally, there'd be two pre-drilled holes here, which align perfectly with the original holes in the edge of the arch, and you'd just fit some screws. In the real world, we have to drill our own.

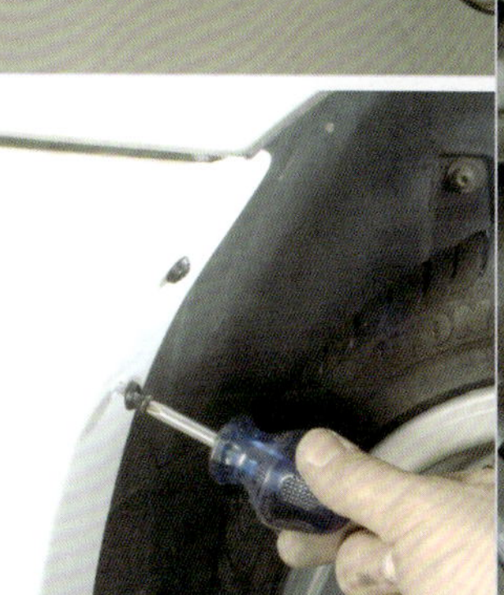

13 Two self-tappers each side, and that bumper's on. Break out the beer.

14 Before you celebrate too much, don't forget to plug in all your new wiring, and see whether the bumper lights work as planned. If all's well, the bumper can come off again, for spraying.

Don't mesh with me, boy

A meshed grille or bumper is just one way to demonstrate who's the daddy of the cruise, and it does a great job of dicing any small insects or rodents foolish enough to wander into the path of your motor. So if you're sick of scrubbing off insect entrails from your paint, and fancy getting even, read on...

Which style of mesh to choose? Classic diamond-shape, or round-hole? In our humble opinion, the round-hole mesh works best on modern roundy-shaped cars (like say, a Corsa) - for everything else, we'll settle for the original and best. But wait - the choice doesn't end with what shape you want. Mesh can now be had in various anodised colours too, to match or contrast with the rest of your chosen paint scheme.

Meshing a bumper

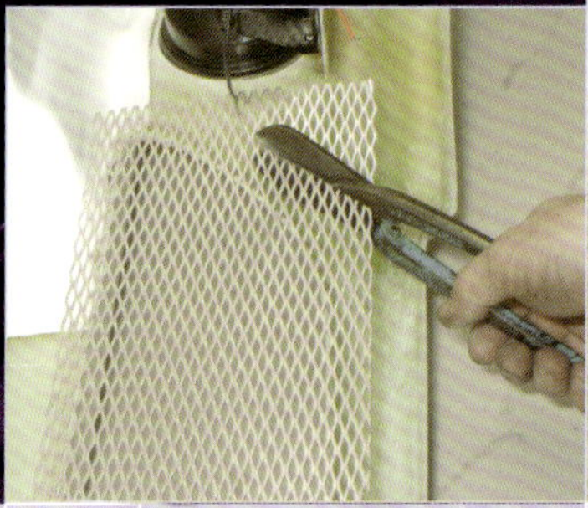

01 Anyone can mesh a hole. Ab-so-lutely anyone - it's dead easy. First, measure your hole, then cut out a roughly-sized piece of mesh, leaving some over the sides to bend around the edges of your hole.

02 Of course, holes usually have corners - and some of the sides you'll encounter aren't exactly straight. Make small cuts in the edge of the mesh at strategic points . . .

03 . . . and bending over the edges will be much easier. The main mesh panel will also stay flatter, and you'll be less stressed, too.

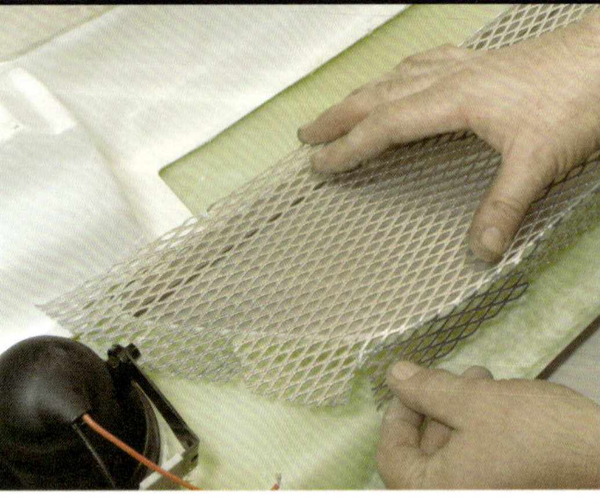

04 There's loads of ways to secure your mesh. One of the most permanent is to use small self-tapping screws, but this won't always be possible. Our hot-glue gun method worked a treat, as the glue flows into place. You can use mastic (quick-setting, exterior-use type) or even builder's 'no-nails' adhesive, but you squirt on a bead of the stuff, and then have to smooth it on by hand, to 'squidge' it over the mesh. Very meshy - sorry, messy.

Meshing a Mk 6 bonnet

01 Open the bonnet (we cheated, and took ours off completely) and take the old grille off by undoing the three plastic nuts from inside.

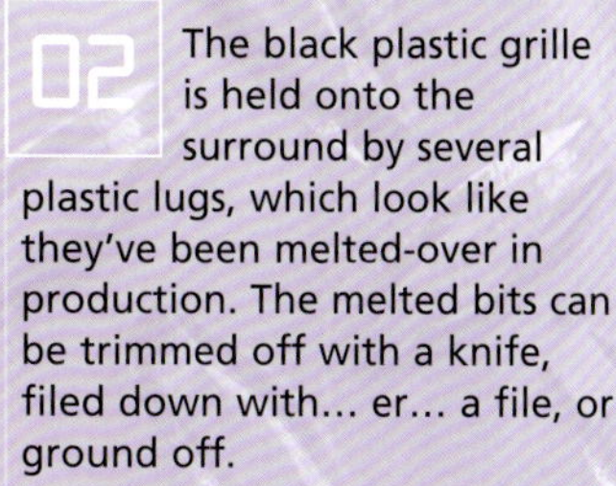

02 The black plastic grille is held onto the surround by several plastic lugs, which look like they've been melted-over in production. The melted bits can be trimmed off with a knife, filed down with... er... a file, or ground off.

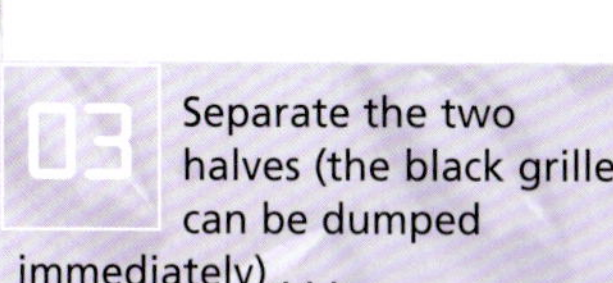

03 Separate the two halves (the black grille can be dumped immediately) . . .

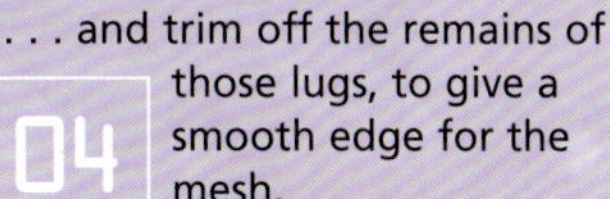

04 . . . and trim off the remains of those lugs, to give a smooth edge for the mesh.

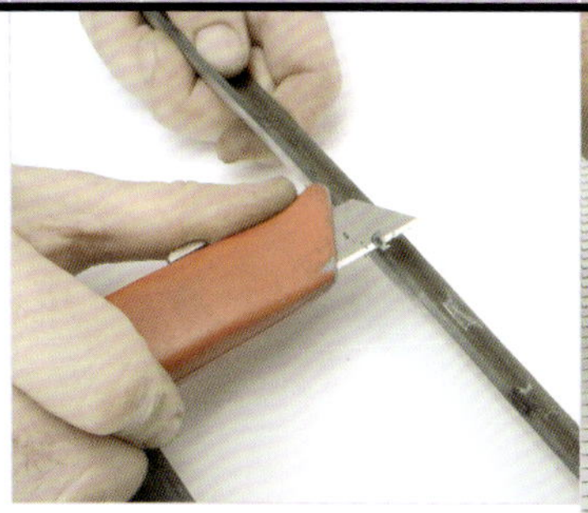

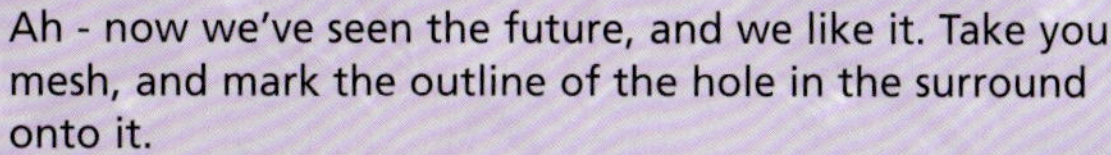

05 Ah - now we've seen the future, and we like it. Take your mesh, and mark the outline of the hole in the surround onto it.

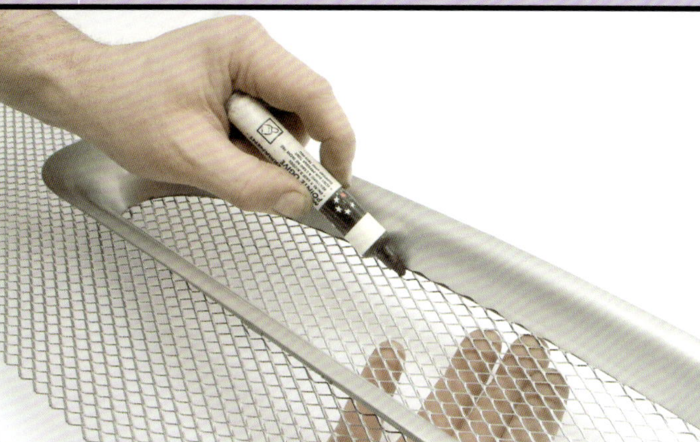

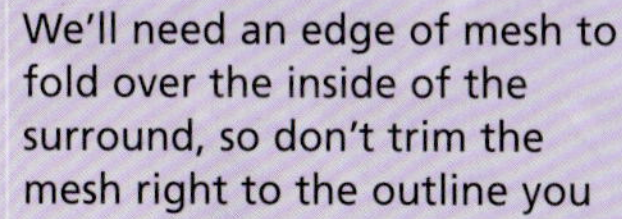

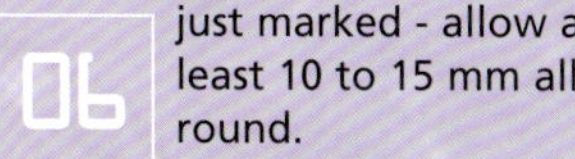

06 We'll need an edge of mesh to fold over the inside of the surround, so don't trim the mesh right to the outline you just marked - allow at least 10 to 15 mm all round.

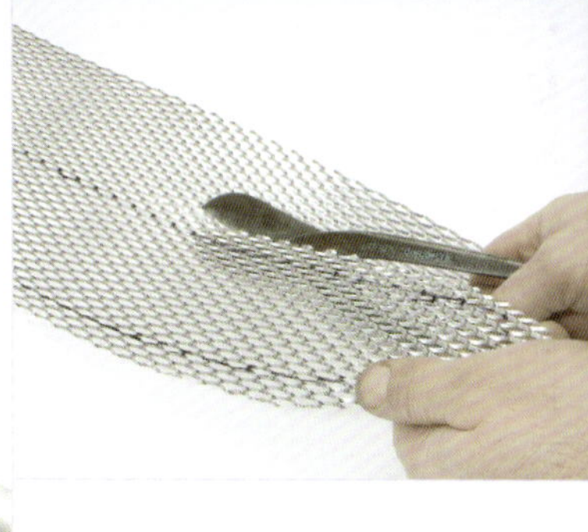

>>

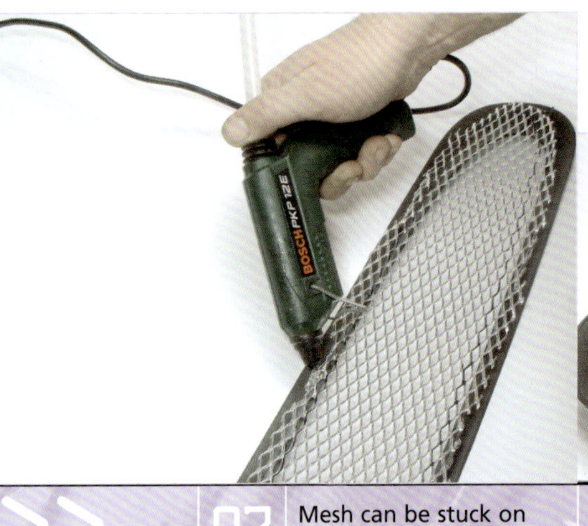
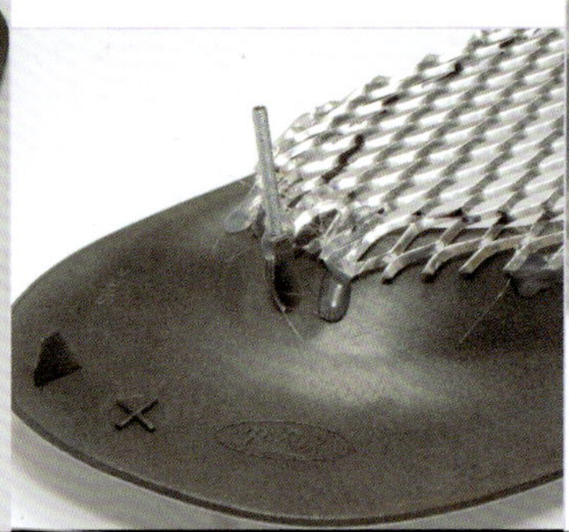

07 Mesh can be stuck on in all sorts of ways - once the edges have been bent over the backside of the hole you're meshing, it almost stays there on its own. Mastic, fibreglass and even 'no-nails' adhesives have all been tried, and they all work. But - we've got a new hot-glue gun, and we want to see if that works too. Guess what? It does.

08 So how do we stick the meshed grille back on the bonnet? Not with hot glue, that's for sure. At each side of the meshed hole, there are two black plastic blocks with neat holes in the centre. DIY stores sell threaded rod (like a bolt without the head), and the smallest size (M4) fits these holes a treat - you can even glue them in place.

09 One more obstacle before fitting the new grille - that centre brace in the bonnet looks a bit lame. Cutting it out is one option, but we figured that might weaken the bonnet. Spraying it matt black hides it nicely.

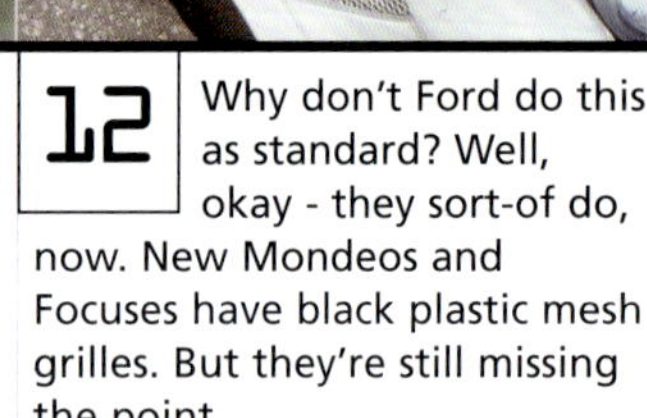

10 A good thing about this approach is that you know, absolutely know, that the grille will fit back on - it came off your own car, after all.

11 It's not essential, but while you're out shopping for the threaded rod (and right-size nuts to go with it), get some 'panel' washers too. These oversize washers come in handy for all sorts of modding stuff, and in this case, prevent the smaller-than-standard nuts from pulling through the holes. Trim off the excess 'bolt', and the job's a winner.

12 Why don't Ford do this as standard? Well, okay - they sort-of do, now. New Mondeos and Focuses have black plastic mesh grilles. But they're still missing the point.

Side skirts

So what's the deal with side skirts, then? Well, they're an 'artificial' way of visually lowering the car, making it seem lower to the ground than it really is, and they also help to 'tie together' the front and rear sections of a full bodykit. This much we know from our magazines. But where did skirts really come from?

As with so much else in modifying, it's a racing-inspired thing. In the late 70s, the Lotus 'ground-effect' F1 cars ran very, very low (for the time) and had side skirts made of rubber (or bristles), to give a flexible seal against the track. With a clear downforce advantage, Lotus blew the opposition away.

So will fitting skirts to your Escort give you race-car levels of downforce, greatly increasing your overtaking chances at the next roundabout? You already know the answer, I'm afraid...

01 If the skirts you've got are of decent quality, fitting is a piece of - very easy indeed. With the help of a willing accomplice, offer one on, making sure you've got it the right way round. We're so confident, we've got the drill out already (well, these are RS 2000 skirts from ESP Design, so we've got reason to be).

02 One self-tapper later, and the skirt's starting to look made for the car. You only need three or four along the top edge.

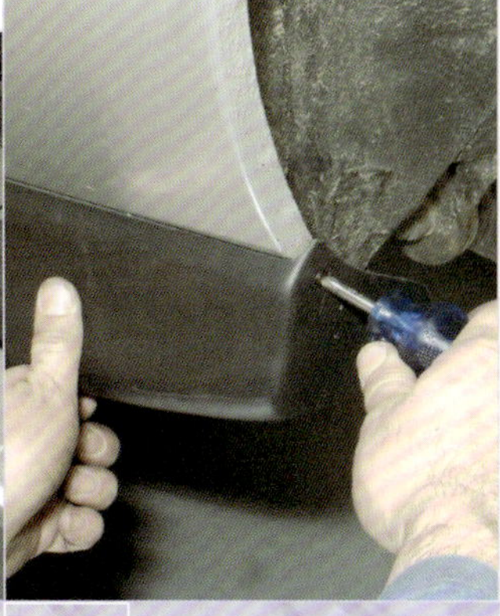

03 Similar straightforward story in the wheelarch, either end (as long as your arch edges haven't gone brown and crumbly). Two screws should do the job nicely. To fit the last screw at the front, the skirt needed quite a bit of twisting - time to call in the handy assistant again.

04 It's also worth popping a screw or two in from below (after removing the cover provided for the jacking point). Screws are used to locate the skirts, but they're really stuck on using screws and mastic, so the next job is to actually undo all the screws you just fitted.

05 Bathtub sealant is not an option for body jobs - get some proper mastic designed for the job (try a bodyshop or car paint suppliers). Wear gloves (or at least one glove, like our man here) when using the good stuff, as it's hell to get off hands. Using masking tape, give yourself a line for the bead of mastic, behind the door.

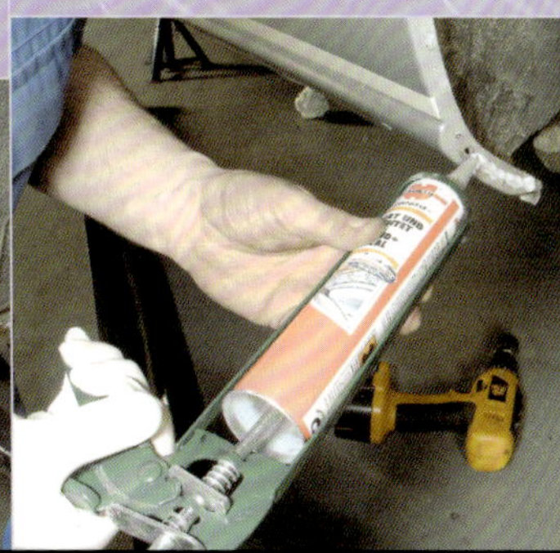

06 Not forgetting to do the wheelarch ends, apply a not-too-heavy bead of the sticky stuff. The mastic will 'splurge' everywhere when the skirt goes back on, so make sure you've a good supply of thinners to get it off everything.

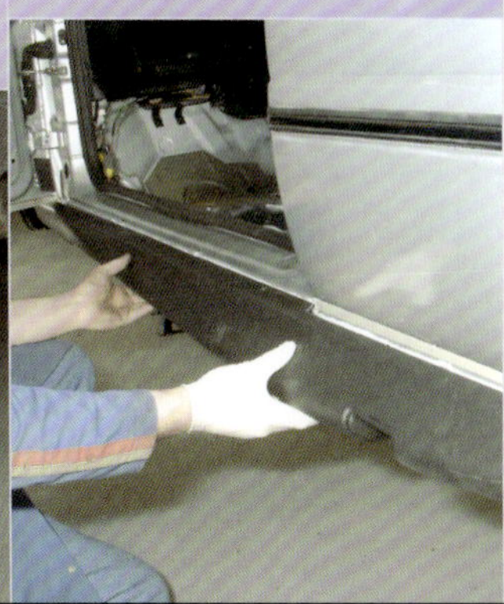

07 Try to line the skirt up accurately when it first goes back on - this will reduce the mess from the mastic. Press it firmly on, then get the screws back in to hold it. For the perfect finishing touch, apply another thin bead of mastic along the body joint behind the door, and smooth it off.

Tailgate smoothing

Achieving the complete 'smooth-tailgate' look isn't too involved a procedure, providing you know someone who can weld, and are handy with filler and spray.

Completely smoothing the tailgate is a logical extension of de-badging - the first thing to go is the rear wiper. Rear wipers are undoubtedly useful, and were put there for a good reason, but hey - that's just boring. Remove the rear wiper and the lock button, and fill over the holes - easy, eh?. Well, yes, except that most of the holes are too big to just filler over, and will probably need glassfibre matting or welding.

Later Escorts have another tailgate-related 'problem' - those naff rear light 'extensions' which some bright spark in the design department thought were a trendy styling feature. Jeez. At least they're only your rear foglights, so they can be lost quite easily (as long as you come up with a better rear foglight solution, for the MOT).

If you're going to de-lock the tailgate, you'll need to devise a means of opening the thing afterwards, if only so your mates can admire your ICE install. Posher Escorts (like ours) come with a remote release as standard, and you can buy a remote release kit from a Ford dealer, for about £30 - even comes with decent instructions. Otherwise, fit a boot solenoid kit and wire it up to a convenient switch.

Tailgate lights

01 If you haven't already, remove the tailgate trim panel. Lots of small Philips screws around the edge, and a little prising, and off she comes.

02 Not much to removing the foglights, thank goodness - just one nut to undo . . .

03 . . . one plug to disconnect . . .

04 . . . and the later Escort's most unattractive rear styling feature is history - even the resulting hole looks better.

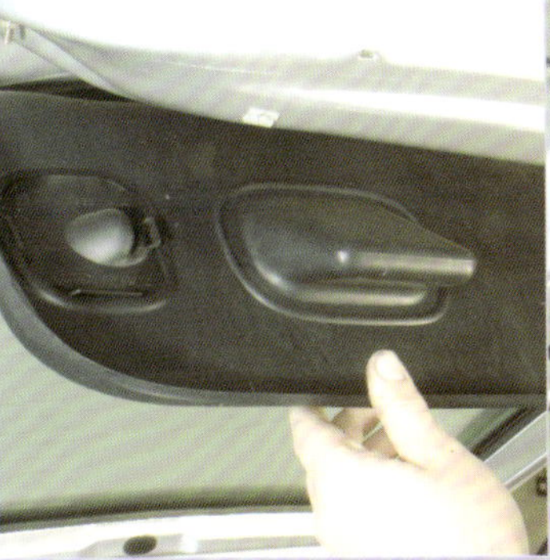

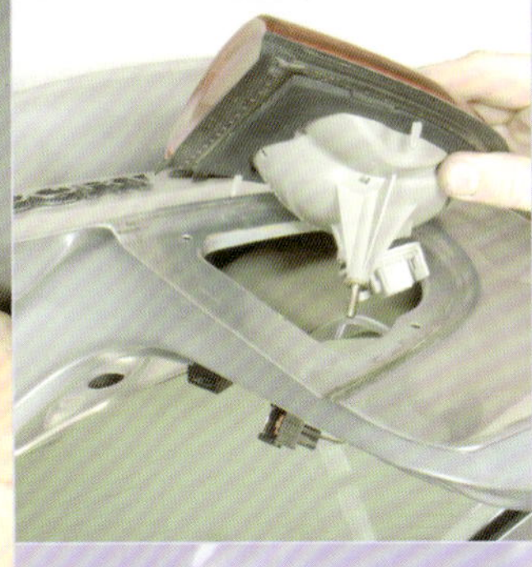

Tailgate wiper

01 A rear wiper has no place on a racing Escort, sort-of useful though it admittedly is. First, undo the nut and prise off the wiper arm (if it's badly rusted-on, serious force might be needed to shift it, but don't wreck the top of the tailgate in the process).

02 Inside, separate the wiring plug halves, and unclip the wiring from the tailgate.

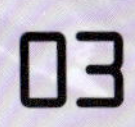

03 It all looks so easy, doesn't it? And it is - as long as you work out which three bolts to undo (it's the three round the outside with the big washers).

04 And the wiper motor is no more (don't forget to pull out the plastic grommet left in the top of the tailgate). We're saving some weight now, eh? That motor's another kilo or two off the kerb weight, so it's another fraction shaved off the 0-60, surely?

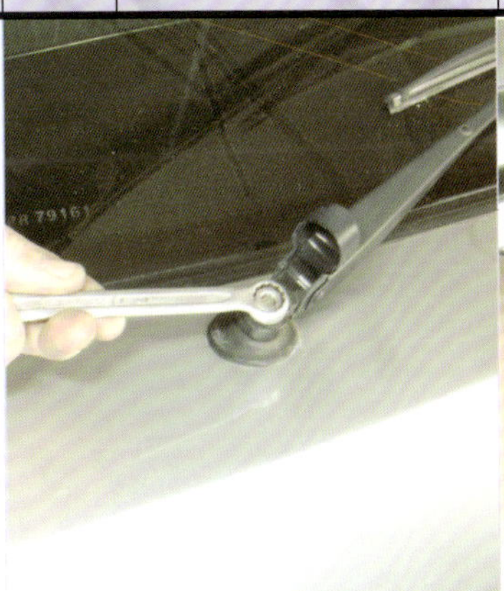

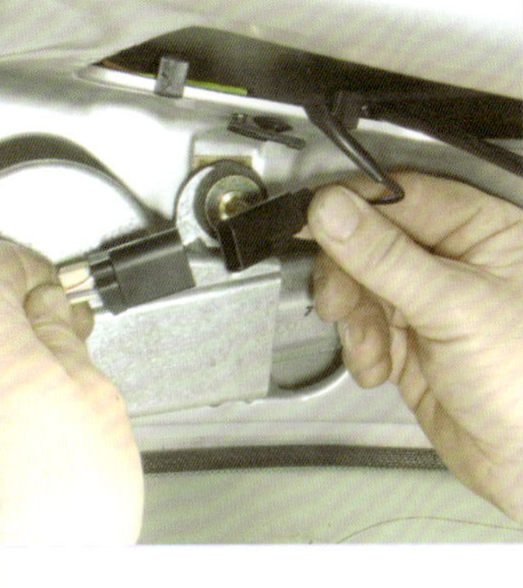

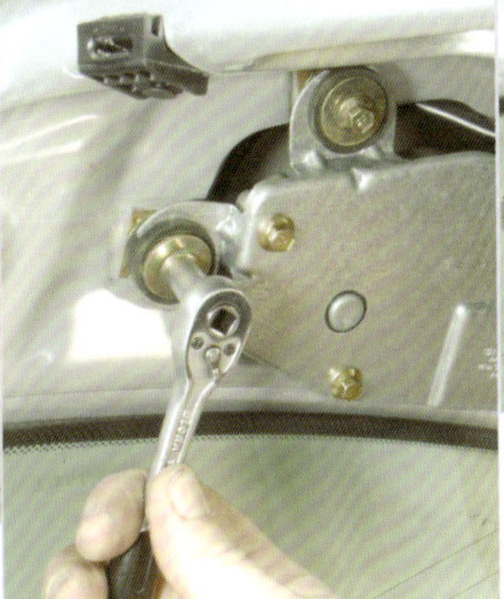

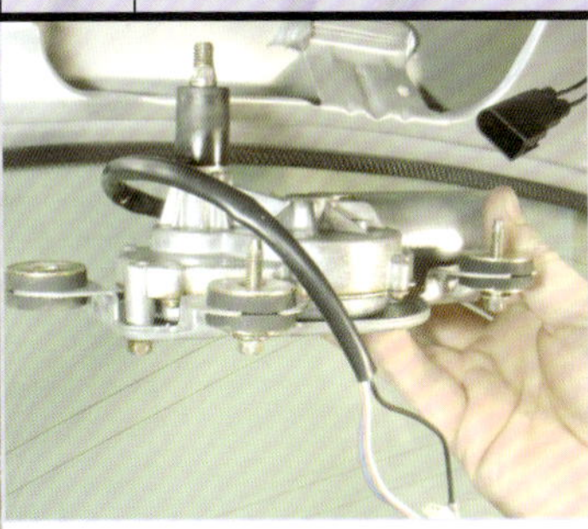

Tailgate lock

01 A word of warning - if you choose to de-lock your Escort tailgate, you sure do leave yourself a lot of holes to fill in. Inside the trim panel once more, and we find four nuts holding the lock trim in place . . .

02 . . . and off it comes. Was that really necessary, Mr Ford? One useless piece of plastic, and now we've got four holes. Great.

03 The lock barrel's held on by two bolts from outside . . .

04 . . . and it comes off inside, once you've unclipped the lock operating rod. The rod isn't needed any more, but it's not so easy to remove completely (and you don't want to leave it in there - the rattling will drive you mad) . . .

05 . . . so you have to temporarily unbolt the tailgate catch, to get at it.

06 As you can see, with the catch off, the rod unhooks easily. Refitting the catch is not optional, assuming you want your hatch to stay shut, of course. If you haven't yet fitted your solenoid kit (or you find that your remote release button has packed up), you can release the tailgate from inside the boot, with a screwdriver. It's just not very cool as a long-term solution, that's all.

Spoil your Escort rotten

If you've 'only' got a base 1.3 Escort, you might kill to have a stock Escort rear spoiler on your car.

But only if you're very sad. The standard Ford item is hardly a thing of great style and beauty - and besides, it's standard, so it's got to go. So - will it be a Cosworth replacement, or something even more impressive, like a tech-looking alloy job. We chose an E-Tech alloy monster, supplied by our friends at ESP Design, and one of the best-quality items we've ever had the pleasure to fit. If only it was always like this.

01 The offending stock item is held by six nuts inside - two at each end, and two more in the centre. The centre ones, and the inner two at the ends (after prising out a rubber grommet), are easy to undo . . .

02 . . . but the outermost two appear to be totally hidden. Luckily, you just unbolt the tailgate bump-stop, get in there with your socket and extension again . . .

03 . . . and the stock spoiler can soon be sent to the scrapyard (or sold for loadsamoney to someone with a base 1.3 Escort).

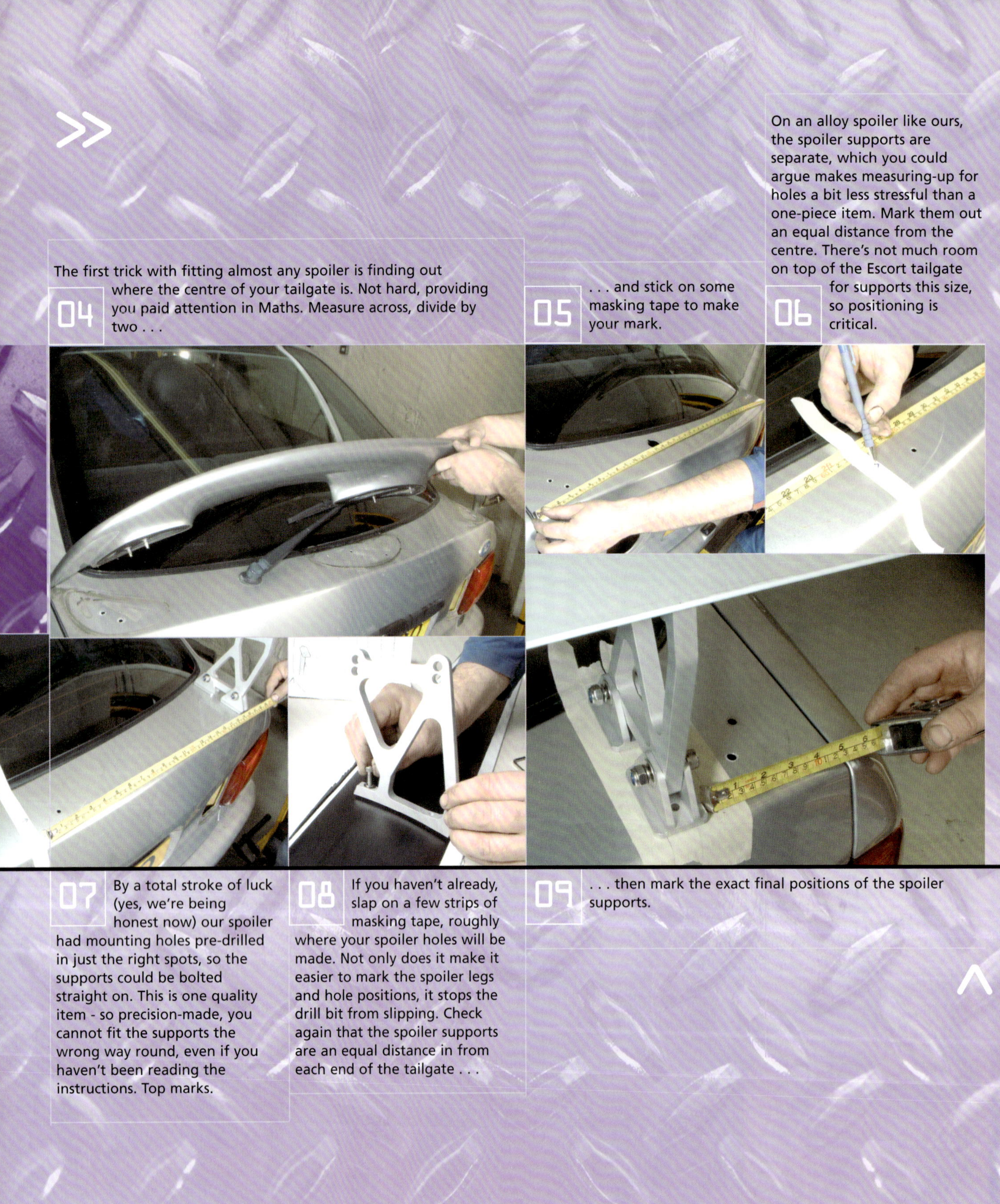

The first trick with fitting almost any spoiler is finding out where the centre of your tailgate is. Not hard, providing you paid attention in Maths. Measure across, divide by two . . .

04

. . . and stick on some masking tape to make your mark.

05

On an alloy spoiler like ours, the spoiler supports are separate, which you could argue makes measuring-up for holes a bit less stressful than a one-piece item. Mark them out an equal distance from the centre. There's not much room on top of the Escort tailgate for supports this size, so positioning is critical.

06

07

By a total stroke of luck (yes, we're being honest now) our spoiler had mounting holes pre-drilled in just the right spots, so the supports could be bolted straight on. This is one quality item - so precision-made, you cannot fit the supports the wrong way round, even if you haven't been reading the instructions. Top marks.

08

If you haven't already, slap on a few strips of masking tape, roughly where your spoiler holes will be made. Not only does it make it easier to mark the spoiler legs and hole positions, it stops the drill bit from slipping. Check again that the spoiler supports are an equal distance in from each end of the tailgate . . .

09

. . . then mark the exact final positions of the spoiler supports.

Depending on your chosen spoiler, you might now have to work out where the holes need to be drilled, relative to the support outlines you just drew (usually, you aim for the middle). Our spoiler has alloy feet you can unbolt from the supports, so we could mark

10 the holes with ease. We really like this spoiler.

11 Some precision drilling later, and we've got our new spoiler mounting holes . . .

12 . . . the trouble is, it's hard to keep track of the new ones, with so many old ones lying about. Don't forget to treat the new holes to some paint, so they've got some chance of not rusting.

13 One slightly unfortunate fact to share with you at this late stage - the top of the Escort tailgate is not flat. Which means that when your spoiler supports are bolted to it, they won't be vertical, and may not line up with the holes in the spoiler. Use rubber pads to fit under the supports, we had to shape ours to get the supports vertical.

14 Bolt the feet to the tailgate, and the supports to the feet, and we're nearly there - just the endplates to bolt on . . .

15 . . . and the second wing element to set, for optimum downforce. Get a heavy smoker to stand next to the car on a windy day, and set the spoiler according to the airflow observed over the wing elements. Or perhaps not.

Wheelarch mods

The law states that your wide rubber shouldn't be so wide that it sticks out from your arches, and the MOT crew will not be impressed if your new rubber's rubbing, either. This presents something of a problem, if you're determined to get 18s or 19s on, especially if the car's also having a radical drop job (like our Escort, on coilovers). If you've exhausted all possibilities with spacers (or wheels with a more friendly offset - see *'Wheels n' tyres'*), further work will be needed.

Sometimes, all you need to stop those nasty grinding noises is to remove the plastic wheelarch liners. These are usually held on by a few simple clips and screws. Tyres can sometimes be rubbing on the liner clips alone - once they're trimmed off, problem gone. Any non-vital protrusions into the under-arch area can be trimmed off or flattened with a hammer - but we don't advise the hammer approach with the arch lips (you'll crack the paint, and probably distort the wing).

Serious wheelarch mods are best done at a bodyshop - but if you're brave and reasonably talented, there's nothing to stop you having a go yourself. The best approach with problem arch lips is to trim off the offending metal - get the wheel off, and get right under there. If you can borrow (or hire) an air hacksaw, the job's as good as done. If, however, the problem is rubbing on suspension bits, trimming isn't really an option, and it's time to start swapping components - see 'Suspension'. The best answer to arches which aren't roomy enough is, of course, a wide-arch bodykit. And bank loans are so cheap these days.

Bonnet vents

Once you've got your bodykit on, it's only natural you'll want a bonnet vent, isn't it? Respect.

But this is one SCARY job to tackle yourself, unless you're really that good, or that brave. Plenty of options - you can get little louvres stamped in as well, to complement your Evo, Impreza, Integrale or Celica GT4 main vent. A more recent trend is the F50 vent, and there's even been a feature car with a bonnet scoop from a (sensible) Kia Sedona people carrier! Truly, anything goes.

Most common option chosen by the Escort elite? Cosworth vents, of course - the original and still the best. Companies like RGM (makers of our vents) do Cosworth vents in two flavours - pretend and (fer) real. Or in other words, stick-on (no cutting) and genuine (ohmigawd, we're going to cut holes in our bonnet). So - are you feeling lucky?

Cosworth vents

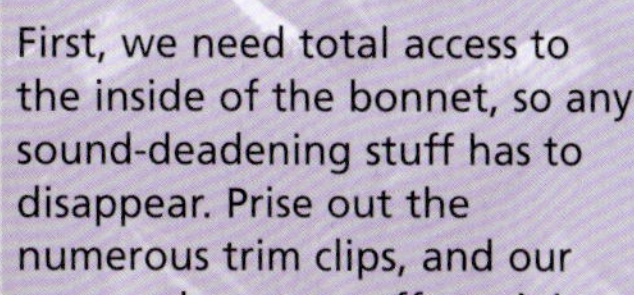

First, we need total access to the inside of the bonnet, so any sound-deadening stuff has to disappear. Prise out the numerous trim clips, and our bonnet muff can join the growing pile of scrap standard bits.

01

Okay, we all know roughly where Cossie vents are meant to go from the outside, but it really pays to look inside the bonnet too. With all those strengthening beams around, it's pretty obvious there's a limited area where that vent can go - chopping those beams is not an option.

02

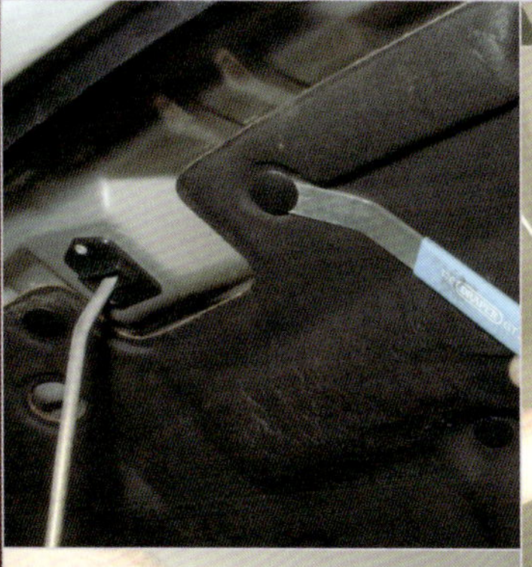

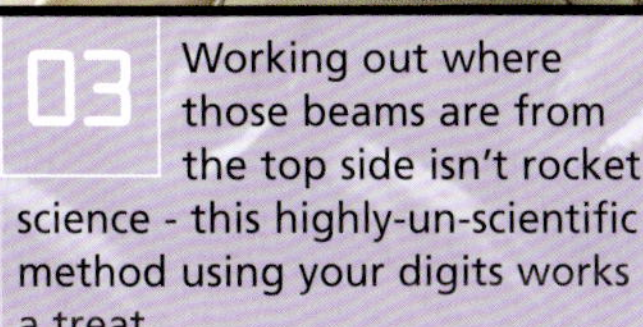

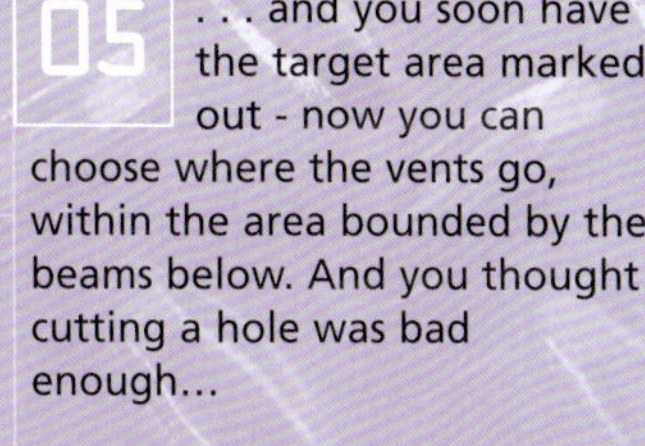

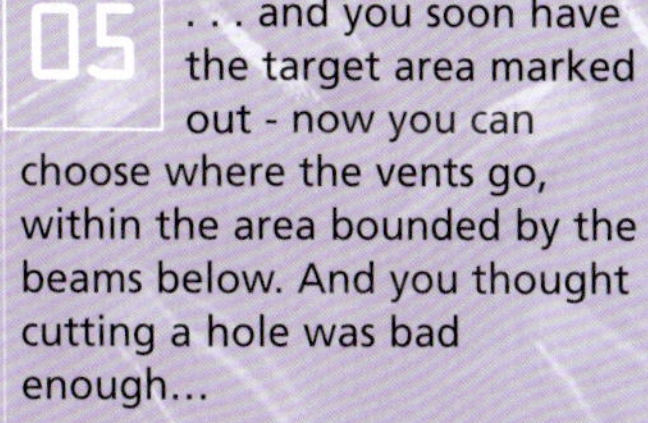

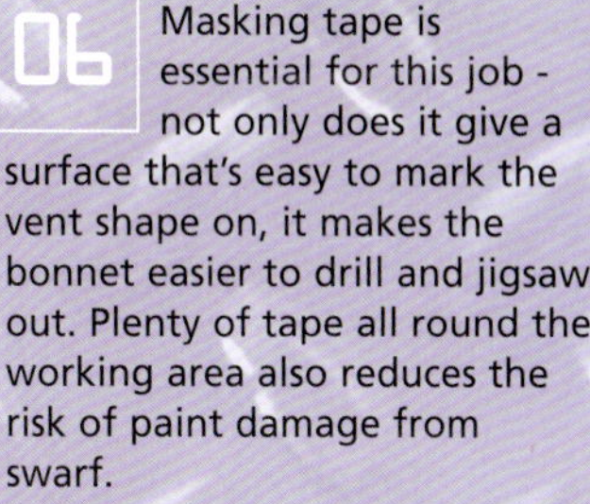

03 Working out where those beams are from the top side isn't rocket science - this highly-un-scientific method using your digits works a treat . . .

04 . . . apply tape where your fingers end up, top side . . .

05 . . . and you soon have the target area marked out - now you can choose where the vents go, within the area bounded by the beams below. And you thought cutting a hole was bad enough...

06 Masking tape is essential for this job - not only does it give a surface that's easy to mark the vent shape on, it makes the bonnet easier to drill and jigsaw out. Plenty of tape all round the working area also reduces the risk of paint damage from swarf.

>>

07 To give yourself a chance of getting both vents set at the same angle, measure the rough distance from the crease (swage line) up the bonnet to the centre-line of the vent. If you get this distance the same at the top and bottom of the vent, it will follow the line of the bonnet. If, of course, this is how you want your two vents to look.

08 When the vent's in the right spot, tape it to the bonnet, and draw round it. Keep the pen vertical all the way round, or you'll draw a distorted shape.

09 Important decision now - does the vent fit on top, or up from below? We chose from below, for a neater job - don't think you can filler over the raised edge of a vent, as the thin skim will crack with engine heat and bonnet flex. The hole we want to cut is 10 to 15 mm INSIDE the shape we've just drawn. How do we get an even 10 mm? By using a 10 mm bolt head, and joining the dots.

10 We'll be using drills and jigsaws next, which will stick through the bonnet. Yeah, so? Well, these sharp cutting tools will make a mess of any wires and hoses they touch under there, so raise the bonnet on blocks beforehand, and check before cutting too far that nothing's in the way.

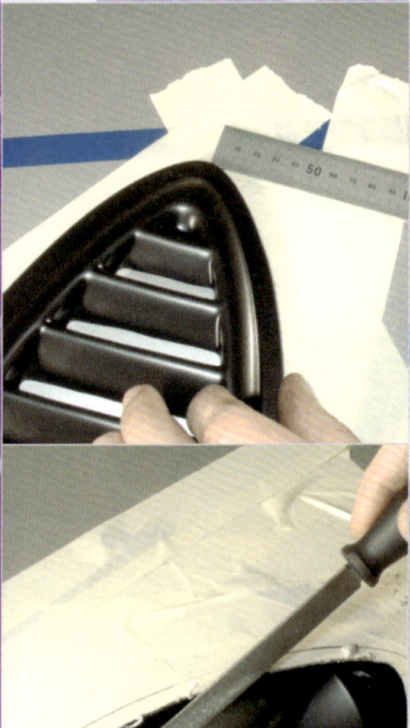

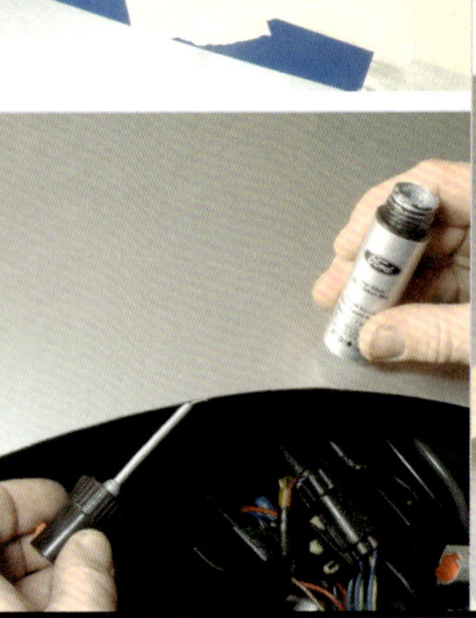

15 Don't get too fussy, trying to get an absolutely perfect shape - by the time the vent's in, secured with the mastic and painted, a slight imperfection in the hole shape won't matter.

16 Our whole bonnet's being resprayed later, but yours might not be. Either way, it pays to protect that cut-and-filed edge of metal with some paint. How cool will rust bubbles look, around your vents? Not very.

17 Our vent's going in from below - how to hold it in place while the mastic goes off? This splendid device is our idea. Two wood blocks to sit on the bonnet, a strip of thick MDF along the vent, and four long bolts with nuts and washers. The bolts fit through the vent slots and holes in the MDF, with washers to stop them pulling through. The vent goes into the bonnet, then the nuts are tightened evenly to pull the vent up into place. Works a treat, and easy to make.

18 Before the mastic comes out, clean round the inside of the bonnet to help make sure it sticks.

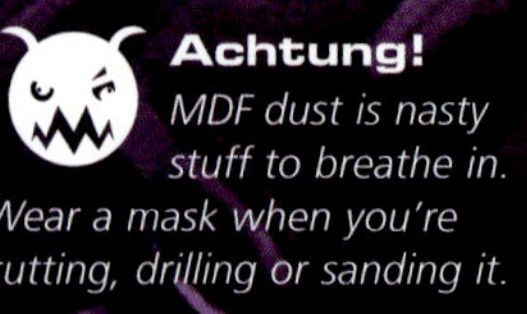

Achtung!

MDF dust is nasty stuff to breathe in. Wear a mask when you're cutting, drilling or sanding it.

11 A hole for our jigsaw blade is the first requirement. If it's a 10 mm drill bit you're using, mark the drill hole centre 5 mm in from the edge of the vent hole.

12 Yes, we really cut our own hole - no bodyshop pros for us. Use a fine-tooth blade (tooth pattern similar to a normal hacksaw blade) for cutting metal, and take it slowly, especially on the curves.

13 Well, that's a hole. The vent had better fit, 'cos there's no going back now.

14 Try the vent in the hole now, and see how good a job you did. There's bound to be some uneven metal, so mark up the worst bits for attention with a file.

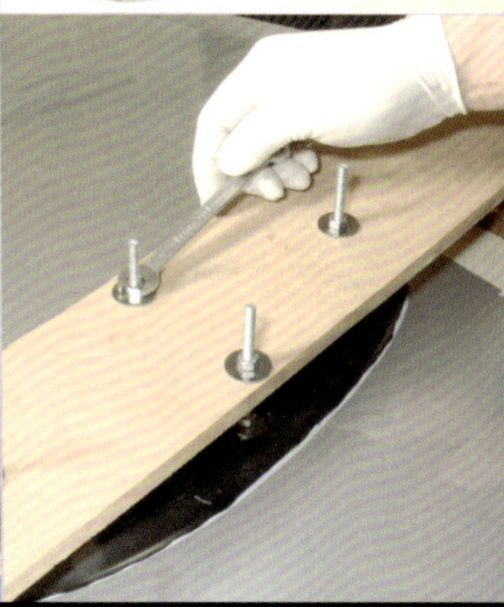

19 If the mastic you've chosen is any good, it should smell like pear drops (fast-setting, suitable for external use). The right stuff is also hell to get off your hands, so do like our mechanic, and wear gloves.

20 In with the vent, fit our bolts securely, and press it into place.

21 Topside, we're now evenly tightening up our bolts, to squeeze the mastic up through. The MDF bends a bit when you do this, but not enough to be a problem. If you don't fancy our idea, you could get away with resting the bonnet down onto some wood blocks, placed on top of the engine. Our way means the vent sits in nice and evenly. Up to you.

22 Before the mastic goes off, it's time to use those magic fingers and smooth it off. You'll probably need some solvent to clean off the excess mastic (if the mastic's any good). This stuff can be painted over, so perhaps another light skim of mastic (when the first lot's dry) would do the job. What we're trying to say is - don't try to get it perfectly smooth, in one go.

06

Lights & bulbs

Lights & bulbs

Being scene

Lights - one of the easiest and coolest ways to trick up your Escort. Several options here, so we'll start at the front, and work back.

Headlights

Almost nothing influences the look of your Escort more than the front end, so the headlights play a crucial role.

Before we go any further, it's worth pointing out there's several different stock items out there. The XR and RS models have a wider headlight unit than the rest, with a sidelight alongside (where lesser Escorts have their front indicators) - make sure you know what you're ordering. The later (Mk 7) headlights are totally different again, with a much rounder shape.

What's available?

For most people, there's several popular routes to modding the Escort headlights - some cheap, and... well... some rather less cheap (but more effective).

The popular cheap option is stick-on headlight "brows", which do admittedly give the rather bland Escort front end a tougher look. The brows are best sprayed to match the car, before fitting - most are fitted using stick-on velcro pads. Street-cred on the cheap, and (if you choose the Fox-style brows) a cheap alternative to a proper "badboy" bonnet.

Another cheap option is again stick-on - this time, it's stick-on covers which give the twin-headlight look. This is basically a sheet of vinyl (shaped to the headlights, and colour-matched to your car) with two holes cut in it. Dead easy to fit, but dare we say, a bit tacky? Just our opinion. A cheap and simple way to get close to the Morette look.

If you want tinted headlights, you could try spray-tinting them, but go easy on the spray. Turning your headlights from clear glass to non-see-through is plain daft, even if it's done in the name of style. A light tint is quite effective, and gives you the chance to colour-match to your Escort. Unlike newer cars, there don't seem to be any companies offering ready-made tinted replacement lights for the Escort. At least, not yet. With tinted headlights, you'd be wise to tint those clear front indicators too, of course.

If you've got a really early Escort with orange indicator lenses, the clear ones became standard-fit from late 1991 onwards - a cheap upgrade, if you find some in a scrapyard.

Getting more expensive, we're looking at complete replacement lights - "proper" twin-headlights, available as a kit from the French company Morette. Typically around £300 a set at time of writing, these are for those who're seriously into their cars - maximum cred, and no-one's gonna accuse you of owning a "boring" Escort ever again! The light surrounds have to be sprayed to match your car, and fitting is not without some difficulties, but the finished result is SO worth it.

Another "headlight" option often featured on Escorts actually belongs in the bodywork section - it's the "badboy" bonnet. By cunningly welding-in a couple of triangular plates to your standard Escort bonnet, a bodyshop (or handy DIY-er) can create a really mean look, using just the standard lights. Excellent.

Finally, there's one more adventurous option for those who really want their car to look something different. Definitely one for the bodyshop, but you won't beat it for effect - try fitting standard headlights from another car altogether. A popular choice are the "crystal" headlights from the Mk 4 VW Golf, but there's no limit if you use your imagination.

Pub trivia

The popular twin-headlight look was derived from a cunning tweak first employed in the Touring Cars, years ago. Some teams homologated a twin-headlight unit, but for racing, turned one pair of the "headlights" into air inlets, to direct air from the front of the car to brake ducts or into the engine air intakes, as required. Think about it - why else would the touring cars bother with headlight mods? Until recently, there were no night races!

Morette twin headlights

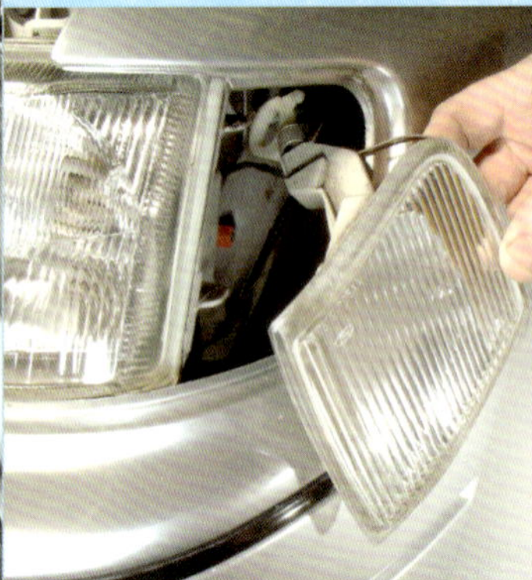

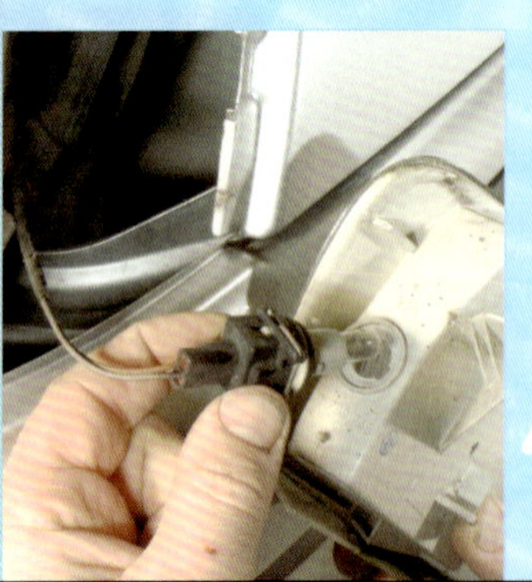

01 In the name of bringing you better photos, we cheated a little here, and took out the air cleaner box (covered in the section on fitting an induction kit, so don't moan). Just gives more room behind the headlight. Of course, on a lesser 'scort, you won't have this problem. Take out the indicator/sidelight unit (if you've got one) by pulling and unhooking the spring catch . . .

02 . . . removing the unit from the wing . . .

03 . . . and twisting out the bulbholder.

Achtung!

Our Escort was a Mk 6 - for those of you with a Mk 7, prepare for bad news. Removing the headlights on a Mk 7 Escort means taking off the front bumper and radiator grille. Yes, 'fraid so - but it's not so bad - taking the bumper off's similar to how we removed our Mk 6 bumper (in the bodywork section) except that the radiator must be tied in place, as you'll also be removing the radiator support brackets. The grille's got an air deflector over the top (four screws), then one screw either side. The good news is, once you're over that, there's just three screws to undo (and the wiring to disconnect), and the headlight's at your mercy. And don't stick the old bumper back on afterwards, okay? Do us all a favour, and get a bodacious bodykit.

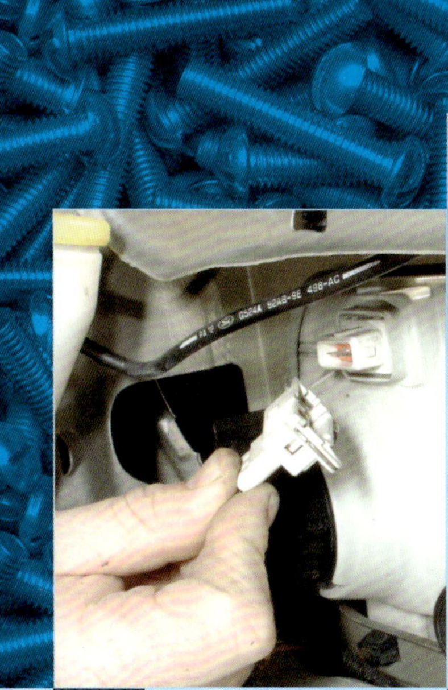

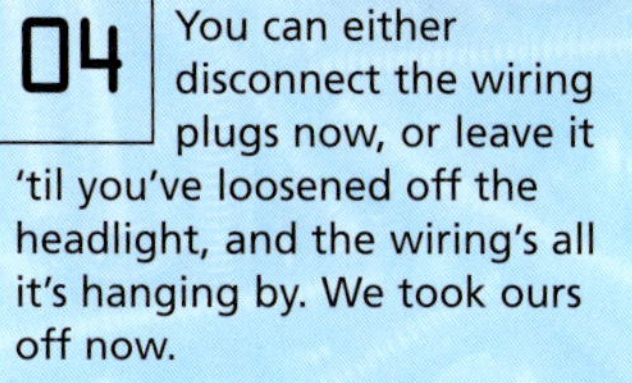

04 You can either disconnect the wiring plugs now, or leave it 'til you've loosened off the headlight, and the wiring's all it's hanging by. We took ours off now.

05 The two bolts holding the headlight at the top are easy to undo, but wait - there's a third bolt hiding inside the hole left by the indicator/sidelight, and it's a bit harder to reach. Still no real challenge to the competent Maxer, though.

06 And that's the last we'll need to see of that. So are you keeping the old lights, to swap it back to standard, or are they off to the next car boot sale? Could be £20 the pair, which would sort you out some blue bulbs...

07 Usually, Morette lights set very high standards for how they fit. Ours weren't bad, but we were surprised they didn't quite go in first time (maybe our Escort wasn't quite straight - not unlikely for an XR3i to have a light frontal in its history).

08 Best to mark up the offending plastic first, and if you can, trim away with the light in position, to get a perfect fit. This, by the way, is why you don't paint your surrounds first...

09 The new light mounting nuts don't have to be done up murder-tight now, especially not if the surrounds have to come off again for painting.

10 The earth wire (brown) for the new Morettes is wired up in a snap, thanks to a handy earth point which Ford have provided just behind each headlight. Just add your brown wire to the one that's there already, and re-tighten the bolt.

11 The live feed (red, with an in-line fuse) must be run up to the battery. Fortunately, there's plenty of other wiring to tape your live to, on the way up there, and it's best to make a neat job of it. When you get near the battery, there's a bulkhead in the way - after some investigating, we chopped off the live's wiring plug . . .

12 . . . then pulled down the sound-deadening, and fed the wire through a small hole already there. On a sharp-edged hole, you should really use a grommet, to stop the wire rubbing through and putting your lights out.

13 Our Escort being a bit posh, it has a fusible-link bracket mounted on the battery positive terminal - we took ours off for a better look.

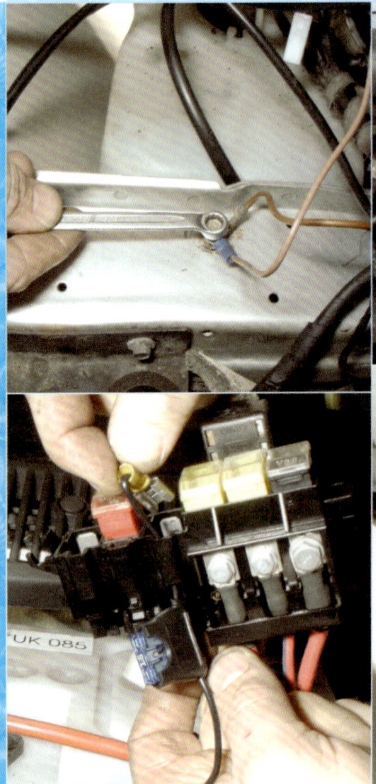

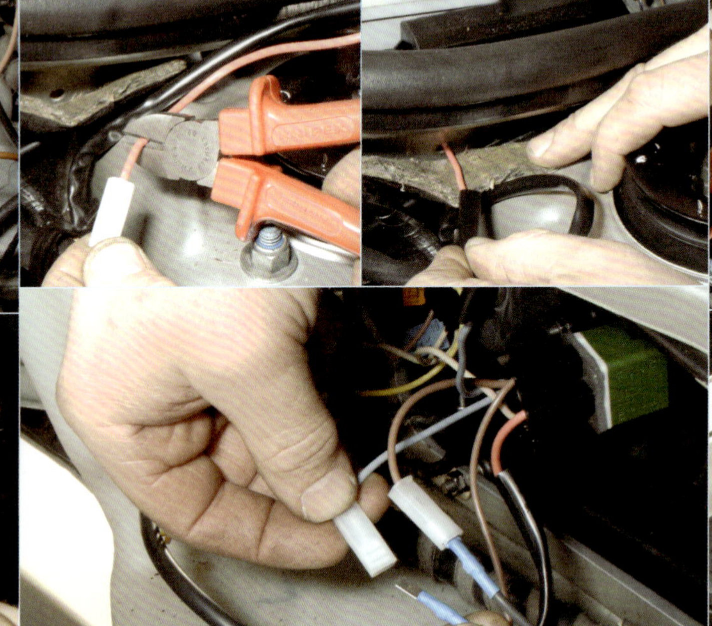

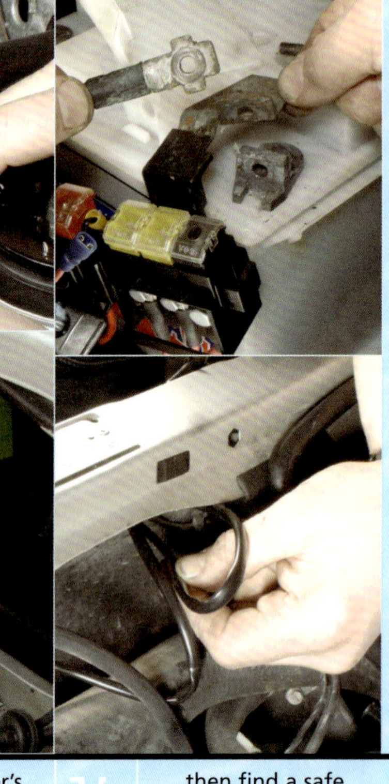

14 There's a spare live spade connection already in there, so we fitted a large spade to our previously-chopped live feed, and connected it straight on. Neat, or what? Otherwise, fit a ring terminal to your wire, and fit to the battery lead bolt. Make sure the in-line fuse can be got at easily, if it blows.

15 With one headlight working, it's time to rig up the driver's side. Morette provide a "loom", which you plug into the spade-equipped blue and brown wires . . .

16 . . . then find a safe passage for the wiring, across to the other side. We cable-tied ours to the front crossmember, keeping it away from anything moving or hot. The wires plug into the other light, and there's another earth to connect up - you should then have fully-functioning lights again, with added style. Back of the net!

You should, of course, refit your indicator or sidelight to finish the job. But if you've got sidelights like us, there's another option here - Morette provide a sidelight bulbholder in their lights (no bulb, but that's easily sorted). So if you re-wire the sidelight to the Morettes, you can colour-code the old sidelight big-time. You could also use this method to lose your indicators, if you get some new ones, and cut them into your front bumper (try motorbike fairing indicators - cheap and legal).

17

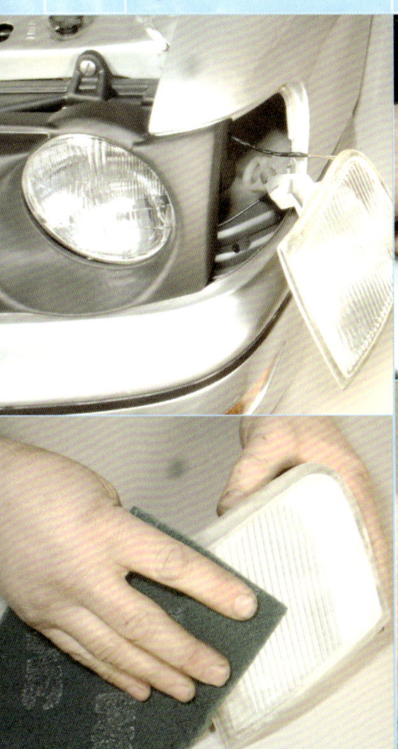

18 If you're going the let's-ditch-the-sidelights route, chop off the old wiring plug . . .

19 . . . and crimp on some suitable spades. If you're fitting new indicators, you might need a different wiring plug to make them work, depending on what new light units you've chosen.

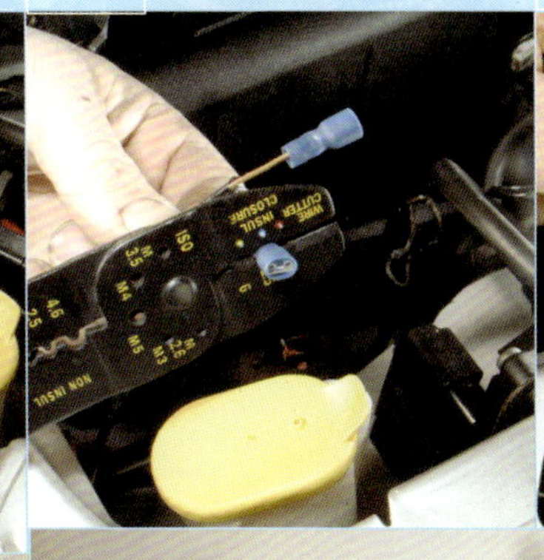

20 This is the Morette sidelight bulbholder, to which we fit our spades (and a bulb) to give us a sidelight inside the headlight (if you see what we mean).

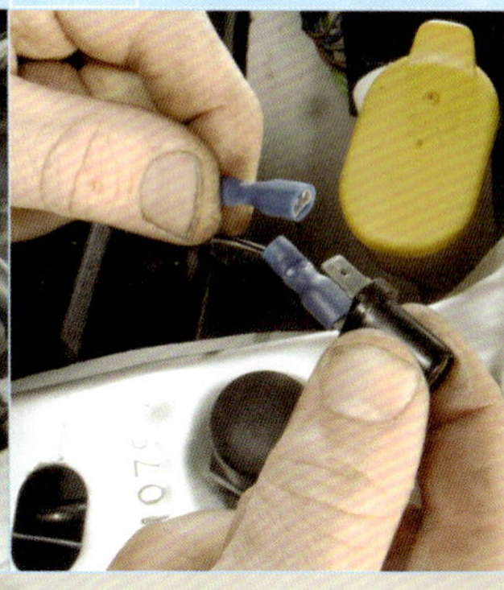

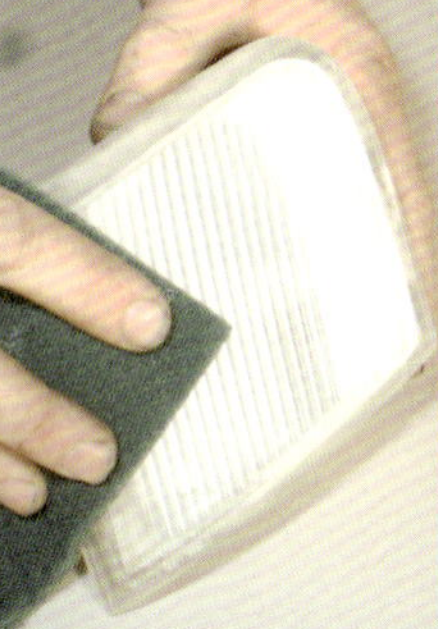

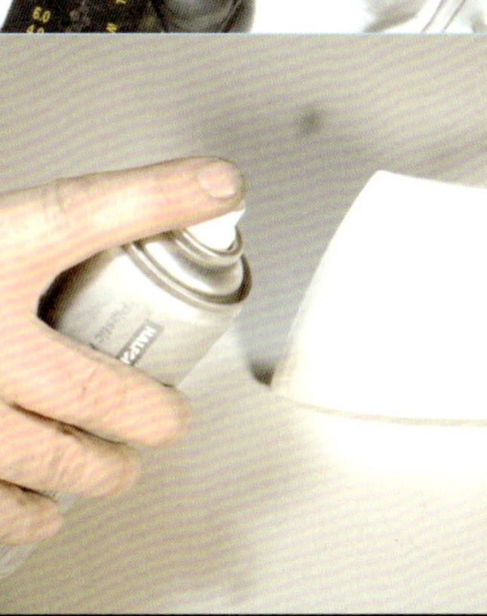

21 So - what are we doing with our old sidelights, then? Can't just leave them out - bit of an unsightly hole. We quite like the idea of painting our Morette surrounds black (to go with our satin-black bonnet), so why not match the sidelights, and give a wrap-round headlight effect? Give the plastic lenses a clean and rubdown with Scotchbrite . . .

22 . . . then a coat of plastic primer . . .

23 . . . and finally, the black topcoat. Very moody - and, because we've got sidelights in our Morettes now, no worries on the legal/MOT front. If your lights are still functional, just a light coat of colour-coding paint (no primer) should just keep you on the right side of the law.

Headlight **bulbs**

Make your Escort look like an Audi or a Beemer, the easy way. Bad-weather and "blue" headlight bulbs are an excellent way to boost headlight performance, and are perfect with other blue LED accessories like washer jets and number plate screws. The blue bulbs you buy in most accessory shops will be legal, 60W/55 bulbs, and are no problem. Don't be tempted to buy the mega-powerful bulbs you can get from rallying suppliers (any over 60W/55 are in fact illegal for use in this country) - as with all other non-standard lights, the boys in blue will love pulling you over for a word about this, so ask before you buy.

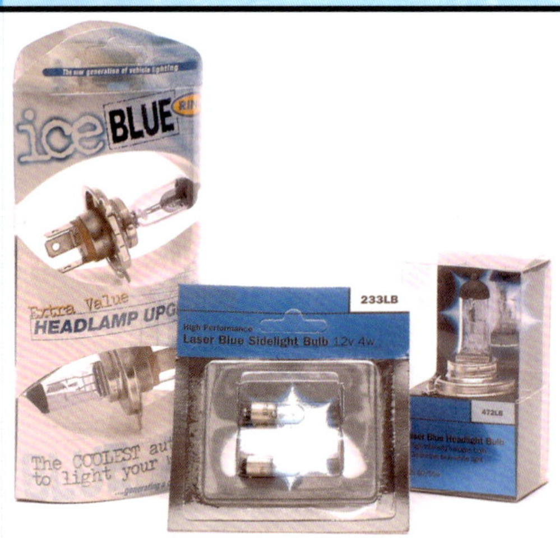

Even if you're not bothered about the legality of over-powerful bulbs (and you might well argue that being more powerful is the whole point of fitting), there's other problems with monster bulbs. First, they give off masses of heat, and loads of people have melted their headlights before they found this out. Don't believe us? Try fitting some 100W/90s and put your hand in front of the light, close to the glass. Hot, isn't it? The excess heat these bulbs generate will damage the headlights eventually, either by warping the lens, burning off the reflective coating, or melting the bulbholders. Maybe all three.

The increased current required to work big bulbs has also been known to melt wiring (this could lead to a fire) and will almost certainly burn out your light switch. There's no headlight relay fitted as standard, so the wiring and switch were designed to cope only with the current drawn by standard-wattage bulbs; if you're going for high power, a relay must be fitted (much as you'd have to, to fit foglights or spots).

Side repeaters

There's a range of "standard" colours that side reps come in (clear, red, smoked, green, and blue). If you're going for the same colour rear clusters, try to buy your lights from the same source, to get the same shade. Clear lenses can be coloured using special paint, but the paint must be applied lightly and evenly to the lens, or this will invite an easily-avoided MOT failure. Bodyshops can colour clear lenses to the exact shade of your car, by mixing a little paint with loads of lacquer - very trick.

Side repeaters must still show an orange light, and must be sufficiently bright (not easy to judge, and no two coppers have the same eyesight!). The stock bulbs are clear, so make sure you get orange bulbs too. You can actually get orange bulbs that look clear, to avoid the "fried egg" effect. Alternatively, get LED side repeaters, like we did on our Fiesta project car.

Besides the various colour effects, side repeaters are available in many different shapes. Any shape other than standard goes, really - one popular choice for now are the Focus-style triangular lights. Bad news on the Escort Mk 7 - the oval side reps are recessed into the front wings, leaving you little choice but to stay oval.

Or how about ditching the repeaters altogether, and get some tasty Merc-style mirrors, with side reps built-in? You could smooth your front wings, then…

01 Fitting new side repeaters, in theory, is dead easy. On older models, twist the old unit clockwise, and pull it out of the wing. On Mk 7s with the oval side reps, carefully push the light sideways, and prise it out of the wing.

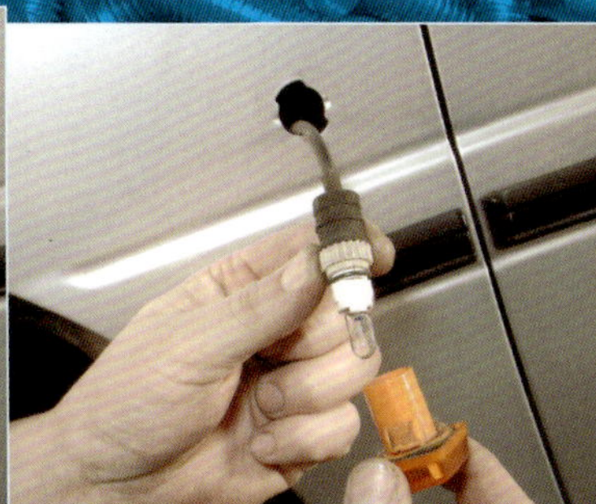

02 Time to remove the naff orange lens. You might want to keep this, if the car's ever going back to standard. Our car, as you'll see, isn't.

03 In theory, all you do now is fit an orange bulb into the holder, slip on your new lens, and pop back into the wing. But - oh dear - our Focus-style reps seem to be for a Focus, not an Escort. We're not scared - we drew round the odd shape on the back of the light, then trimmed the shape out. Stick the template to the wing, mark out the shape.

04 Yes - we're going to cut metal. This is Draper's excellent multi-tool we're using. Think about it - how else are you going to cut a shape like this?

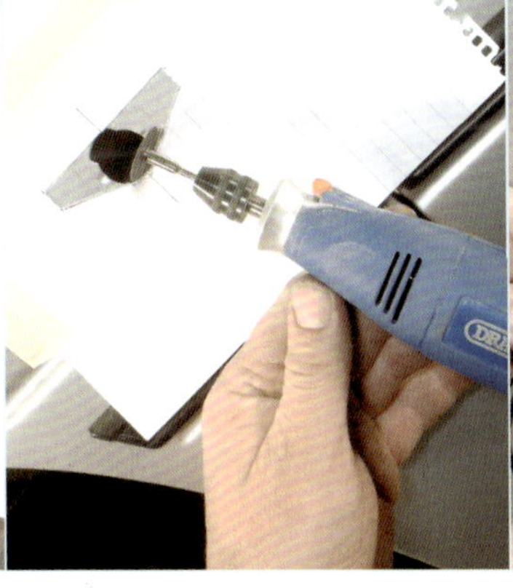

05 A little 'adjustment' with a needle file later, and the new light was a perfect fit. Honestly. It really clicks into place, just like it presumably does on a Focus. Removing the wheelarch liner gives you plenty of access to the back of the light, in case you get the fit too perfect, and can't get it out to fit the bulb. Treat the cut edge to some paint, or you'll end up with a self-enlarging hole, of the rusty kind.

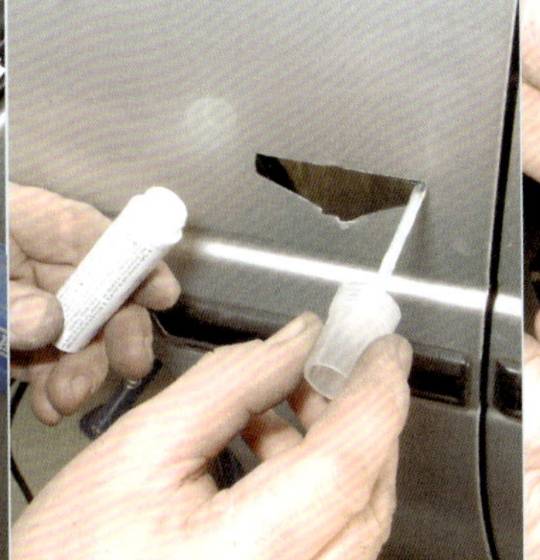

06 Anything other than an orange lens will need an orange bulb fitted. That bulb looks pretty orange to me. Clip it all back together, and feel very chuffed. If Focus lights are too common for you, remember this method would also let you fit the coolest side reps ever - BMW M3s.

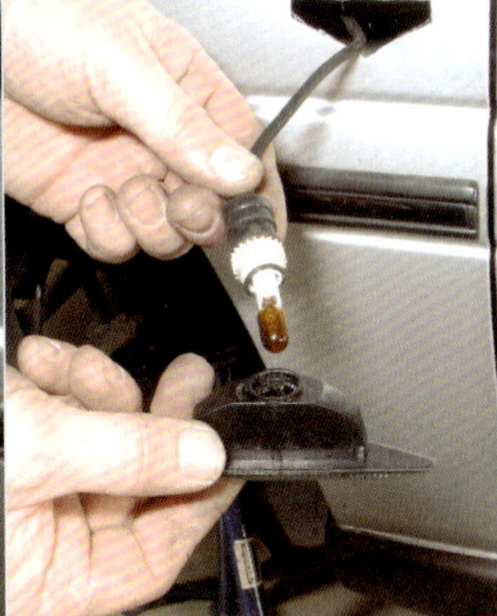

Rear foglight

Many aftermarket rear lights don't have a foglight in. Bothered? You should be, since your not-so-friendly MOT man will fail your beloved motor if you don't have one. Yeah, but who's heard of a rear foglight that's both legal and cool? One that may actually enhance your car's rear end?

01 Tell me that's not the sauciest foglight you ever saw. Of course, it's not Ford, but it is standard - on a Peugeot 206, anyway. Our plan is to mount that sexy little light in the mesh strip at the base of our ST24 rear bumper.

02 With the bumper yet to be finally fitted, our job was much easier. Draw round the light on the inside . . .

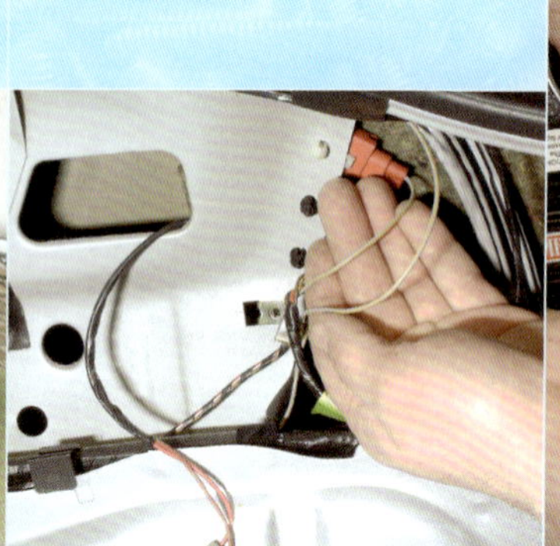

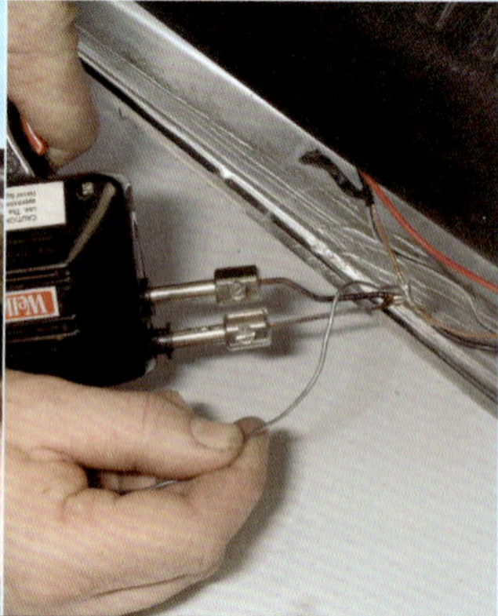

03 . . . snip out the required hole, leaving enough mesh to fold up the sides of the light . . .

04 . . . then glue it in place.

05 Now for the wiring. Our original rear fogs were in the tailgate - so did we have a long hard search for the foglight live, and a nightmare feeding it down to the bumper? Not really - the grey/yellow wire needed comes down to a plug on the right-hand side of the boot, and can be spliced as easy as you like.

06 That's the live - all we need for some red light action is an earth. Well, any good chassis earth point would do, with the aid of a self-tapper, but there's a perfectly-good brown wire going to the number plate light, so let's splice that. Solder the live and earth to the two pins on the new foglight connector, and it's a go.

Afterburner rear lights

When buying any rear light clusters, it's not a good idea to go for the cheapest you can find, because you'll be buying trouble. Cheap rear light clusters don't have rear foglights or rear reflectors, so aren't really legal. Mr. Plod is well-informed on this point, and those sexy rear lights are way too big a come-on for him to ignore.

You can buy stick-on reflectors, but these are about as sexy as NHS specs (you'd have to be pretty unlucky to get pulled just for having no rear reflectors, but don't say we didn't warn you). And what happens if your car gets crunched, parked at night with no reflectors fitted? Will your insurance try and refuse to pay out? You betcha.

The rear foglight problem could perhaps be solved by spraying the clear bulb itself red, but it won't fool every MOT man.

The best solution? Only buy UK-legal lights. Any questions on light legality? Why not check out the ABC Design website tech tips page, at www.abcdesignltd.com - if you've any questions after that, you can E-mail them. We're so good to you.

01 Before we can start dreaming of how sexy our Escort's going to look with its new afterburners on, those gakky old rear lights have to go. Open the boot, and detach the wiring plug - this releases by pressing down a wire clip on the plug.

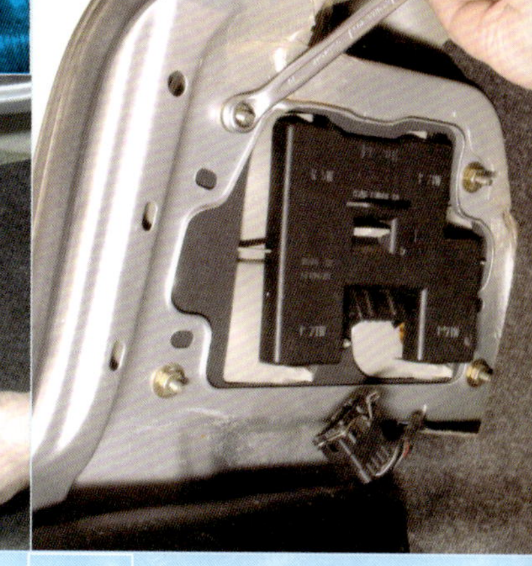

02 Now there's four nuts to remove . . .

03 . . . before the light parts company from the car. It might be 'stuck' on, if it's been there a while. Persuade it.

04 This is more like it - we've seen the future, and it's looking good. For now though, we've got to separate the front and rear sections of our lights, to try them in place. Remove the two screws holding the larger light units in place . . .

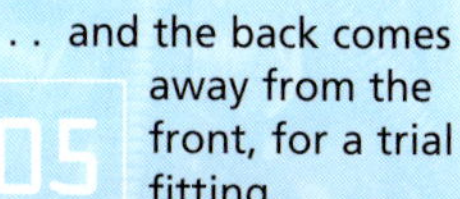

05 . . . and the back comes away from the front, for a trial fitting.

Oh whoops - Houston, we have a problem. There seems to be rather a large chunk of Escort in the way of one of our light units, and it's got to go. Mark it up with a pen . . .

06

. . . then it's out with a hacksaw blade (or, if you're well-equipped, a powered multi-tool makes life easier).

07

As we don't want to encourage rust (and this is a Ford we're dealing with here), a little paint on that cut edge is a mighty good plan.

08

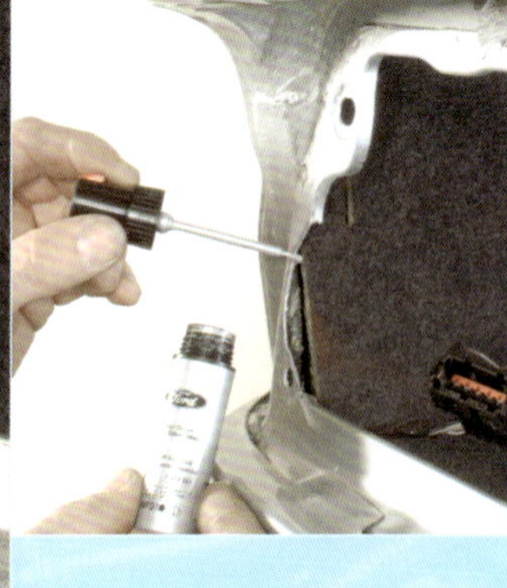

Ah, and here we have problem number two - there's a mounting bolt hole in the light which should line up with one in the car. Yes, you guessed it - it doesn't line up, so we'll be drilling that later. For now, we're just marking up.

09

Cordless drills - how did we manage before these beauties came along? If you don't have one, invest now.

10

We don't want to bore you with any more problems, but it appears one of the other mounting holes isn't quite in the right spot either. Not too serious this time - just a touch with a round file.

11

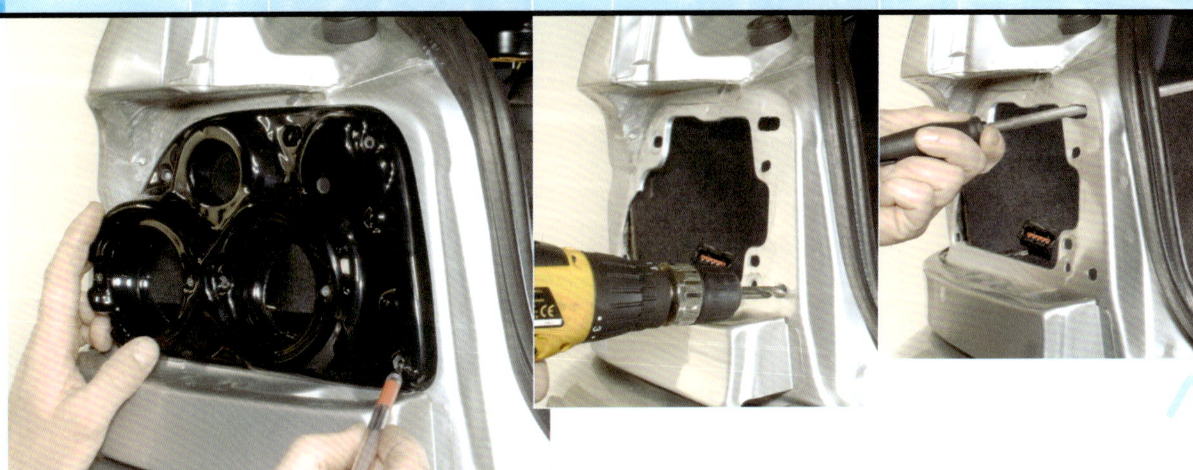

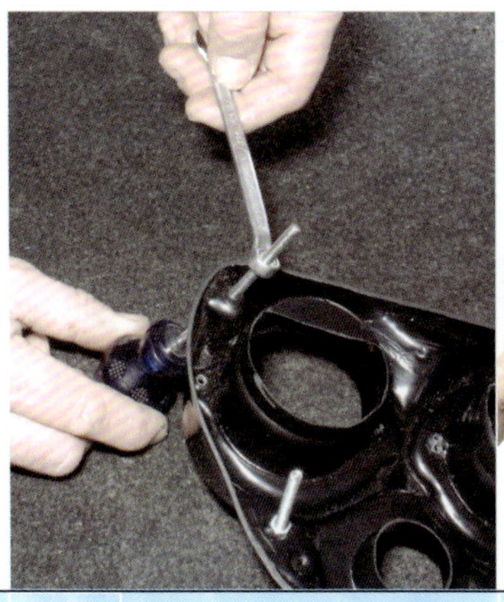

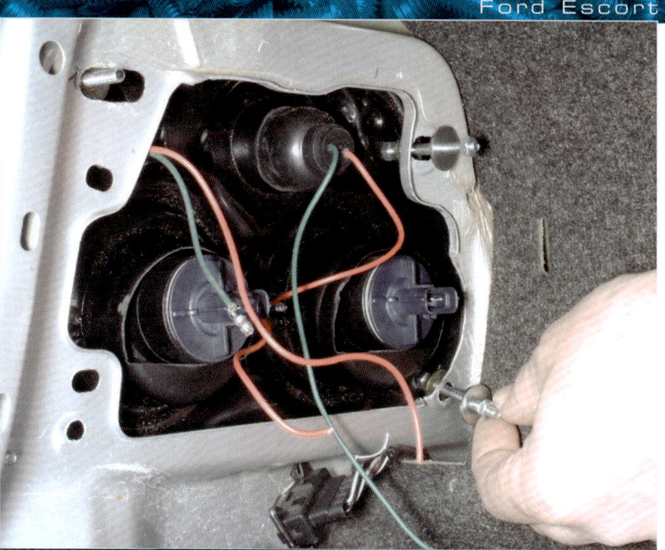

12 Now we're reasonably confident of success, it's time to fit the light mounting bolts. Just fit the bolt through from the front, and tighten one of the nuts up to it. When the light's fitted to the car, another nut will go on, and hold it on the inside (like before).

13 So did we get it right? Do all the bolts line up? Only one way to find out . . .

14 . . . looks like we're there. On with the oversize washers, then the nuts, and tighten it all up. Of course, if that light isn't a tight fit to the car body, water's going to get in our boot. Were they a good fit? Have they been a good fit, so far? We'll let you work it out. Fortunately, mastic's nice and cheap, and does the job a treat - take the light off again, and put a good bead of the stuff round, to keep the water out.

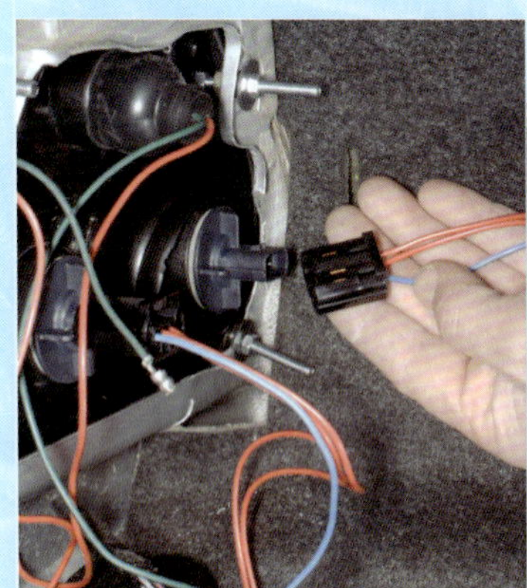

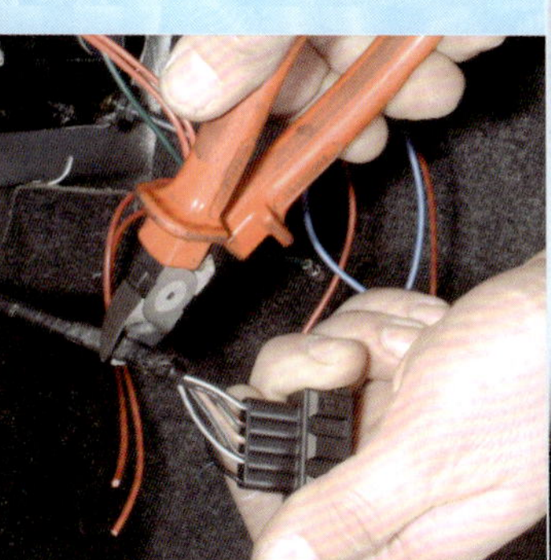

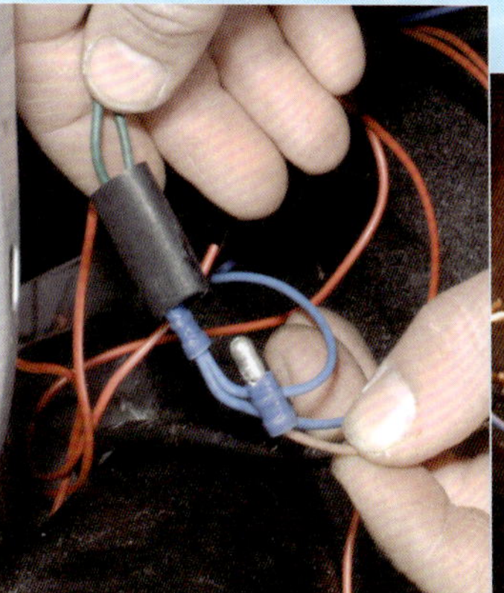

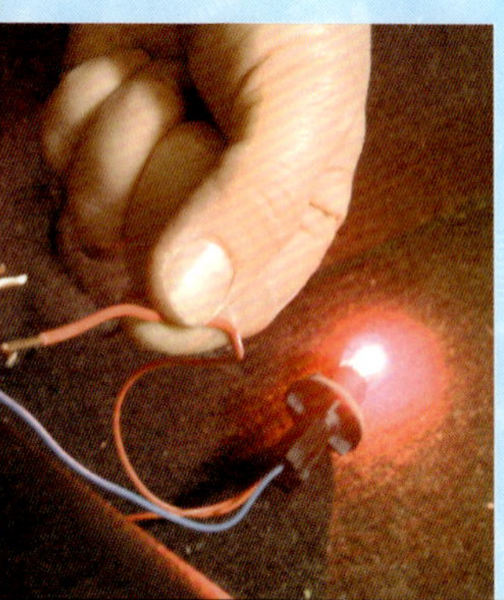

15 All that remains now is the wiring-up, which for many of you is the scary bit. Well, don't panic - there's really not much to it. First, plug on the supplied wiring harness to each of the large light units.

16 Time for some butchery. Chop off the old multi-plug for the rear lights (but leave enough wire attached to the plug so's you could re-connect it, if the car gets put back to standard later).

17 You'll have noticed by now that, apart from the red wires off your new lights (obviously the live wires), there's green and blue too - these are the earths. Would be less confusing if they were all one colour, like black, but there we are. All the greens and blues can be joined together (make it a large bullet, or even two), and these go onto one of the black wires from the car's original rear light wiring.

18 Doing the red wires is great fun. First, bare the ends of any non-black wires from the car's original wiring. Now bare the ends of the red wires. Have an assistant work each of the lights in turn (switch on the lights, press the brake pedal, that kind of thing), while you put the wires together, to see what comes on. Not perhaps the most scientific way to do it, but it's simple and it works. Use the bullets supplied, and the job's done.

07

Wheels & tyres

Wheels & tyres

Your most **important decision** ever?

This is where it's at - alloy wheels are the most important styling decision you'll ever make. No matter how good the rest of your car is, choose the wrong rims and your car will never look right. Choose a good set and you're already well on the way to creating a sorted motor. Take your time and pick wisely - wheel fashions change like the weather, and you don't want to spend shedloads on a set of uncool alloys.

None of the standard alloys cut it (with the possible exception of genuine Cosworth items, but not on an unmodded 1.3, please), and should very quickly be dumped. Advice on which particular wheels to buy would be a waste of space, since the choice is so huge, and everyone will have their own favourites - for what it's worth, though, we reckon anything in a five-spoke or multi-spoke design seems to look best on an Escort, but go for something a little more original by all means. Beyond those words of dubious wisdom, you're on your own - car colour and your own chosen other mods will dictate what will look right on your car.

Fitting 17s or 18s will be a great deal less stressful if you get wheels with exactly the right offset - otherwise, your arches won't just have to be "trimmed" - they'll be butchered! Fitting wheels with the wrong offset may also do unpleasant things to the handling. The correct offset for all Mk 5/6/7 Escorts is anything in the range 36 to 41, meaning alloys from Fords of a similar age should fit. Escort Cosworth rims have a 25 offset, so try (on the car) before you buy.

Lead us not into temptation

Before we go any further into which wheels are right for you, a word about insurance and security. Fitting tasty alloys to your Escort is one of the first and best ways to make it look cool. It follows, therefore, that someone with dubious morals might very well want to unbolt them from your car while you're not around, and make their own car look cool instead (or simply sell them, to buy spot cream and drugs).

Since fitting a set of top alloys is one of the easiest bolt-on ways to trick up any car, it's no surprise that the market in stolen alloys is as alive and kicking as it currently is - your wheels will also look very nice on any number of other cars, and the owners of those cars would love to own them at a fraction of the price you paid... It's not unknown for a set of wheels to go missing just for the tyres - if you've just splashed out on a set of fat Yokohamas, your wheels look even more tempting, especially if you've got a common-size tyre.

Tell your insurance company what you're fitting. What will probably happen is that they'll ask for the exact details, and possibly a photo of the car with the wheels on. Provided you're happy to then accept that they won't cover the extra cost of the wheels if they get nicked (or if the whole car goes), you may find you're not charged a penny more, especially if you've responsibly fitted some locking wheel bolts. Not all companies are the same, though - some charge an admin fee, and yes, some will start loading your premium. If you want the rims covered, it's best to talk to a company specialising in modified cars, or you could be asked to pay out the wheel cost again in premiums. The worst thing you can do is say nothing, and hope they don't find out - we don't want to go on about this, but there are plenty of documented cases where insurance companies have refused to pay out altogether, purely on the basis of undeclared alloy wheels.

How cheap are you?

Hopefully, you'll be deciding which wheels to go for based on how they look, not how much they cost, but inevitably (for most ordinary people at least), price does become a factor. Surely buying a cheaper wheel must have its pitfalls? Well, yes - and some of them may not be so obvious.

Inevitably, cheaper wheels = lower quality, but how does this manifest itself? Cheap wheels are often made from alloys which are more "porous" (a bit like a sponge, they contain microscopic holes and pockets of air). Being porous has two main disadvantages for a wheel, the main one being that it won't be able to retain air in the tyres. The days of tyres with inner tubes are long gone (and it's illegal to fit tubes to low-profile tyres), so the only thing keeping the air in are the three "walls" of the tyre, with the fourth "wall" being the inside of the wheel itself. If you like keeping fit by pumping up your tyres every morning, go ahead - the rest of us will rightly regard this as a pain, and potentially dangerous (running tyres at low pressure will also scrub them out very effectively - what was that about saving money?).

Porous wheels also have difficulty in retaining their paint or lacquer finish, with flaking a known problem, sometimes after only a few months. This problem is made worse by the fact that porous wheels are much harder to clean (brake dust seems to get ingrained into the wheels more easily) - and the more you scrub, the more the lacquer comes off.

The final nail in the coffin for cheap wheels is that they tend to corrode (or "fizz") more. This not only looks crap if visible from outside, but if you get corrosion between the wheel and the hub, you won't even be able to take the damn things off! Yes seriously, grown men with all the specialist tools in the world at their disposal will be scratching their heads when faced with wheels which simply **will not** come off.

Tricks 'n' tips

Whenever you have your wheels off, clean off any hub corrosion with wet-and-dry paper, then coat the hub mating surfaces with copper (brake) grease. There's no way you'll suffer stuck-on wheels again. "Proper" alloys come with a plastic collar which fits inside the wheel - an essential item, it centres the wheel properly and reduces wheel-to-hub corrosion. Do not chuck out.

Buying an established, popular make of wheel has another hidden benefit, too. Choosing a popular wheel will mean more suppliers will stock it, and the manufacturers themselves will make plenty of them. And if you're unlucky enough to have an accident (maybe a slide on a frosty road) which results in non-repairable damage to one wheel, you're going to need a replacement. If you've chosen the rarest wheels on the planet, you could be faced with having to replace a complete set of four, to get them all matching... A popular wheel, even if it's a few years old, might be easier to source, even second-hand.

The Sunday morning ritual

It's a small point maybe, but you'll obviously want your wheels to look as smart as possible, as often as possible - so how easy are they going to be to clean?

The real multi-spokers and BBS-style "wires" are hell to clean - a fiddly toothbrush job - do you really want that much aggro every week? The simpler the design, the easier time you'll have. For those who like nothing better than counting their spokes, though, there are several really good products out there to make your life less of a cleaning nightmare.

Tricks 'n' tips

It's worth applying a bit of car polish to the wheels - provided it's good stuff, and you can be sure of getting the residue out of the corners and edges, a polished wheel will always be easier to clean off than an unpolished one. You can also buy waxes which are tailor-made for the job.

Bolt from the blues

Don't forget about locking wheel bolts (see "Hold on to your wheels" further on) - bargain these into a wheel/tyre package if you're buying new.

A word of warning about re-using your existing wheel bolts, should you be upgrading from steel wheels. Most steel-wheel bolts are not suitable for use with alloy wheels (and *vice-versa*, incidentally). Make sure you ask about this when buying new wheels, and if necessary, bargain a set of bolts into the price. Most bolts for use with alloys will have a washer fitted, for two very good reasons - 1) the bolt will pull through the wheel hole without it, and 2) to protect the wheel finish.

Another point to watch for is that the new wheel bolts are the correct length for your fitment, taking into account whether you've fitted spacers or not. Bolts that are too short are obviously dangerous, and ones that are too long can foul on drum brakes, and generally get in the way of any turning activities. If in doubt ask the retailer for advice. Always check that the wheels turn freely once they've been put on, and investigate any strange noises before you go off for a pose.

Tricks 'n' tips

If you're keeping a steel wheel as your spare (or even if you're keeping an original alloy), keep a set of your original wheel bolts in a bag inside the spare wheel. Locking bolts especially might be too long when fitted to a thin steel wheel, and might jam up your brakes!

Other options

If you're on a really tight budget, and perhaps own a real "basic" model Escort, don't overlook the possibility of fitting a discarded set of standard alloys, possibly from another Ford entirely - check that the stud pattern's the same, obviously. Getting the right wheel bolts also applies here, not just with aftermarket wheels.

If the Ford range of wheels is too limiting, don't be too quick buying (for instance) alloys suitable for other makes altogether. For instance, some Peugeot and Citroën alloys have the same stud pattern (4x108), so they'll go on alright, but the offset is more than a bit different (like, 16 for Saxo VTS rims, where it should be at least 36 for a Ford - have fun). In the case of some alloys (BMW, VW, or Vauxhall, for example), the stud pattern may be only fractionally different (4x100), but if you put these on, the strain on the bolts is too great, and they can fracture or work themselves loose...

Size **matters**

For us Brits, biggest is best - there are Escorts out there with 18s and up. And yes, the mags all say you can't be seen with anything less than 17-inchers. In Europe, meanwhile, they're mad for the small-wheel look, still with seriously dropped suspension of course.

The Escort isn't really a small car, which means you can look down on people in Saxos, for whom fitting 17s means loads of arch-work. Escorts have nice roomy arches, and even a basic model can take a set of 17s with virtually no work being needed - so "it's only a Ford", eh, Saxo-boy?

Without touching the arches, 17s really are the biggest you'll do easily, unless you can find some 7x18 rims. By the time you get to a 7.5J rim (like many 18s), you'll be rubbing on the rear arch lip, and you could well be having trouble on the inside edges, on the strut lower spring plates. The strut problems you can get over by fitting a set of coilovers - most coilover struts are much slimmer than

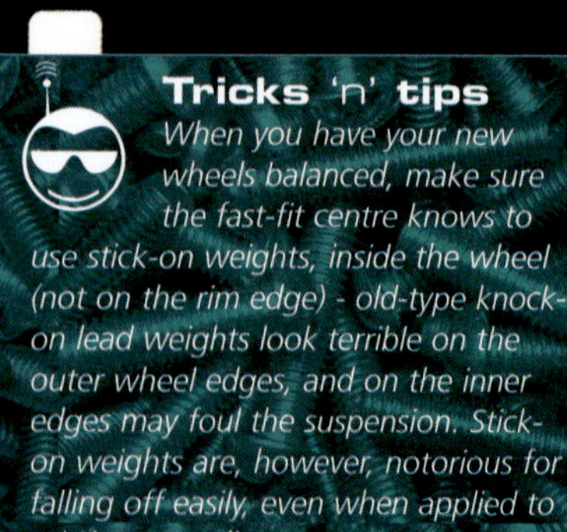

Tricks 'n' tips

When you have your new wheels balanced, make sure the fast-fit centre knows to use stick-on weights, inside the wheel (not on the rim edge) - old-type knock-on lead weights look terrible on the outer wheel edges, and on the inner edges may foul the suspension. Stick-on weights are, however, notorious for falling off easily, even when applied to pristine new alloys.

stock items, giving better clearance for huge rims. The rear arches will probably need bodyshop attention, unless you fancy being brave with a hacksaw.

We like a challenge

To be honest, successfully fitting big wheels in combination with lowered suspension is one of the major challenges to the modifier. At least the Escort has reasonably roomy front arches (or they can be made to be easily, by taking out the plastic wheelarch liners). As much as anything, tyre width is what ultimately leads to problems, not so much the increased wheel diameter.

If the tyres are simply too wide (or with wheels the wrong offset), they will first of all rub on the suspension strut (ie on the inside edge of the tyre). Also, the inside edges may rub on the arches on full steering lock - check left and right. Rubbing on the inside edges can be cured by fitting offsets or spacers between the wheel and hub, which effectively pull the wheel outwards, "spacing" it away from its normal position (this also has the effect of widening the car's track, which may improve the on-limit handling - or not). Fitting large offsets must be done using special longer wheel studs, as the standard ones may only engage the bolts by a few threads, which is highly dangerous.

Rubbing on the outside edges is a simple case of wheelarch lip fouling, which must be cured by rolling up (or trimming off) the wheelarch return edge, and other mods. If you've gone for REALLY wide tyres, or have already had to fit offsets, the outer edge of the tyre will probably be visible outside the wheelarch, and this is a no-no (it's illegal, and you must cover it up!).

The other trick with fitting big alloys is of course to avoid the "Escort 4x4 off-road" look, which you will achieve remarkably easily just by popping on a set of 17s with standard suspension. The massive increase in ground clearance is fine for Farmer Palmer, but won't win much admiration on cruises - guilty of having "fistable" arches, M'lud! Send him down! Overcoming this problem by lowering can be a matter almost of inspired guesswork, as much as anything (see "Suspension").

Speedo error? Or not?

One side-effect of fitting large wheels is that your car will go slower. Yes, really - or at least - it will appear to go slower, due to the effects of the mechanically-driven speedometer.

As the wheel diameter increases, so does its circumference (distance around the outside) - this means that, to travel say one mile, a large wheel will turn less than a smaller wheel. Because the speedometer is driven from the gearbox final drive, the apparent vehicle speed is actually based on the number of complete revolutions of the wheel. Therefore, for a given actual speed, since a larger-diameter wheel will be turning at a slower rate than a smaller wheel, and the method for measuring speed is the rate of wheel rotation, a car with larger wheels will produce a lower speedo reading than one with smaller wheels - but it's not actually going any slower in reality. So don't worry if you think you've reduced your Escort's performance somehow with the monster rims, 'cos you 'aven't.

With the ever-increasing number of those lovely grey/yellow roadside boxes with a nasty surprise inside, spare a thought to what this speedo error could mean in the real world. If (like most people) you tend to drive a wee bit over the posted 30s and 40s, your real speed on 17s or 18s could be a bit more than the bit more you thought you were doing already, and you could get an unexpected flash to ruin your day. What we're saying is, don't drive any faster, to compensate for the lower speedo reading. Actually, the speedo error effect on 17s and 18s really is tiny at around-town speeds, and only becomes a factor over 70. But then, Officer, you couldn't possibly have been going over 70, could you? Officer?

Jargon explained

Rolling Radius - You may have come across the term "rolling radius", which is the distance from the wheel centre to the outer edge of the tyre, or effectively, half the overall diameter. The rolling radius obviously increases with wheel size, but up to a point, the effects are masked by fitting low-profile tyres, with "shorter" sidewalls. Above 16-inch rims, however, even low-profiles can't compensate, and the rolling radius keeps going up.

PCD - this isn't a banned substance, it's your Pitch Circle Diameter, which relates to the spacing of your wheel holes, or "stud pattern". It is expressed by the diameter of a notional circle which passes through the centre of your wheel studs, and the number of studs/bolts. Unlike the offset, the PCD often isn't stamped onto the wheels, so assessing it is really a matter of eyeing-up and trying them on the studs - the wheel should go on easily, without binding, if the stud pattern is correct. On a Mk 5/6/7 Escort, the PCD is 108 mm with four studs, which is given as 108/4, or 4 x 108.

Offset - this is determined by the distance from the wheel mounting face in relation to its centre-line. The offset figure is denoted by ET (no, I mustn't), which stands for einpress tiefe in German, or pressed-in depth (now I KNOW you're asleep). The lower the offset, the more the wheels will stick out. Fitting wheels with the wrong offset might bring the wheel into too-close contact with the brake and suspension bits, or with the arches. Very specialised area - seek advice from the wheel manufacturers if you're going for a very radical size (or even if you're not). The correct offset for Escorts of all sizes is in the range ET 36 to 41.

Hold on to your wheels

The minute you bang on your wicked alloys, your car becomes a target. People see the big wheels, and automatically assume you've also got a major stereo, seats and other goodies - all very tempting, but that involves breaking in, and you could have an alarm. Pinching the wheels themselves, now that's a doddle - a few tools, some bricks or a couple of well-built mates to lift the car, and it's easy money

The trouble with fitting big wheels is that they're only screwed on, and are just as easily screwed off, if you don't make life difficult for 'em. If you're unlucky enough to have to park outside at night (ie no garage), you could wake up one morning to a car that's literally been slammed on the deck! Add to this the fact that your car isn't going anywhere without wheels, plus the damage which will be done to exhaust, fuel and brake pipes from dropping on its belly, and it's suddenly a lot worse than losing a grand's worth of wheels and tyres...

The market and demand for stolen alloys is huge, but since most people don't bother having them security-marked in any way, once a set of wheels disappears, they're almost impossible to trace. Thieves avoid security-marked (or "tattooed") wheels (or at least it's a pretty good deterrent) - and it needn't look hideous!

When choosing that car alarm, try and get one with an "anti-jacking" feature, because thieves hate it. This is sometimes now called "anti-tilt", to avoid confusion with anti-hijacking. Imagine a metal saucer, with a metal ball sitting on a small magnet in the centre. If the saucer tilts in any direction, the ball rolls off the magnet, and sets off the alarm. Highly sensitive, and death to anyone trying to lift your car up for the purpose of removing the wheels - as we said, the crims are not fond of this feature at all. Simply having an alarm with anti-shock is probably not good enough, because a careful villain will probably be able to work so as not to create a strong enough vibration to trigger it - mind you, it's a whole lot better than nothing, especially if set to maximum sensitivity.

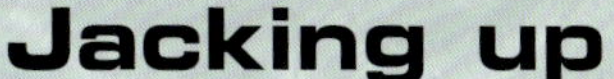

Locking nuts/bolts

Locking wheel bolts will be effective as a deterrent to the inexpert thief (kids, in other words), but will probably only slow down the pro.

Thieves want to work quickly, and will use large amounts of cunning and violence to deprive you of your stuff. If you fit a cheap set of locking bolts, they'll use a hammer and thin chisel to crack off the locking bolt heads. Some bolts can easily be defeated by hammering a socket onto the bolt head, and undoing the locking bolt as normal, while some of the key-operated bolts are so pathetic they can be beaten using a small screwdriver. So - choose the best bolts you can, but don't assume they'll prevent your wheels from disappearing. Insurance companies seem to like 'em - perhaps it shows a responsible attitude, or something...

There seems to be some debate as to whether it's okay to fit more than one set of locking bolts to a car - some people we know value their wheels so highly that they've fitted four sets of bolts - in other words, they've completely replaced all the standard bolts! The feeling against doing this is that the replacement locking bolts may not be made to the same standard as factory originals, and while it's okay to fit one set on security grounds, fitting more than that is dangerous on safety grounds (bolt could fail, wheel falls off, car in ditch, owner in hospital...).

Obviously, you must carry the special key or tool which came with your bolts with you at all times, in case of a puncture, or if you're having any other work done, such as new brakes or tyres. The best thing to do is rig this onto your keyring, so that it's with you, but not left in the car. The number of people who fit locking bolts and then leave the key to them cunningly "hidden" in the glovebox or the boot... You don't leave a spare set of car keys in your glovebox as well, do you?

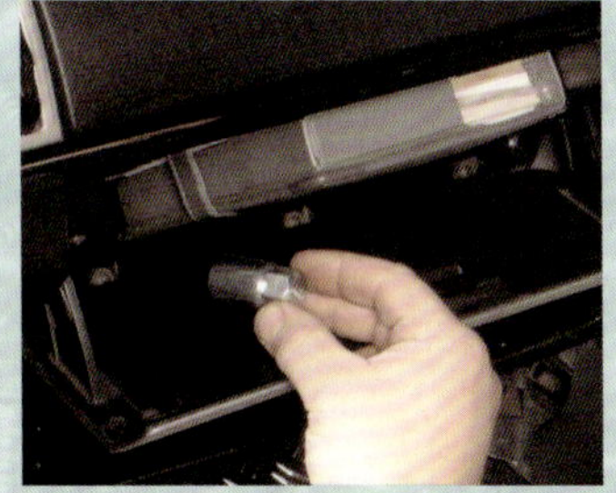

Jacking up

You might think you know all about this, but do you really?

Okay, so you know you need a jack and wheelbrace (or socket and ratchet), but where are the jacking points? If you want to take more than one wheel off at a time, have you got any axle stands, and where do they go? If you've only ever had wheels and tyres fitted by a garage, chances are you're actually a beginner at this. It's surprising just how much damage you can do to your car, and to yourself, if you don't know what you're doing - and the worst thing here is to think you know, when you don't...

What to use

If you don't already have one, invest in a decent hydraulic (trolley) jack. This is way more use than the standard car jack, which is really only for emergencies, and which isn't really stable enough to rely on. Lifting and lowering the car is so much easier with a trolley jack, and you'll even look professional. Trolley jacks have a valve, usually at the rear, which must be fully tightened (using the end of the jack handle) before raising the jack, and which is carefully loosened to lower the car down - if it's opened fully, the car will not so much sink as plummet!

Axle stands are placed under the car, once it's been lifted using the jack. Stands are an important accessory to a trolley jack, because once they're in place, there's no way the car can come down on you - remember that even a brand new trolley jack could creep down (if you haven't tightened the valve), or could even fail completely under load (if it's a cheap one, or knackered, or both).

Under no circumstances use bricks, wooden blocks or anything else which you have to pile up, to support the car - this is just plain stupid. An Escort weighs plenty (like we said, it's not really a small car) - if you want to find out just how solidly it's built, try crawling under it when it's resting on a few bricks.

Where to do it

Only ever jack the car up on a solid, level surface (ideally, a concrete or tarmac driveway, or quiet car park). If there's even a slight slope, the car's likely to move (maybe even roll away) as the wheels are lifted off the ground. Jacking up on a rough or gravelled surface is not recommended, as the jack could slip at an awkward moment - such as when you've just got underneath...

How to do it - jacking up the front

Before jacking up the front of the car, pull the handbrake on firmly (you can also chock the rear wheels, if you don't trust your handbrake).

If you're taking the wheels off, loosen the wheel bolts before you start jacking up the car. It's easily forgotten, but you'll look pretty silly trying to undo the wheel bolts with the front wheels spinning in mid-air. Standard alloys have a prise-off cover fitted over the bolts - well, at least they tried.

We'll assume you've got a trolley jack. The next question is - where to stick it? Up front, there's a subframe just behind the front wheels which will do nicely, and behind that, there's a chunky-looking square-section chassis member running back along the car, inside the sill. If you use these as support points, always put a nice flat offcut of wood on your jack head first, to spread the load. You can jack on the sill jacking points (which are marked by little notches on the sill edges), but it's better to leave those for your axle stands.

Once you've got the car up, pop an axle stand or two under the front sill jacking points. These points are shown by having a notch cut in the sill flange, and this is the only part of the sill it's safe to jack under or rest the car on. On the XR and RS models, you'll have to unclip a cover for access to the sill jacking points, and even then, access to them might not be all you'd like. With the stands in place, you can lower the jack so the car's weight rests on the stands. For maximum safety, spread the car's weight between the stands and the jack - don't lower the jack completely unless it's needed elsewhere.

I'm sure we don't need to tell you this, but don't jack up the car, or stick stands under the car, anywhere other than kosher jacking and support points. This means - not the floorpan or the sump (you'll cave it in), not the suspension bits (not stable), and not under the brake/fuel pipes (ohmigawd).

How to do it - jacking up the rear

When jacking up the rear of the car, place wooden chocks in front of the front wheels to stop it rolling forwards, and engage first gear.

If you're taking the wheels off, you don't have to loosen the wheel bolts before lifting the car, but you'll be relying on your handbrake to hold the wheels while you wrestle with the bolts. Much cooler (and safer) to loosen the rear wheel bolts on the ground too.

Jacking and supporting the Escort back-end is a little trickier. Have a good look under there before making your choice. The rear "axle" running across the car is a possible jacking point, but it's made awkward by its triangular shape, so you will need a block of wood here, or the jack will slip.

Although Ford certainly wouldn't recommend it, you can jack under the rear shock absorber mounting, on the suspension arm - just go slowly, as the arm will move and compress the suspension as the jack rises. Jacking under the suspension arm is obviously no use if you're working on the rear suspension itself.

Another support point is the box section which runs from the rear towing eye - you'll need some axle stands which extend pretty high to use this one, though.

Remember not to put your axle stands under any pipes, the spare wheel well, or the fuel tank, and you should live to see another Christmas.

Finally...

As far as possible, don't leave the car unattended once it has been lifted, particularly if kids are playing nearby - football goes under your car, they go under to get it, knock the jack, car falls... it would almost certainly be your fault.

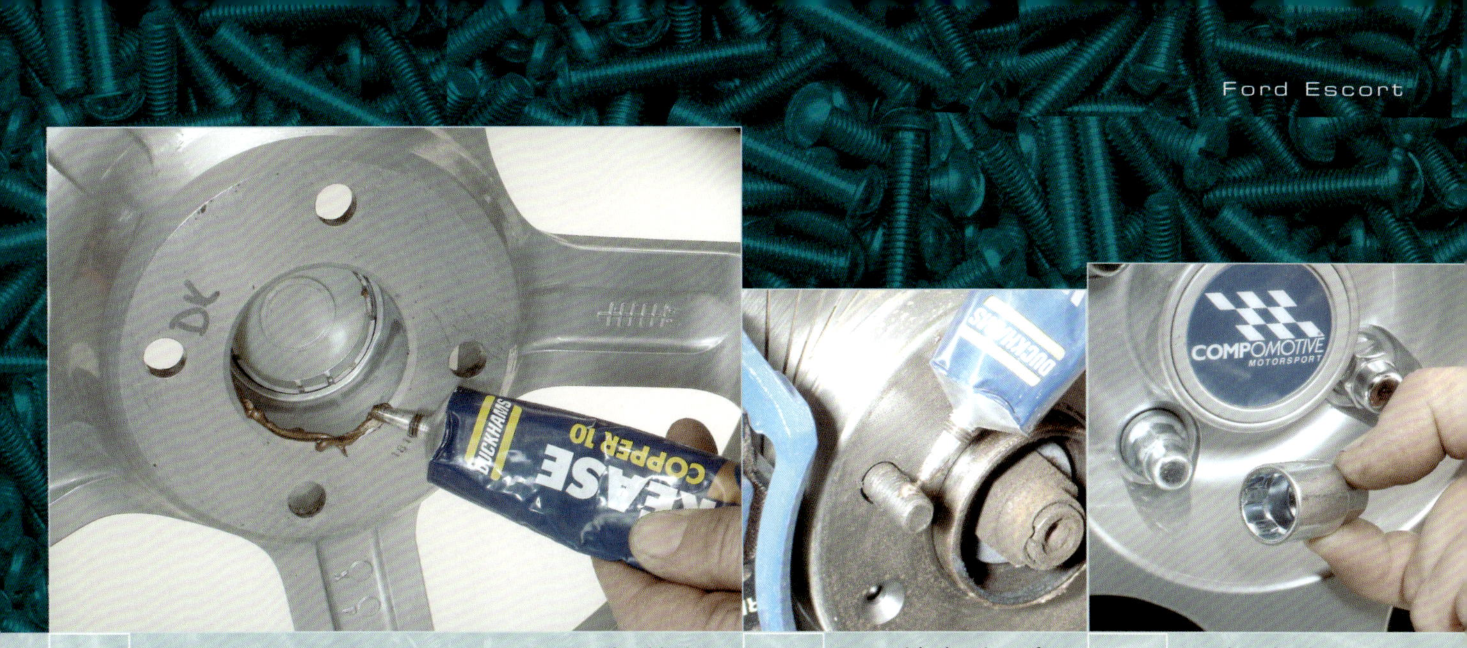

01 Have you got a nice ally/plastic ring inside the wheel hub? Make sure it's there, as it acts to centre the wheel properly, and may help to stop the wheel rusting on. Ever had a rusted-on wheel? Your local fast-fit centre will have, and they'll tell you it ain't funny. Our Compomotives were unusual in not having this ring, so we used copper grease instead.

02 Even with the ring of plastic confidence, the metal bits can still corrode on. Equip yourself with some copper brake grease, and smear some on the wheel boss, inside. It's not a bad idea if some of that grease finds its way onto the wheel studs, too.

03 Pop the wheel onto the studs, then on with the nicely-greased nuts (oo-er), and tighten up as far as possible by hand. You have got some locking nuts, haven't you? Keep your locking wheel nut tool somewhere safe, but not obvious. The glovebox is convenient, but way too obvious!

Changing wheels

04 Always tighten the wheel bolts securely (ideally, to the correct torque - 90 Nm). This can only be done properly with the wheel back on the ground. Don't over-tighten the bolts, or you'll never get them undone at the roadside, should you have a flat! D'oh!

05 If you've really blown some serious cash on your new rims, why not treat them to a special protected socket for tightening the nuts? Companies like Draper do a set of special sockets with plastic protector sleeves fitted, to stop the metal scratching your fine alloys. Makes sense to us.

Always nice to see a good brand of tyre on a decent alloy. How cool do cheap tyres look?

Tyres

To some people, tyres are just round and black - oh, and they're nearly all expensive, and don't last long enough. When you're buying a new set of wheels, most centres will quote prices with different tyres - buying a tyred-up set of rims is convenient, and usually quite good value, too.

Some people try and save money by fitting "remould" or "re-manufactured" tyres. These aren't always the bargain they appear to be - experience says there's no such thing as a good cheap tyre, with wheel balancing problems a well-known downside, for starters.

Choosing a known brand of tyre will prove to be one of your better decisions. Tyres are the only thing keeping you on the road, as in steering, braking and helping you round corners - what's the point of trying to improve the handling by sorting the suspension if you're going to throw the gains away by fitting naff tyres? Why beef up the brakes if the tyres won't bite? The combination of stiff suspension and cheap tyres is inherently dangerous - because the front end dives less with reduced suspension travel, the front tyres are far more likely to lock and skid under heavy braking.

Cheap tyres also equals more wheelspin - might be fun to disappear in a cloud of tyre smoke, but wouldn't you rather be disappearing up the road? Another problem with really wide tyres is aquaplaning - hit a big puddle at speed, and the tyre skates over

Tricks 'n' tips

When buying tyres, look out for ones which feature a rubbing strip on the sidewall - these extend over the edge of the wheel rims, and the idea is that they protect the rim edges from damage by "kerbing". Any decent tyre has them - discreet and very practical, and much better than a chewed-up rim.

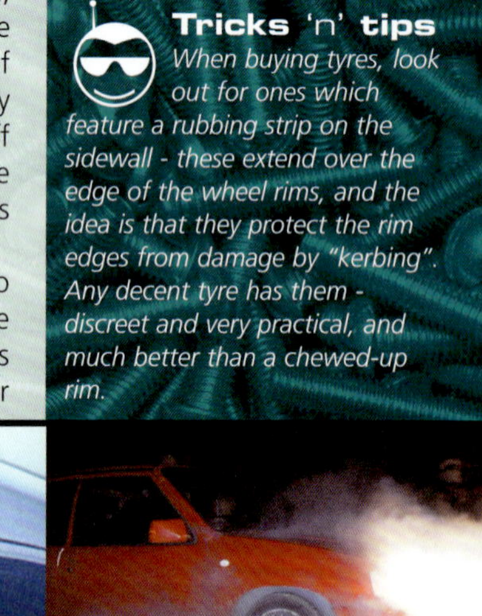

The size markings are obviously the most important, but take note of the directional marks too, if swapping wheels round. Most of the other markings are for anoraks only.

the water without gripping - it's seriously scary when your car starts steering for you. Fitting good tyres won't prevent it, but it might increase your chances of staying in control. The sexiest modern low-profile tyres have a V-tread pattern, designed specifically to aid water dispersal, which is exactly what you need to prevent aquaplaning - try some, and feel the difference!

Finally, cheap tyres ruin your Escort's appearance - a no-name brand emblazoned in big letters on your tyre sidewalls - how's that going to look? If you're spending big dosh on wheels, you've gotta kit 'em out with some tasty V-tread tyres, or lose major points for style. Listen to friends and fellow modifiers - real-world opinions count for a lot when choosing tyres (how well do they grip, wet or dry? How many miles can you get out of them?) Just make sure, before you splash your cash on decent tyres, that you've cured all your rubbing and scrubbing issues, as nothing will rip your new tyres out faster.

Marks on your sidewalls

Tyre sizes are expressed in a strange mixture of metric and imperial specs - we'll take a typical tyre size as an example:

205/40 R 17 V

for a 7-inch wide 17-inch rim

205 width of tyre in millimetres

40 this is the "aspect ratio" (or "profile") of the tyre, or the sidewall height in relation to tyre width, expressed as a percentage, in this case 40%. So - 40% of 205 mm = 82 mm, or the height of the tyre sidewall from the edge of the locating bead to the top of the tread.

R Radial.

17 Wheel diameter in inches.

V Speed rating (in this case, suitable for use up to 150 mph).

Pressure situation

Don't forget, when you're having your new tyres fitted, to ask what the recommended pressures should be, front and rear - it's unlikely that the Ford specs for this will be relevant to your new low-low profiles, but it's somewhere to start from. If the grease-monkey fitting your tyres is no help on this point, contact the tyre manufacturer - the big ones might even have a half-useful website! Running the tyres at the wrong pressures is particularly stupid (you'll wear them out much faster) and can be very dangerous (too soft - tyre rolls off the rim, too hard - tyre slides, no grip).

Speed ratings

Besides the tyre size, tyres are marked with a maximum speed rating, expressed as a letter code:

T up to 190 km/h (118 mph)

U up to 200 km/h (124 mph)

H up to 210 km/h (130 mph)

V inside tyre size markings (225/50 VR 16) over 210 km/h (130 mph)

V outside tyre size markings (185/55 R 15 V) up to 240 km/h (150 mph)

Z inside tyre size markings (255/40 ZR 17) over 240 km/h (150 mph)

If you've got marks on your sidewalls like this, you're in trouble - this has almost certainly been caused by "kerbing".

08 Suspension

If your Escort's still sitting on standard suspension, it's probably safe to say it doesn't cut it - yet. If you've decided you couldn't wait to fit your big alloys, the chances are your Escort is now doing a passable impression of a tractor. An essential fitment, then - so how low do you go, and what nasty side-effects will a lowering kit have?

The main reason for lowering is of course, to make your car look cool. Standard suspension nearly always seems to be set too soft and too high - a nicely lowered motor really stands out instantly. Lowering your car should also improve the handling. Dropping the car on its suspension brings the car's centre of gravity closer to its roll and pitch centres, which helps to pin it to the road in corners and under braking - combined with stiffer springs and shocks, this reduces body roll and increases the tyre contact patch on the road. BUT - if improving the handling is really important to you, choose your new suspension carefully. If you go the cheap route, or want extreme lowering, then you could end up with a car which don't handle at all...

As for what to buy, there are basically three main options when it comes to lowering, arranged in order of ascending cost below:

1. *Set of lowering springs.*
2. Matched set of lowering springs and shock absorbers (suspension kit).
3. Set of "coilovers".

Lowering springs

The cheapest option by far, but with the most pitfalls and some unpleasant side-effects. Lowering springs are, effectively, shorter versions of the standard items fitted to your Escort at the factory. However, not only are they shorter (lower), they are also uprated (stiffer) - if lowering springs were simply shorter than standard and the same stiffness (the same "rate"), you'd be hitting the bump-stops over every set of catseyes. With lowering springs, you just fit the new springs and keep the original shock absorbers ("dampers"), so even if the originals aren't completely knackered, you're creating a problem caused by mis-matched components. The original dampers were carefully chosen to work with the original-rate springs - by increasing the spring rate without changing the dampers, you end up with dampers that can't control the springs properly. What this usually does before long is wreck the dampers, so you don't even save money in the end.

The mis-matched springs and dampers will have other entertaining side-effects, too. How would you like a Escort which rides like a brick, and which falls over itself at the first sign of a corner taken above walking pace? A very choppy ride and strange-feeling steering (much lighter, or much heavier, depending on your luck) are well-documented problems associated with taking the cheap option, and it doesn't even take much less time to fit, compared to a proper solution. Even if you're a hard man and don't object to a hard ride if your car looks cool, think on this - how many corners do you know that are completely flat (ie without any bumps)? On dodgy lowering springs, you hit a mid-corner bump at speed, and it's anyone's guess where you'll end up.

If cost is a major consideration, and lowering springs the only option for now, at least try to buy branded items of decent quality - some cheap sets of springs will eat their way through several sets of dampers before you realise the springs themselves have lost the plot. Needless to say, if riding around on mis-matched springs and shocks is a bit iffy anyway, it's downright dangerous when they've worn out (some inside 18 months!).

Assuming you want to slam your suspension so your arches just clear the tops of your wicked new rims, there's another small problem with lowered springs - it takes some inspired guesswork (or hours of careful measuring and head-scratching) to assess the required drop accurately, and avoid that nasty rubbing sound and the smell of burning rubber. Springs are generally only available in a very few sizes, expressed by the amount of drop they'll produce - most people go for 60 mm or more, but there's usually 35 to 40 mm springs too if you're less brave (or if you've simply got massive rims). Take as many measurements as possible, and ask around your mates - suppliers and manufacturers may be your best source of help in special cases.

Suspension **kit**

A far better choice, Sir - a matched set of springs and dampers is a genuine "upgrade", and respect is due. There are several branded kits available, and most of the Ford specialists do their own. With a properly-sorted conversion, your Escort will handle even better, and you'll still be able to negotiate a set of roadworks without the risk of dental work afterwards. Actually, you may well be amazed how well the Escort will still ride, even though the springs are clearly lower and stiffer - the secret is in the damping.

Some of the kits are billed as "adjustable", but this only applies to the damper rates (don't mistake them as being cheap coilovers), which can often be set to your own taste by a few minutes' work. This Playstation feature can be a good fun thing to play around with, even if it is slightly less relevant to road use than for hillclimbs and sprints - but don't get carried away and set it too stiff, or you'll end up with an evil-handling car and a CD player that skips over every white line on the road!

Unfortunately, although you should end up with a fine-handling car, there are problems with suspension kits, too. If you don't have your steering geometry (camber and tracking) reset, you'll eat tyres, and once again, you're into guesswork territory when it comes to assessing your required drop for big wheels. Generally, most suspension kits are only available with a fairly modest drop (typically, 35 to 40 mm).

Coilovers

If you've chosen coilovers, well done again. This is the most expensive option, and it offers one vital feature that the other two can't - true adjustability of ride height, meaning that you can make the finest of tweaks to hunker down on your new rims (coilovers are an almost-essential choice if you're trying for 18s). Coilovers give you more scope to fit those big rims now, lower it down as far as poss, then wait 'til next month before you have the arches rolled, and drop it down to the deck. Coilovers are a variation on the suspension kit theme - a set of matched variable-rate springs (some have separate 'helper' springs too) and shocks, but their adjustability might not guarantee as good a ride/handling mix as a normal kit.

A coilover set replaces each spring and shock with a combined unit where the coil spring fits over the shocker (hence 'coil' 'over') - nothing too unusual in this, because so far, it's similar to a normal front strut. The difference lies in the adjustable spring lower seat, which can lower the spring (and car) to any desired height, within limits.

Unfortunately, making a car go super-low is not good for the ride or the handling. Coilover systems have very short, stiff springs, and this can lead to similar problems to those found with cheap lowering springs alone. If you go too far with coilovers, you can end up with a choppy ride, heavy steering and generally unpleasant handling. Combine a coilover-slammed car with big alloys, and while the visual effect may be stunning, the driving experience might well be very disappointing. At least a proper coilover kit will come with shock absorbers (dampers) which are matched to the springs, unlike a 'conversion' kit.

Tricks 'n' tips

Another bonus with coilovers is that the new struts and springs are usually slimmer than stock items. One problem with the stock Escort struts is that super-wide rims rub on the strut lower spring seat, front and rear. Even a new "ordinary" suspension kit might not be the answer, but all the coilovers we've seen do the trick.

Coilover conversion

A better-value option is the 'coilover conversion'. If you really must have the lowest, baddest machine out there, and don't care what the ride will be like, these could be the answer. Offering as much potential for lowering as genuine coilovers (and at far less cost), these items could be described as a cross between coilovers and lowering springs, because the standard dampers are retained (this is one reason why the ride suffers). What you get is a new spring assembly, with adjustable top and bottom mounts - the whole thing slips over your standard damper. Two problems with this solution (how important these are is up to you):

1 Your standard dampers will not be able to cope with the uprated springs, so the car will almost certainly ride (and possibly handle) like a pig if you go for a really serious drop - and okay, why else would you be doing it?

2 The standard dampers are effectively being compressed, the lower you go. There is a limit to how far they will compress before being completely solid (and this could be the limit for your lowering activities). Needless to say, even a partly-compressed damper won't be able to do much actual damping - the results of this could be… interesting…

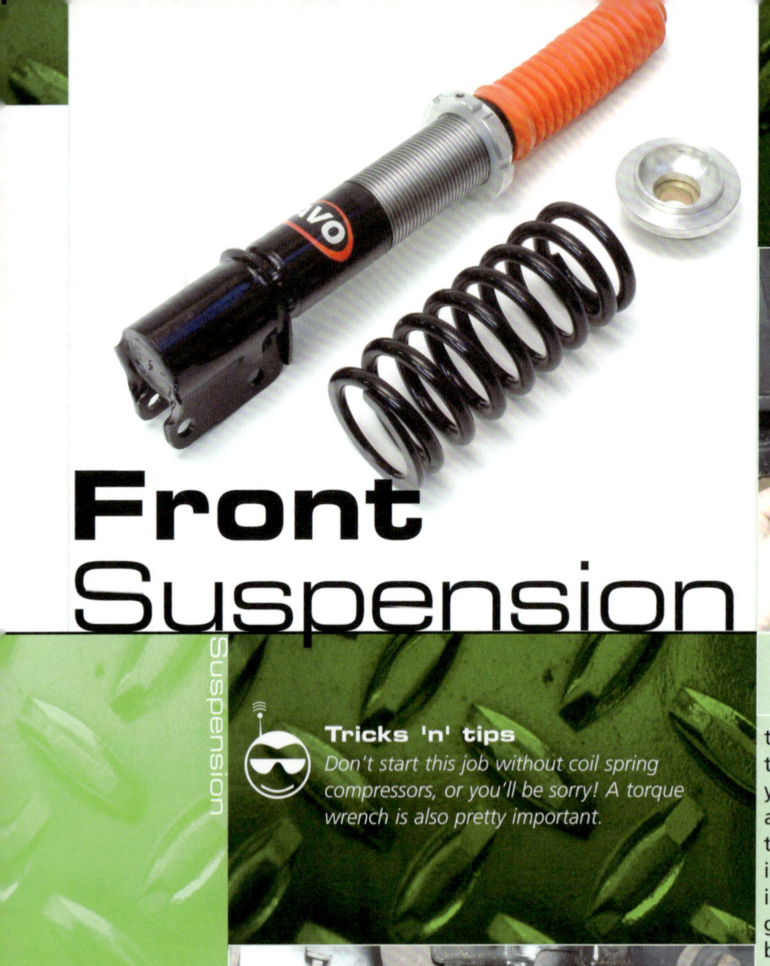

Front Suspension

Tricks 'n' tips

Don't start this job without coil spring compressors, or you'll be sorry! A torque wrench is also pretty important.

01 Start with the fronts. Loosen the wheel bolts, jack up the corner of the car you're working on, and take off the wheel. Make sure you've got an axle stand under a solid part of the car in case the jack gives out. Have a look in "Wheels & tyres" for more info on jacking up. First, we've got to undo the nut holding the brake hose support bracket (easy) . . .

02 . . . followed by the nut and bolt for the anti-roll bar droplink (your Escort DOES have an anti-roll bar?). This isn't quite as easy, as you'll need a very slim 17 mm spanner to hold the flats on the back.

03 Now for some more fun. To remove the strut from the hub, we first need to undo the 19 mm hub clamp bolt . . .

04 . . . note which way round the bolt is fitted when you take it out.

05 Getting the bolt out is the easy bit, so if you struggled with that, stop reading now. To give us a slightly better chance of separating the hub from the strut, a shot or two of WD-40-type spray was applied.

06 For those of you not into physical violence, look away now. These hubs are tough to separate off the bottoms of the struts, but that's what's got to happen next - smack them downwards and off. You definitely will need a large heavy tool, and a bucketful of welly.

07 When it comes free, it won't happen all at once - you'll be inching that hub down the strut, until finally, you'll have something that looks like this. To free the last bit, you have to grab the brake disc and heave downwards against the pressure from the lower arm - or else get a crowbar in there. Modifying like this is hard work.

08 When the bottom end's free, it's all downhill. Up at the top, undo the two small nuts (avoid undoing the large one in the middle, unless you want to find out your old spring's 0-60 time) . . .

09 . . . and lower the old strut out from under the wheelarch.

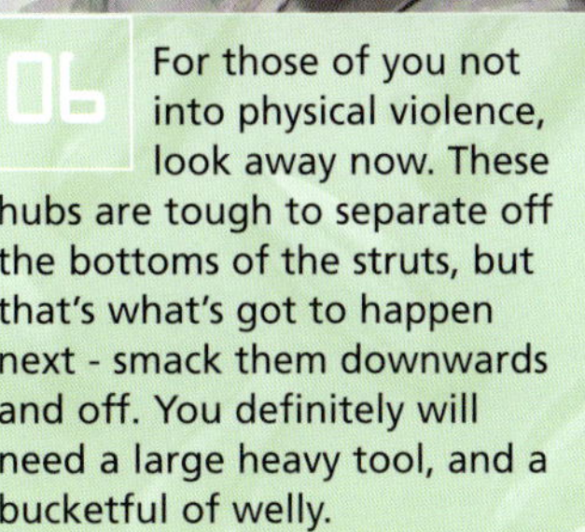

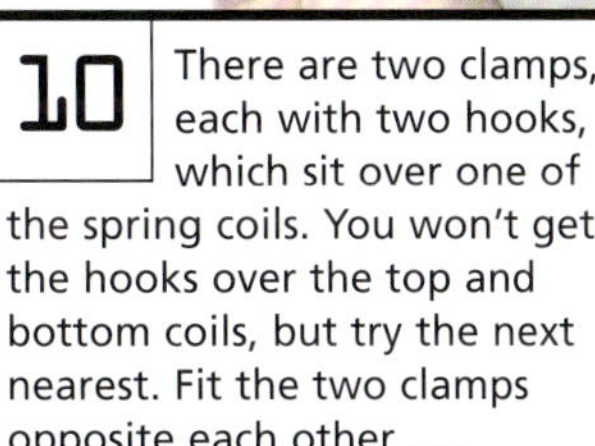

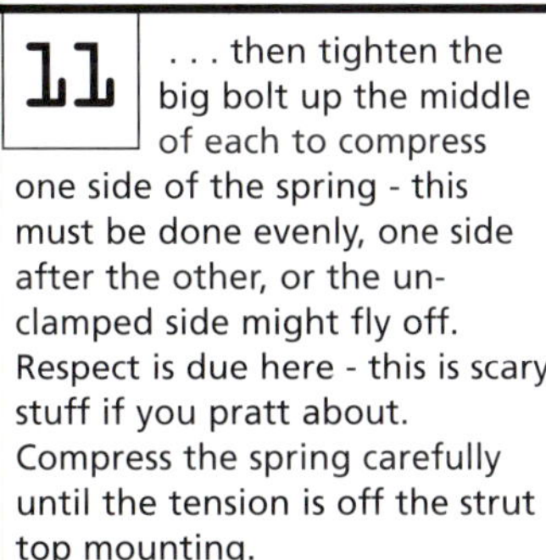

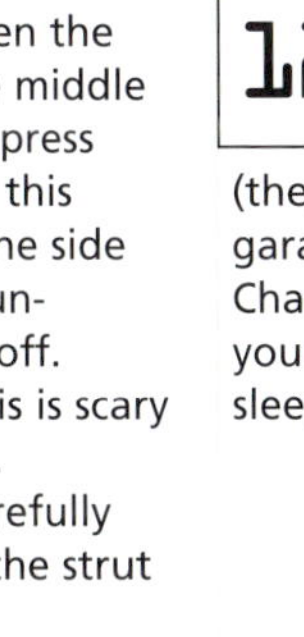

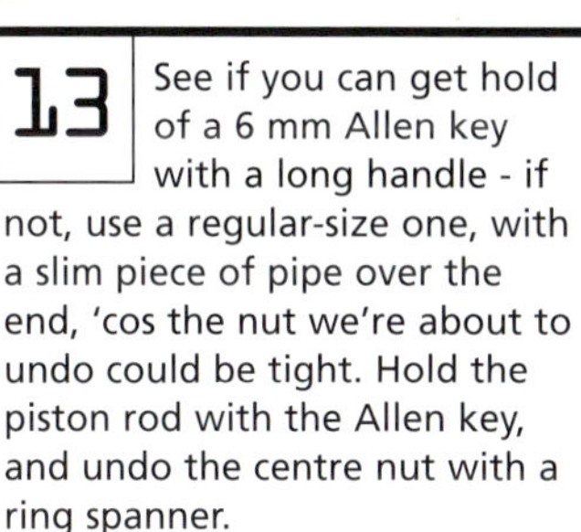

10 There are two clamps, each with two hooks, which sit over one of the spring coils. You won't get the hooks over the top and bottom coils, but try the next nearest. Fit the two clamps opposite each other . . .

11 . . . then tighten the big bolt up the middle of each to compress one side of the spring - this must be done evenly, one side after the other, or the un-clamped side might fly off. Respect is due here - this is scary stuff if you pratt about. Compress the spring carefully until the tension is off the strut top mounting.

12 If your Escort still has the plastic cap fitted over the centre nut (they tend to wander off at garages), take it off now. Chances are, it won't fit back on your new struts, but don't lose sleep over it.

13 See if you can get hold of a 6 mm Allen key with a long handle - if not, use a regular-size one, with a slim piece of pipe over the end, 'cos the nut we're about to undo could be tight. Hold the piston rod with the Allen key, and undo the centre nut with a ring spanner.

Respect

For the next bit, you MUST use coil spring compressors ("spring clamps"). Medical attention will be required if you don't. Do we have to draw you a diagram? The spring's under tension on the strut, even off the car - what do you think's gonna happen if you just undo it? The spring-embedded-in-the-forehead look is really OVER, too.

When the nut's free, the dismantling process can start. Depending on your suspension kit, you might be needing a few of the rusty old bits you were about to chuck out - find those kit instructions now.

14 First to go with the top nut is the top plate . . .

15 . . . then the upper mounting . . .

16 . . . strut top bearing . . .

17 . . . and finally, the spring top seat and the spring (which is still compressed, with the clamps). Remove the spring clamps slowly, and above all, do it evenly - if you try and loosen one side completely, the clamps will slip, and you'll have a spring like a banana (sounds funny, actually v. dodgy).

18 By now, you'll have had a sneaky peek at your shiny new suspension bits - and you may be wondering how all those bits are meant to fit such a short strut. To get all the bits in the smallest possible box, the makers compress the struts before packing them in, so the first job is to get a workout, by pulling the tops of the pistons right out. Game on.

19 First, slip on the spring. Our AVO jobs didn't have any markings on, to show which way up the springs were meant to go, and after looking at the instructions, we decided it didn't matter - your springs could be different. If they've got writing on, make sure the writing's the right way up (seems like a good guess to us).

20 Now the spring top seat can go on - and it looks like we're about to run out of space again, once it's on . . .

21 . . . but these being coilovers, all we need to do is wind down the spring lower seat.

22 With this kit (it might be different on yours), we have to re-use the old strut top bearing. If yours is the same, make sure the bearing's worth re-using - if it's obviously leaking grease, is stiff/rough to turn, or you know it's been on there for ages, it's probably time for a new one. On both sides.

23 We're also re-using the old upper mounting (no great surprise there - it fits the car perfectly) . . .

24 . . . and the old top plate as well.

25 At last - some new bits. Many suspension kits have you re-using the old top nut, which is okay as long as it's in good nick - if not, a new one would be a very sound move.

26 The proper torque for the top nut is 58 Nm, which is all very well, but you try getting a torque wrench on there. And then the feeble little 8 mm spanner you have to use (to hold the flats on the piston while you tighten) wants to slip off. Nightmare. Just do the big nut up tight, as best you can.

27 AVO give you a second nut, to use as a locknut on the first nut you just tightened. Makes sense - but why not supply one Nyloc nut, like the Ford original? Lots less hassle, probably safer. Oh well. To be absolutely sure it all stayed done-up, we added a little thread-lock before fitting the second nut (not essential). Using the same method as before, fit and tighten the second nut up against the first.

Suspension

28 Though it can be done at any time, we chose to set the lower spring seats on our coilovers roughly now. Setting them equal on both sides before fitting will make life easier, too, later on - measure the thread above or below the spring seat, and note it down.

29 Time to offer in that shiny new strut under the wheel arch (shame to hide it under there, really), and poke the two mounting studs up through the holes in the wing . . .

30 . . . fit the two nuts loosely at this stage - this is just to stop the strut falling straight out on your foot. We don't want it tight yet, as there's some fiddling to do...

31 Before even trying to get the bottom end of the strut mated with the hub, get some lube on there. Copper grease is the stuff of choice, but almost anything slippery's better than nothing. Lube up the inside of the hub as well.

32 There's two things to remember when fitting the strut into the hub.
1) - It won't go in very well if you don't keep it vertical.
2) - There's a rib on the inside of the strut which fits into the slot in the hub. Getting it started is the worst bit - once it's going in, use a jack underneath to help it, or give it a bash with the hammer.

33 Most new struts have a ridge around, so you can see when it's all the way in. Give the old pinch-bolt a bit of a clean-up, and screw it back in from the front.

34 This is one bolt not to be shy of doing up properly. The torque is 85 Nm, which is pretty tight - make sure the car's well-supported before heaving on it.

35 Any Escort worth having will have an anti-roll bar, and now it's time to reconnect the roll bar drop link. More fun and games here, as you'll probably have to prise up the end of the bar itself, to get the drop link threads to engage with the mounting hole on the strut. We did.

36 Don't forget to refit the brake hose support bracket to the strut front mounting hole - it's an MOT fail to have a flexible brake hose flapping about. Some kits don't give you a mounting hole, so you might have to get a bit inventive here. Or get on the phone and complain…

37 Got coilovers? Then get lowering. This is a bit trial-and-error, but don't set them to the lowest setting and work upwards, or you might find you've got wheels and tyres wedged under your arches. You'll need several attempts with the special C-spanner they provide to get the setting just perfect.

38 When you're happy, nip the spring seat up to hold it. These use an Allen key to pin the spring seat in place, but most kits give you a second lock ring, which you tighten up under the spring seat.

39 A dose of lubricant (Waxoyl's even better, if you've got some) on the coilover threads should stop them rusting up and being impossible to adjust in a few months' time.

40 In case you haven't already done it, tighten the two strut mounting nuts (50 Nm, if you've got a torque wrench) - this is best done with the car sat back on the ground. Job done.

41 You don't get a suspension kit with adjustable damping, and then not fiddle with it, do you? But - your new suspension's going to be way-stiff anyhow, so making it much stiffer's possibly not advisable unless you're shaving a few tenths off your lap time at Silverstone. Set both sides the same, to avoid getting strange handling quirks you can live without.

Rear Suspension

Loosen the rear wheel bolts, then jack the whole back end of the car, and support with axle stands under the sill rear jacking points. Have a look in "Wheels & tyres" for more info on jacking up. Remove the first rear wheel, then place a trolley jack directly under the suspension arm and raise the rear arm slightly, so it's supported. Phew. Make sure that jack's secure, as the shock lower mounting bolt will be tight.

01

Tricks 'n' tips

You'll be making life a lot easier for yourself if, a few days before attacking your rear suspension, you spray some WD-40 on the shock absorber lower mounting nut, which is on the side nearest the wheel. If the nut's rusted-up, it'll slip round. And we're not talking about a hex nut with flats here - if it turns, there's not much to grab hold of with Mole grips. You have been warned.

Respect

Coil spring compressors ("spring clamps") are needed on the back suspension too, so don't be taking them back to the hire shop just yet.

02

Yes, that is an oxy-acetylene torch. No, we're not suggesting you try this at home. The photo's in to demonstrate just how much of a pig these things can be to undo. If you don't give them some WD-40 a few days before . . .

03

. . . heat, followed by some fairly unsubtle work with a large pair of Mole grips, could be required to get anywhere. The bolt you can see is almost out. The nut is supposed to be round, and has a square flange at the base which is meant to locate against raised edges in the suspension arm - ours slipped round.

Anyway, where were we? Assuming you haven't had the same nightmare we did, you can now slide out the lower mounting bolt - you might have to adjust the height of the trolley jack if the bolt binds up as it's withdrawn. Lower the jack temporarily, and unhook

04 the bottom end of the shock absorber from the suspension arm.

05 Inside the boot, pull off the plastic cap fitted over the top mounting.

06 First of all, ignore the horizontal centre nut and bolt - if you undo that, things will go off bang (like the strut ejecting itself at high speed from under the wheel arch, straight on your foot). Undoing the two top nuts instead is far less dramatic . . .

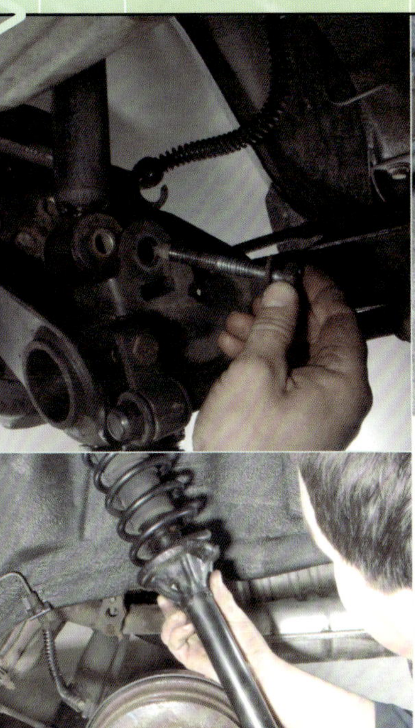

07 . . . though you'll still end up with a strut on your foot if you're not careful.

08 Here we go with the spring clamps again, as we need that top mounting (and would quite like to live a bit longer). Fit the clamps either side of the spring . . .

09 . . . winding them up evenly until the pressure's relieved from the top mount . . .

>>

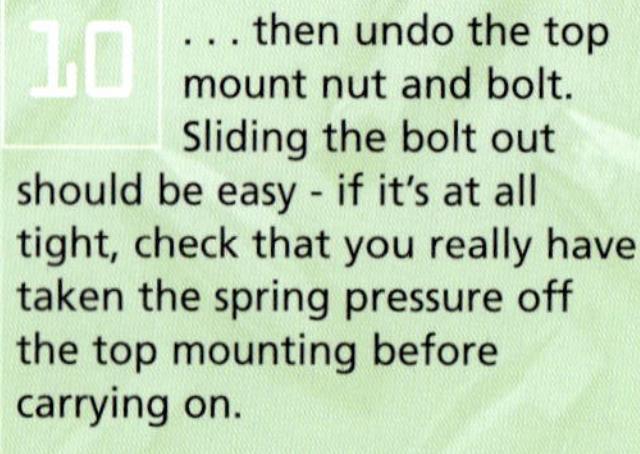

>>

10 . . . then undo the top mount nut and bolt. Sliding the bolt out should be easy - if it's at all tight, check that you really have taken the spring pressure off the top mounting before carrying on.

11 Take off that top mounting, and keep hold of the nut and bolt. With this AVO kit, everything else gets dumped. And about time too.

12 Before you can start fitting stuff to the new strut, you'll probably have to play with it a little. Feeling strong? First, you have to pull out the piston rod at the top of the strut, and (assuming you've got coilovers, like us) you might also have to wind down the lower spring seat. Now the spring slips over a treat . . .

13 . . . and, once you've slid the rubber bump stops down a tad, the spring top mount slips in too.

14 Now wind the lower spring seat up, to hold everything together for fitting. Look at the amount of threads you've got left for ride-height adjustment - awesome!

15 Back at the top end again, it's time to fit the old Ford top mounting - but lose the rubber insert first . . .

16 . . . before popping it on . . .

17 . . . and securing with the old nut and bolt - done up suitably tight, of course. By the way, this is just what our coilover kit's instructions say to do - always check your instructions, and go by them if there's any doubts.

18 Looking better already - shame no-one's really gonna see the new struts once they're bolted in.

19 If your new struts have adjustable damping, make sure you fit them so the damper adjuster's easy to get at - there's a right and wrong way round, in other words. When you're sure, fit and tighten the strut top mounting nuts (torque to 35 Nm, if you've got a wrench).

20 At the bottom end, it's a case of first getting the shock lower mounting to slide into the suspension arm. You might need a hand from the jack now, to raise the arm, especially with shorter (lowering) struts fitted. The lower mounting should have a bush inside - some makers provide these in a separate bag inside the box, so check whether yours are pre-fitted.

21 When the arm's raised to the right height, the old bolt should slip in . . .

22 . . . and we strongly recommend using a new, proper, nut. Even if your old nut didn't have to be butchered like ours, you'll have a much easier time with a new hex nut fitted - though you will need a socket and a spanner to tighten it up, of course. If you can get a Nyloc nut (with a plastic insert) like ours, even better.

23 The lower mounting nut/bolt is a pretty important item, so make sure it's done up well-tight. If you've got a torque wrench, it's 120 Nm, which is pretty tight.

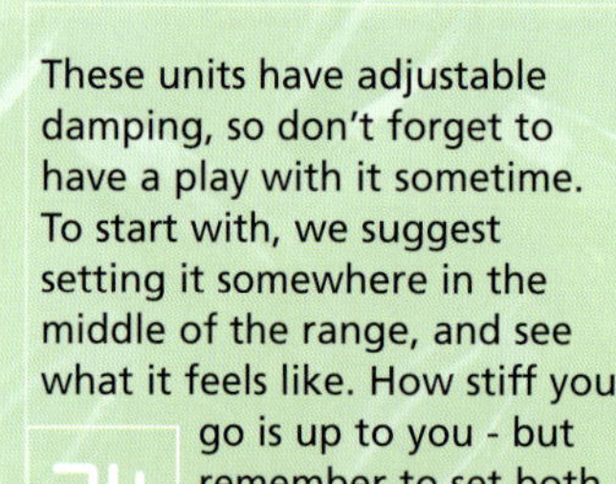

24 These units have adjustable damping, so don't forget to have a play with it sometime. To start with, we suggest setting it somewhere in the middle of the range, and see what it feels like. How stiff you go is up to you - but remember to set both sides the same.

25 Oh, and we nearly forgot - the whole point of fitting coilovers is to slam that car as low as you can possibly get away with. And then perhaps a bit more? Use the C-spanner supplied to set the height of the lower spring seat . . .

26 . . . then lock it up - this kit uses an Allen key to pinch the spring seat in place, but most of the other kits we've seen use a second locking ring, which tightens up against the seat.

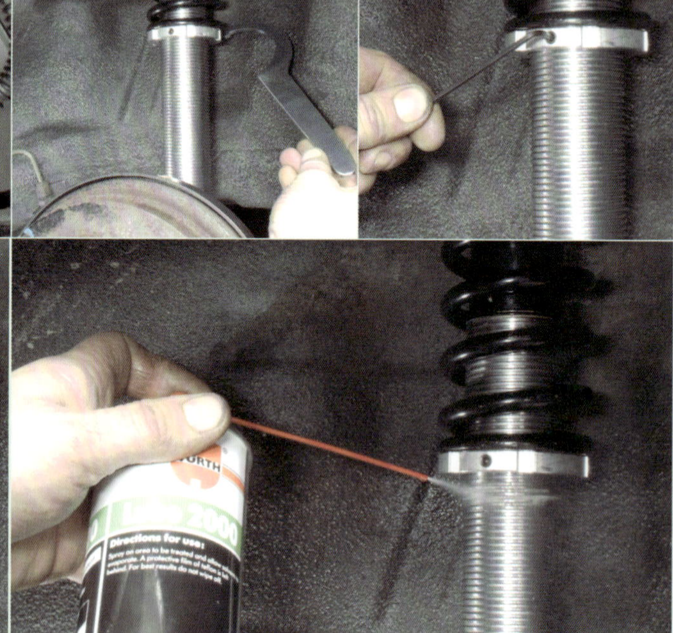

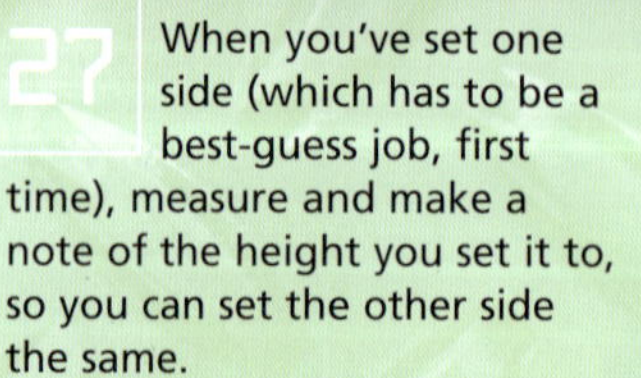

27 When you've set one side (which has to be a best-guess job, first time), measure and make a note of the height you set it to, so you can set the other side the same.

28 Before dropping the car down off the jack, spare a thought to what the winter weather's likely to do to those coilover threads. Will they corrode up, and be impossible to adjust in a few months' time? Some WD-40 (or better still, some Waxoyl) should keep things rust-free.

Nasty side-effects

Camber angle and tracking

With any lowering "solution", it's likely that your suspension and steering geometry will be severely affected - this will be more of a problem the lower you go. This will manifest itself in steering which either becomes lighter or (more usually) heavier, and in tyres which scrub out their inner or outer edges in very short order - not funny, if you're running expensive low-profiles! Sometimes, even the rear tyres can be affected in this way, but that's usually only after some serious slammage. Whenever you've fitted a set of springs (and this applies to all types), have the geometry checked ASAP afterwards.

If you've dropped the car by 60 mm or more, chances are your camber angle will need adjusting. This is one reason why you might find the edges of your fat low-profiles wearing faster than you'd like (the other is your tracking being out). The camber angle is the angle the tyre makes with the road, seen from directly in front. You'll no doubt have seen race cars with the front wheels tilted in at the top, out at the bottom - this is extreme negative camber, and it helps to give more grip and stability in extreme cornering (but if your car was set this extreme, you'd kill the front tyres very quickly!). Virtually all road cars have a touch of negative camber on the front, and it's important when lowering to keep as near to the factory setting as possible, to preserve the proper tyre contact patch on the road. Trouble is, there's not usually much scope for camber adjustment on standard suspension, which is why (for some cars) you can buy camber-adjustable top plates which fit to the strut tops. Setting the camber accurately is a job for a garage with experience of modified cars - so probably not your local fast-fit centre, then.

Load-apportioning valve (ABS models)

If your Escort is sufficiently posh to have ABS brakes on it, there's something lurking under the rear end you probably didn't know about - until now. Part of the ABS is a load-apportioning valve, which is linked to the rear suspension, and limits the amount of braking pressure applied to the rear wheels. Without this valve, when the car's lightly loaded at the back end, the rear wheels might lock up and spin the car if full rear brakes were applied, so this valve restricts the flow of brake fluid to the back brakes. With the motor full of hefty mates or luggage, the back end sinks down, and the valve lets full braking pressure through to the rear.

When you slam the suspension, the valve is fooled into thinking the car's loaded up, and you might find the rear brakes locking up unexpectedly - could be a nasty surprise on a wet roundabout! The valves aren't generally intended to be easy to adjust, but they are quite simple devices - the best idea would be to get underneath and see how it looks when unloaded (on standard suspension), and try to re-create the same condition once the car's been dropped.

On the Escort, the valve assembly is mounted centrally under the car, above the rear "axle". The nut and bolt on the adjuster quadrant can be loosened and re-positioned in the slot to give a limited amount of ride-height adjustability - don't touch the threaded adjusters on the ends of the springs, though. With no load in the car, the two valve springs should only be slightly compressed, so the valve's just open by a small amount. If the springs are seriously compressed, the valve will already be letting too much braking effort through to the back wheels. You could always take the car to the dreaded MOT centre, and ask them to brake-test it on the rollers, or if you're really worried, let a Ford dealer reset the thing for you. Isn't technology wonderful?

Even with the compensator adjusted, the valve still won't work as Ford intended. It was meant to operate based on the full suspension travel originally available with the standard springs. Now the car's been lowered, the amount of travel will be less, so the valve will probably never be fully open, in fact. Just as well that 90% of the braking is done by the front wheels!

Brace yourself

Another item which is inspired by saloon racing, the strut brace is another underbonnet accessory which you shouldn't be without. Some of them might even work...

The idea of the strut brace is that, once you've stiffened up your front suspension to the max, the car's "flimsy" body shell (to which the front suspension struts are bolted) may not be able to cope with the "immense" cornering forces being put through it, and will flex, messing up the handling. The strut brace (in theory) does exactly what it says on the tin, by providing support between the strut tops, taking the load off the bodyshell.

Where this falls down slightly (for road use) is that

1) no-one's going to have the car set that stiff,
2) no-one's going to drive that hard, and
3) the Escort shell isn't exactly made out of tin foil (allegedly). The strut brace might have a slight effect, but the real reason to fit one is for show - and why not? They look great in a detailed engine bay, and are available in lots of designs and finishes. You're looking at parting with about a hundred of your finest English pounds, but your mates will be impressed and the girls will love it - and you can't put a price on that!

Strut brace

Put the brace in its place - by doing this, you can see how much stuff it interferes with. Quality-made strut braces fit with minimal disturbance to other components in the engine bay. The one we're fitting's from the good guys – E-tech. And ours fitted a treat - the only thing that threw us slightly was the logo being upside-down, but it won't fit any other way, so ignore it.

01

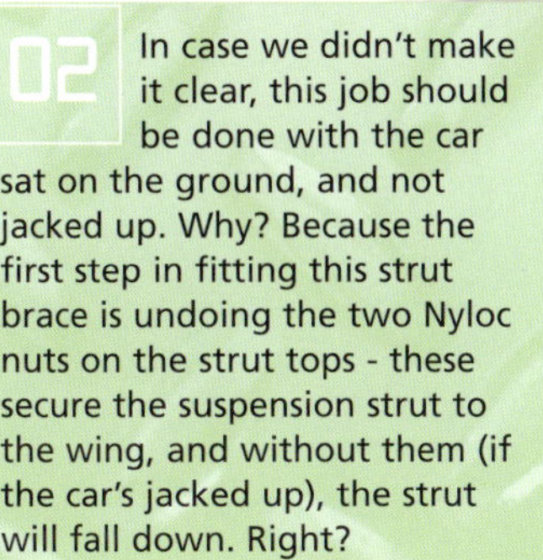

02 In case we didn't make it clear, this job should be done with the car sat on the ground, and not jacked up. Why? Because the first step in fitting this strut brace is undoing the two Nyloc nuts on the strut tops - these secure the suspension strut to the wing, and without them (if the car's jacked up), the strut will fall down. Right?

03 Place the strut brace plate over the two strut studs, and see how it fits. In our case, it didn't sit down tight to the car body - the plate was resting on the raised lip around the suspension strut top. Not good. Remember, the nuts you're going to refit for the strut brace also secure the suspension itself, so wobbly brace plates we cannot have.

04 Spacers were needed under the plates, and we made our own by trimming up a couple of big washers - two for each stud. Don't build the spacers up too high, or you'll have no threads left on the studs, and the nuts won't go back on.

05 Now the strut plate can go back on top of the two washers. Add a further washer, then fit the Nyloc nut (you're really supposed to use new ones) and tighten fully. The torque for these nuts is 46 Nm, but it's equally important that the nut is tightened down enough for the blue plastic thread insert to do its job. Do the same for the other brace plate, and we're ready for the brace itself.

06 Slip the brace into position, and loosely fit the nut and Allen bolt. With the end bolts loose, you can now take any slack out of the brace itself, using a spanner on the adjuster nut at each end. Try and get roughly the same amount of thread showing at each end of the brace, then tighten the nuts.

07 Finally, tighten the nut and Allen bolt at each end of the brace. Time to stand back and admire your handiwork - remember to give the brace a quick clean to make it shine, so people notice it as soon as you lift the bonnet!

09 Brakes

Brakes

Remember the middle pedal?

It's the one next to the throttle - some people don't use it much. Uprating the brakes is actually a very easy bolt-on upgrade, but there are some points to consider.

One of the strangest, given that improving the brakes should in theory also improve your chances of avoiding an accident, is that insurance companies do not like performance brakes. You should still tell them, but be prepared for bad news. To them, it seems that fitting sporty brakes must automatically make you drive like Colin McRae - the clear implication is that if you need better brakes, you've either also uprated the engine (and not told them?), or you simply drive on the limit everywhere. Shame. We just like to know our cars will stop quickly. That, actually, might be another reason why they don't like better brakes - you stop better, but does the old dodderer behind you? Crunch.

Uprating the brakes will be a complete waste of time if you're a cheapskate on tyres. Cheap, no-name tyres (or ones with no tread left) won't always be able to translate extra braking power into actual vehicle-stopping power - they'll give up their grip on the tarmac and skid everywhere. Something like 90% of braking is done by the front wheels - ie the ones you steer with. If you consider that locked-up wheels also don't tend to steer very well, you'll begin to see why top brakes and lame tyres are a well-dodgy mixture.

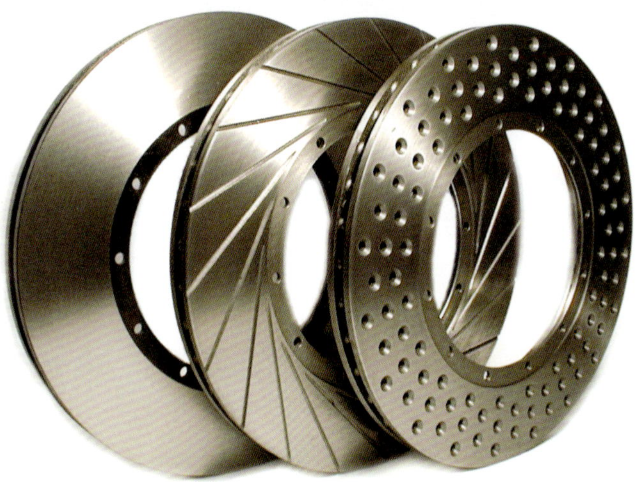

Groovy discs

Besides the various brands of performance brake pads that go with them, the main brake upgrade is to fit performance front brake discs and pads. Discs are available in two main types - grooved and cross-drilled (and combinations of both).

Grooved discs (which can be had with varying numbers of grooves) serve a dual purpose - the grooves provide a "channel" to help the heat escape, and they also help to de-glaze the pad surface, cleaning up the pads every time they're used. Some of the discs are made from higher-friction metal than normal discs, too, and the fact that they seriously improve braking performance is well-documented.

Cross-drilled discs offer another route to heat dissipation, but one which can present some problems. Owners report that cross-drilled discs really eat brake pads, more so than the grooved types, but more serious is the fact that some of these discs can crack around the drilled holes, after serious use. The trouble is that the heat "migrates" to the drilled holes (as was intended), but the heat build-up can be extreme, and the constant heating/cooling cycle can stress the metal to the point where it will crack. Discs which have been damaged in this way are extremely dangerous to drive on, as they could break up completely at any time. Only fit discs of this type from established manufacturers offering a useful guarantee of quality, and check the discs regularly.

Performance discs also have a reputation for warping (nasty vibrations felt through the pedal). Is this fair? Well, the harder you use your brakes (and we could be talking serious abuse), the greater the heat you'll generate. Okay, so these wicked discs are meant to be able to cope with this heat, but you can't expect miracles. Cheap discs, or ones which have had a hard time over mega-thousands of miles, will warp. So buy quality, and don't get over-heroic on the brakes.

Performance pads can be fitted to any brake discs, including the standard ones, but are of course designed to work best with heat-dissipating discs. Unless your Escort's got an over-boosted Cossie lump under the bonnet, don't be tempted to go much further than "fast road" pads - anything more competition-orientated may take too long to come up to temperature on the road. Remember what pushbike brakes were like in the wet? Cold competition pads feel the same, and old dears always step off the pavement when your brakes are cold!

Lastly, fitting all the performance brake bits in the world is no use if your calipers have seized up. If, when you strip out your old pads, you find that one pad's worn more than the other, or that both pads have worn more on the left wheel than the right, your caliper pistons are sticking. Sometimes you can free them off by pushing them back into the caliper, but this could be a garage job to fix. If you drive around with sticking calipers, you'll eat pads and discs. You choose.

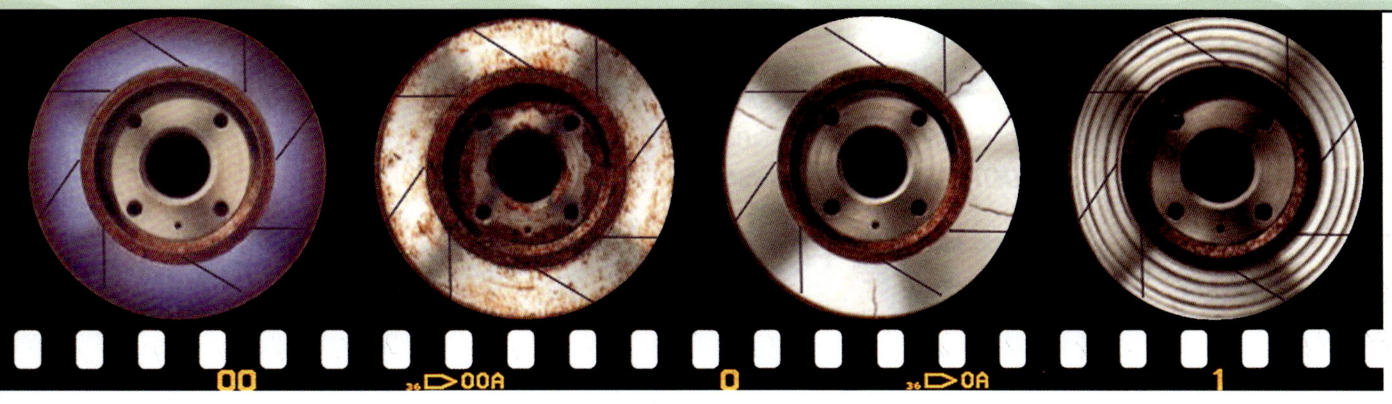

Brake discs and pads

01 Loosen the wheel bolts, jack up the corner of the car you're working on, and take off the wheel. Make sure you've got an axle stand under a solid part of the car in case the jack gives out. Have a look in "Wheels & tyres" for more info on jacking up. First job is to pull out the tiny wire R-clip holding the pad retaining plate in place - has someone had bodged in a split pin instead of the real thing, on your car? Or left it out/lost it? It happens.

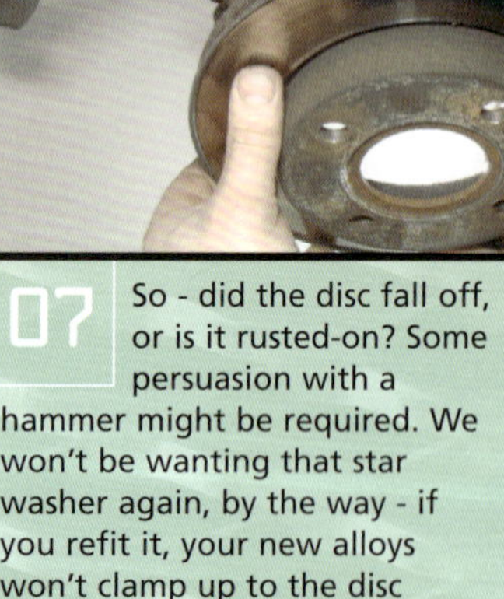

05 If you're going the whole way, and fitting new discs, we salute you. Now the brake caliper anchor bracket has to be unbolted, to get the old discs off. Not too hard - just two big bolts on the inside. They're just done up real tight, is all - make sure that front end's well-supported on the jack and axle stands before heaving on the cracker bar.

06 Lift the caliper and its bracket off the disc, then "unscrew" the star washer which locates the brake disc. Not much holding it on, is there? Don't forget - when the wheel's bolted up, it clamps the disc in place.

07 So - did the disc fall off, or is it rusted-on? Some persuasion with a hammer might be required. We won't be wanting that star washer again, by the way - if you refit it, your new alloys won't clamp up to the disc properly (as we found out).

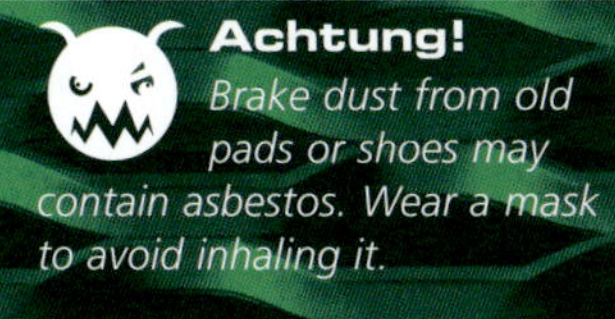

Achtung! *Brake dust from old pads or shoes may contain asbestos. Wear a mask to avoid inhaling it.*

02 Now you'll need a thin pin-punch (a small screwdriver could be used as a bodgy substitute) to tap out the pad retaining pin (the pin's tapered, so tap from the outside inwards) . . .

03 . . . remove the pin (don't lose it, or the R-clip), and swing the front part of the caliper upwards, for your first view of the pads. If you look closely, you can also see the round caliper piston - this will have to be pushed back inside the caliper body, to make room for the new pads. Don't worry - you'll soon understand what we mean.

04 As always, we seem to be removing perfectly-good pads yet again! Yours for a fiver.

08 Any rust on the hub now has to go, along with any other crud. If the wheel hub isn't totally pristine, the new disc won't sit on quite straight, and will eat its way through the new pads in no time. All for the sake of a few minutes with a wire brush and sand paper.

09 Like the hubs, the new discs must be clean before fitting. Most discs are coated with a sticky or oily substance, to stop them rusting in the box - any decent brake-cleaning solvent will shift it.

Remember! *It's a good idea to have your brake mods MOT-tested once you've fitted new discs and pads, and you might even be able to "blag" a free brake check at your local fast-fit centre if you're crafty! Brakes are a serious safety issue, and unless you're 100% confident that all is well, demo-ing your car's awesome new-found stopping ability could find you in the ditch...*

10 You might think your new discs are identical. Chances are, they're not, and they should only be fitted with the grooves facing a certain way (this is the left front). Check your paperwork - our new multi-grooved discs were supplied by Red Dot Racing Ltd, with matching pads. Cheers, chaps!

>>

Now it's back on with the caliper anchor bracket, in with the two bolts, and tighten them up GOOD. If you've got a torque wrench, it's 58 Nm, which is tight.

11

Before we get to fitting the new pads, let's deal with that caliper piston. Two methods for pushing this back in - use a pair of slip-joint ("water pump") pliers and a block of wood, and squeeze the piston back in. Watch the fluid level in the reservoir. Works fine, 99% of the time. Or there's the "proper" way . . .

12

. . . which is really the same, but you connect a brake bleeder kit to the caliper bleed screw, and open the screw slightly with a spanner, before squeezing the piston in. Makes the job a bit easier, and prevents possible damage to the brake fluid seals, from the reverse-flow of brake fluid.

13

14 Smearing a bit of copper grease on the pad backplate shows you're serious about not having annoying squealing brakes. The pads will only fit one way round - and we don't just mean friction-material-to-brake-disc. No pad should have to be forced in - try all four in the box.

15 When they're all in, slide in the pad retaining pin (from the inside, outwards), and peg it in place with a proper wire clip, which fits through a small hole in the pin itself. If your R-clip has wandered off, brake pad fitting kits can be had from outlets such as Halfords, and they're cheap!.

Remember!

New pads of any sort need careful bedding-in (over 100 miles of normal use) before they'll work properly - when first fitted, the pad surface won't have worn exactly to the contours of the disc, so it won't actually be TOUCHING it, over its full area. This will possibly result in very under-whelming brakes for the first few trips, so watch it - misplaced over-confidence in your brakes is a fast track to hospital...

Cool coloured **stoppers**

One "downside" to fitted massive multi-spoked alloys is that - shock-horror - people will be able to SEE your brakes! So don't be shy about it - paint some of the brake components so they look the biz, possibly to match with your chosen colour scheme (red is common, but isn't the only choice). Red brake calipers are often seen on touring cars, too, which may well be where the initial inspiration came from. Escorts with less than 130 bhp under the hood don't have rear discs, but painting the brake drums is acceptable under the circumstances - but then, do you paint 'em black, to de-emphasise them, or in your chosen colour for the fronts? It's all tough decisions, in modifying. If you're really sad, you can always buy fake rear discs... For the less-sad among you, Ford performance specialists may be able to sell you a rear disc brake conversion kit (or you could swap the whole back axle from a 130-brake XR3i) but surely that's going a bit far, just to have red calipers front and rear? Remember, the rear brakes don't do much actual stopping...

Tricks 'n' tips

If you have trouble reassembling your brakes after painting, you probably got carried away and put on too much paint. We found that, once it was fully dry, the excess paint could be trimmed off with a knife.

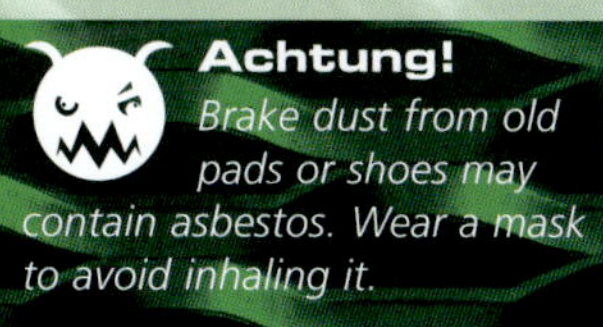

Achtung!

Brake dust from old pads or shoes may contain asbestos. Wear a mask to avoid inhaling it.

Painting the calipers requires that they are clean - really clean. Accessory stores sell aerosol brake cleaner, which (apart from having a distinctive high-octane perfume) is just great for removing brake dust, and lots more besides! Some kits come complete with cleaner spray. Many of the kits advertise themselves on the strength of no dismantling being required, but we don't agree. Also, having successfully brush-painted our calipers, we wouldn't advise using any kind of spray paint.

We know you won't want to hear this, but the best way to paint the calipers is to do some dismantling first. The kits say you don't have to, but trust me - you'll get a much better result from a few minutes' extra work. We took off the new brake pads and disc we'd just fitted - stopping halfway through the new disc fitting process would have been a really sound move, but nobody thinks that far ahead.

Interiors

The Escort dash is best described as functional. It does the job, and that's about it. It might have no style whatsoever, but at least it doesn't feel like it's about to fall apart, or come off in your hands, unlike certain popular French superminis we could mention. Yes, the Escort interior (with the exception of some really awfully-nice seat fabrics - not) is pretty damn dull. But you need suffer no longer, because the interior really is one area where most of the goodies are pretty easy to fit, and provided you go for one particular 'theme' (rather than a mixture), the end result can certainly help you forget you're in a base model, if indeed you are...

To be fair to the Escort, not many standard interiors are anything to shout about, particularly when you compare them with the sort of look that can easily be achieved with the huge range of product that's out there. As with the exterior styling, though, remember that fashions can change very quickly - so don't be afraid to experiment with a look you really like, because chances are, it'll be the next big thing anyway. Just don't do wood, ok? We've a feeling it's never coming in, never mind coming back...

Removing stuff

Take it easy and break less

Many of the procedures we're going to show involve removing interior trim panels (either for colouring or to fit other stuff), and this can be tricky. It's far too easy to break plastic trim, especially once it's had a chance to go a bit brittle with age. Another 'problem' with the Escort is that the interior trim is pretty well-attached (and the designers have been very clever at hiding several vital screws), meaning that it can be a pig to get off. There's more than a few Torx screws - invest in a set or Torx keys (like Allen keys), otherwise you'll come across one screw that won't come out using any other type of screwdriver. We'll try and avoid the immortal words 'simply unclip the panel', and instead show you how properly, but inevitably at some stage, a piece of trim won't 'simply' anything.

The important lesson here is not to lose your temper, as this has a highly-destructive effect on plastic components, and may result in a panel which no amount of carbon film or colour spray can put right, or make fit again. Superglue may help, but not every time. So - take it steady, prise carefully, and think logically about how and where a plastic panel would have to be attached, to stay on. You'll encounter all sorts of trim clips (some more fragile than others) in your travels - when these break, as they usually do, know that many of them can be bought in ready packs from accessory shops, and that the rarer ones will be available from a Ford dealer, probably off the shelf. Even fully-trained Ford mechanics aren't immune to breaking a few trim clips!

Door trim panel

You'll find plenty of excuses for removing your door trim panels - fitting speakers, re-trimming the panel, de-locking, even window tinting, so we'd better tell you how ...

01 Open the window, by whatever means you have. Now, if you've got wind-up windows:
a) Prise the winder handle to open a gap between it and the circular disc behind. Work the edge of a piece of (clean) cloth/rag into the gap behind the handle.

b) Using a 'sawing' action, work the cloth side to side, and also pull the ends of the cloth. It may take some time, but what you're trying to do is snag the ends of the spring clip holding the handle in place - when you do, the sawing action should work the clip off, allowing the handle to be pulled from the splines. With patience, it does work - just watch for that spring clip flying off into the blue!

c) Alternatively, use this special window winder tool (no, don't panic, it's available v. cheap) which makes removing the winder handles so much easier, and makes you look all professional.

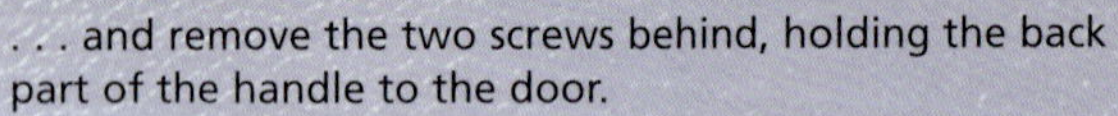

05 . . . and remove the two screws behind, holding the back part of the handle to the door.

06 Another screw lurks at the front of the door pocket.

07 Unlike most cars, the door trim panel on the Escort is not secured by clips (which break eventually, when the panel's been on and off a few times). Instead, there's a total of five tiny screws around the back and bottom edges of the panel to remove - much better (as long as you don't lose them). Later models have eight screws, hidden under plastic covers which you just prise out.

Tricks 'n' tips

Find something like an old ice-cream or margarine tub to keep all the little screws and bits in, as you take them off. This approach is far superior to the chuck-them-all-on-the-floor method most people use, until they lose something vital.

02 Now there's a single screw to remove from the door lock interior handle . . .

03 . . . before the handle surround can be taken out (pull the handle open slightly, to give room for the surround to come past).

04 Prise out the centre section of the door pull handle - try not to chew the plastic edges up too much (use a small screwdriver, carefully) . . .

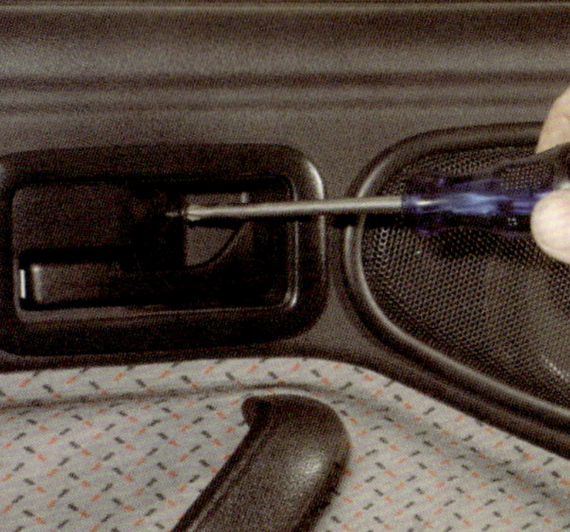

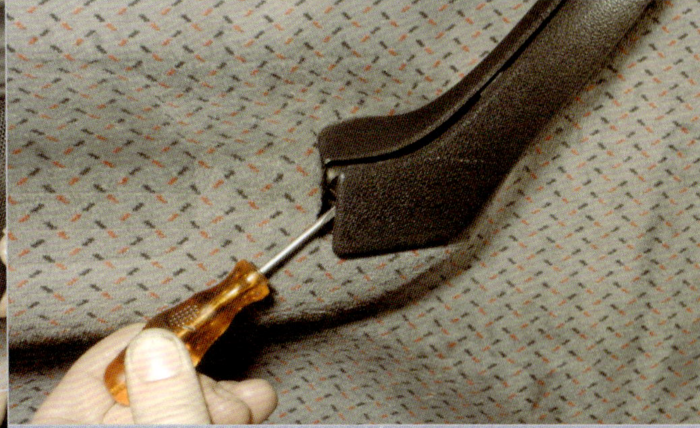

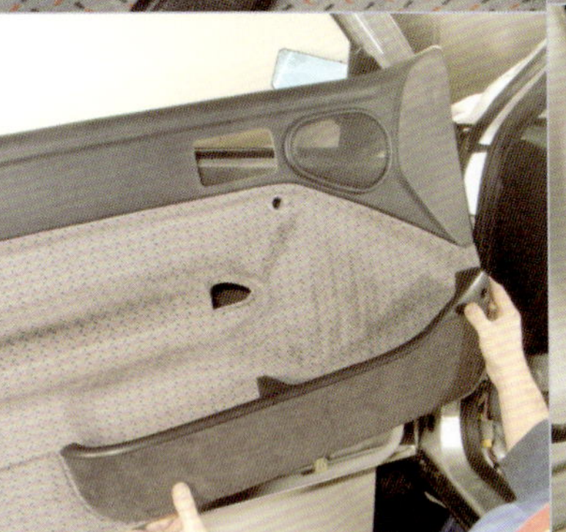

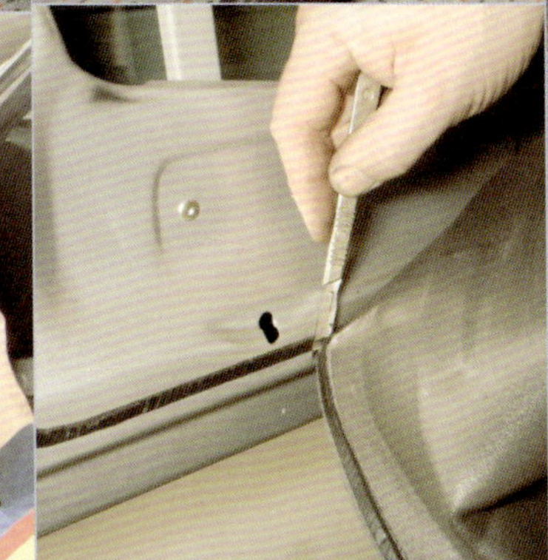

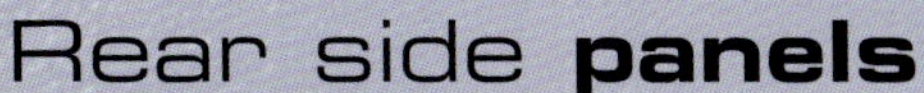

Rear side **panels**

01 There's not an awful lot to removing these, really - they just unclip, after removing the seat belt (see the section on harnesses). Saves you wasting time looking for hidden screws, anyway. But take your time, or they might not re-clip again.

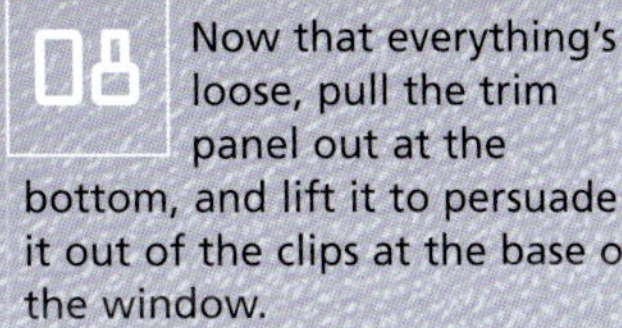

08 Now that everything's loose, pull the trim panel out at the bottom, and lift it to persuade it out of the clips at the base of the window.

09 If you need to get at the door innards - for de-locking, for instance - there's a foam membrane (or what's left of one) to remove first. If it's already been wrecked, tough. If it's still intact, there's no need to wreck it. Usually, the membrane's stuck on with a bead of mastic - if you slice through the mastic with a v. sharp knife, you'll be able to re-stick it. Which is nice.

Sill trim panels

01 At the front of each sill trim panel is a footwell kick panel, which has to come off first. There's a sort-of screw holding the panel in place, which you turn through 90° and remove . . .

02 . . . then the panel itself is hooked into three lugs on the sill panel. Some careful wiggling will free it.

03 Removing the sill trims themselves seems easy - there's six (plastic) screws to remove, which seems pretty obvious . . .

04 . . . then you pull up the weatherseal strips along the base of the door opening . . .

05 . . . and remove the trim. However, the trim is actually pegged into the sill itself - where there was a screw, there's a peg - and it takes a heck of an effort to persuade them out. A large screwdriver may be needed, especially on the one right at the back. Good luck.

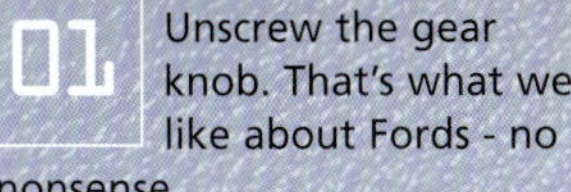

01 Unscrew the gear knob. That's what we like about Fords - no nonsense.

02 Prise the lovely Ford gaiter surround out of the console, slide it up the lever, and throw it away - please.

03 If you've got a cheapo Escort (ok, tell me they're not all like that) with a short console, you'll now have four screws to undo, and the console will slide up 'n' over the gear stick. The price you pay for owning a posher Escort is there's a bit more work to do yet - first there may be window switches to push/prise out and disconnect . . .

Centre console

04 . . . then two screws inside the storage box behind the handbrake. Later (Mk 7) models may only have one screw inside the box, or may have no box at all, in which case the rear screw is hidden below a small trim cap, which you prise out. Clear so far?

05 Now there's four nuts to undo, round the base of the gear lever . . .

06 . . . these nuts not only secure the console, they also hold the gear lever itself up in the car. Once you remove the support plate, don't play with the gear lever.

07 Make sure the handbrake's pulled up as far as you can, then slide the console back and upwards, over the gear and handbrake levers. Again on later (Mk 7) models, there may be a surround on the handbrake lever to unclip and slide off first.

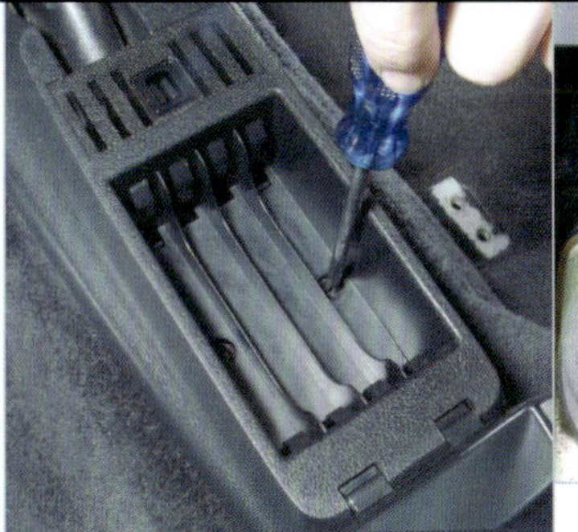

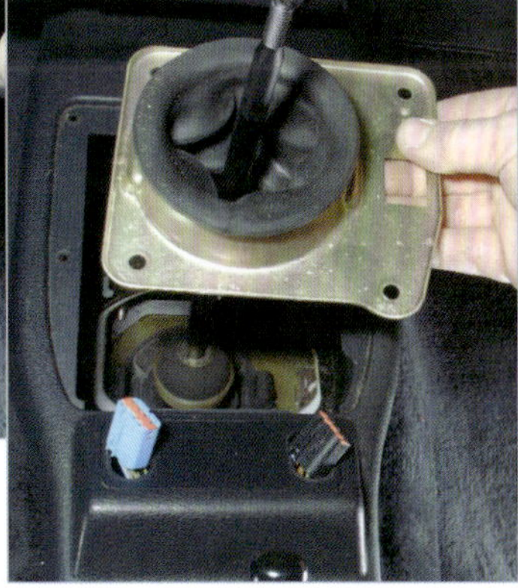

Window winders

01 Okay, so not everyone's got 'em, but they're never the most attractive door furniture! Removing the old ones is covered in the section on removing your door trim panel.

02 The curse of 'universal-fit' falls on us once again with our new handles - very nice items from Richbrook. Before you can fit them to your Escort, you have to pull them to bits. That's right - the new handles contain all the possible fittings required for all different cars, including ones which have a screw in the centre. On an Escort, you have to undo the four Allen screws holding the handle to the base, and remove the centre screw hidden inside . . .

03 . . . before re-assembling and tightening the four Allen screws fully. That's not another free Allen key, to add to our collection?

04 Now slide the handle onto the splines, making sure you've got it at the right angle for when the window's closed, and tighten the grub screw so the handle can't fall off.

05 Now tell me that chunky chrome item's not miles better than wobbly grey plastic. You can't, can you.

Anything but black?

The interior trim on the Escort at least hides its age well, and doesn't rattle much. And that's about it - for a lover of elephant-hide grey, it's heaven, but for more normal people, it's something else. Fortunately, there's plenty you can do to personalise it, and there are three main routes to take:

1) Spray paint - available in any colour you like, as long as it's... not black (see Painting by numbers). Folia Tec stuff actually dyes softer plastics and leather, and comes in a multi-stage treatment, to suit all plastic types. Don't try to save money just buying the top coat, because it won't work! Special harder-wearing spray is required for use on steering wheels. Ordinary spray paint for bodywork might damage some plastics, and won't be elastic - good primer is essential. Make sure you also buy lots of masking tape.

2) Adhesive or shrink-fit film - available in various wild colours, carbon, ally, and, er... walnut (would YOU?). Probably best used on flatter surfaces, or at least those without complex curves, or you'll have to cut and join - spray is arguably better here. Some companies will sell you sheets of genuine carbon-fibre, with peel-off backing - looks and feels the part (nice if you have touchy-feely passengers).

3) Replacement panels - the easiest option, as the panels are supplied pre-cut, ready to fit. Of course, you're limited then to styling just the panels supplied.

If you fancy something more posh, how about trimming your interior bits in leather? Very saucy. Available in various colours, and hardly any dearer than film, you also get that slight 'ruffled' effect on tighter curves.

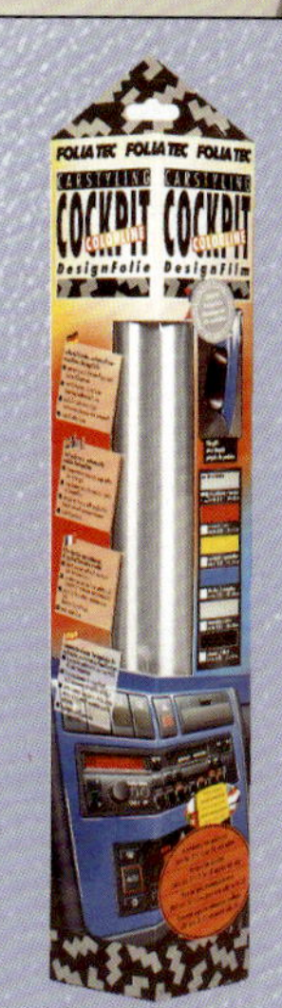

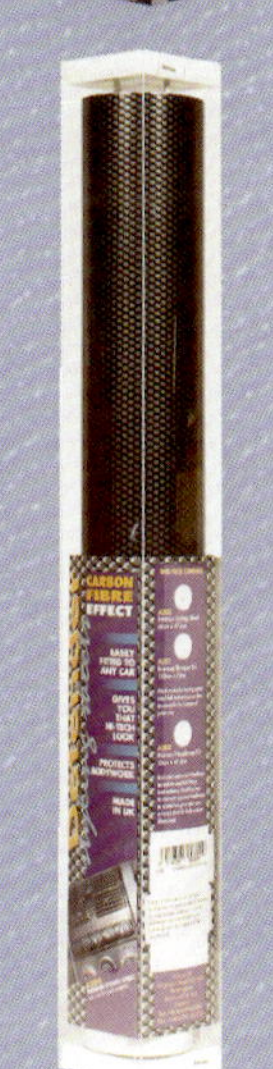

Get the cans out

For our race/rally theme, we found that the silver carbon-fibre film was the best way to lift the black interior out of the ordinary - but that's just us, and for our chosen look. For variety, we tried spraying some things, and a Dash Dynamics kit to break up the rest.

Any painting process is a *multi-stage* application. With the Folia Tec system (thanks to Eurostyling for supplying ours), many of you apparently think you can get away just buying the top coat, which then looks like a cheap option compared to film - WRONG! Even the proper interior spray top coat won't stay on for long without the matching primer, and the finish won't be wear-resistant without the finishing sealer spray. You don't need the special foaming cleaner - you could get by with a general-purpose degreaser, such as meths. Just watch the cloth doesn't suddenly turn black - if it does, you're damaging the finish! This might not be too important to you, as it's being sprayed over anyway, but if you take out the black too far on a part that's not being sprayed all over, you'll have to live with a cacky-looking white-black finish to any non-painted surface...

Providing you're a dab hand with the masking tape, paint gives you the flexibility to be more creative. For instance, you could try colour-matching the exterior of the car - but will ordinary car body paint work on interior plastics? Course it will, as long as you prep the panels properly.

Choice of paint's one thing, but what to paint? Well, not everything - for instance, you might want to avoid high-wear areas like door handles. Just makes for an easier life. The glovebox lid and instrument panel surround are obvious first choices, as are the ashtray and fusebox lid. The centre console's not lighting anyone's fire in standard Ford black, so hit it with some spray too. Any panels which just pop out are targets, in fact (lots less masking needed) - just make sure whatever you're dismantling was meant to come apart, or it'll be out with the superglue instead of the cans.

Don't be afraid to experiment with a combination of styles - as long as you're confident you can blend it all together, anything goes! Mix the painted bits with some tasteful carbon-fibre sheet or brushed-aluminium film, if you like - neutral colours like this, or chrome, can be used to give a lift to dash bits which are too tricky to spray.

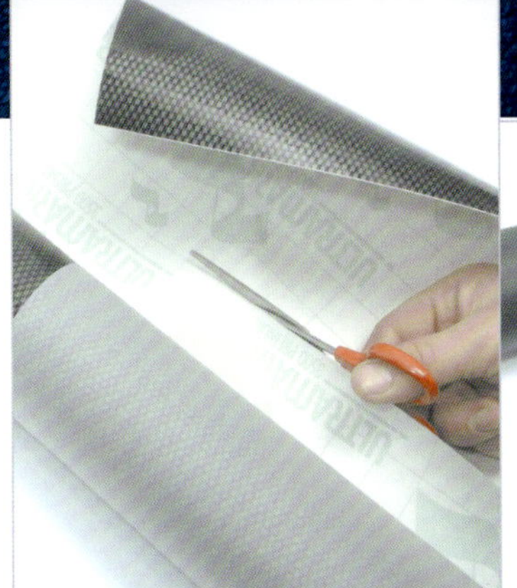

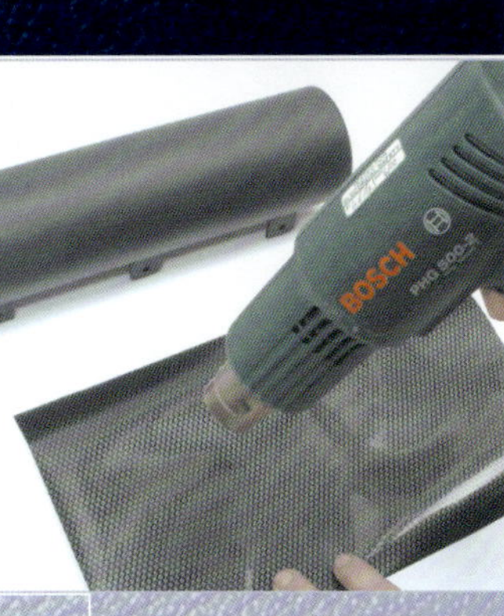

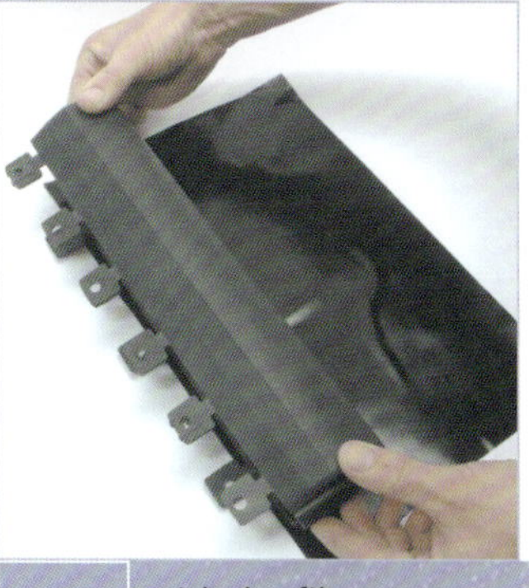

01 Cut the film roughly to size, remembering to leave plenty of excess for trimming - it's also a good idea to have plenty to fold around the edges, because thin film has a nasty habit of peeling off, otherwise.

02 Next, we gently warmed up both the panel, and the film itself. Just following the instructions provided, and who are we to argue?

03 Peel off the backing, being careful that the film stays as flat as possible. Also take care, when you pick the film up, that it doesn't stick to itself (our stuff seemed very keen to do this!).

04 Stick the film on straight - very important with any patterned finish. Start at one edge or corner, and work across, to keep the air bubbles and creases to a minimum. If you get a really bad crease, it's best to unpeel a bit and try again - the adhesive's very tacky, and there's no slide-age available.

Applying **film**

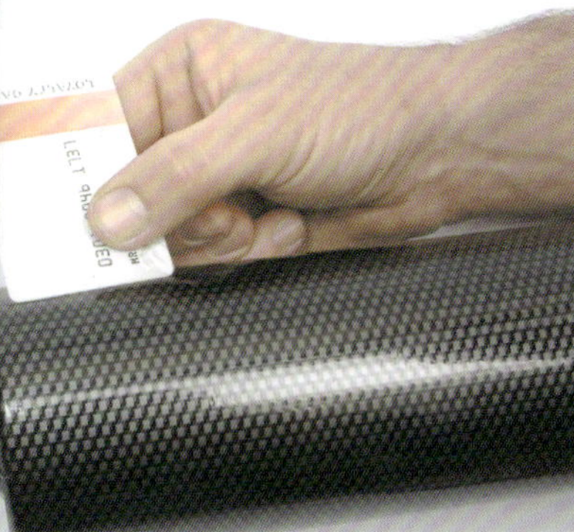

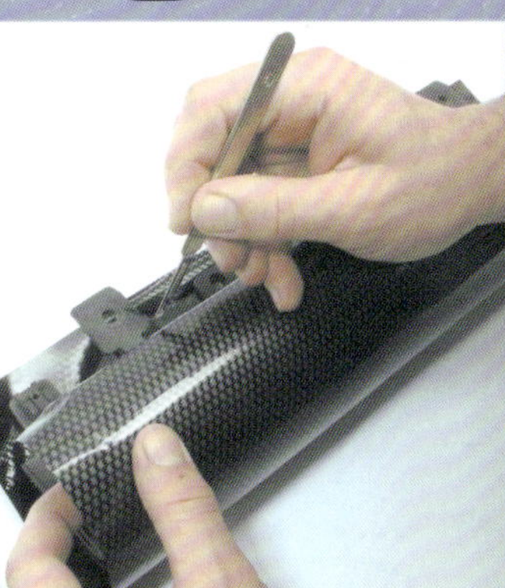

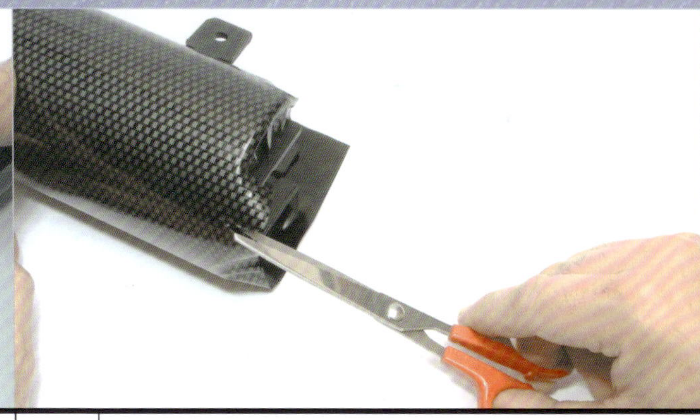

05 Work out the worst of the air bubbles with a soft cloth - get the stuff to stick as best you can before trimming, or it'll all go horribly wrong. To be sure it's stuck (especially important on a grained surface), go over it firmly with the edge of your least-important piece of 'plastic' - ie not a credit card.

06 Once the film's basically laid on, it's time for trimming - which as you've possibly guessed is the tricky bit. We found it was much easier to trim up the tricky bits once the film had been warmed up using a hairdryer or heat gun, but don't overdo it! Make sure you've also got a very sharp knife - a blunt one will ripple the film, and may tear it (one good thing about film is that blood wipes off it easily!).

07 To get the film to wrap neatly round a curved edge, make several slits almost up to the edge, then wrap each sliver of film around, and stick on firmly. If the film's heated as you do this, it wraps round and keeps its shape - meaning it shouldn't try and spring back, ruining all your hard work.

Bum notes

There are limitations to using film, and the quality of the film itself has a lot to do with that. We had major problems doing any kind of job with one particular make of brushed-aluminium-look film - it was a nightmare to work with, and the edges had peeled the next day. Buying quality film will give you a long-lasting result to be proud of, with much less skill requirement and lots less swearing. But it still pays not to be too ambitious with it.

Dash **kit**

Interiors

A far easier route to the brushed-ally or carbon look, pre-finished ('here's some we did earlier') panels are available from suppliers. Dash kits are available for the Escort from companies like Dash Dynamics, and offer a simpler way of livening-up the dull Escort dash.

Did we say simple? It's sometimes not too obvious where the various kit bits are supposed to go! A trial fitting isn't a bad idea, before peeling off the backing. Make sure your chosen trim piece is lined up nice and square, and keep it square as you press it on - the adhesive's usefully-sticky, meaning it will stay stuck whether you get it right or wrong. Still, it's easier by far than trying to mask up and spray the edges of the vents, which is what you'd have to do otherwise.

01 As you might expect, the first thing is to get that dash clean - really clean. To avoid you damaging the finish with unsuitable solvents, you usually get supplied with a bottle of cleaner in the kit. If you (or a previous owner) had a fetish for silicone-based cockpit sprays, clean the required area twice.

02 You might not expect the next bit - it's recommended that you heat the area you're about to dress up. Or maybe move to Florida.

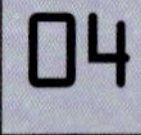

03 We're not done with the heat gun yet. Next to feel its warming blast are the dash kit components themselves.

04 Before it all goes cold again, peel off your chosen section . . .

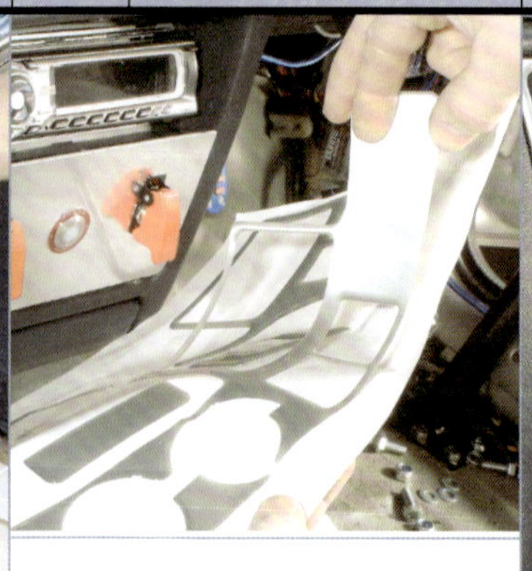

05 . . . line it up carefully, and stick it on - press it on firmly by smoothing a cloth over the whole surface. And you're really telling us you'd rather spray that heater control panel?

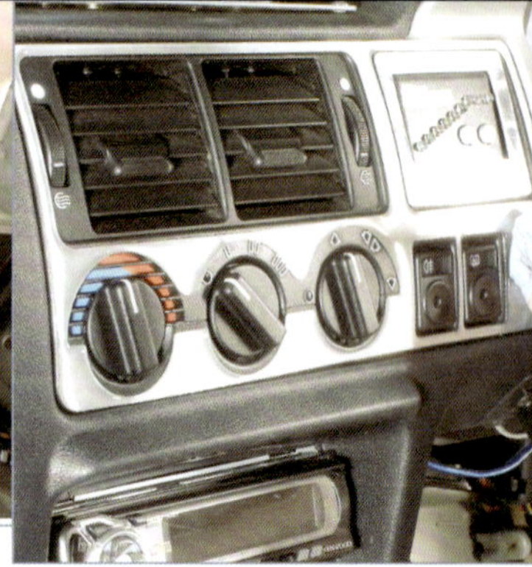

Gear knob jobs

01 Begin by unscrewing that nasty Ford knob. Anyone who doesn't agree that this is a good idea - get your coat.

02 Next, prise the gaiter trim plate from the console, and lift the gaiter over the gear lever.

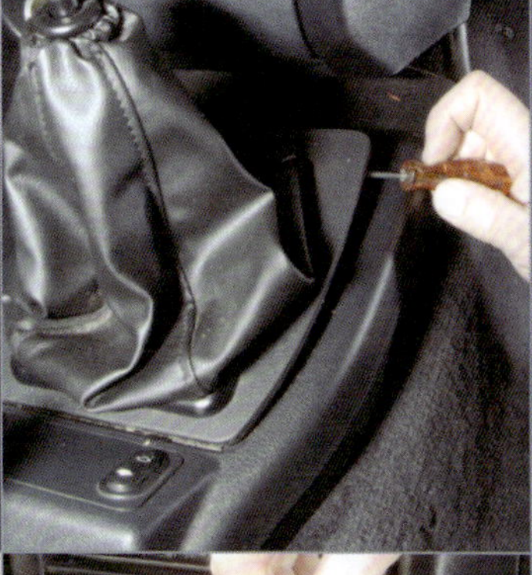

03 Using a screwdriver, prise out the staples that retain the old gaiter to the plastic trim, then separate the inner and outer trim pieces and remove the old gaiter.

04 Taking your sexy new gaiter, stretch the fabric over the base of the inner trim - ours was elastic and held itself, but if yours isn't, glue or staple it to the trim.

05 Build up the unit by fitting the outer gaiter trim. This can be quite a tight fit - be careful not to snap the plastic surround. When it's on, fit the whole gaiter assembly back into the trim plate, and then back into the console.

06 Now for a new knob (well, you wouldn't refit the Ford effort, would you?). Most knobs have a trim ring of some kind, which screws up to the base of the knob - pop it on the lever first. Gear knobs are also usually supplied with different-sized collars - little plastic tubes to you and me - which are for locating the knob on the lever. Choose a tube that will give the tightest fit.

07 Slip the knob on and tighten the grub screws, then tighten the base ring to the knob to make it look nice. Finally, adjust your gaiter to sit around the base of the knob properly - some have Velcro, some have laces.

Handbrake knobs & gaiters

01 A new handbrake gaiter and handle are great for adding detail to standard nasty interiors. Your sexy new gear knob and gaiter's making the sad black stick behind look even worse, so get it sorted. First, remove the centre console as described in 'Removing stuff', then grab hold of the handbrake and pull off the lovely plastic handle.

02 At the base of the lever, there's a plastic grommet that secures the trim retaining pin - prise it off with a screwdriver . . .

. . . then, using a pin punch (a small screwdriver will do, but don't be too violent), tap out the pin.

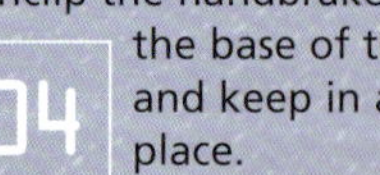

Unclip the handbrake spring at the base of the lever, and keep in a safe place.

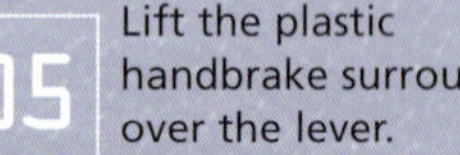

Lift the plastic handbrake surround over the lever.

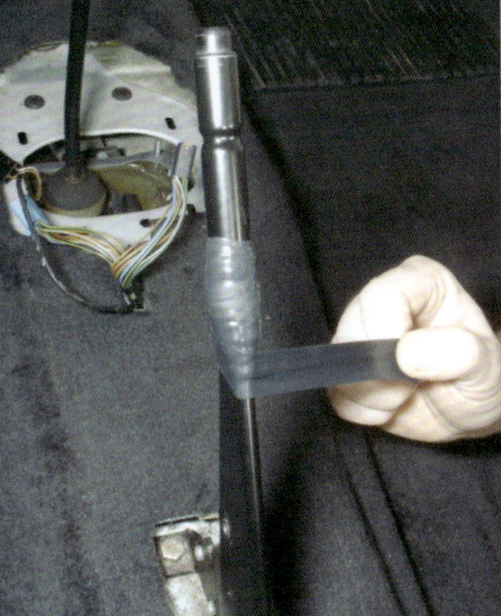

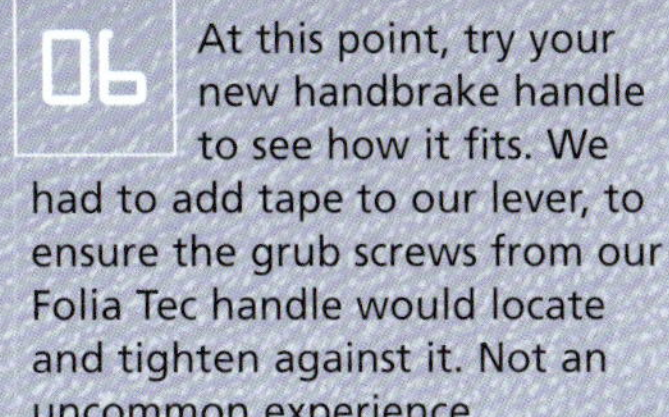

06 At this point, try your new handbrake handle to see how it fits. We had to add tape to our lever, to ensure the grub screws from our Folia Tec handle would locate and tighten against it. Not an uncommon experience.

07 Slip your new gaiter and handle over the lever - our kit was an all-in-one item, which makes life easier, as long as you're in love with both handle and gaiter. Using the Allen key and grub screws supplied, tighten the handle to the lever.

08 You could just tuck the gaiter into the slot in the carpet, but for a more permanent solution, use staples or spray glue. Refit the centre console, and admire your handiwork.

09 Hmmm... Our Escort had a very black, dull interior. The all-in-one gaiter and handle we used kind-of faded into this sea of black. The chrome handle we like, but the black gaiter's got to go. Leaving the new handle attached to the handbrake lever, pull the gaiter up until you reveal the cable-tie that holds the fabric to the handle. Give the clip the snip.

10 Remove the black gaiter by pulling it up over the handle. Our slightly more colourful little blue number from Richbrook slips over the lever, and fits beautifully, with plenty of excess to tuck into the carpet. The new gaiter's also elasticated at the base, which helps to locate it.

11 Tie the strings at the top of the gaiter, to hold the fabric to the handle - and job done! Not everyone gets a job right first time - you've got to be persistent to achieve your ideal look.

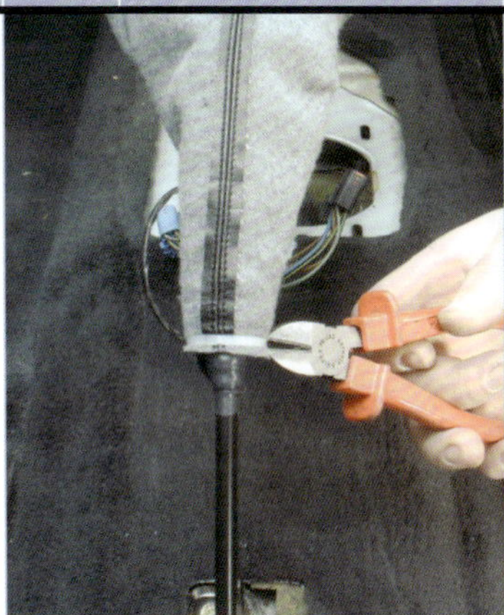

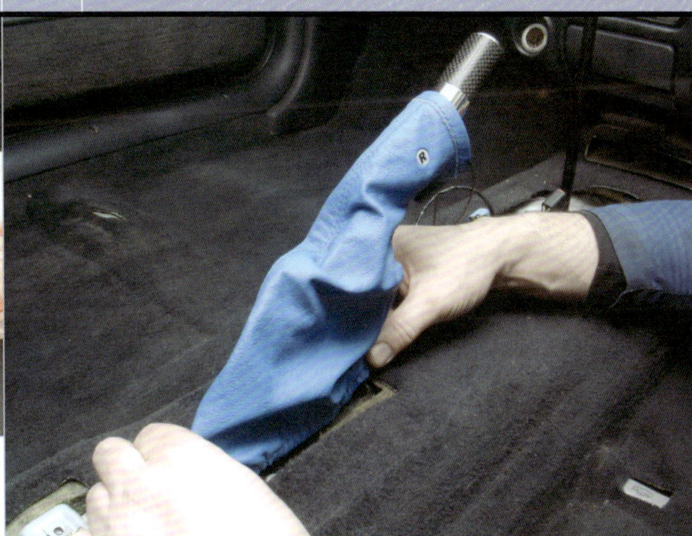

The personal touch - re-trimming

Okay, so you're definitely not happy with how the inside of your Escort looks, but you're not sold on any of the off-the-shelf options for tricking it up, either. You know how you want it to look, though, so get creative!

There are any number of upholstery companies in Yellow Pages, who will be able to create any look you want. If your idea of Escort heaven is an interior swathed in black and purple leather, these guys can help. Don't assume that you'll have to go to Carisma, to get a car interior re-trimmed - they might well be the daddies at this, but any upholsterer worth the name should be able to help, even if they normally only do sofas!

Of course, if you're even slightly handy with things like glue and scissors, you might be inspired to get brave and DIY. An upholsterers will still be a useful source for your materials

Door trim **panels**

What applies to seats can also be applied to your door cards. If you're gonna DIY, practice on something old first.

If you've had your seats trimmed, you'll obviously choose the same stuff for your doors - but here's a tip. Say you've gone for some nice bucket seats, in maybe a red-and-black pattern cloth. Would be nice to match your seats to the door panels here, too, wouldn't it? So how about doing what we did for another of our project cars, and contacting the seat manufacturer for a few square metres of the actual cloth they use to make the seats with? Should match then, shouldn't it? Hand material and cash to your upholstery experts, with cash, and wait. Or do it yourself.

There's no place for luxury items like leather and wicked-colour fabrics in our race/rally Escort, so we went for something a little more radical. Our new 'door trims' are going to be smooth, shining alloy - very trick, very cheap, and ridiculously easy to make.

To stand any chance of making the door trim panels the right size and shape, you'll need to start with a card template. When you're trimming this to size, remember to allow enough at the edges for screws - Escort inner doors are not flat.

01

Transfer your card template to your chosen metal. We went for 'ordinary' aluminium, but there's brushed, chequer, and some very cool patterned stainless to choose from. Aluminium's cheapest. If you're stuck where to source it from, look under Sheet Metal Work or Trailer Manufacturers in the Yellow Pages.

02

This ally's as easy to cut as MDF (even if the rough edges are sharper).

03

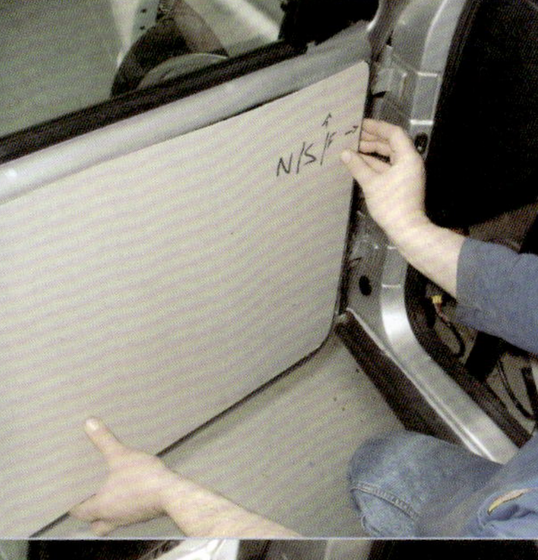

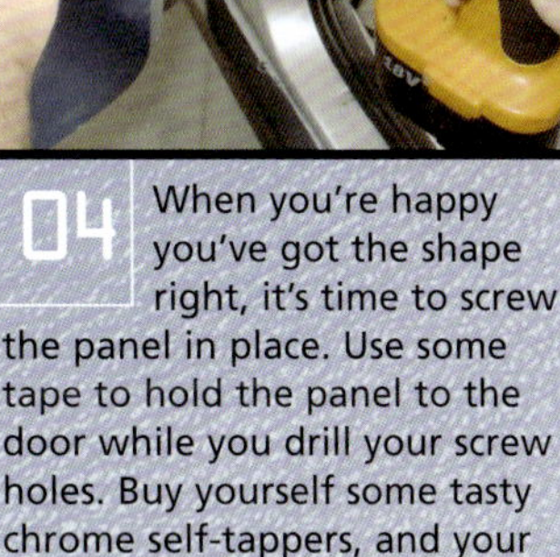

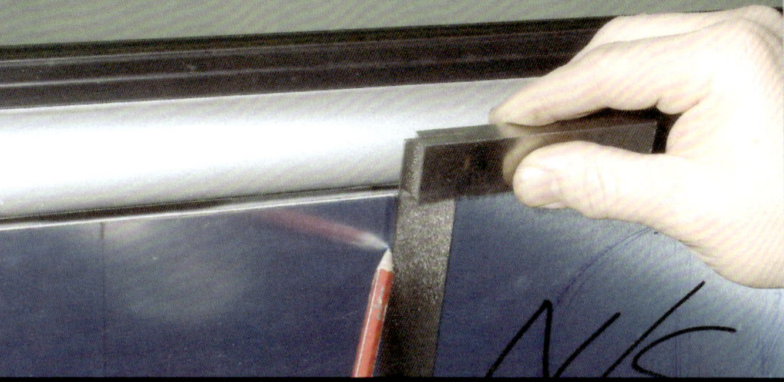

04

When you're happy you've got the shape right, it's time to screw the panel in place. Use some tape to hold the panel to the door while you drill your screw holes. Buy yourself some tasty chrome self-tappers, and your trim panel will look techy and lush at the same time.

05

Of course, you will need at least one more hole in your new panel, for the door-opening handle. You'll also need to source a new door pull (DIY stores sell some quite saucy handles, these days). Getting the hole for the door-opening handle in the right spot means pulling the top of the panel back, and marking the position by eye. Measure how far down the door panel the handle is, and use a square to get the hole in the right spot.

06

Drill a hole at one corner, then work the jigsaw round until you've got a door-handle-sized rectangular hole. It doesn't have to be a perfect fit - enlarge the hole as necessary until the panel fits over flush. Sound-deadening the panel can be achieved with stick-on draught excluder around the edges where the panel touches the door. To see more of our finished results, go to the ICE section (yes, we fitted speakers to them, too).

Are your dials **all white?**

White or coloured dial kits aren't that difficult to fit, but you will need some skill and patience not to damage the delicate bits inside your instrument panel - the risk is definitely worth it, to liven up that dreary grey Escort dash, anyway. Just make sure you get the right kit for your car, and don't start stripping anything until you're sure it's the right one - look carefully. Most dial kit makers, for instance, want to know exactly what markings you have on your speedo and rev counter. If they don't ask, be worried - the kit they send could well be wrong for your car, and might not even fit.

01 If you haven't yet removed the steering wheel - don't! You don't really need to for this. The surround comes off first, held by two screws in the inside top edge . . .

02 . . . and persuaded off with a small screwdriver - possibly the single most-useful tool you'll ever... um... spend all your time looking for. Buy two.

03 That's one ugly-looking bit of plastic to be looking at all the time - and it came off so easily, too. Why not get creative with it, while it's off?

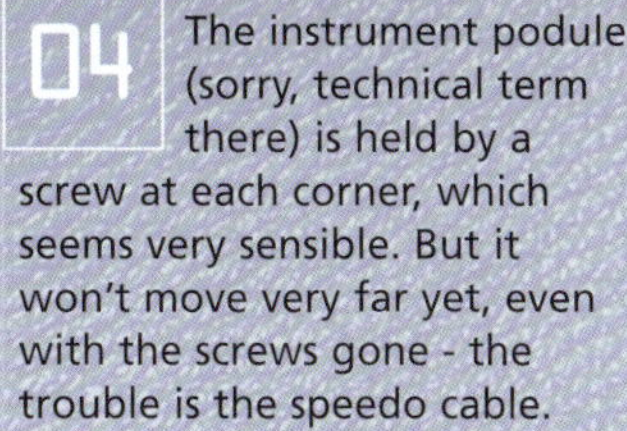

04 The instrument podule (sorry, technical term there) is held by a screw at each corner, which seems very sensible. But it won't move very far yet, even with the screws gone - the trouble is the speedo cable.

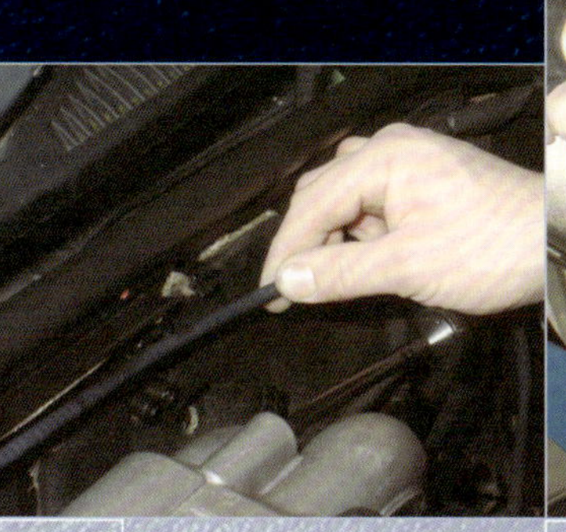

05 Moving quickly under the bonnet, we find the speedo cable is clipped to the bulkhead - pull it out of these clips, and suddenly, there's be a lot more movement in our clocks, inside the car.

06 It's not absolutely essential, but taking off the steering column top shroud will make getting the clocks in and out easier. And it's only two screws.

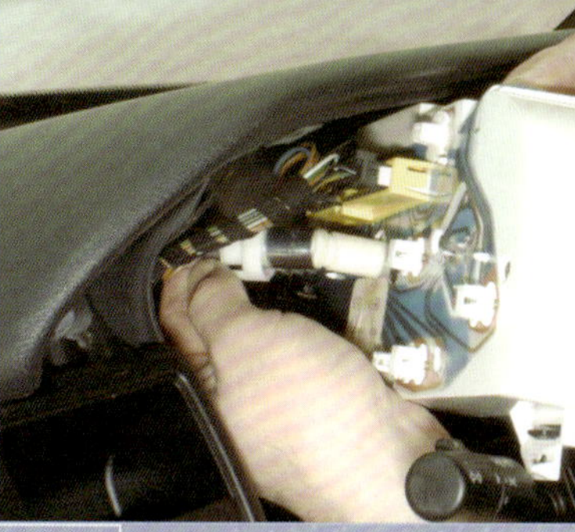

07 Reach in behind the speedo, then squeeze the white plastic collar and pull the cable end fitting down until it detaches. Take the time to notice how it all fits, 'cos you'll have to reconnect this later, and it's tricky. While you're in there, disconnect the long wiring plug from the yellow socket.

08 As the clocks finally emerge, disconnect one more wiring plug on the right-hand side, and they're free.

09 The first item to remove from our recently ripped-out instrument panel? Its knob, I'm afraid.

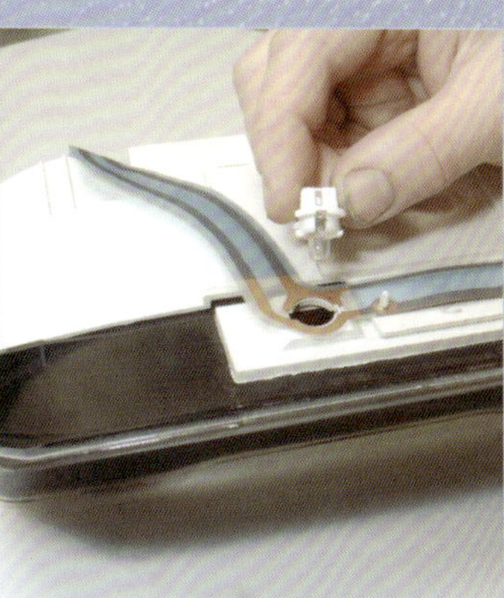

10 Flip it over, and take its two bulbs out from behind . . .

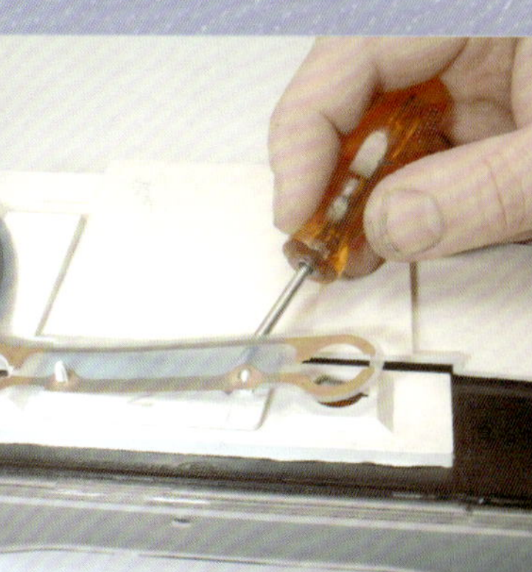

11 . . . before carefully lifting off the printed circuit from the locating pegs. There's that screwdriver again.

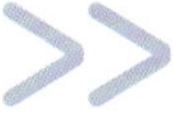

12 The plastic 'lens' over the panel is clipped in place - two catches top and bottom, and we have lift-off.

13 On the bigger clocks, the first job is pulling out the needle stop with pliers. Bet you didn't even know you had one. Put it somewhere safe.

14 Nurse, the screens - this man's attacking his speedo dial with a scalpel, and he isn't even a proper doctor. The idea is to slice the old dial from the centre, out to the edge (which means you don't have to take off the needle, so don't try) . . .

Interiors

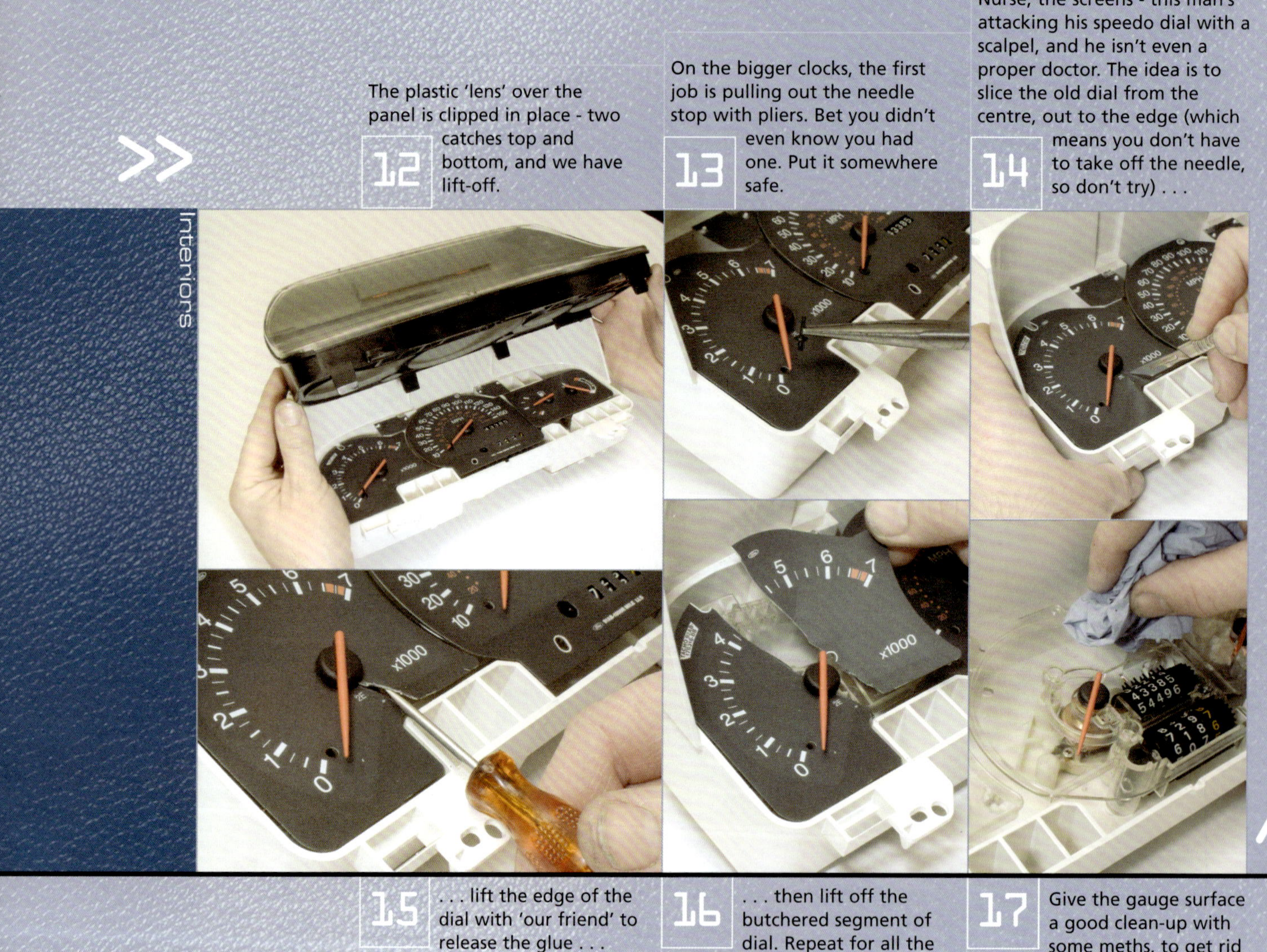

15 . . . lift the edge of the dial with 'our friend' to release the glue . . .

16 . . . then lift off the butchered segment of dial. Repeat for all the others - and remember - take your time.

17 Give the gauge surface a good clean-up with some meths, to get rid of the excess sticky.

Tips 'n' tricks
Before peeling off the backing, and sticking the dials in place, have a trial run at it. Fitting the dials over the needles isn't easy when you first try - with practice, it ain't so bad!

The makers of our kit supply a packet of what they charmingly refer to as 'banjos'. These black stick-on bits are meant to go around the needle hubs, and stop the light from the illumination bulbs from shining up through at night. Sounds fair to us. It's all a bit fiddly, though - peel off the backing,

18 then hook them over the needle hub (there's a slit in the banjo) . . .

. . . use something like a screwdriver to press the banjo onto the gauge, and then trim

19 off the banjo 'handle', to leave a black circle around the needle.

This is what you've paid to see - let's get those dials on. Peel

20 off the backing from the rather weedy-looking adhesive strips . . .

. . . then, keeping the dial face slightly curved between your fingers (to stop it sticking to everything), slide the dial sideways onto the end of the needle, so the needle goes under and over. When it gets all the way up, get the dial to go under the needle hub, and

21 hook the inner end of the needle over the dial.

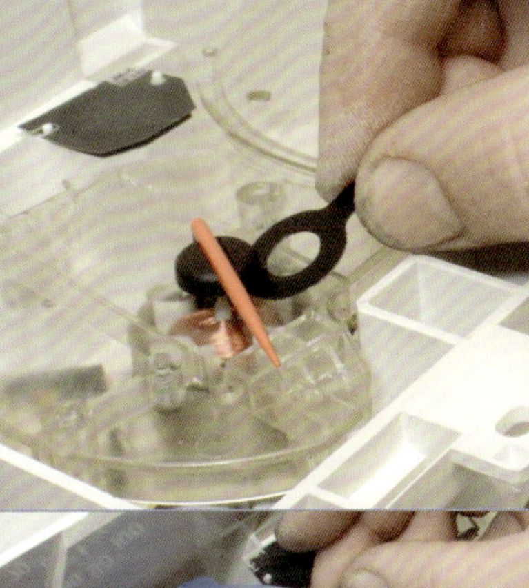

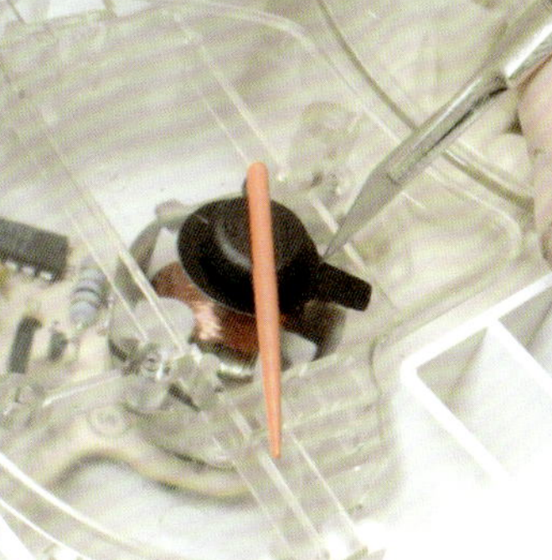

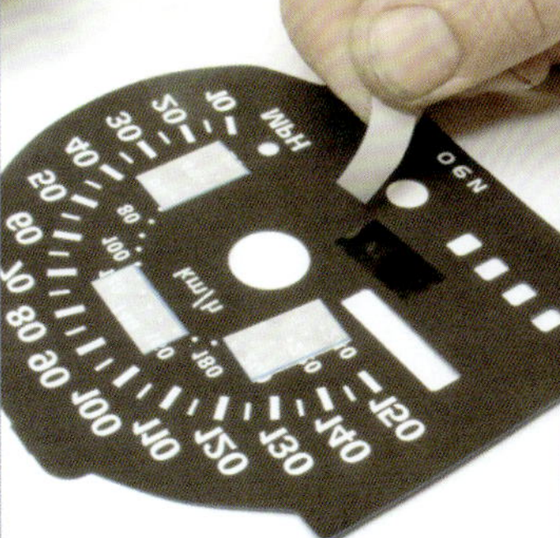

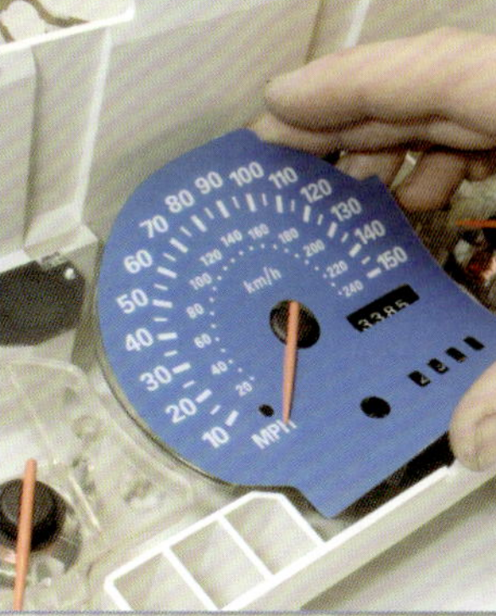

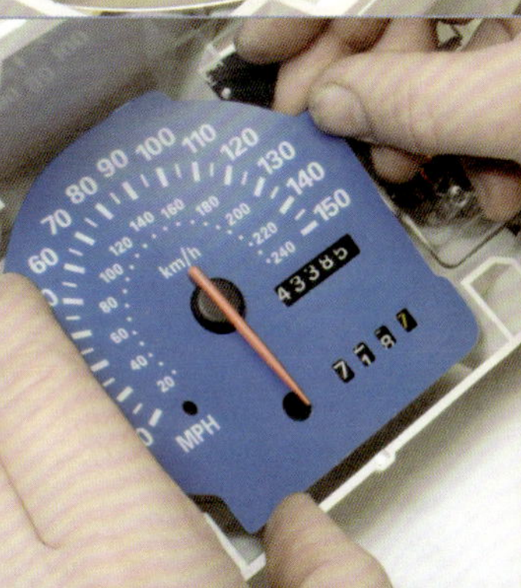

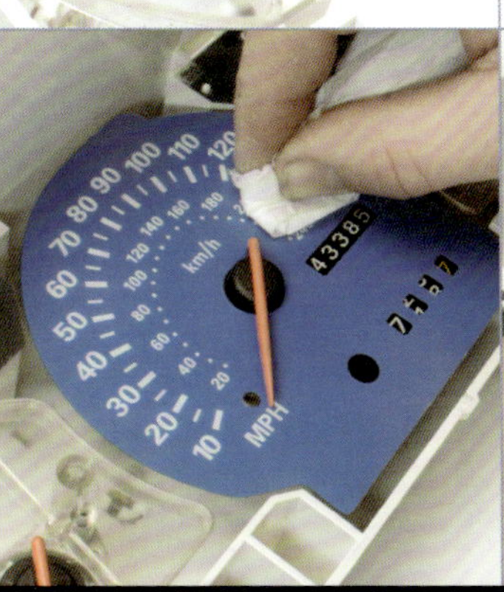

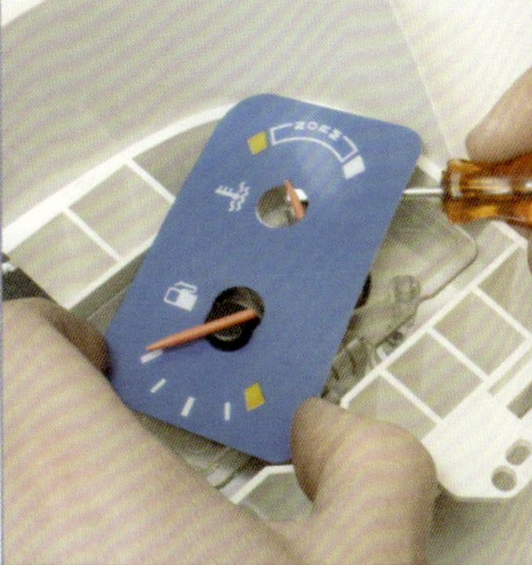

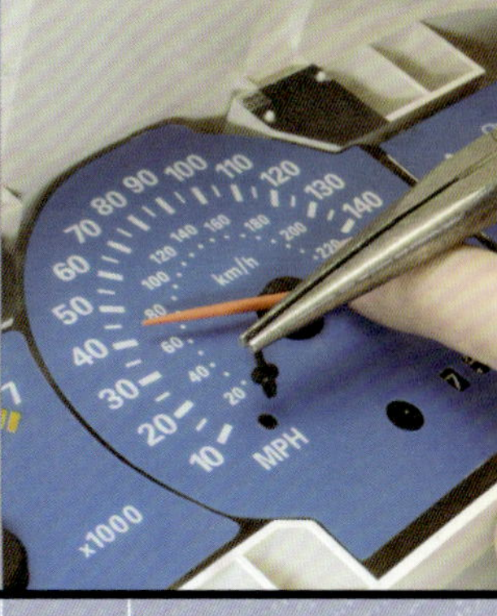

22 Unstick the dial from wherever it landed, and position it using the various holes as a guide . . .

23 . . . before sticking it down firmly - wipe a cloth over the whole dial.

24 There's a knack to getting the dial over the smaller gauges. First, slip the dial over the fuel gauge needle.

25 Don't forget to refit the needle stops to your new dials before refitting the 'lens', or the trip reset knob once it's on.

Rev counter

Those of you who already have a rev counter (or tacho), ignore this bit. Or perhaps not - you might want a tidy little tacho mounted somewhere more helpful than in the instrument podule. If so, we're here to help. Having one separate gauge mounted on the A-pillar, centre of the dash or centre console adds hugely to the racing look - so how smart will three look?

If you don't want to give yourself a hard time, choose extra gauges which are easy to wire in - rev counter, voltmeter, water temperature, that kind of thing. Oil pressure and temperature gauges need dedicated sender units fitted, which makes things trickier (though not impossible). Then again, if you're just going for the look, who cares if they actually work or not?

01 A bit like doing the starter button, the most-fun part of fitting new dials is figuring out where they'll go. Getting them working is the boring bit. The area in front of the Escort clock is a bit of an instrument desert, so we thought we'd fill it up. To match our ally kill switch panel, we chose to mount our clocks on another plate, which meant first trimming the shallow tray surround down, to give a flat surface.

02 One card template later, we'd cut our piece of ally, and we're well into mounting the gauge holder mounting brackets in place. What we'll have, hopefully, is three clocks in a staggered row, angled at the driver.

03 It's important to check the spacing when you're fitting a group of clocks like this. As well as the gauge shells, there's the extra width of the dial bezels (front trims - blue in our case) to allow for. Note that we've also thought ahead, and drilled a big hole in the plate, to feed the new wiring down through (and that the hole's fitted with a rubber grommet - very important where wires pass through metal).

04 Oh man - they're not even slightly finished yet, and we're already getting excited. Our plate can be fitted using four self-tappers, straight into the dash (just make them nice and shiny, that's all). We forgot to mention that we drilled a big hole in the top of the dash, to match the big 'un in the plate, to feed the wires down through (you've seen enough holes drilled, in this book).

05 Fitting the dials to the bezels means laying the bezel on some cloth, and pressing the dial onto it. Some pressure is needed for this.

06 Before our rev counter gets fitted to its shiny chrome shell on the dash, there's a bit of wiring to tidy up. The gauge needs two earths - one for the gauge, one for the lighting. We cheated, and joined ours together with a quick soldered joint. Note that the lighting earth comes straight off one of the mounting studs (not used in our case).

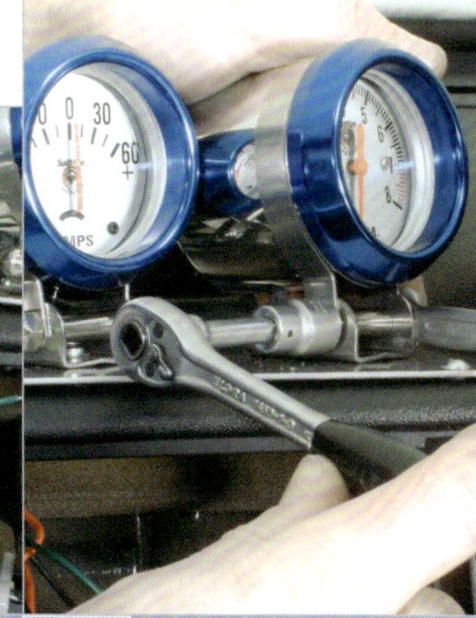

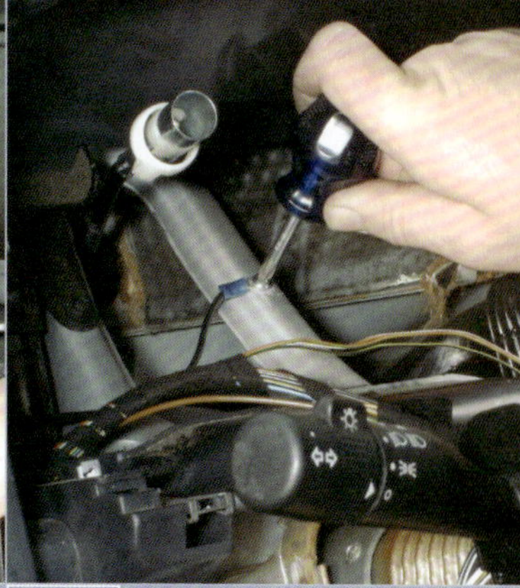

07 In it goes, making sure none of the wiring gets pinched-up . . .

08 . . . and all the wiring gets fed down behind the dash. Our original idea of a grommet fitted to the plate didn't work, so we passed another one up the bunch of wires, and pressed it in from below.

09 When the dials have been set to the driver's liking, don't forget to tighten the mounting clamps which hold the gauge shells in place.

10 And so to the boring bit we mentioned earlier - the wiring. First, our joint earth. With the clocks out, we spotted a likely hole in this bracket behind the steering wheel. One ring terminal, one self-tapper, one good earth.

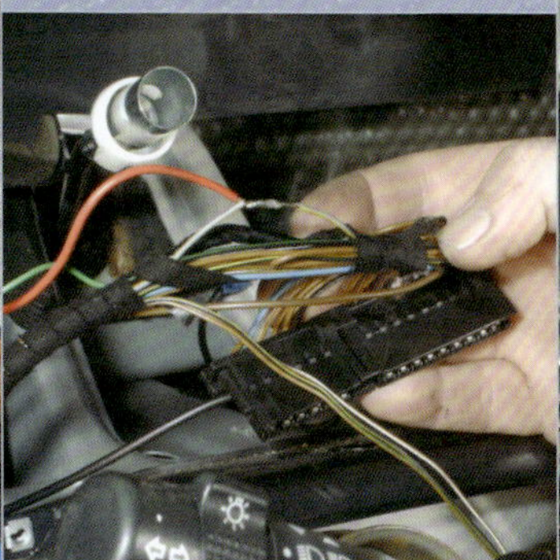

11 Next is the green wire for the rev counter signal (confusingly, our tacho had two green wires - one was the live for the lighting, off the bulb). Even if your Escort has no tacho as standard, it's still got a green wire on the big plug at the back of the instrument panel. Strip and solder the new green to the old green, not forgetting to insulate the joint.

12 The red wire is an ignition live, taken from any wire that's live when the ignition's on (obviously). Either probe around the fusebox with a test light/meter, or splice a new wire straight onto the big black wire on the back of the ignition switch (see the starter button section for details). We were able to cheat, and just added another wire to the ones on the kill switch terminals.

13 Last, the wire from the rev counter's bulb has to be spliced into the dash lighting circuit. On an Escort, you're looking for a grey wire with a yellow stripe (almost any standard switch or gauge will have one). As we were in the instrument area anyway, we chose the grey/yellow off the now-famous big plug behind the clocks.

14 Fire the engine up, and see if it works. For the record, this shot was taken with the engine running. Say hi to Mr voltmeter, ammeter and rev counter - lookin' good, fellas.

For true touring-car feel inside, you won't beat a fully-functioning gearshift light to impress your mates. Plenty to choose from in Demon Tweeks - ours is the super-sexy Micro Dynamics sequential shift light, which has a row of different-colour LEDs that light as the engine speed rises. Top stuff.

Owners of 1.3 HCS Escorts don't really need a shift light, unfortunately - the rattly old pushrod engine tells you loudly when it's time to change up. Sorry lads.

Shift light

01 This is a tidy little unit - where can we fit it, to show it off best, and still be useful to the driver? How about this coin tray-thingy, next to the clocks? Looks an ideal size.

02 To get the most from our chosen hole, we need to enlarge it slightly. Luckily, Ford have thought of this, by making the lower section removable, with the help of our trusty screwdriver.

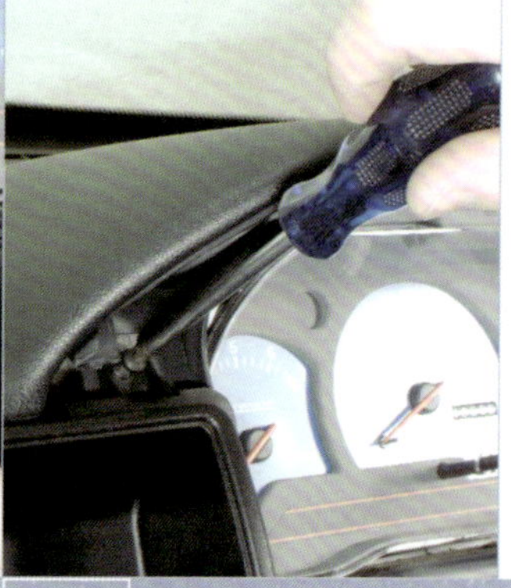

03 Sooner or later, you'll find an excuse to remove the heater control panel - this was ours. With the instrument surround out of the way (see 'dials'), there's a screw above the coin tray . . .

04 . . . and one alongside it to remove . . .

05 . . . then you prise off all the control knobs . . .

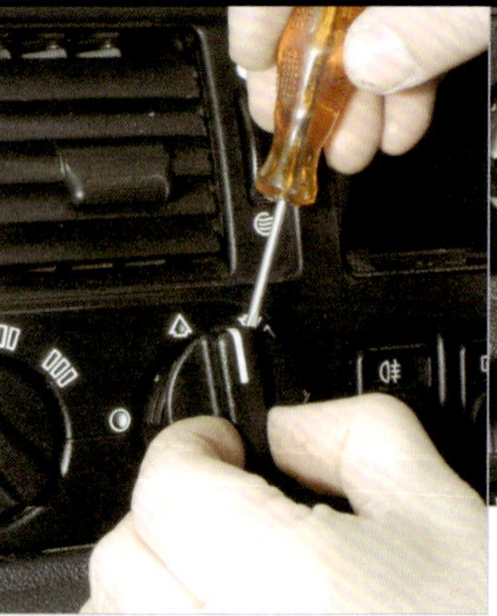

06 . . . and switches, disconnecting them as you go.

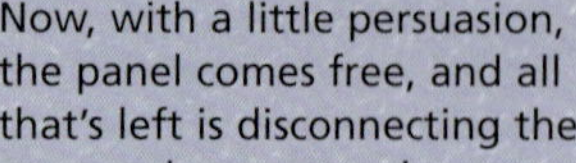

07 Now, with a little persuasion, the panel comes free, and all that's left is disconnecting the heater panel illumination before it's yours to play with.

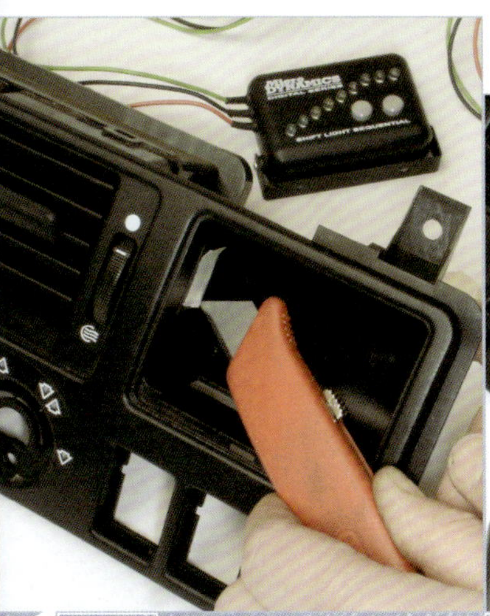

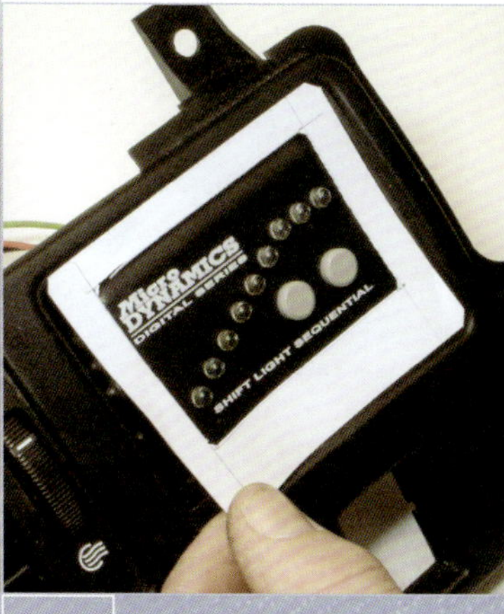

08 The first task was to cut a hole for the three wires to pass through - not too hard with a little help from Stanley the knife.

09 To stick the unit in place, use a few strips of double-sided tape . . .

10 . . . and in she goes. You could, of course, leave it at that, and it would still look the business. But we're here to give you ideas, so . . .

11 . . . how about making up a surround for the unit, from ally? Gives a far more 'finished' look to the whole thing. All you need is a paper/card template, a small section of metal, and a jigsaw.

12 Now a little mastic to hold it in place . . .

13 . . . and on with a shiny surround. Very trick, very touring-car, very easy.

14 Okay, so it looks nice, but how about getting it to work, eh? Well, there's only three wires - red, black and green. Red goes to an ignition live feed, which you could tap off the back of the ignition switch (see 'Racing starts'). Black is earth, so choose a convenient screw into the car body, or do like us, and splice into a brown wire on one of the heater control panel switches.

15 The green wire is the tacho (rev counter) feed. Remove the instrument pack (see 'Blue dials') and seek out the green wire which goes into the long wiring plug. Even if your Escort doesn't have a tacho as standard, the green wire will still be there - trust us. Tap the shift light green into the wiring plug green (solder is a preferred choice here), and the shift light should burst into life. Refer to you instructions to set it up, and prepare to impress.

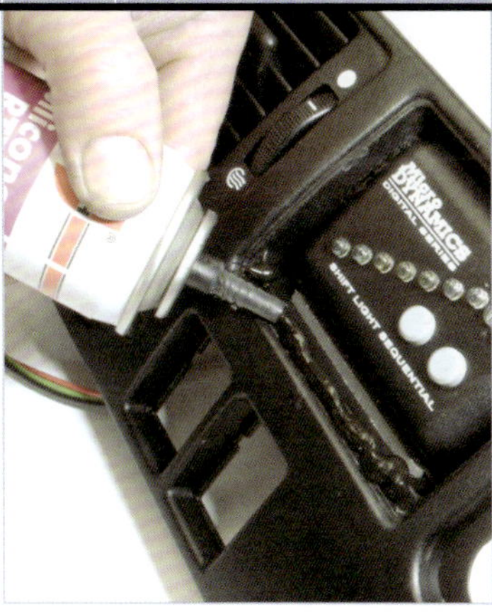

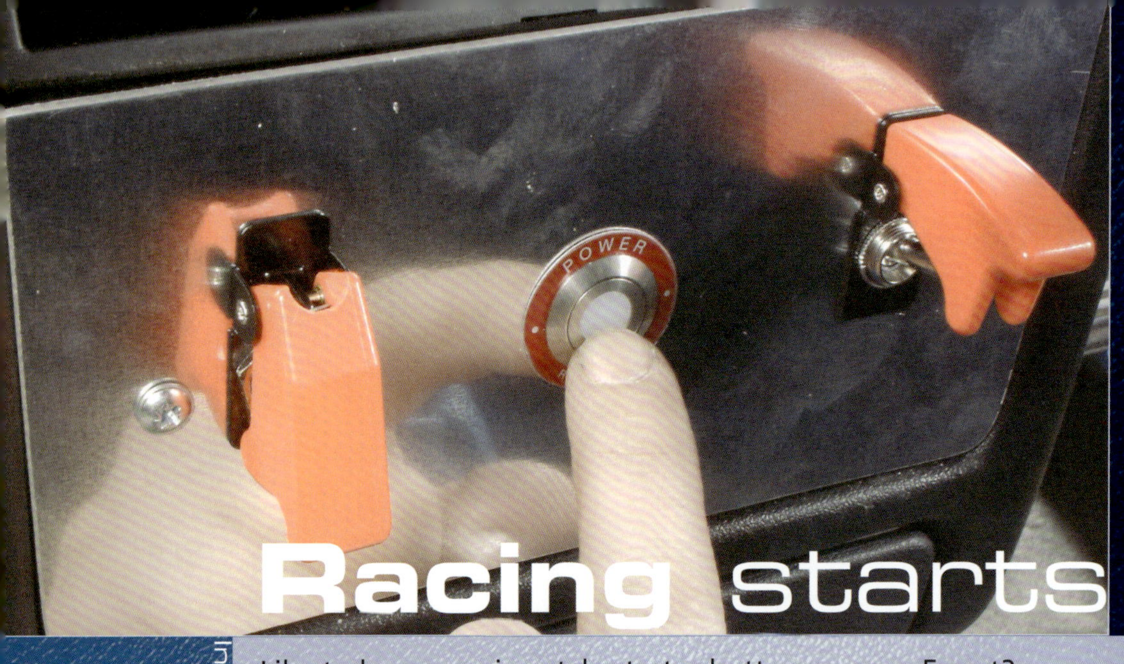

Racing starts

Like to have a racing-style starter button on your Escort? Read on! A very cool piece of kit, and not too bad a job to wire up - the most difficult bit's deciding where to mount the button (somewhere easy to get at, but still in full view so's you can impress your passengers!). The idea of the racing starter button is that the ignition key is made redundant, beyond switching on the ignition lights (it'd be a pretty negative security feature, if you could start the engine without the key at all).

This is one job where you'll be messing with big wires, carrying serious current - more than any other electrical job, don't try and rush it, and don't skimp on the insulating tape. Do it properly, as we're about to show you, and there's no worries. Otherwise, at best, you'll be stranded - at worst, it could be a fire.

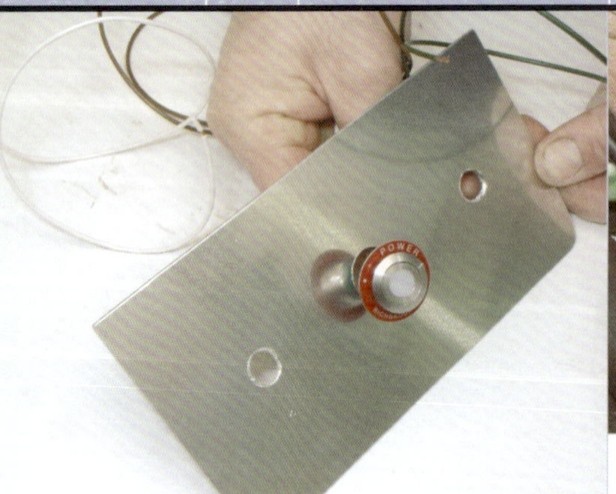

01 Our Prostart button was supplied by Richbrook, but the instructions here should be good for most makes. The best (and easiest) part of fitting one of these babies is - deciding where the button's going to go. Must be somewhere highly-visible, for maximum pose value. Our alloy kill switch panel was an obvious choice - why not make something like it, yourself?

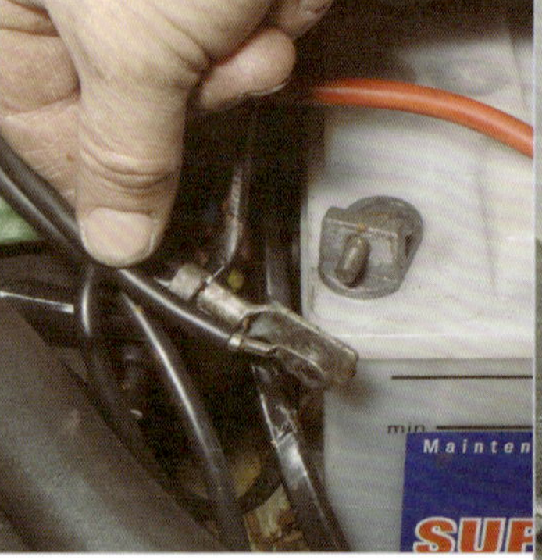

02 Now for the wiring. First, DISCONNECT THE BATTERY. You may have ignored this advice before. You may not. Don't do so now.

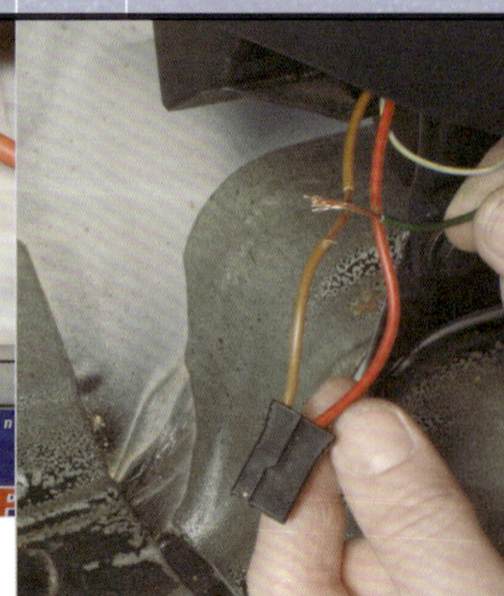

03 The green wire from the starter button has to go to a decent earth. Luckily, just below our new switch panel, there's the cigar lighter, which has a luvverly great big brown wire off its wiring plug. That says 'earth' to us - strip a little insulation off the brown, bare the end of the green, and join with solder. Don't forget to tape it up afterwards.

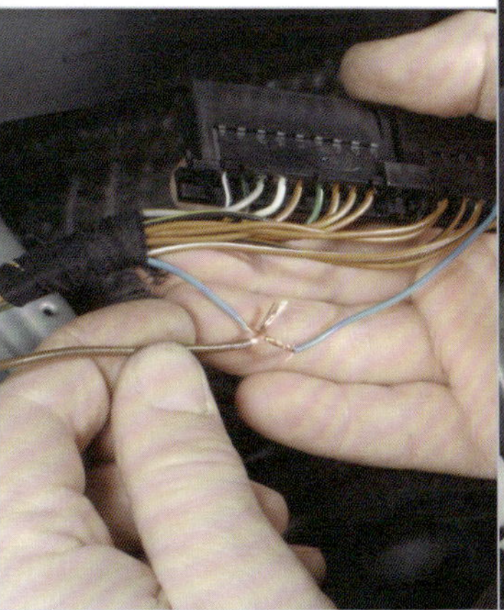

04 The black wire from the starter button joins to the black wire from the relay supplied in the kit. A relay is an electrically-operated switch, for switching big loads (like starter motors, foglights, etc) on and off. It's an important item, which should first be mounted securely, somewhere out of the way (we hid ours behind the new switch panel).

05 If your pro-start is an 'illuminated' one, take out the instruments (see 'dials'). The brown wire from the starter button has to be spliced onto the blue wire in the long wiring plug on the back of the clocks. The blue is the alternator warning light wire - connecting the brown to it means the starter button light goes out when the engine starts. Neat.

06 Remove the steering column lower shroud for access to the ignition switch wires, on the left-hand side. Cut the black/blue wire as shown . . .

07 . . . and join it to the blue wire from the new relay. Notice we say 'cut' rather than 'cut into' - once the black/blue wire has been cut, leave it cut. This is the starter solenoid wire, and leaving it cut means that the ignition key will no longer start the engine, which is the whole point of a starter button.

08 Now we need an ignition live feed, to join to the white wire which goes to one side of the fuseholder. Slice off a little insulation from the black wire on the back of the ignition switch plug, then strip the end from the white wire, wrap the wire around the stripped section of black, and use solder to make the joint permanent. Wrap the finished joint with insulating tape.

09 Take the white wire from the starter button, and the white wire from the relay, and join them together using a female spade connector. Plug this onto one side of the fuseholder, then join on the white wire which you just soldered onto the ignition live, using another spade connector.

10 The relay and fuseholder must be mounted somewhere reasonably easy to get at - our experience has been that the fuses can have a nasty habit of blowing. You could just tuck it under the dash somewhere, but our new switch panel's designed to be removable, so we stuffed our fuse in there. Apply one finger, and the racing Escort bursts into life. Fantastic stuff.

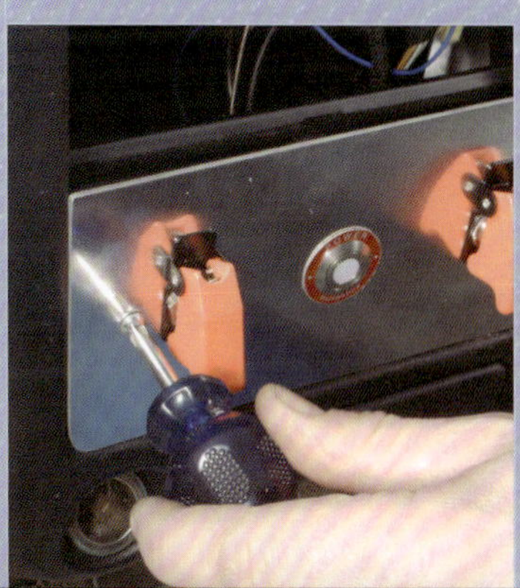

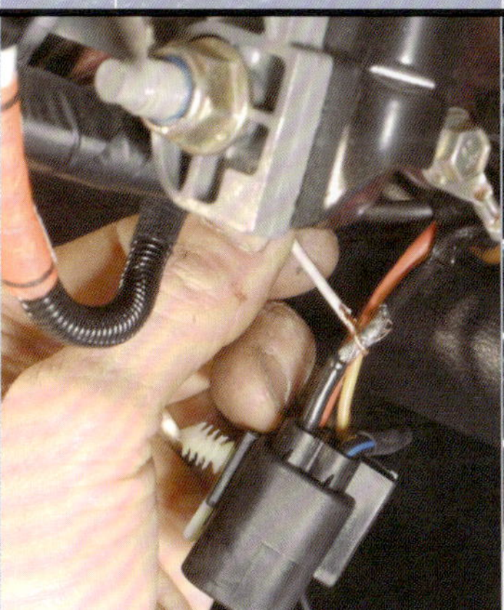

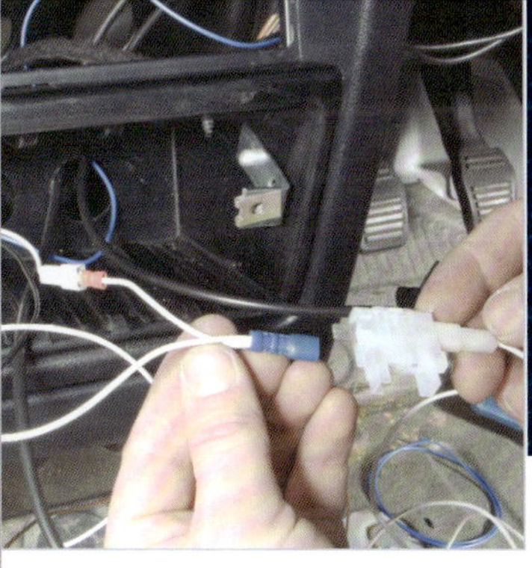

Tips 'n' tricks

We fitted an ignition kill switch to our racing Escort, so the black ignition switch wire was cut, and the wire sent over to one side of our kill switch. From the new switch, the wire went back across the car, and was joined back into the original ignition wiring, which runs on into the fusebox. The original ignition switch now apparently does nothing - no lights come on, and the starter doesn't turn. The key has to be in the ignition position, then you flick up the kill switch, and press the starter. To stop the engine, flick the kill switch down. Tell me that's not seriously cool.

Kill switches

A big part of creating the race/rally look, the kill switch is an icon. Find any excuse you can for fitting one - these things are as cool to use as they are to look at (readily available from places like Demon Tweeks - try and buy the proper racing ones, rather than fakes).

Mount a row of kill switches on an ally panel, and we're talking saucy. A sauce overload, in fact - and it's really easy to achieve.

01 What are we going to do with that desperately-dull cassette storage box under the radio? Rip it out, and treat it to a home-made switch panel, that's what. Two screws hold it in, and they're inside the top edge

02 Take one piece of alloy, cover in masking tape, and draw round using the front of the cassette box as a template . . .

03 . . . then cut out using a jigsaw.

04 The new panel can be mounted to the cassette box using a pair of right-angled brackets, available in packs from any DIY store. Fit a U-clip to each bracket, and they'll take a (nice, chrome) self-tapping screw inserted through the front of the panel.

05 Mark a hole for the kill switch . . .

06 . . . drill it out (in this case, using a cone-shaped hole-cutting tool that we call the 'mole') . . .

07 . . . and fit the switch to the panel. Use it to wire in anything you like. We fitted two - one for our pace-car strobe lights, and one which really is an ignition kill switch, wired-in when we fitted our pro-start button (which you can see lurking in the background).

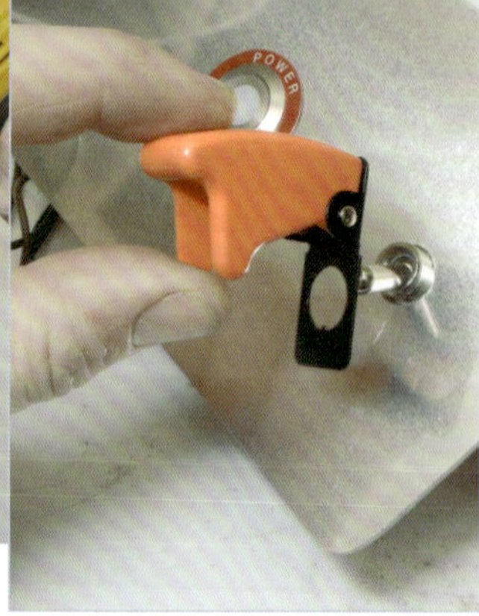

Boring **flooring?**

Alright, so carpets have always been a dull colour because they have to not show the dirt - when was the last time you heard of a car with white carpets? What goes on the floor needn't be entirely dull, though, and can still be easy to clean, if you're worried.

Ripping out the old carpets is actually quite a major undertaking - first, the seats have to come out (you might be fitting new ones anyway), but the carpets and underfelt fit right up under the dashboard, and under all the sill trims and centre console, etc. Carpet acts as sound-deadening, and is a useful thing to hide wiring under, too, so don't be in too great a hurry to ditch it completely. Unless, of course, your Escort is having a full-on race/rally style treatment, in which case - dump that rug!

Chequerplate is the current fashion in cool flooring, and it's easy to see why it'll probably have an enduring appeal - it's tough but flexible, fairly easy to cut and shape to fit, has a cool mirror finish, and it matches perfectly with the racing theme so often seen in the modified world, and with the ally trim that's widely used too.

Tips 'n' tricks

If you're completely replacing the carpet and felt with, say, chequerplate throughout, do this at a late stage, after the ICE install and any other electrical work's been done - that way, all the wiring can be neatly hidden underneath it.

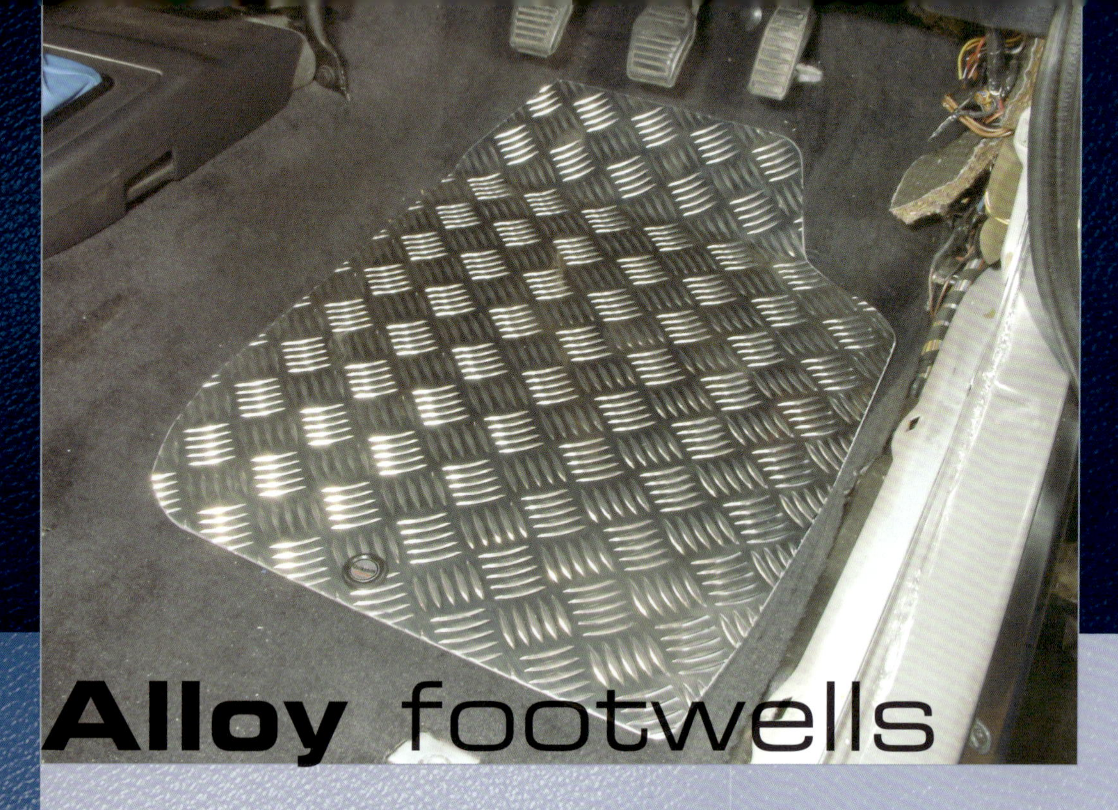

Alloy footwells

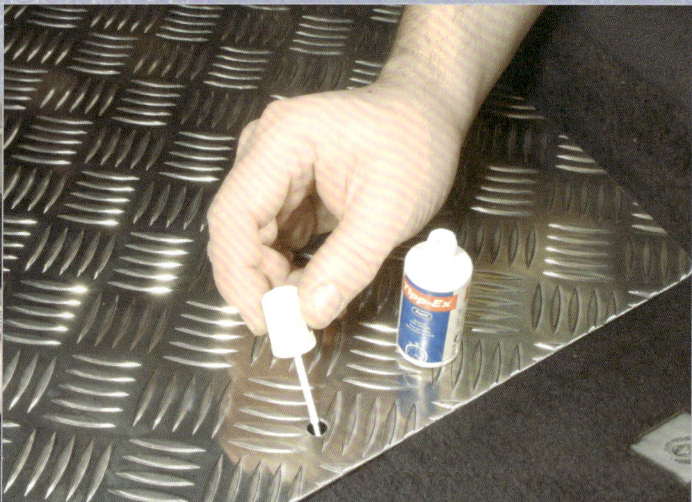

01 The halfway-house to a fully-plated interior is to make up your own tailored mats (or you can buy ready-mades if you're not allowed to play with sharp knives). Unless you buy real ally chequer, what you'll get is actually plastic, and must be supported by mounting it on hardboard. These footwells are the real deal, however - and not that pricey. First, lay them in, and see how they fit.

02 These Quikshift plates from Demon Teweks have a clever two-part screw mounting at the back. When you're happy that the plates are in the right spot, use Tipp-Ex through the mounting hole in the plate to make a spot on the carpet.

03 The lower half of the screw mounting has a pin attached, which you poke into the carpet, so that the centre of the mounting ends up in the spot you just marked. As the mounting's speared into the carpet, the plate shouldn't slip. In theory.

04 Lay the plate back in, fit over the lower mounting, and screw on the top. To make them less slippery when wet (so to speak), try sticking on a few strips of skateboarder's grip tape. Job done - or is it? We found the plate was still pretty unstable using this approach, so we thought about it, and tried again.

Instead of just marking the carpet, use the Tipp-Ex dot to mark for cutting a small hole in the carpet . . .

. . . then use the white paint through the hole in the carpet to make a dot on the sound-deadening underneath.

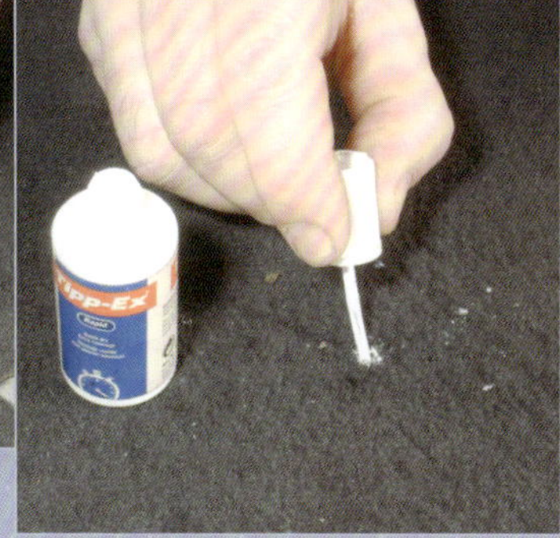

With the door sill trims removed (described elsewhere in this Chapter), you can peel back the carpet, and stick the lower mounting into the more substantial sound-deadening. Fold the carpet back into place, making sure the mounting pokes up through the hole you made, and fit the plate as before. Much better.

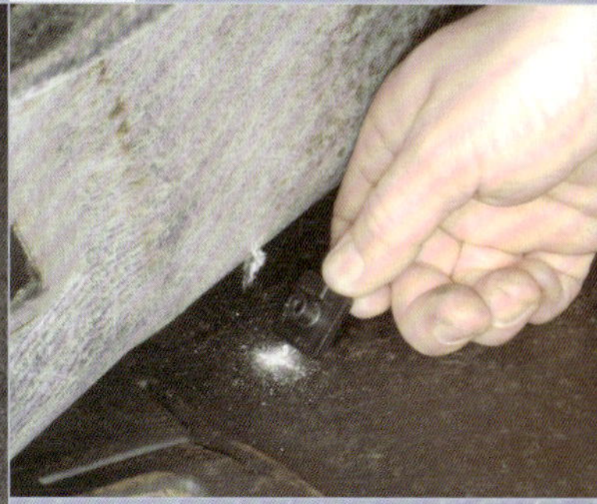

Removing the **carpet**

01 If you're really serious about doing this, there's lots of other stuff to take out first. Start with the seats, door sill trims and centre console (removing all of these is covered in this Chapter). You might also need to remove the seat belts (see the section on fitting harnesses). With all that gone, it's pretty easy - prise out the plastic plugs in the front footwells . . .

02 . . . and start 'peeling' the carpet away, around the base of the dash.

03 Under that, you'll find two sections of sound-deadening, which lift out without too much hassle.

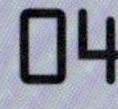

Finally, to see the bare metal floor, there's still more sound-proofing in the front footwells - this reaches right up behind the bulkhead, and might have to be sliced free. Ripping it is more satisfying, though.

A new steering wheel is an essential purchase in personalising your Escort. It's one of the main points of contact between you and the car, it's sat right in front of you, and the standard ones are dull and massive!

Don't be tempted to fit too small a wheel if you've not got power steering. Escort steering can be a tad heavy anyway, and a tiny-rimmed steering wheel will make manoeuvring very difficult, especially with phat tyres.

One bit of good news is that, once you've shelled out for your wheel, it may be possible to fit it to your next car, too. When you buy a new wheel, you usually have to buy a boss (or mount) to go with it - the mounts are less pricey, so one wheel could be fitted to another completely different car, for minimum cost.

A trick feature worth investigating is the detachable wheel/boss. This feature comes in handy when you park up and would rather the car was still there when you come back (something most people find a bonus). It's all very well having a steering wheel immobiliser or steering lock, but I doubt many thieves will be driving off in your car if the steering wheel's completely missing! Also, removing the wheel may remove the temptation to break in and pinch... your wheel!

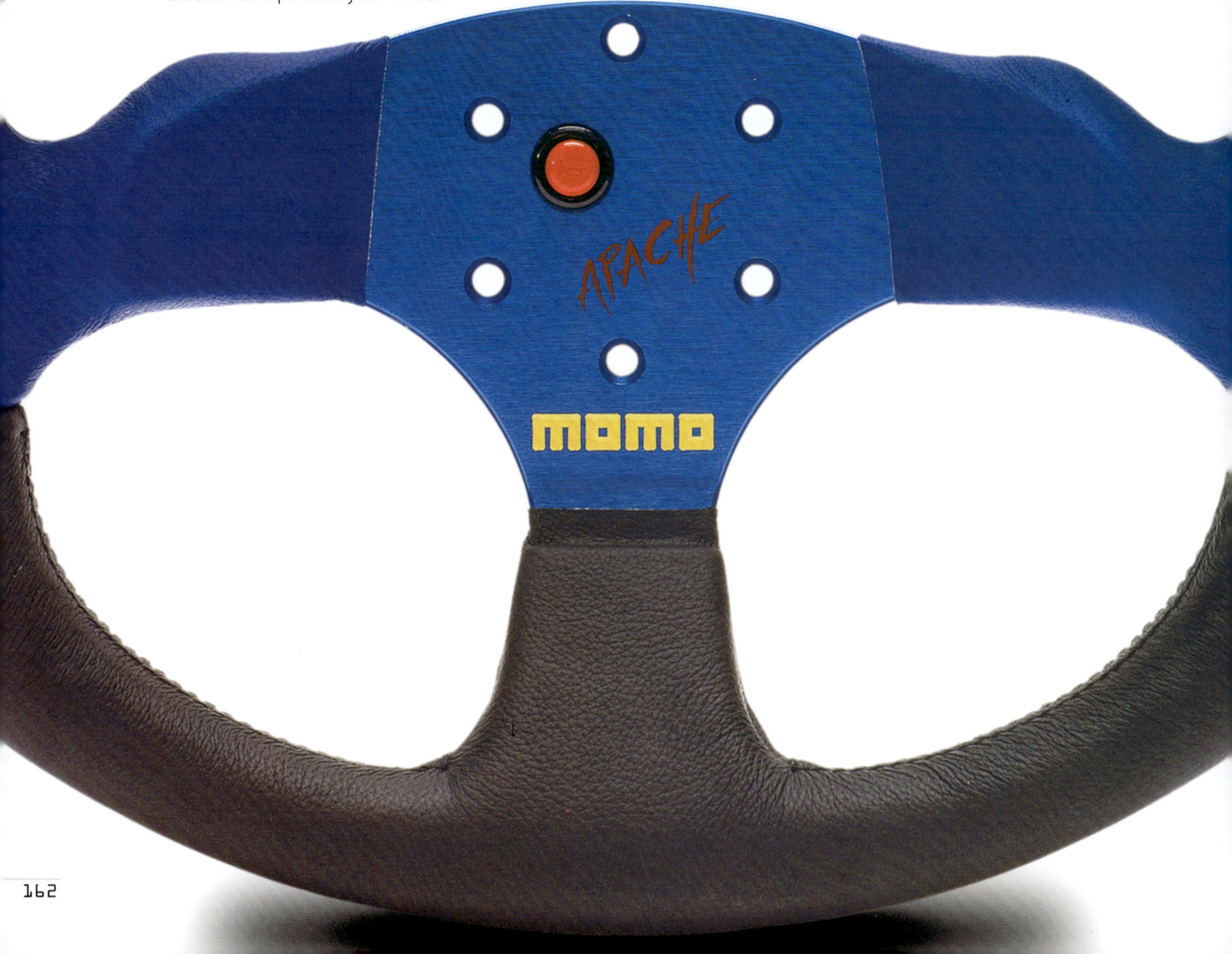

A word about **airbags**

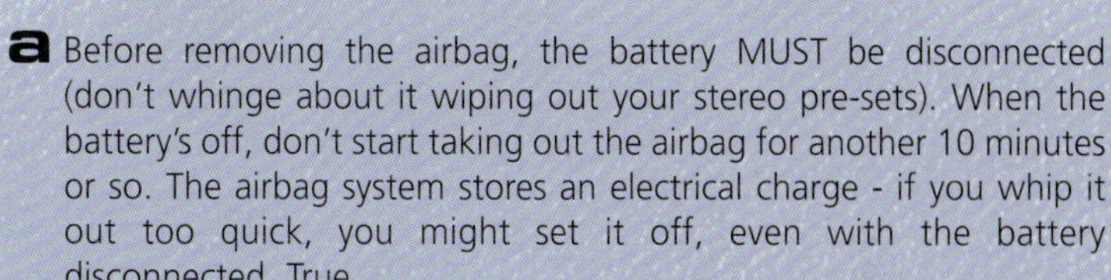

Some Mk6, and all Mk7 Escorts will have a driver's airbag fitted to the original wheel. So far, the market for replacement wheels with airbags hasn't materialised, so fitting your tasty new wheel means losing what some (old) people think is a valuable safety feature. So just disconnect the damn thing, right? Wrong.

Then your airbag warning light will be on permanently - not only is this irritating, your newly-modded motor will fail the MOT (having the airbag itself isn't compulsory, but if the warning light's on, it's a fail - at least at the time this was written). Two ways round this - either take out the clocks (see the section on fitting dials) and remove the offending warning light bulb, OR bridge the airbag connector plug pins with two lengths of wire attached to either side of a 5A fuse. Bridging the pins this way 'fools' the test circuit (which fires up every time you switch on the ignition) into thinking the airbag's still there, and the warning light will go out as it should.

Disabling the airbag is yet another issue which will interest your insurance company, so don't do it without consulting them first. We're just telling you, that's all.

Warning: Airbags are expensive to replace (several £100s), and are classed as an explosive!!! Funny, that - for a safety item, there's any number of ways they can CAUSE injuries or damage if you're not careful - check this lot out:

a Before removing the airbag, the battery MUST be disconnected (don't whinge about it wiping out your stereo pre-sets). When the battery's off, don't start taking out the airbag for another 10 minutes or so. The airbag system stores an electrical charge - if you whip it out too quick, you might set it off, even with the battery disconnected. True.

b When the airbag's out, it must be stored the correct way up.

c The airbag is sensitive to impact - dropping it from sufficient height might set it off. Even if dropping it doesn't actually set it off, it probably won't work again, anyway. By the way, once an airbag's gone off, it's scrap. You can't stuff it back inside.

d If you intend to keep the airbag with a view to refitting it at some stage (like when you sell the car), store it in a cool place - but bear in mind that the storage area must be suitable, so that if the airbag went off by accident, it would not cause damage to anything or anyone. Sticking it under your bed might not be such a good idea.

e If you're not keeping the airbag, it must be disposed of correctly (don't just put it out for the bin men!). Contact your local authority for advice.

f Airbags must not be subjected to temperatures in excess of 90°C (194°F) - just remember that bit about airbags being an explosive - you don't store dynamite in a furnace, now do you? Realistically in this country, the only time you'll get that hot is in a paint-drying oven.

Removing an Escort airbag

Our Mk6 XR3i didn't have an airbag, but we're not leaving you poor guys with them out in the cold. First, in case you hadn't already got the message, disconnect that battery, then wait a while (like 10 minutes or so).

You can always use the time to undo the two screws holding the steering column top shroud on, and removing the shroud. From straight-ahead, spin the wheel round about 90°, and you should be able to feel one screw hole in the back of the steering wheel. The Torx screw is well-recessed inside this hole, and might well be tight. Undo the first screw, then spin the wheel through 180° and remove the other one.

All you have to do now is lift the airbag unit out of the wheel, and disconnect the yellow wiring plug behind.

Fitting a **sports wheel**

01 Escorts without airbags have it easy. Prise out the horn push . . .

02 . . . then simply pull the red and black wires from their connectors. It's not unknown for the Escort horn push to give trouble (like suddenly coming on permanently, which is a bit embarrassing), so you might be familiar with this bit already.

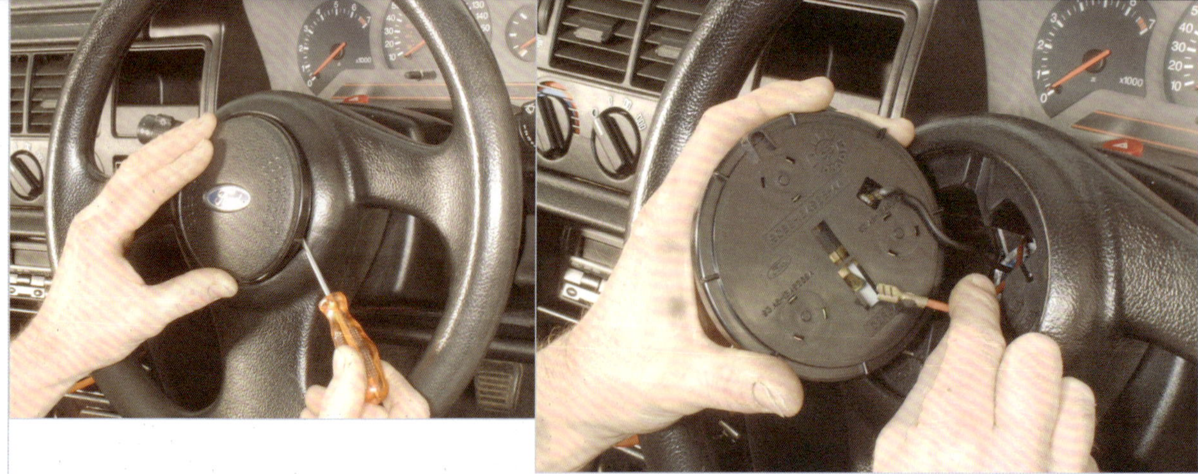

03 Getting the old wheel off is a bit of a challenge. Using a 22mm socket and bar, remove the bolt. Hold onto the wheel to stop it turning while you undo the bolt - don't just let the steering lock take the strain, as you might bust it. Before you go much further, make sure that the steering wheel's straight - as confirmation, look to see that the front wheels are pointing straight-ahead.

04 If you're lucky, the wheel will pull off its splines without effort. But with an old Ford, life's never that simple. If you're struggling, first put the bolt back on, but only by a few threads (to stop the wheel smacking you in the face when it finally gives up). Then persuade it free.

05 Lay the wheel face down and remove the indicator self-cancelling ring, which is held on by three screws. This ring also acts as the horn contact plate, so we'll be needing it again.

06 Now to your new boss (unlike the one at work, you can't possibly hate this one, it's your friend). Using the three old screws you removed earlier, fit the self-cancelling ring to the new boss, then feed the two horn wires through (one through each hole).

07 This Momo boss comes with a lovely rubber cover, which you just slip on - you know, for extra protection. Or something. You know, fitting a steering wheel is very much like making love to a beautiful woman...

08 Check that the front wheels are still straight, then fit the new wheel boss, with the 'TOP' mark - duh-uh - at the top!

09 Firstly, finger-tighten the wheel bolt so you can feel when the boss locates and centralises itself on the splines. Try and keep the wheel on straight - there's nothing more annoying than fitting it one spline out.

10 Place your new sexy steering wheel onto the boss, making sure the horn wires go through the hole in the middle and don't get crushed. Many companies use Torx screws to attach the wheel to the boss, so get to it - tighten those screws!

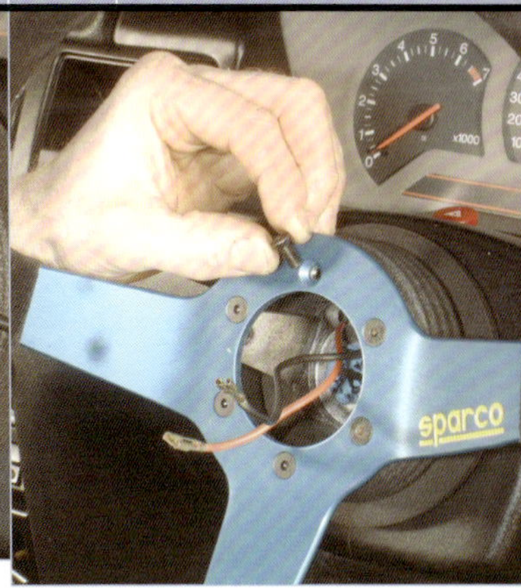

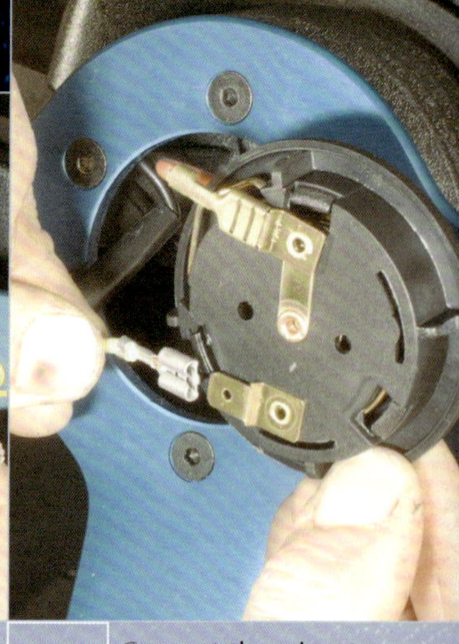

11 Now that you've got a wheel to hold onto again, you can tighten the wheel bolt - 50 Nm if you've got a wrench. If you haven't, do it up as if your life depended on it... which of course, it does! Again, don't rely on the steering lock to tighten against, or you'll bust it. It would be a terrific idea to fit a **new** bolt.

12 The Sparco wheel from Demon Tweeks came with an odd-looking piece of black wire, and now's the time to use it. The red and black horn wires we removed earlier have different size connectors on the ends. The Ford red wire is the daddy, but the black is a wiener in comparison. Size matters - and the new wire sorts us out.

13 Connect the wires to the horn plate on the new wheel. The red wire fits to the connector plate feeding the middle of the wheel.

14 Press the horn plate into the wheel . . .

15 . . . and add the shiny sticker as a finishing touch. Speaking of touch, you won't beat the feeling of running your hands over this sexy little number. Suede-covered wheel rims do it for us.

Pedalling your Escort

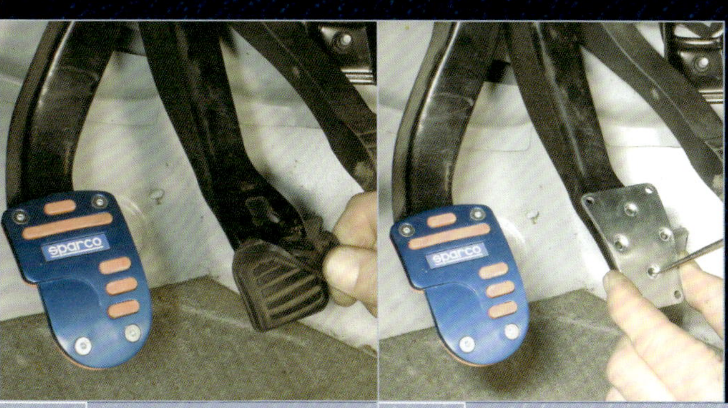

Ford cars often have nasty cheapo pedals, so it's a must to change them, and it's so simple to do.

Aftermarket pedals are a great way of making your motor look trick. They're inexpensive and are available in lots of cool colours - match the colour scheme of your interior, and the better it looks, the more the ladies will want to ride with you! Why not ring Demon Tweeks to request a catalogue? We did, and we have some very sexy Sparco pedals to show for it.

Achtung!

Check your insurance company's position regarding pedal extensions. A while ago there was a big fuss after a couple of cars fitted with pedal extensions crashed, which resulted in pedal extensions being withdrawn from sale at a lot of places.

01 Just to prove how easy this whole process is, our mechanic fitted the clutch pedal extension all on his own. But we stopped him with the brake pedal. The clutch and brake pedals have rubber covers, which just peel off. For safety, your new extensions should also be non-slip, or the MOT crew will have something to say. For drilled extensions, try sourcing some little rubber grommets from a motor factors (or just don't buy any extensions that don't come with them in the first place).

02 Place the metal backplate on the brake pedal, and hold in place while you mark the holes ready for drilling.

03 Drilling through the plates into the pedals means there's less chance of mucking it up. But we're feeling lucky. Placing an old piece of wood behind the pedal means there's less chance of drilling the carpet. But we haven't got any.

04 The backplates are held on by four Allen bolts, with nuts fitted behind. The more observant among you may have noticed we could only drill three out of four holes in our Escort pedal, owing to the rather large hole fitted to the pedal as standard! Still, three bolts will do the job.

05 Place the gorgeous extension on top of the pedal . . .

06 . . . and using the same Allen key and spanner, tighten the four nuts and bolts. The same process is also applied to the loud pedal, except there's no rubber cover to start with. Every so often, check that the nuts and bolts are still tight.

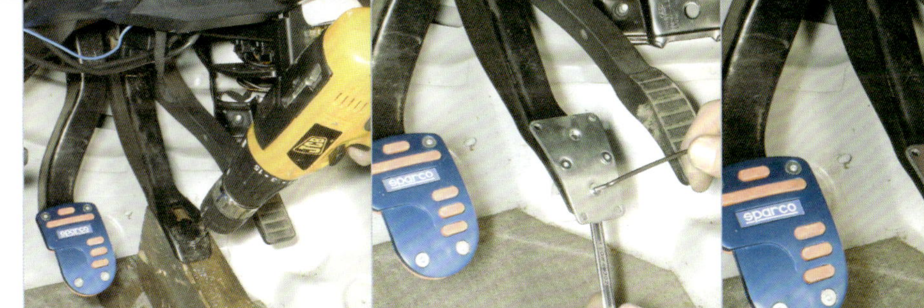

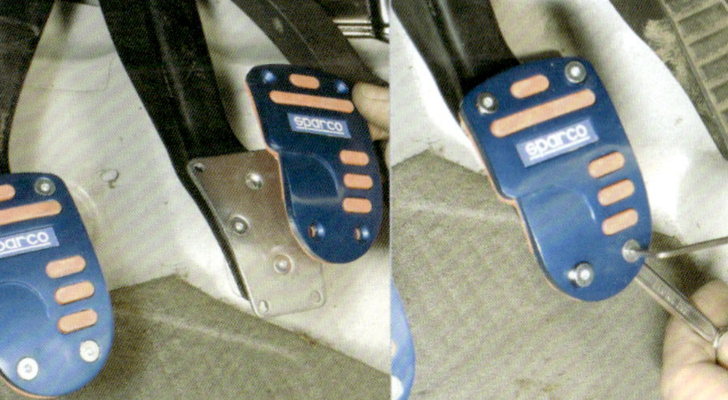

Tips n' tricks!

It's a good idea at this point to put all the pedals in place using Blu-tac or tape to ensure that the spacing between the pedals is ok. By doing this, the pedals won't look pants and more importantly, you won't hit the juice and the brakes at the same time – d'oh!

Are you **sitting stylishly?**

The perfect complement to your lovingly-sorted suspension, because you need something better than the standard seats to hold you in, now that you can corner so much faster... and they look brutal, by way of a bonus. Besides the seat itself, remember to price up the subframe to adapt it to the mounting points in your car. Most people also choose the three- or four-point harnesses to go with it (looks a bit daft to fit a racing seat without it), but make sure the harness you buy is EC-approved, or an eagle-eyed MOT tester might make you take 'em out.

Reclining seats are pricier than non-recliners, but are worth the extra. With non-adjustable seats, how are your mates meant to get in the back? Through the tailgate? Or maybe there is no back seat... You can get subframes which tilt, so that non-reclining seats can move forward. Non-reclining racing seats should be tried for fit before you buy.

An alternative to expensive racing seats would be to have your existing seats re-upholstered in your chosen colours/fabrics, to match your interior theme. You might be surprised what's possible, and the result could be something truly unique. If you've got a basic model, try sourcing RS or XR seats from a breakers. A secondhand interior bought here will be a lot cheaper than buying new goodies, and you know it'll fit easily (all Escorts are the same underneath) - but - it won't have that unique style. Specialist breakers may be able to supply something more rad, such as a wicked leather interior from a top-spec Mondeo/Granada - might take some persuading to get it in, though!

01 If your Escort has an airbag, bad luck - you've also got seat belt tensioners. Some Escorts have mechanical tensioners, while later cars have electronically-triggered units. To be on the safe side, you should disconnect the battery and wait two minutes before proceeding. Removing the front chairs is easy - remove all the bolts . . .

02 . . . and lift them out. Check before lifting the seat that there aren't any wires attached underneath.

03 The back seat removal process isn't hard either - in front of the seat cushion, there's a screw each side . . .

04 . . . then the cushion unclips at the back edge, and lifts out.

Removing **seats**

05 Once the cushion's gone, the backrests are a doddle - unscrew the backrests from the hinges . . .

06 . . . remove the backrests from the car . . .

07 . . . then remove the hinges from the floor.

Fitting new **Corbeaus**

We had a bit of a challenge fitting our Corbeau Pro-Series seats - because they were too sporty! Being proper race buckets, they don't come with Escort subframes, which gave us some head-scratching. We decided to mount them on the old front chair bases, so these had to come off first. Under

01 the front of the seat are two large crosshead screws . . .

02 . . . which is all that's holding the seat cushion in place. Bit scary, that.

03 With the seat cushion removed, there's a bolt at each corner holding the seat base in place.

04 Lifting away the 'scrap' part of the seat, we're left with a base we can adapt for our splendid new blue babies.

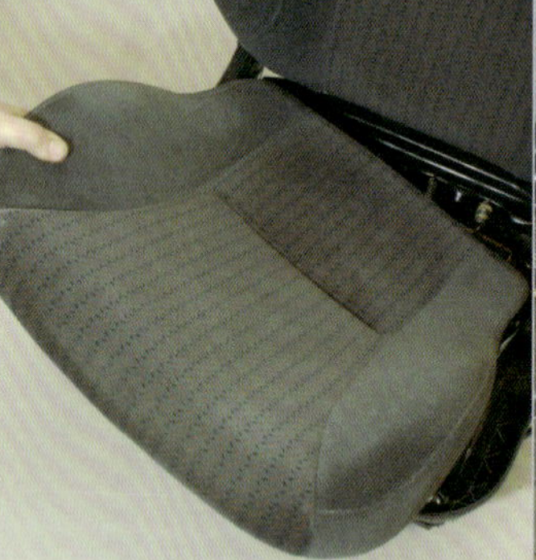

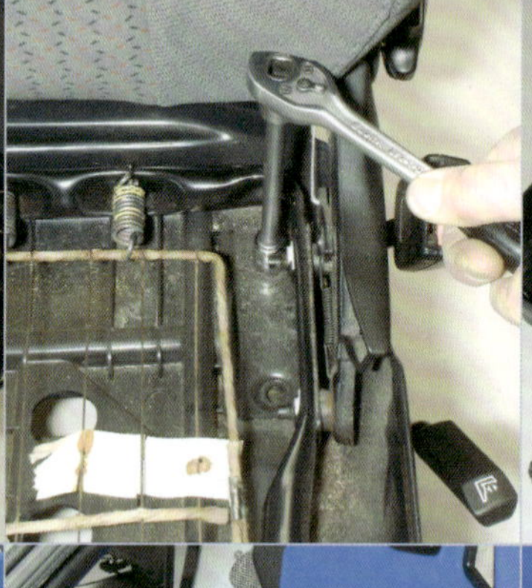

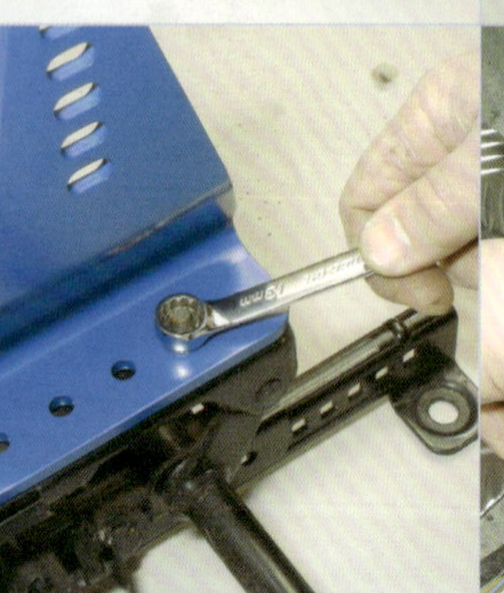

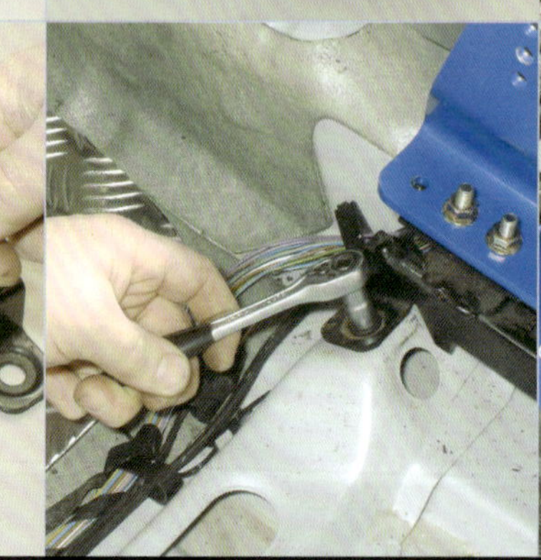

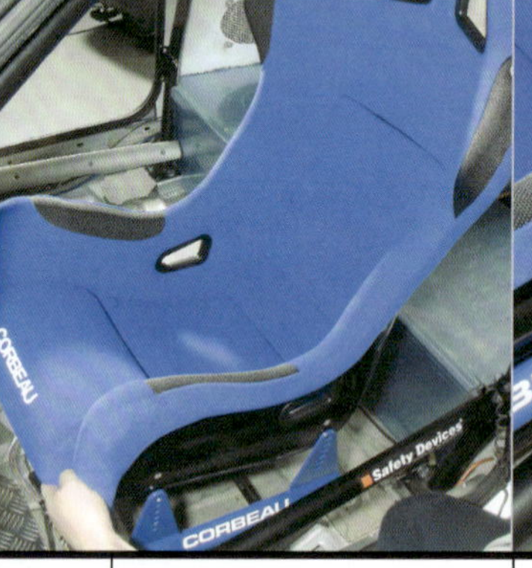

05 These race seats come with two side-mounts, which you're supposed to drill and mount direct to the car floor - not easy on an Escort, since the floor's not flat. Our method means bolting the side mounts to the old Escort seat base, which is only easy if the holes in both items line up. But then, you're not afraid of a little drilling (unless it's at the dentist). Just use decent bolts, and tighten them like you mean it.

06 Now we're bolting our adapted Escort bases to the floor. The mounting bolts are, of course, the old ones you took out. Which are probably rusty as hell, so treat them to some copper grease, instead of just bunging them straight back in. The bolts should really be tightened using a torque wrench (25 Nm), but if you haven't got one handy, just do them up good 'n' tight.

07 At last, a proper look at these very proper Corbeau buckets. Worth all the trouble we've gone to, to make them fit? Hell yes. Lesser seats will give you an easier time, with custom-made subframes which just bolt to the seat and the Escort floor with almost no effort. But, as with so much else in modding, the look you get is proportional to the work you put in.

08 The side mounts use two large Allen bolts to fix them to the seats. No torque given for these, but we don't want them coming undone... And the verdict? As you'd expect , really - top looks, top quality, and they even manage to be comfortable (while still pinning you in place like an upholstered vice, of course).

How strapped are you?

It's true that not everyone likes racing harnesses, but the majority of those who don't are boring. You don't fit sexy race seats and then not fit race belts, do you?

The only problem with harnesses is caused by where you have to mount them. Even with a three-point harness, you end up using one of the rear seat belt mounts, and it seriously reduces your ability to carry bodies in the back seats (webbing everywhere). The MOT crew say that, if you've got rear seats, you must have rear seat belts fitted, so you either 'double-up' on your rear belt mounts (use the same mounts for your harnesses and rear belts), or you take the back seats out altogether. Removing the rear seats leaves the rear deck free for chequerplate, speakers, roll cages - whatever you like. It's just important to understand how fundamental harnesses can end up being, to the whole look of your car - there's almost no half-measures with race belts, so you've got to really want 'em.

One thing you must **not** do is to try making up your own seat belt/harness mounting points. Ford structural engineers spent plenty of time selecting mounting points and testing them for strength. Drilling your own holes and sticking bolts through is fine for mounting speakers and stuff, but you're heading for an interview with the Grim Reaper if you try it with seat belts. The forces in a big shunt are immense. We're not convinced either that the practice of slinging harnesses round a rear strut brace is kosher, from the safety angle - the poxy strut braces available are so flimsy (they're usually ally) you can bend them in your hands. Nuts to trusting MY life to one of those!

Removing seat belts

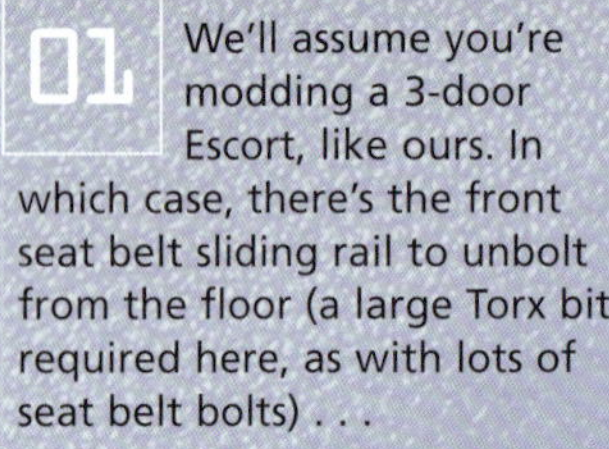

01 We'll assume you're modding a 3-door Escort, like ours. In which case, there's the front seat belt sliding rail to unbolt from the floor (a large Torx bit required here, as with lots of seat belt bolts) . . .

02 . . . then the rear end unhooks from the floor, and you can slip off the end of the belt.

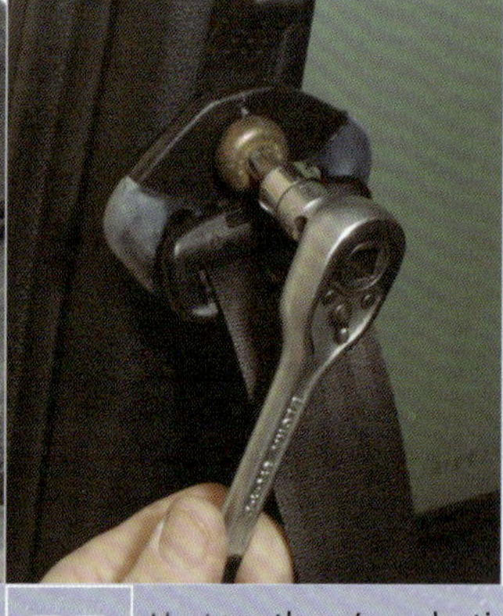

03 Up top, there's a plastic cover over the belt upper mounting, which flicks off, revealing a reassuringly-large bolt underneath.

04 Work round the edges of the rear side panel, and release all the clips holding it on. With the panel folded down, the seat belt reel is within sight.

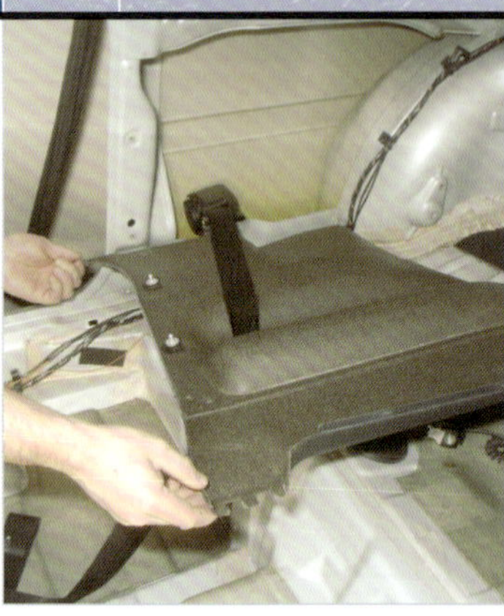

05 Unbolt and remove the belt reel, then release the belt from the trim panel (there's a removable plastic clip for this).

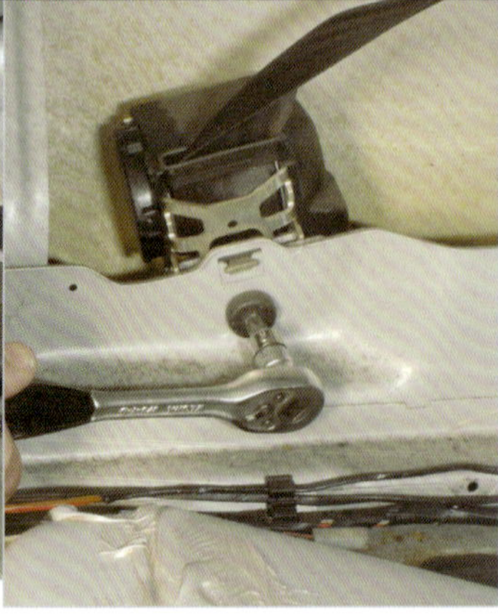

06 Removing the rear seat belt involves plenty of dismantling, too. The belt reel itself unbolts easily enough.

07 No great brain power needed to remove the rear seat belt buckles (or the front seat belt stalks, come to that) - they just unbolt, leaving you with an ideal mounting point for the new harnesses.

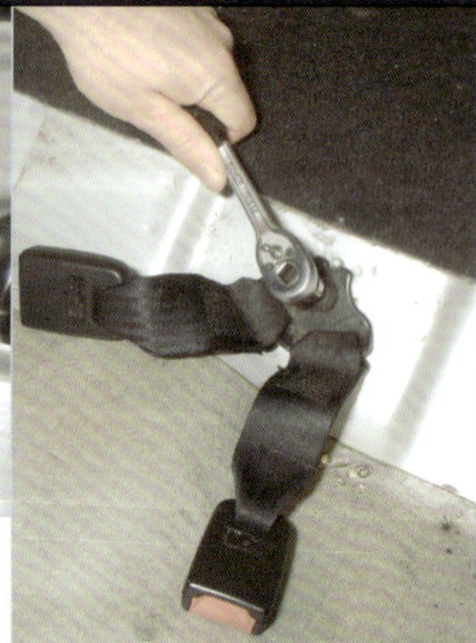

Harnesses

01 Fitting the new harnesses is a walk in the park, compared to taking out the naff old belts. The harnesses clip onto 'eyes', which you screw in, in place of the old seat belt bolts. This means you'll be using the hole for the old seat belt stalk, next to the centre console . . .

02 . . . as well as the old belt outer rail mounting hole, by the door sill (you'll also need both pairs of rear belt mounts, for a four-point harness). The only trick is tightening the eyes sufficiently to be safe - they must go in all the way down to the shoulder. Use an adjustable spanner to help with final tightening, as shown.

03 Hooking-on the new harness is made very easy by the spring-loaded tag which you pull back. These are some quality Luke harnesses, looking very saucy in silver, supplied by our friends at Corbeau seats.

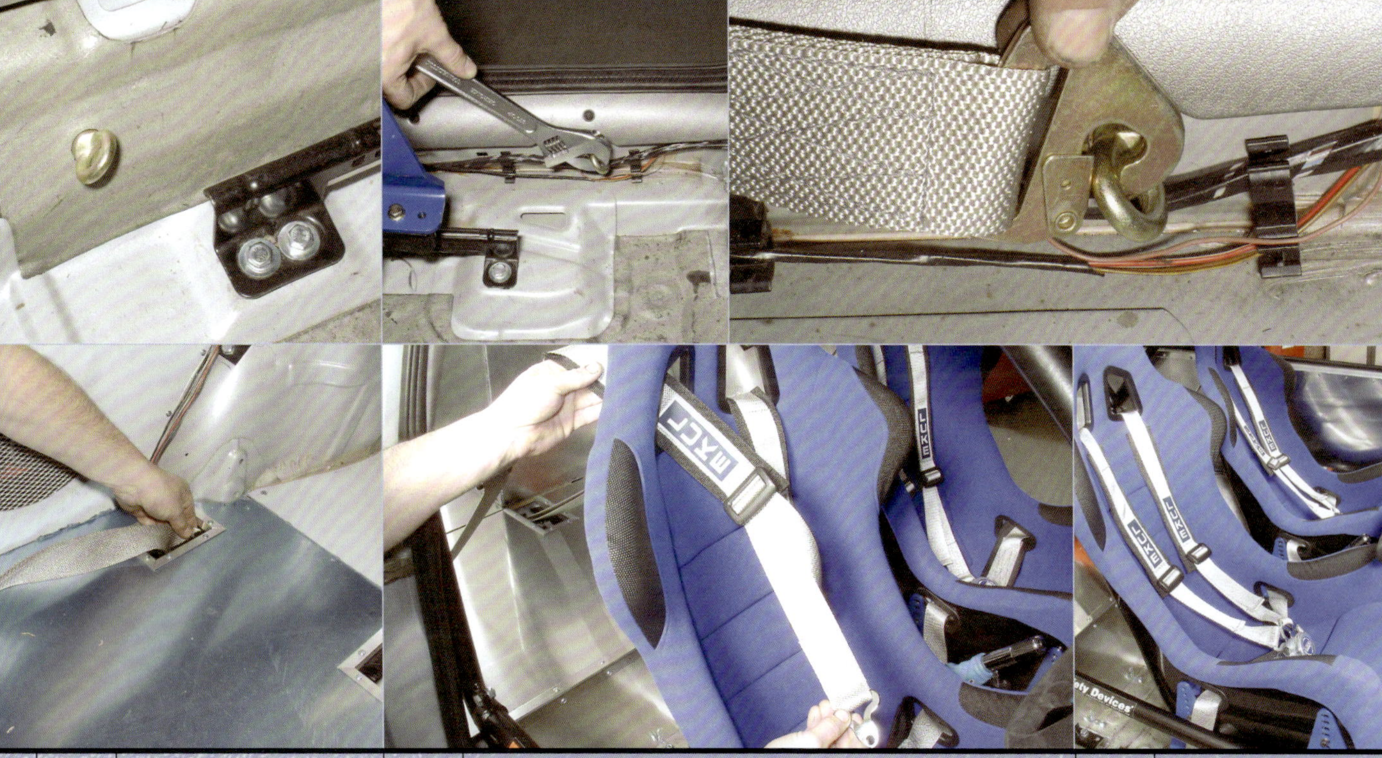

04 Our race-look Escort has an alloy rear floor - we cut holes for the harness rear mounting points, but didn't stop there. A trip to the local DIY store later, we had some brush-type letterbox draught excluders, and it's the black brushes you see here, used as edging on the holes. Looks trick, saves fraying the belts on a metal edge.

05 Oh, so that's what the big holes in the tops of the seats are for... Feed the belts through . . .

06 . . . and connect them together. That's what a race car looks like.

Keep rollin', rollin'

A rollcage is essential equipment for the 'motorsport' look - full-on sports seats and harnesses look a bit half-hearted without a cage to back them up. The same way a strut brace works for the front suspension, a rollcage stiffens up the rest of the bodyshell, as well as providing all-important protection should you lose it big-time and stick your Escort on its roof (not that we advise trying out this theory). None of this really matters, though - we fit cages 'cos they look well-'ard.

One word of warning - test the water with your insurance company before rushing out and fitting a cage. The sad fact is, most insurance companies do not like rollcages. Surely only someone who drives like Colin McRae needs a cage?

No weedy 'show-cage' for us (though these are easier to fit). Our totally pukka cage came from cage maestros Safety Devices - properly fitted, it's fully up to pro motorsport standards. So there. They do various standard cages for Escorts (ours is a six-point cage, with rear diagonal and removable door bars), but if it's a cage you want, they'll make anything to your own spec.

01 If you want a proper cage, you've got some work to do. A cage deserves to be fitted right, so pay attention. The carpets and sound-deadening have to go (though you could refit these afterwards). We have to weld in a cage mounting plate just inside the B-pillars, so even the tar-like floor covering has to be chipped away to the bare metal.

02 Mark round the mounting plate . . .

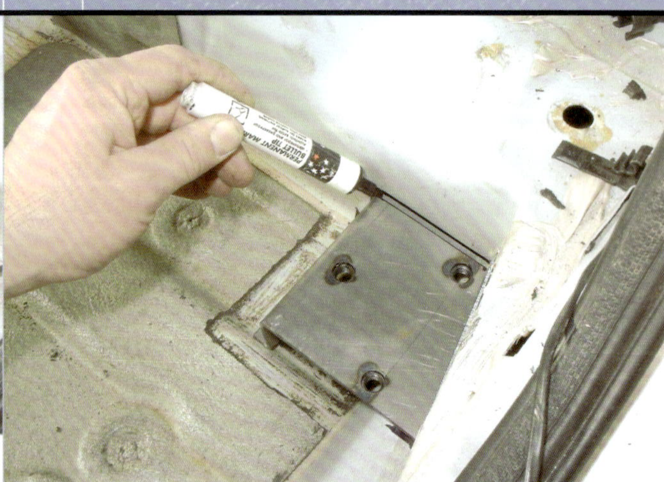

03 . . . then use the line to clean off the paint - a Dremel tool is a great labour-saver here (we're using the Draper equivalent.

04 The sooner the cage actually goes in, the better - and it's not a straightforward job (especially if, unlike our car, most of your interior trim's still there). One vital point, on a six-point cage - as soon as the main cage section is in, loosely fit both the front bars, which run round the doors. Once the main section's fully bolted in, the front bars won't fit.

05 You don't strictly need a welder this size to do the job, so we're just showing off really. That's 230 amps of welding power . . .

06 . . . so mind your eyes, lads. Obviously, you'll have disconnected your battery, and maybe also unplugged your alternator and the injection ECU, if you have one (behind the passenger footwell kick panel).

07 Only the B-pillar mounting points need plates welding-in (for road use) - the rest of the install is a more conventional drill-and-bolt approach. Just make sure everything's absolutely lined up before you go drilling big holes in your Escort rear wheel wells . . .

08 . . . and down in the front footwells, too. Any unintentional holes you happen to spot will need attention with the welder, while you've got it out.

09 Those girly grab-handles get in the way of the front bars, which run round the doors to the front floor, so they've got to go.

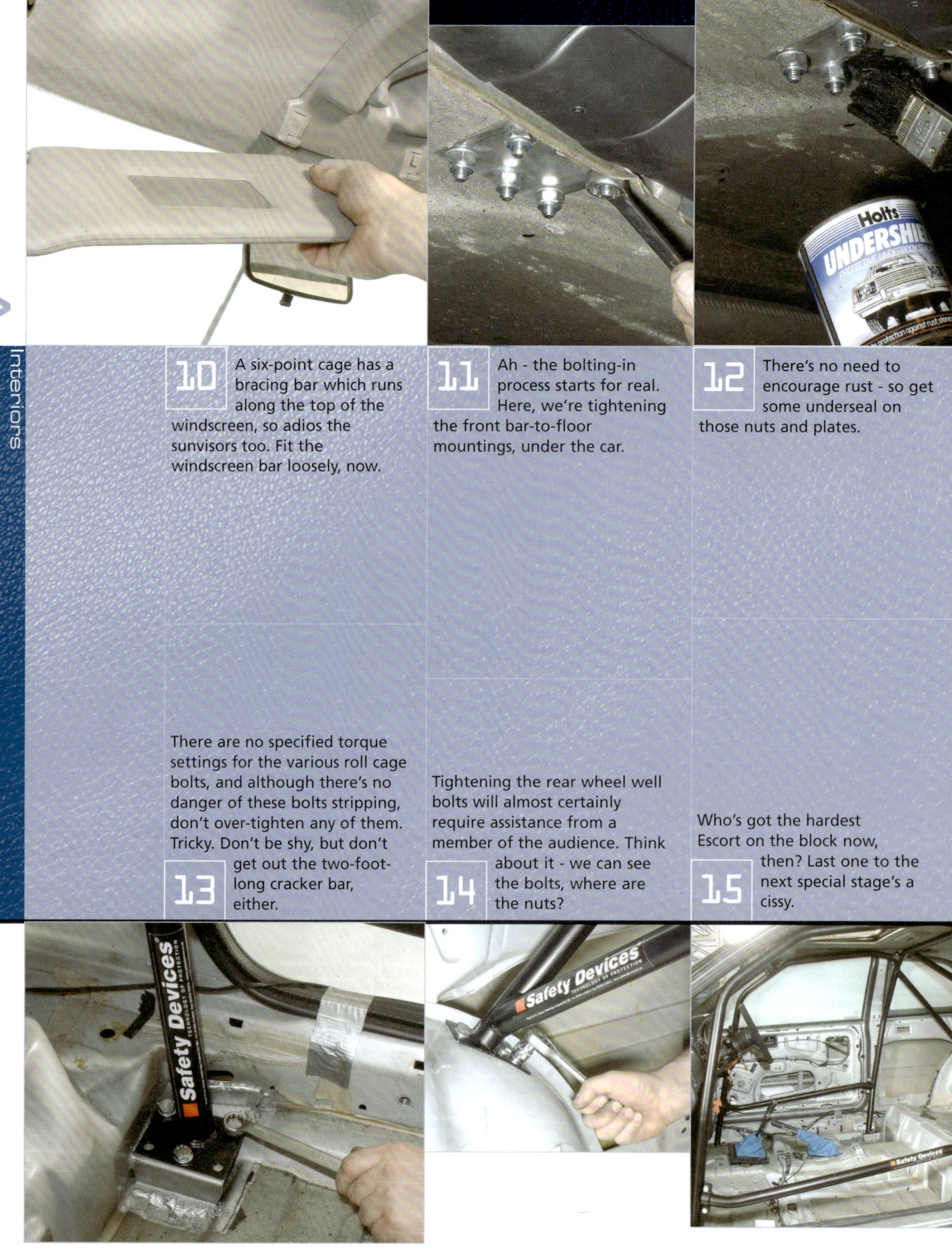

10 A six-point cage has a bracing bar which runs along the top of the windscreen, so adios the sunvisors too. Fit the windscreen bar loosely, now.

11 Ah - the bolting-in process starts for real. Here, we're tightening the front bar-to-floor mountings, under the car.

12 There's no need to encourage rust - so get some underseal on those nuts and plates.

13 There are no specified torque settings for the various roll cage bolts, and although there's no danger of these bolts stripping, don't over-tighten any of them. Tricky. Don't be shy, but don't get out the two-foot-long cracker bar, either.

14 Tightening the rear wheel well bolts will almost certainly require assistance from a member of the audience. Think about it - we can see the bolts, where are the nuts?

15 Who's got the hardest Escort on the block now, then? Last one to the next special stage's a cissy.

Fire **drill**

Looking for more inspiration for racing Escort must-haves? It's over to our friends at Safety Devices once again. Besides being masters of all things cage-y, this one-stop-shop for competition car safety also know fire extinguisher systems intimately. If you've done the race look, and removed the rear seats, that rear floor area could be looking a bit vacant right now. You might plan to fill it with ICE, but we chose fire.

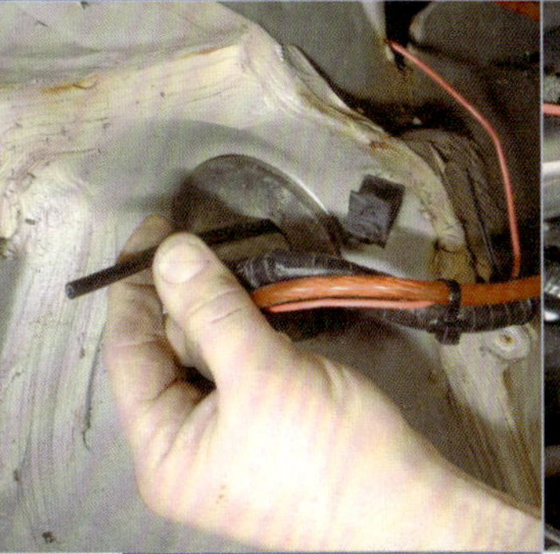

01 The extinguisher bottle has to be mounted in the car. This is the main 'pose' item for us, and it's also the easy bit. To make it work, the CO_2 gas has to be fed into the engine bay, through the armoured tubing supplied. Trickier, but not much - poke it through the same grommet under the wheelarch that we used for our eight-gauge ICE live feed.

02 You get two extinguisher nozzles with this kit - one for the main fuel area, and one for the ignition system. Once the black pipe's in place, feed it round to a point between these two underbonnet areas, and push on the T-piece connector.

03 You'll have to make up a couple of small mounting brackets for the nozzles (not hard). This is the one we've mounted just above our Escort's fuel rail, receiving its section of pipe, which joins back to one side of the T-piece. Fit and connect up the other nozzle, and that's the story under the bonnet - what's inside the car?

04 To trigger the system, proper rally cars have at least one pull-cable fitted to the front wing, but that was a bit much, even for us. Being non-smokers, we decided to do without the fag lighter, and fitted our cable in the resulting hole, using a home-made circle of alloy, and a nut or two, to secure it in place.

05 That extinguisher looks the real deal to us. With the black CO_2 gas pipe already attached, it only requires the trigger cable fitting . . .

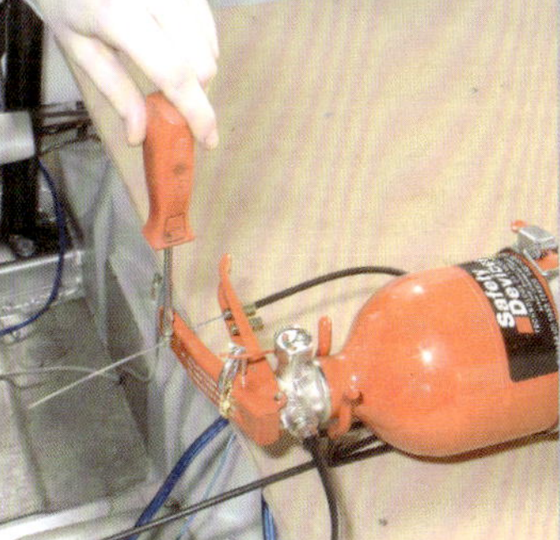

06 . . . and the bottle cage mounting in place. Is your gas pipe long enough to reach to the back seat area, or will you have to mount the bottle under the passenger seat? Bit of a shame to hide it down there...

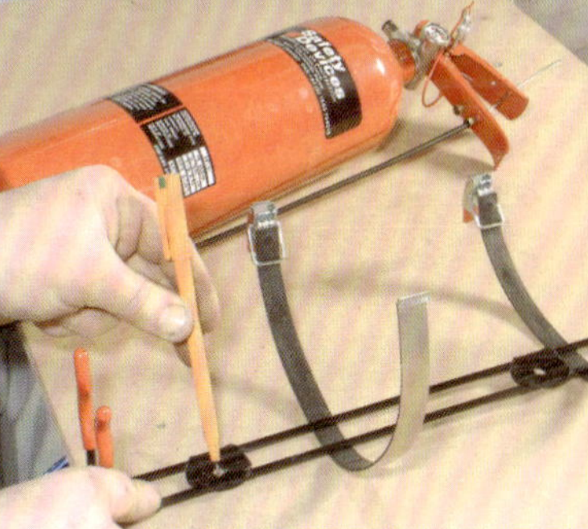

ICE Headset

The cheaper your Escort, the nastier your standard head unit's going to be. Of course, by the time an Escort's passed through several owners, it's pretty unlikely to still have a standard Ford radio in anyway, but if all you've got is a hole, don't feel too bad. Standard sets are fine if all you want to do is aimlessly listen to the radio with your arm out the window, but not - definitely not - if you want to impress your mates with the depth and volume of your bass.

Or, of course, if you want to listen to CDs. It's got to go - and there's plenty of decent headsets out there which will give you a night-and-day difference in sound quality and features.

The headset is the heart of your new install - always go for the best you can afford. Ask the experts which features matter most, if you're building a full system.

Our Kenwood 5021 headset was supplied by Optima of Bristol, and is pretty typical of the current single-CD state of the art - looks decent, good sound, plenty of features. So far, so Kenwood.

01 First, the old set's got to be shifted. Resist the urge to just crowbar the thing out of the dash - you'll be needing two of the standard radio removal tools to do the job with less damage. And you could always sell it, or keep it, to stick back in when you sell the car.

02 Don't just rip out all the old set's wiring - some of it could be useful. This though, is one plug we'd never seen before - it's for the standard Ford amplifier (our XR3i had the Premium sound system fitted, apparently). If yours is like this, it means your standard speaker wiring's mostly tucked up under the passenger footwell, with the amp itself.

03 Told you we could re-use some of that wiring - our 1993 Escort didn't have the now-standard ISO plugs fitted, but yours might. Ripspeed (and others) sell adaptor plugs like this, which take some of the hassle out of wiring-up. One of the ISO plugs does power, the other speakers - the power one has red, yellow and black leads (among others). If you're not using any of the stock speaker wire, you don't need to connect the other ISO plug.

04 See how easy this is? Using the adaptor means there's no butchering the stock wiring, or damaging the ISO loom which comes with the new headset. You just plug it in. Then, when you shift the car on, the old set can just be plugged straight back into its original wiring. Bonus.

05 To complete this part of the wiring-up, the headset's ISO loom gets plugged into the back of the new set. Simple so far.

06 Look at that mass of wiring. But our man's doing the right thing, and consulting the manual. Well, it's a lot better than blowing up your headset.

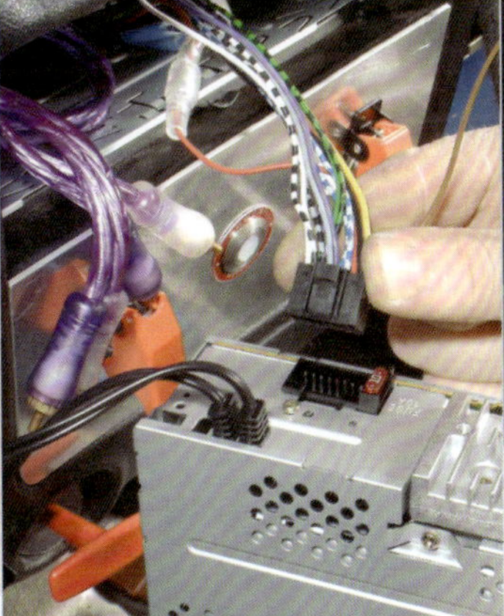

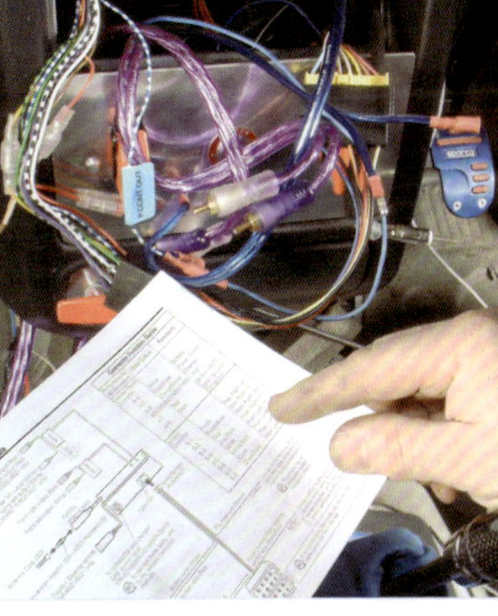

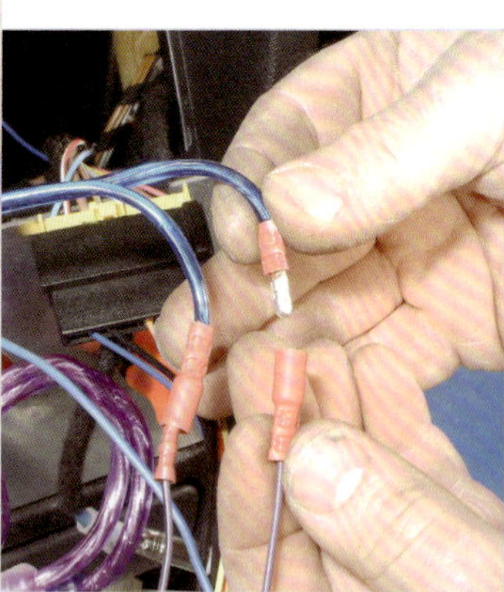

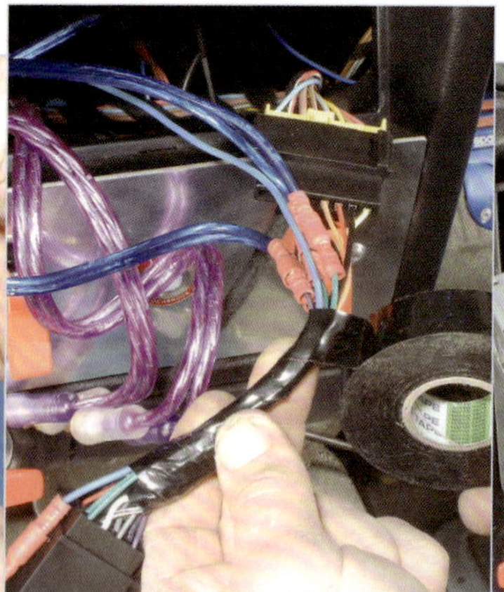

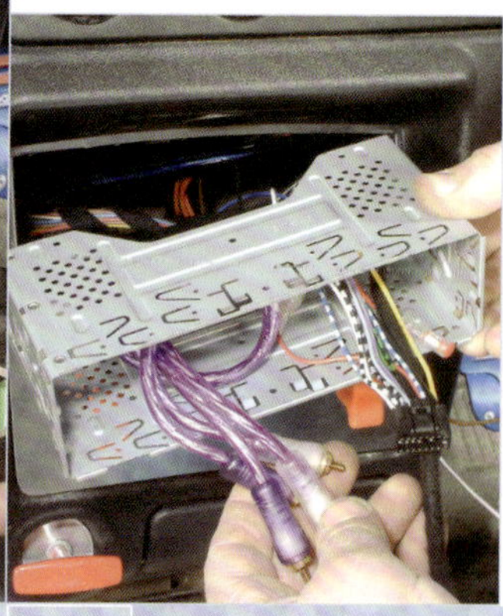

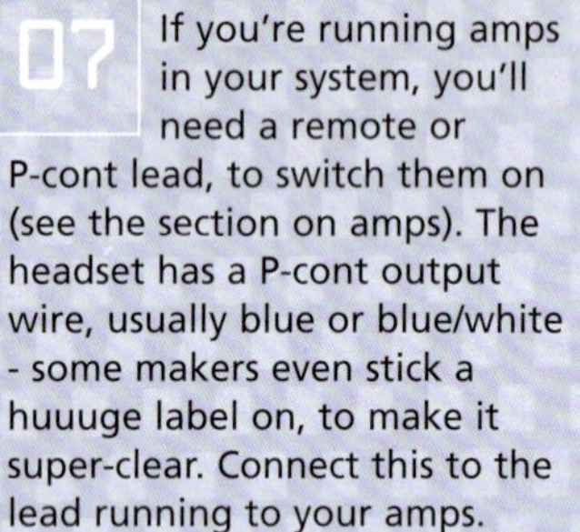

07 If you're running amps in your system, you'll need a remote or P-cont lead, to switch them on (see the section on amps). The headset has a P-cont output wire, usually blue or blue/white - some makers even stick a huuuge label on, to make it super-clear. Connect this to the lead running to your amps.

08 We're running a pair of 6x9s straight off the headset, to give a rear fill to the sound. This means connecting our oxygen-free speaker wire direct to the rear channel wires on the headset - or in our case, direct to the correct wires on the adaptor we plugged in earlier. The adaptor's black striped wires are negative, and the oxygen-free's 'writing' wire's positive, for I.D. purposes.

09 Rather than just stuff it all into the dash, it's more satisfying to 'loom' some of the speaker wiring with tape first. It's also less likely to give trouble later, if it's neatly bundled-up. Just a bit of a pain if you find something's wired-up wrong, that's all. So don't do it wrong.

10 Before getting too carried away with all the wiring, remember there's a new cage to be fitted - no, you can't just use the old one. Feed through all the wires required, and slide the new cage in place - try not to distort it as it goes in.

11 To make sure it doesn't just slide out again (which slightly defeats the idea of having special security removal tools), you need to bend up the cage securing lugs, to pin it inside the radio hole in the dash. Don't bend them all up - just two top and bottom, and one each side, will do the job nicely.

12 Those amps of yours need a signal to work from, and that's what the RCA outputs on the headset provide. Red is for Right, usually, but on these trendy purple RCAs, we're relying on white-to-white as a guide. Also, don't forget the aerial lead... common mistake... or your CD changer lead, maybe...

13 It's not a bad idea to test that everything's working at this point, before pushing the unit right into its cage. If all's well, push the headset home until the cage clips click in. Sounds easy, but you'll almost certainly have to reach in behind the set, and straighten out the wiring before the set will go in. Do not force it in, or you could end up having a very bad day. Success! Now get out the instruction manual again, and set those levels properly. Enjoy.

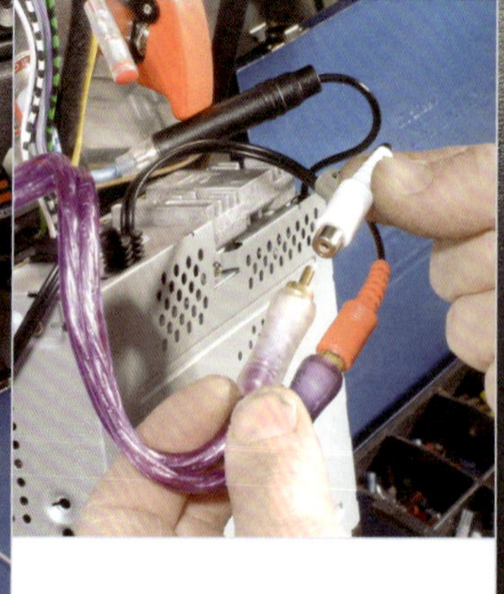

The standard items in the Escort speak volumes (hur-hur) about any car manufacturer's desire to build things down to a price - ie spend as little as poss. What does it cost Ford for the speakers in a Escort? If it's more than a fiver a set, they're being robbed. Low on power, and with nasty paper cones which disintegrate after a few years, fitting ANY aftermarket speakers is going to be an upgrade. But we don't want to give you that - how about showing you how to fit some tasty components?

Boss - the name's familiar, if you've ever shopped at the budget end of the market. But do not be fooled - Boss make several ranges, and until now, we've only seen the very cheapest range in the UK (for more info, check the DD Audio website - www.ddaudio.co.uk). These very tasty-looking items very obviously come from their more expensive range - so let's see if the sound matches the looks...

Front **speakers**

01 Once you've got the door trim panel off, and have removed (and burnt) the old speaker, it's time to think vibration. If you don't want all that kicking power to set your door panel tizzing, you need to invest in some sound-deadening. Yes, the market leader's Dynamat - but - it comes at a price. What else is out there? Brown Bread. Sounds dead. Clean up the door panel with some decent solvent . . .

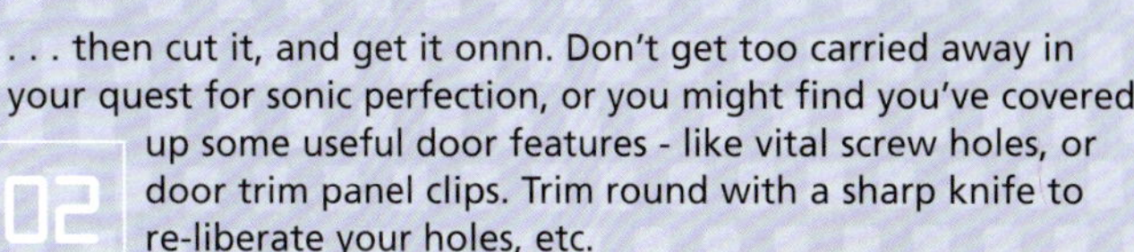

02 . . . then cut it, and get it onnn. Don't get too carried away in your quest for sonic perfection, or you might find you've covered up some useful door features - like vital screw holes, or door trim panel clips. Trim round with a sharp knife to re-liberate your holes, etc.

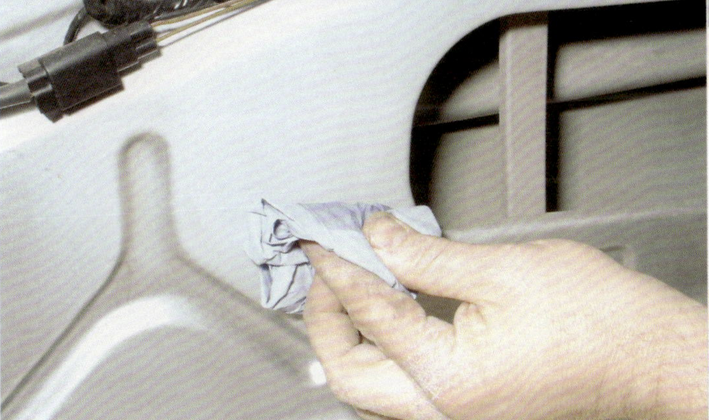

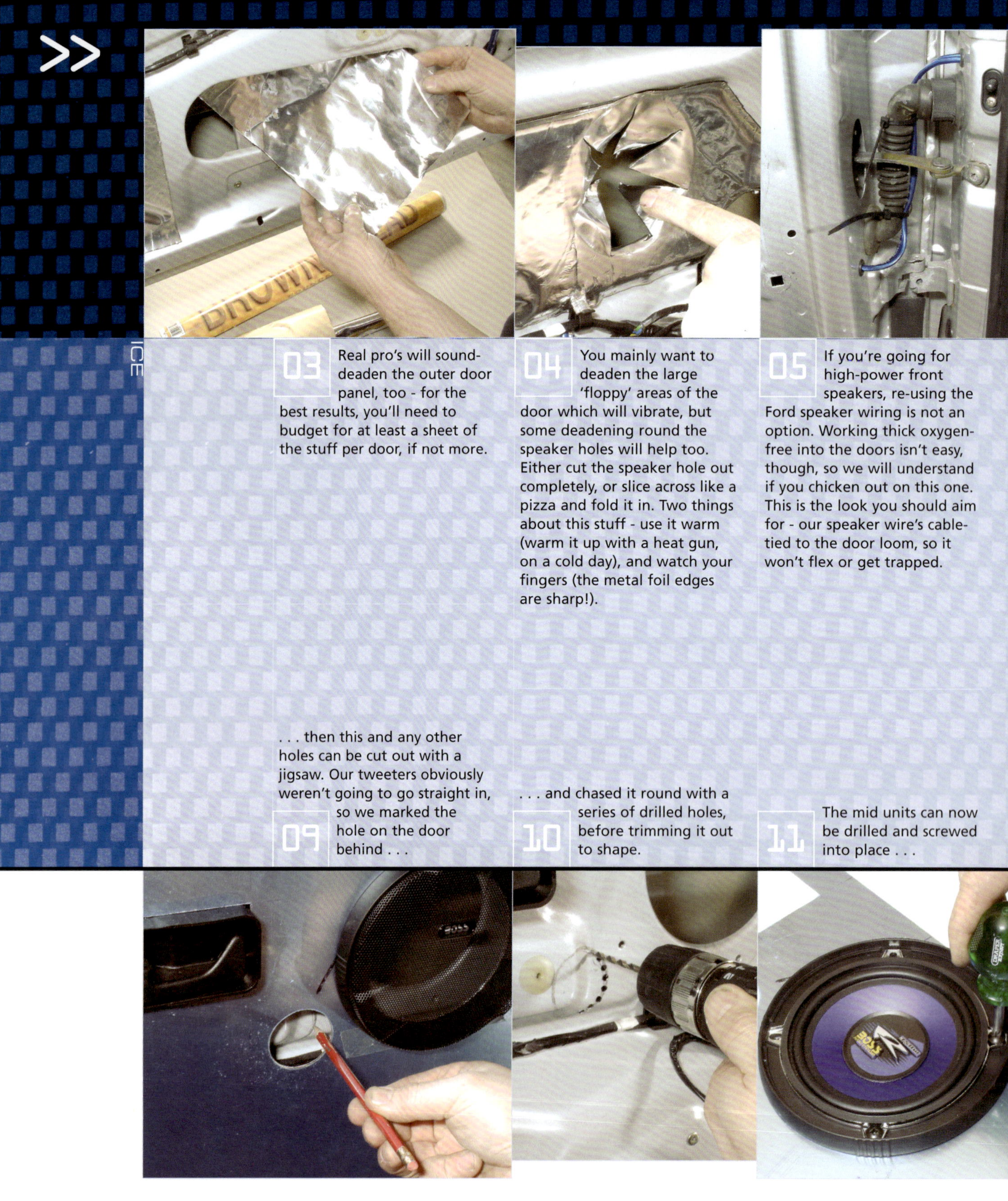

03 Real pro's will sound-deaden the outer door panel, too - for the best results, you'll need to budget for at least a sheet of the stuff per door, if not more.

04 You mainly want to deaden the large 'floppy' areas of the door which will vibrate, but some deadening round the speaker holes will help too. Either cut the speaker hole out completely, or slice across like a pizza and fold it in. Two things about this stuff - use it warm (warm it up with a heat gun, on a cold day), and watch your fingers (the metal foil edges are sharp!).

05 If you're going for high-power front speakers, re-using the Ford speaker wiring is not an option. Working thick oxygen-free into the doors isn't easy, though, so we will understand if you chicken out on this one. This is the look you should aim for - our speaker wire's cable-tied to the door loom, so it won't flex or get trapped.

09 . . . then this and any other holes can be cut out with a jigsaw. Our tweeters obviously weren't going to go straight in, so we marked the hole on the door behind . . .

10 . . . and chased it round with a series of drilled holes, before trimming it out to shape.

11 The mid units can now be drilled and screwed into place . . .

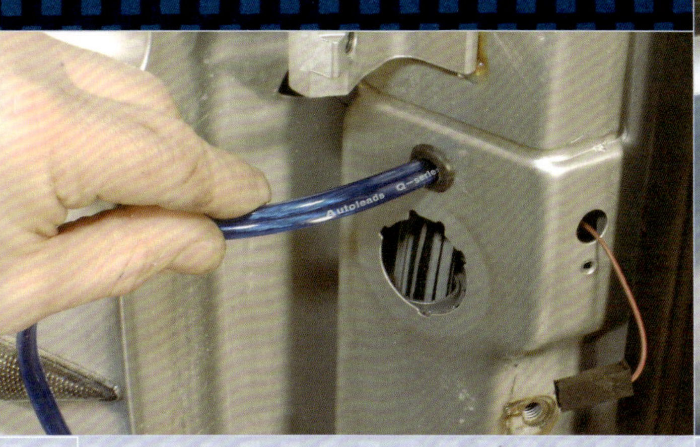

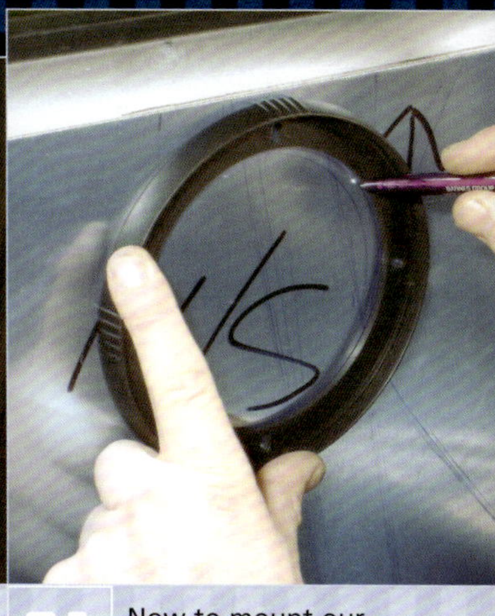

06 Drilling holes in the A-pillar for door speaker wiring is much easier with those pesky doors out of the way - and removing them isn't hard (see your trusty Haynes manual for details). While the door's off, drill a similar hole in that, below where the door loom plugs in.

07 Feed the speaker wiring through your new hole, and please use a grommet on the sharp edges. If you don't, the best that might happen is your tunes will suddenly stop. At worst, you might blow a channel on your system.

08 Now to mount our components onto the doors. Of course, our panels are a tad unusual, being home-made alloy, but the ideas are the same. Either use the mounting plate or the template provided to mark your hole, making sure the hole lines up with the one behind, in the door itself . . .

12 . . . while the tweeters have their own clever little mounting bracket which screws on from behind.

13 Most component sets have a separate crossover - our crossovers look like something out of Star Trek, so we couldn't just hide them under the dash. With a hole drilled (and grommeted) in our door panel to take the speaker wires, it's time to wire them up. Check your set's instructions for which speaker connects where, and where the amp feed goes in.

14 Most tweeters come pre-wired, but the mids need terminals. Make sure your speaker connections are secure - it's also worth wrapping them with tape, just in case they touch metal inside the door when the panel goes back on.

Shelf mounting

01 First job with a new ready-made shelf is to mark the speaker positions. Not tricky.

Rear speakers

If we're talking about a set of 6x9s, shelf-mounting is the simplest option. If you don't want to butcher your standard shelf (always a flimsy item), either make a new one from MDF (using your stock shelf as a template), or buy a ready-made acoustic shelf. Either way, make hiding your new speakers a priority - tasty speakers on display in the back window could soon mean no rear window, and no speakers...

While shelf mounting offers top quality sound and an easy life, 3-door Escorts also have another top spot for speakers - the rear side trim panels. Providing you don't go for mahoosive units with huge, heavy magnets, you just cut a suitable-sized hole in the panel, and mount your speaker in from behind. We, of course, had other ideas.

Remember that the length of wire to each speaker should be the same (as near as poss), or you might find the speakers run slightly out of phase. Crimp on the right terminals, and connect up your speakers. For max neatness, use P-clips screwed along the edge of the shelf. To remove the shelf more easily, fit some bullet connectors in the speaker wiring, or ask your ICE dealer for a Neutrik connector plug.

02 With a speaker outline marked, remove the wood from the rest of the shelf, and drill a nice big hole somewhere inside the outline... then get busy with the jigsaw.

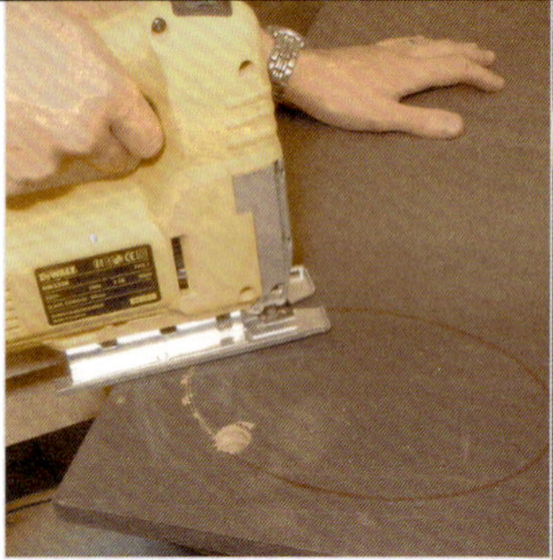

03 Use the speaker mounts (or even the speakers themselves) as a template to drill the mounting holes . . .

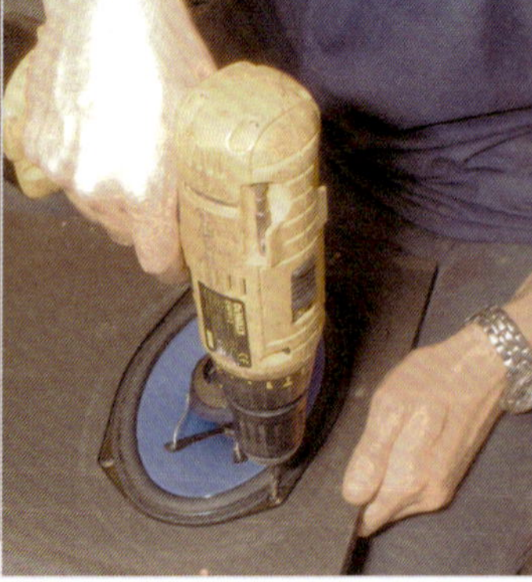

04 . . . then screw on the speakers themselves. Don't forget that 6x9s can be run off the headset, to provide a little "rear fill" - if you have them amped-up, you might find that the sound's too biased to the back of the car.

05

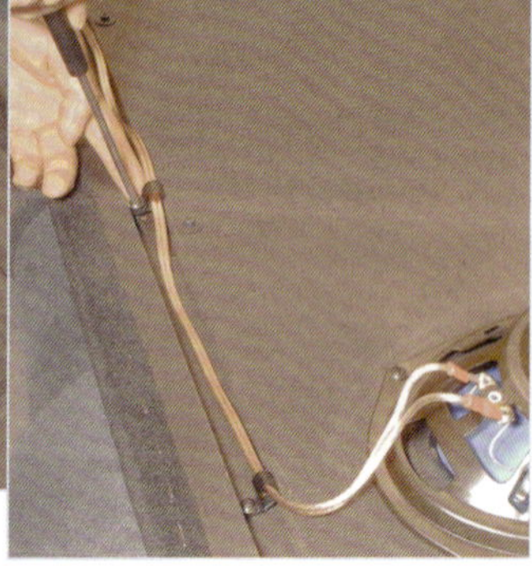

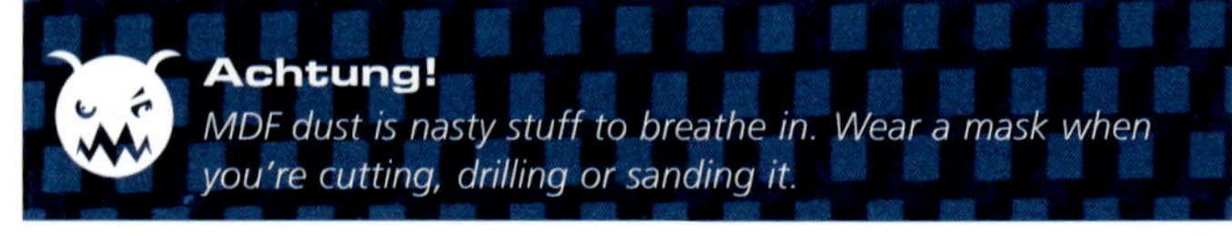

Achtung!

MDF dust is nasty stuff to breathe in. Wear a mask when you're cutting, drilling or sanding it.

Side trim panel mounting

01 We didn't want to keep our old side trim panels, having made our own from (yes, more) alloy plate. We didn't fancy mounting a speaker on tinny alloy, so we cut two strips of thick steel, mounted our speaker plate onto them, and welded the strips to the rear arch and door pillar. Just a bit extreme.

02 A few strips (slices?) of sound-deadening, and our vibration worries from the car disappeared.

03 The 6x9s we chose are being run from the headset (a bit of a waste, as they're rated at 400W), so at least we're keeping something simple. Attach terminals to oxygen-free speaker wiring, and connect up.

04 Oh man - these are some sexy-looking speakers. We're not covering them up too much. We mounted ours rigidly to the metal strips we fitted earlier, using longer-than-necessary bolts. Why? You'll see in a minute.

05 Speaker grilles? Who needs 'em? Certainly not the standard items, anyway. This is a section of grille mesh (the stuff you might normally find in a bumper) which we put to good use. Cut it to shape, make holes for those four over-long bolts we fitted earlier . . .

06 . . . and slide in our new side trim panel, lovingly trimmed from ally (and still wearing its plastic protective coating, which we'll peel off later). In case you're wondering, yes, we did sound-deaden the tinny new panel on the back, before fitting it.

07 Four carefully-drilled holes in the new trim panel later, and now our speaker's rigidly mounted to the car and the panel. And it shouldn't vibrate (especially with only 50W of headset power per channel through it). Yes, the 6x9s do sound lush - as good as they look, in fact.

Subs & boxes

Our unorthodox box has an open base at this stage (we'll be sealing it with a sheet of MDF later), as we still need to line it with sound-deadening. But first - we need another hole. Sort-of round, and speaker-sized. And in the centre of the box - mark the centre using a straight-edge across both diagonals.

01

No system's complete without that essential deep bass boom and rumble. Don't muck about with bass tubes - get the real thing to avoid disappointment. So you lose some of your boot space - so what? Is getting the shopping in an issue? We think not.

Most people opt for the easy life when it comes to boxes, at least until they're ready for a full-on mental install. The Escort at least has a roomy boot, so standard boxes will fit easily. Making up your own box isn't hard though, especially if you were any good at maths and geometry. Oh, and woodwork. Most subs come with instructions telling you what volume of box they work best in, but ask an expert (or a mate) what they think - the standard boxes are just fine, and none are pricey. The only real reason to build your own is if you've got an odd-shaped boot (or want something that looks trick).

Our Escort has a distinct race/rally theme goin' on - and whoever heard of a rally car with a kickin' ICE install? To try and preserve the race look, we came up with a cunning plan. Rally cars often have an ally fuel tank mounted in the rear of the car (it's safer than a plastic tank, slung under the car where the rocks can hit it). Why not build a fake fuel tank from ally, and mount our sub in that? Sounds like the sort of challenge we like.

The alloy tank was supplied courtesy of local firm Holden Engineering (contact details at the back of the book), who can make anything you desire in any metal you like - hand them your specs, and they'll do the rest. For something a little different, give them a try. The only limit is your imagination.

The sub deserves a mention, too. Supplied by DD Audio, this is one of their own-branded subs, made in the land of Uncle Sam. Some of you might think it doesn't look special, but trust us - it is. Love it with your ears, if not your eyes. Made using the highest-quality components, turn this up and no-one needs to apologise.

02 The spec sheet supplied with our DD Audio sub told us what size hole we needed, but it was too big to mark using compasses. We used a small steel rule, with two holes drilled in it, exactly the radius of the hole apart. With the rule pinned by a self-tapper in the centre, and a pen in the other hole, it was easy to mark this huge hole accurately . . .

03 . . . while cutting it out with precision, using our jigsaw, required only a steady hand.

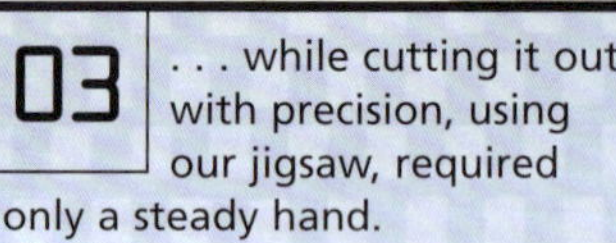

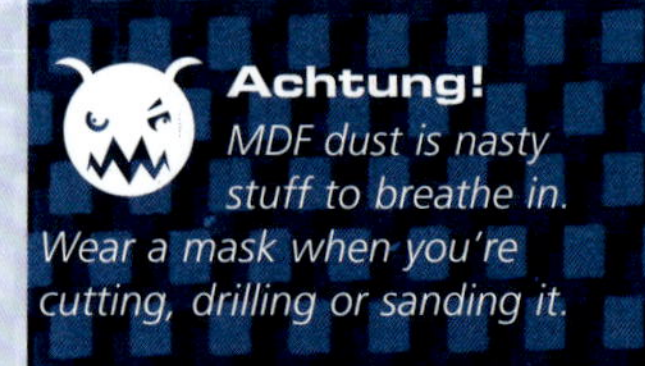

Achtung!

MDF dust is nasty stuff to breathe in. Wear a mask when you're cutting, drilling or sanding it.

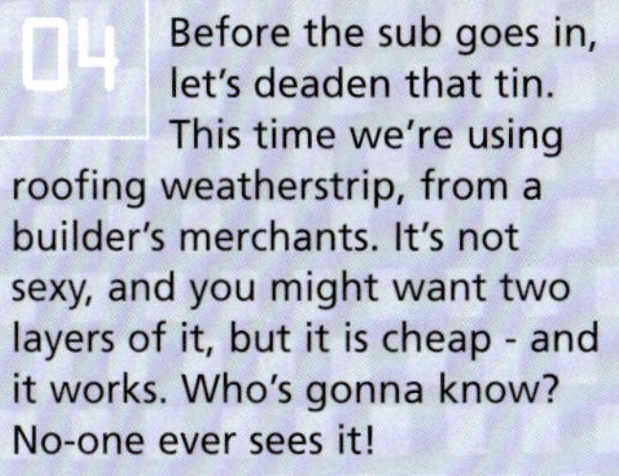

04 Before the sub goes in, let's deaden that tin. This time we're using roofing weatherstrip, from a builder's merchants. It's not sexy, and you might want two layers of it, but it is cheap - and it works. Who's gonna know? No-one ever sees it!

05 Time to try the sub in its new hole. You ordinary folk with a normal sub box can come back in now - mark those mounting holes . . .

06 . . . then take the sub out before drilling (it's just a tad safer without the speaker, in case the drill slips).

07 If your sub comes with a rubber/foam gasket, use it between the speaker and your box, to reduce vibration. You might also consider fitting a 'sensible' plastic grille over the front - might save your sub from destruction by flying tools or shopping.

08 It's not a bad idea to use small nuts and bolts, not screws - decent Nyloc (plastic insert) nuts won't shake loose when you crank it up.

09 Proper sub boxes often have a built-in connection plates, with external screw-on terminals. With these, all you do is connect the internal wires to your sub. Our 'custom' fuel-tank box doesn't have this luxury, so bulleted-on oxygen-free it is.

10 The last job before our open-bottomed box gets sealed to the floor, over its sheet of thick MDF, is more deadening. Packing your sub box loosely with Dacron (available from upholsterers, used for stuffing cushions) is thought by some experts to smoothen the bass sound. Want ruff bass? Then don't bother.

11 The finished item - screwed in place over a precision-cut sheet of MDF. Looks every inch a fuel tank, with fake filler cap and two braided hoses running off. The sound's not hurt by all that tin, either - something a little bit different...

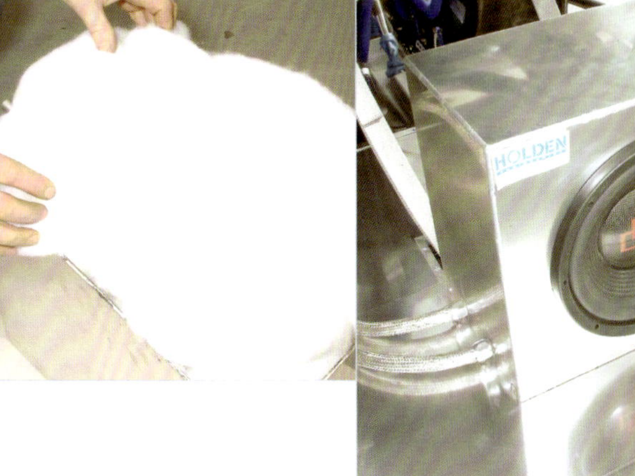

Wiring-up

For most people, this is the scariest part of an install - just the thought of masses of multi-coloured spaghetti sticking out of your dash might have you running to the experts (or a knowledgeable mate). But - if you do everything in a logical order, and observe a few simple rules, wiring-up isn't half as brain-numbing as it seems.

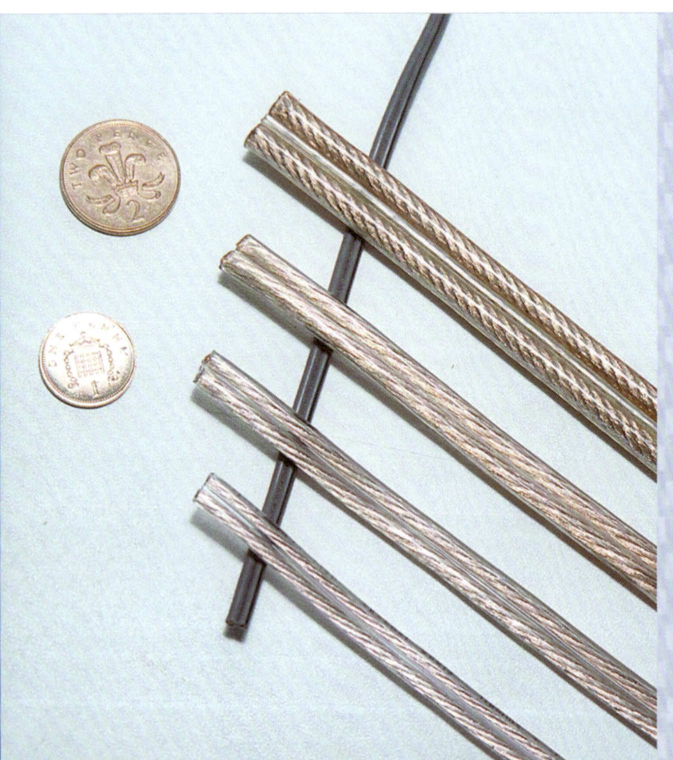

Live feeds

Although a typical head unit can be powered off the standard Ford wiring (the stock wire is good for about 15 amps, tops) running amplifiers means you'll be needing a new live feed, taken straight off the battery.

Get some decent 'eight-gauge' (quite heavy) or 'four-gauge' (getting on for battery cable thickness - serious stuff) wire, and a matching fuseholder. If you're running more than one item off this feed wire, get a distribution block too, which splits the feed up, with a separate fuse for each item - who'd have thought electrical safety can look trick too?

Pub trivia

Hands up, who knows what 'RCA' stands for? We use it every day in ICE-speak, but what does it really mean? Really Clever Amplifier lead? Remote Control Acoustic lead? Well, the answer's a strange one. RCA leads and connectors are also known as 'phono' connectors in the world of TV and hi-fi, and they've been around a long, long time. How long, exactly? We're talking back in the days when you could only get radios - big suckers with valves in them, and long before anyone thought of putting one in a car. RCA actually stands for Radio Corporation of America, who hold the patent on this type of connector and lead. Not a lot of people know that.

Speaker and RCA wiring

As with all wiring, the lesson here is to be neat and orderly - or - you'll be sorry! RCA leads and speaker wires are prone to picking up interference (from just about anywhere), so the first trick to learn when running ICE wiring is to keep it away from live feeds, and also if possible, away from the car's ECUs. Another favourite way to interference-hell is to loop up your wiring, when you find you've got too much (we've all been there). Finding a way to lose any excess lengths of wire without bunching can be an art - laying it out in a zig-zag, taping it to the floor as you go, is just one solution.

Another lesson in neatness is finding out what kinds of cable clips are available, and where to use them. There's various stick-on clips which can be used as an alternative to gaffer tape on floors, and then 'P-clips', which look exactly as their name suggests, and can be screwed down (to speaker shelves, for instance). 'Looming' your wiring is another lesson well-learned - this just means wrapping tape around, particularly on pairs of speaker wires or RCAs. As we've already said, don't loom speaker wire with power cables (or even with earths).

The last point is also about tidiness - mental tidiness. When you're dealing with speaker and RCA wiring, keep two ideas in mind - positive and negative. Each speaker has a pos (+) and neg (-) terminal. Mixing these up is not an option, so work out a system of your own, for keeping positive and negative in the right places on your headset and amp connections. Decent speaker cable is always two wires joined together - look closely, and you'll see that one wire has writing (or a stripe) on, and the other is plain. Use the wire with writing for pos connections throughout your system, and you'll never be confused again. While we're at it, RCA leads have red and white connector plugs - Red is for Right.

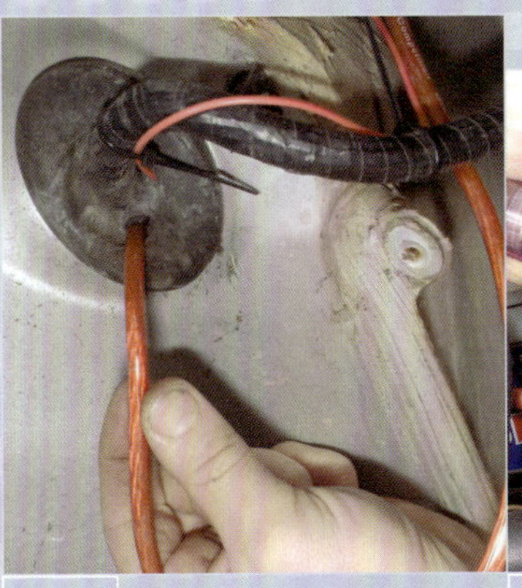

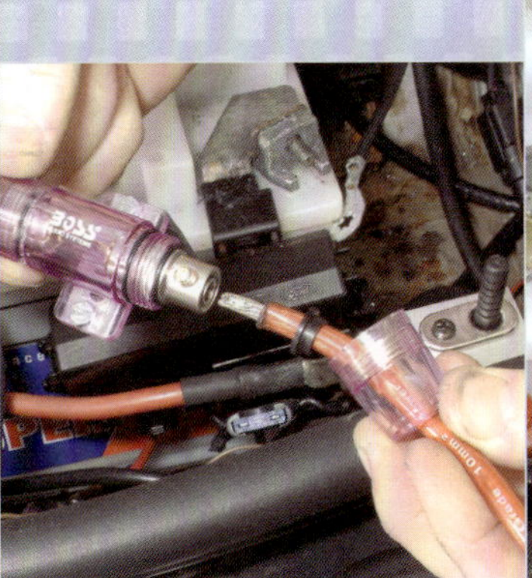

01 First step in running a live feed is deciding where best to run the wire into the car - try and go for the most direct route. On the Escort, rip out the wheel arch liner below the battery tray, and you'll find a large rubber grommet at the back of the arch. Carefully make a new hole (seal it up with silicone sealant later) and feed that large wire into the front footwell.

02 Kit yourself out with a decent fuseholder - ones like this not only look good, they're really excellent to use. Get a fuse the same rating as your amp, or the total load on your distribution block - ask a pro for advice. Make a neat job of fitting the heavy wire into the holder - any stray strands could earth out (we soldered the ends of our wire, but this takes a soldering iron of pretty immense power).

03 Tighten the terminal Allen screws firmly, and screw on the end fittings.

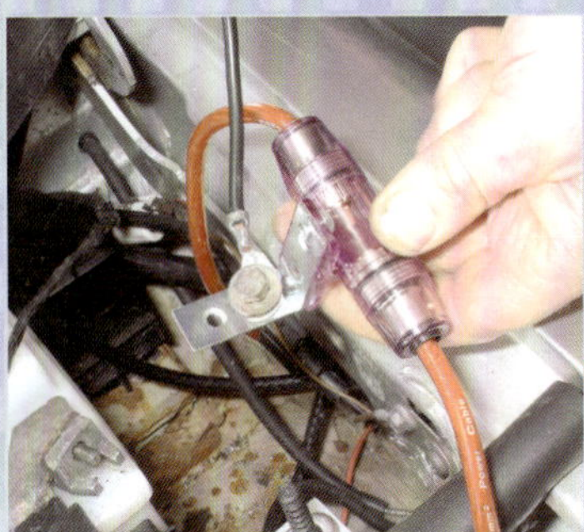

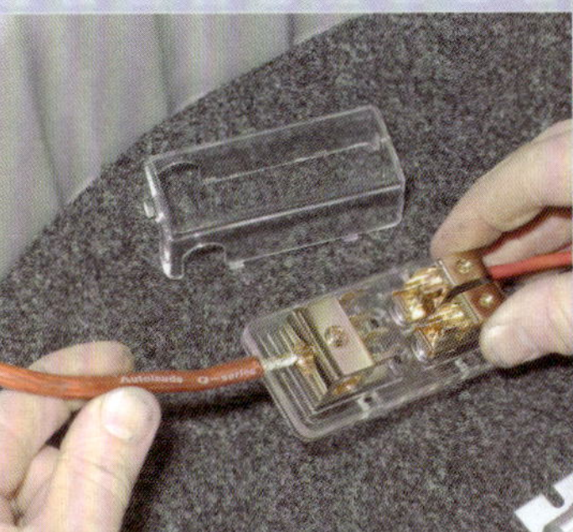

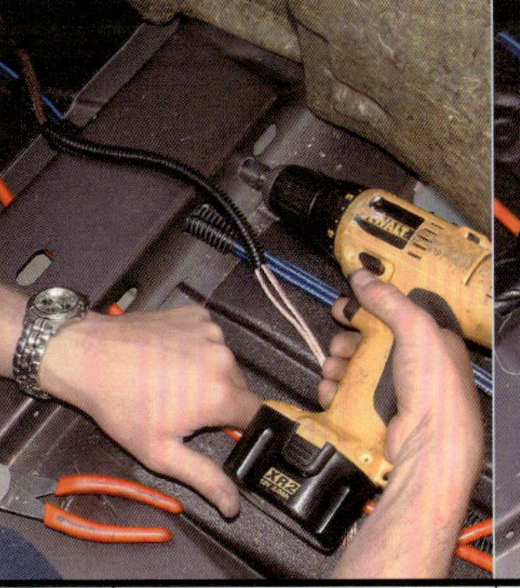

04 The fuseholder ought to be securely mounted, and somewhere you can get at it, if there's ever a meltdown. We made ourselves a mounting bracket from one we bought in a DIY store. Don't get carried away and connect up your live feed until you're ready - remember, this feed is NOT ignition-switched!

05 Here's where your live feed could end up - a distribution block. Here, your power can be split off, usually to separate amps - each amp gets its own fuse (downrated from the large one in the holder up front). This all makes for excellent electrical safety, and the blocks themselves look the nuts too, as a bonus. The wire ends are pinned in by chunky Allen grub screws, and the whole thing has a tidy plastic cover (which must be on tight, or lives will touch earths, and sparks will fly).

06 Here we see just one solution to a little wiring problem. We have two RCA leads, some speaker wiring, and a power feed, all going to our amp in the boot. We can't run all the wires together, so we must separate them. We've removed the passenger seat, to make life easier, but here's the first obstacle - a ridge in the floor. To avoid laying the wires on top, out comes the drill.

07 With strips of gaffer tape to keep it all neatly tied down, this is how a professional wiring install should look. You can also use the Ford clips along the insides of the sills, but keep the power lead away from all the rest.

Amplifiers

Achtung!

MDF dust is nasty stuff to breathe in. Wear a mask when you're cutting, drilling or sanding it.

01 Decide where you'll mount the amp carefully. Amps must be adequately cooled - don't cover it up, and don't hang it upside-down from your shelf. Once the spare wheel on our car had been chucked, we had ourselves a nice hole, which we lined with a circle of MDF, covered in carpet.

02 First to go on is the live feed. This is one amp connection you should really use a ring terminal on, rather than just stuffing a bare wire into the hole. And insulate any bare metal on the terminal - that live touches anything else, and the results won't be good.

So, how many amps do we want in our car? One school of thought says each pair of speakers, and each sub, should have an individual amp - by setting the output from each amp separately, you can control each aspect of the sound, before you even need to think about adding a graphic equaliser. You can also better match your speakers to the level of power they need, to work best. Trouble is, running several amps means doubling-up on wiring, and you could end up drawing an awful lot of power from that battery.

Any starter system can be made to seriously kick, using just one 400W four-channel amp - choose the right one carefully (and the components to go with it), and just one will do. With a 'tri-mode' amp, you could run your front components off one pair of channels, bridge the other two for a sub, and run some 6x9s off the head unit. Don't forget that decent modern headsets chuck out fifty-per-channel now, so don't assume you'll need separate amps for everything.

Our system set-up uses two two-channel amps, one for the front components, and another bridged for the sub, with the 6x9s off the head unit. Again, we're using Boss for the amps (courtesy of DD Audio), and as with all the components supplied for this install, the 'Chaos' amps look the business, with plenty of features. Do they kick? Let's find out.

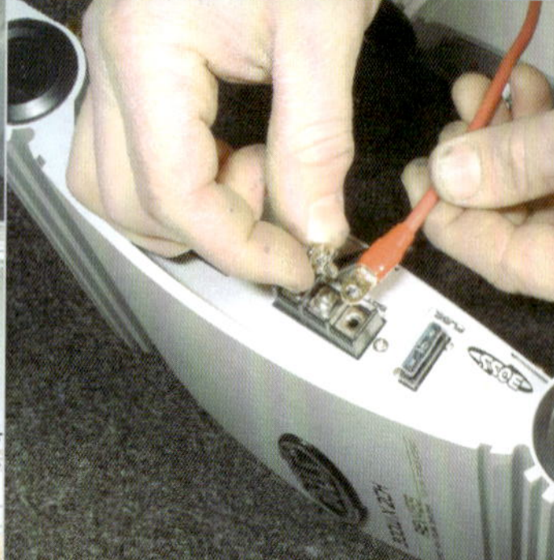

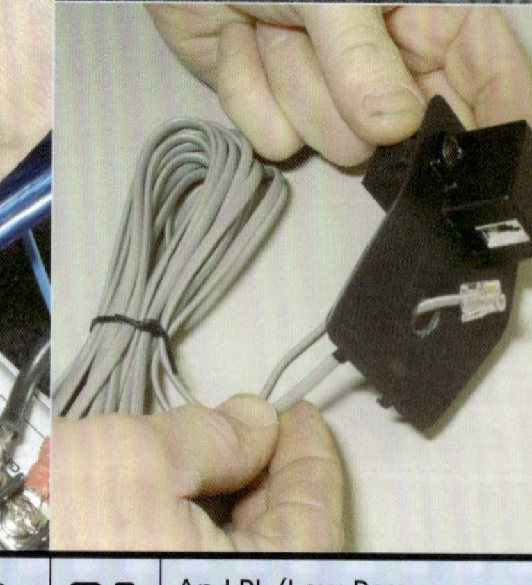

07 . . . while this is a more typical layout, for a pair of speakers (stereo).

08 An LPL (Low Pass Level) controller is effectively a 'volume' control for your sub - make sure you have an amp which accepts one (it should have a socket which looks like a BT phone line). Not much to fitting one of these - we prised off a small trim panel to the left of our Escort steering wheel, mounted the little unit on that, then drilled a hole through to take the 'phone lead' . . .

Tricks 'n' tips

Very few systems work 100%, first time. If the amp LEDs don't light up, for instance, are they getting power? Are the p-cont/remote wires connected properly? If the sub doesn't kick, is the amp switch set to bridged or tri-mode, not stereo? Are the low-pass switches in the correct position? RTFM.

03 Next thing we need is an earth. Don't use skinny wires for earths - ideally, it should be the same-thickness wire as you've used for your live feed. For an earth point, you can use any handy bolt, but seat and seat belt mounting bolts must be re-done up tight, of course. Or you can always make your own hole (just don't go through the fuel tank) . . .

04 . . . and after scratching off the surrounding paint (or rust), you can then fit a large self-tapper, to pin your wire. We went one better, and fitted a bolt in from under the car (self-tappers have been known to work loose, resulting in momentary loss of jive).

05 Next up, it's the humble P-cont (remote) lead going on. This performs the vital function of carrying the 'switch-on' signal from your headset - without this, you won't hear much. The good news is, this is one time when size doesn't matter - it doesn't carry much current, so the wire can be as skinny as you like.

06 Read the amp's instruction book carefully when connecting any wires, or you might regret it, especially if you're using the amp in bridged or tri-mode. Make sure you're happy about your speaker pos and neg/left and right wires, and get them screwed on. Here, we're wiring up the amp running our sub, in bridged mode . . .

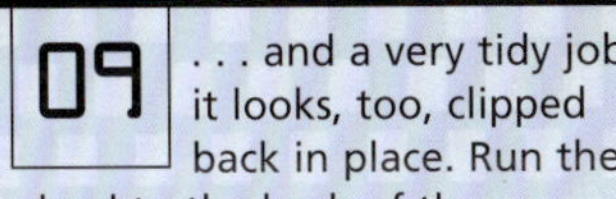

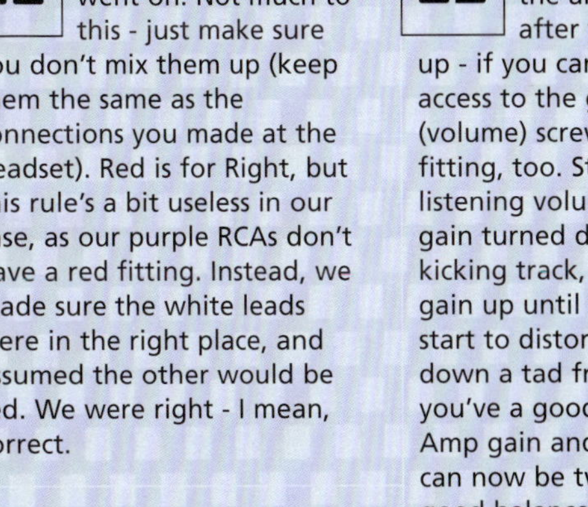

09 . . . and a very tidy job it looks, too, clipped back in place. Run the lead to the back of the car . . .

10 . . . and plug into the socket provided. Told you this was easy - you can't even get it the wrong way round.

11 Time those RCA leads went on. Not much to this - just make sure you don't mix them up (keep them the same as the connections you made at the headset). Red is for Right, but this rule's a bit useless in our case, as our purple RCAs don't have a red fitting. Instead, we made sure the white leads were in the right place, and assumed the other would be red. We were right - I mean, correct.

12 A good tip is to leave the amps loose until after you've set them up - if you can, leave good access to the gain adjustment (volume) screws after final fitting, too. Starting at normal listening volume, with the amp gain turned down, put on a kicking track, then turn the gain up until the speakers just start to distort. Turn the gain down a tad from there, and you've a good basic setting. Amp gain and headset faders can now be tweaked to give a good balanced sound - or whatever tickles your lugholes.

Engines

Faster, faster!

So now your car talks the talk, but does it walk the walk, as in walking away from everything at the next set of lights... Not everyone's into mega-performance, which is why the bolt-on goodies like induction kits and big-bore exhausts are such big business. Serious engine tuning costs, and not just in the initial expense - it goes without saying that your insurance company will throw a wobbly at a gas-flowed head, and might refuse to cover you altogether if you go for that Cosworth conversion.

The induction kit and sports exhaust are an essential first choice, and are as far as you can really go before your insurance company disowns you, or before you need another bank loan to afford the mods in the first place. Both mods help the engine to 'breathe' better, which helps when you go for the accelerator initially, improving the response you feel, while you also get a crowd-pleasing induction roar and rasp from the back box, so everyone's happy.

Now for the harsh and painful truth. On their own, an induction kit and back box will not gain you much extra 'real' power. Sorry, but it's a myth. Time and again, people fit induction kits and back boxes, expecting huge power gains, and those 'in the know' have a quiet chuckle. All these things really do is make the car sound sportier, and improve the response - accept this, and you won't be disappointed. Ask yourself why most insurance companies don't generally increase premiums for the likes of a performance rear box or induction kit. The answer is - because (on their own) they don't make enough difference!

The 'bolt-on' performance goodies have more effect as part of an engine 'makeover' package, and setting-up the engine properly after fitting these parts can make a huge difference. If you're halfway serious about increasing the go of your Escort, talk to someone with access to a rolling road, so you can prove that what's been done has actually made a useful gain. If you've spent time and a ton of money on your car, of course you're going to think it feels faster, but is it?

Fitting all the performance goodies in the world will be pretty pointless if the engine's already knackered, but it might not be as bad as you think. One of the best ways to start on the performance road is simply to ensure that the car's serviced properly - new spark plugs, HT leads, and an oil and filter change, are a good basis to begin from. Correct any obvious faults, such as hoses or wiring plugs hanging off, and look for any obviously-damaged or leaking components, too.

Breathe with me...

Replacement **element**

One of the simplest items to fit, the replacement air filter element has been around for years - of course, now the induction kit's the thing to have, but a replacement element is more discreet (if you're worried about such things).

While we're at it, don't listen to your mates who tell you to simply take out the air filter completely - this is a really foolish idea. The fuel system's air intake acts like a mini vacuum cleaner, sucking in air from the front of the car, and it doesn't just suck in air, but also dust, dirt and leaves - it's also designed to suck in oil fumes from the engine itself (through the 'breather' connection). Without a filter, all this muck would quickly end up in the sensitive parts of the fuel injection system, and will quickly make the car undriveable. Worse, if any of it makes it into the engine, this will lead to engine wear. Remember too, that cheaper performance filters can be of very suspect quality - if your new filter disintegrates completely inside six months, it'll do wonders for the airflow, but it'll also be letting in all sorts of rubbish!

Some performance filters have to be oiled before fitting - follow the instructions provided; don't ignore this part, or the filter won't be effective. If the filter won't fit, check whether you actually have the right one - don't force it in, and don't cut it to fit, as either of these will result in gaps, which would allow unfiltered air to get in.

01 This is obviously one of them posh Escorts with proper fuel injection - if your air cleaner has a more roundy look to it, sit back and watch the fun. The first job here is to unplug the airflow meter - this doesn't just pull off, but is released by pressing down a thin wire clip at the front of the plug.

02 There's always at least one screw to undo. On a rounder air cleaner, there'll be three long screws in the centre.

03 One thing all air cleaners seem to have in common is a dose of wire over-centre clips round the edges, which you flip up and unhook . . .

04 . . . before the top of the air cleaner lifts off and the old element can be taken out.

05 Don't just stick the new filter in - clean out some of the muck that's gathered in the filter box. Use a damp cloth for this, as we don't want the grit and leaves going into the engine, thank you.

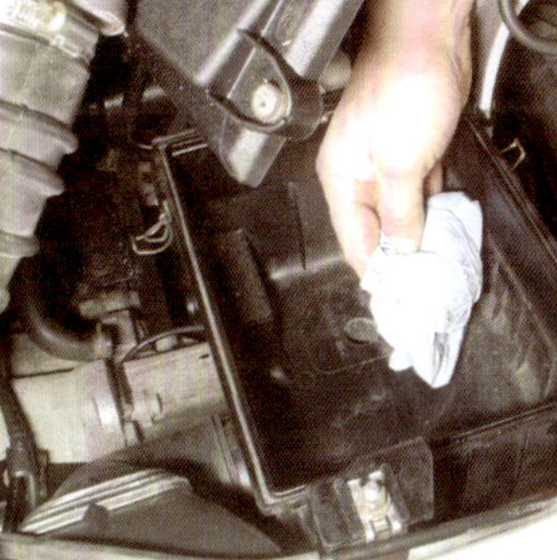

06 Stick in your new K&N (making sure it's the right way up), put it all back together, and feel the difference. Don't forget to find a prominent spot to display your sticker!

Induction kit

Kits can usually only be had for Escorts with multi-point injection (which leaves out those with carbs, or the early 1.3s and 1.4s with CFi). With an induction kit, the standard air filter housing and ducting are junked, and the new filter bolts directly to the airflow meter or throttle body. Most kits also feature special air inlet ducting (hoses) to feed the new filter with the coldest possible air from the front of the car - cold air is denser, and improves engine power. Feeding the filter with cold air is in theory good for maximum performance with a hot engine or in hot weather, but in colder conditions with a cold engine, driveability and fuel economy might suffer.

The fuelling arrangements for fuel injection are based largely on the volume of incoming air. If you start feeding the injection system an unusually large amount of air (by fitting an induction kit, for instance), the management system will compensate by throwing in more fuel. This could result in some more power - or the car will drink petrol and your exhaust emissions will be screwed up, inviting an MOT failure. We're not saying "don't do it", just remember that power gains can be exaggerated, and that there can be pitfalls.

What no-one disputes is that an induction kit, which operates without all the normal ducting provided as standard, gives the engine a real throaty roar when you go for the loud pedal. So at least it sounds fast. Jubbly.

01 There's a fair bit of work fitting an induction kit (or at least there is to a '93 XR3i), so let's get stuck in. First to go is the breather hose, which just pulls off the base of the air cleaner (we'll be needing this hose later, so keep track of it)

06 Let's get rid of that old air cleaner, shall we? First, unplug the airflow meter - release the plug by pressing down the wire clip at the front, before pulling it out.

07 There's a nut in front of the air cleaner to remove . . .

02 Next on the hit list is all the old inlet trunking from the air cleaner to the engine. Unscrew the large Jubilee clip next to the airflow meter . . .

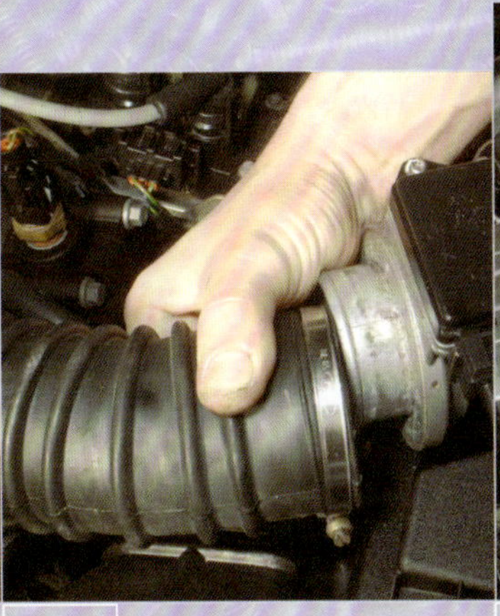

03 . . . and pull off the big hose.

04 Two screws hold a strap which pins the flat section of the inlet hose to the top of the engine - remove the screws, take off the strap, and the whole section of hose should be free to come off (and go in the nearest bin).

05 Now unbolt the engine lifting eye from in front of the oil filler cap - this clears the way for our new inlet hose, later on.

>>

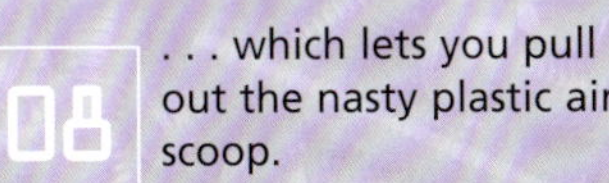

08 . . . which lets you pull out the nasty plastic air scoop.

09 The air cleaner lid is secured by one screw at the front . . .

10 . . . and by several over-centre wire clips round the edge.

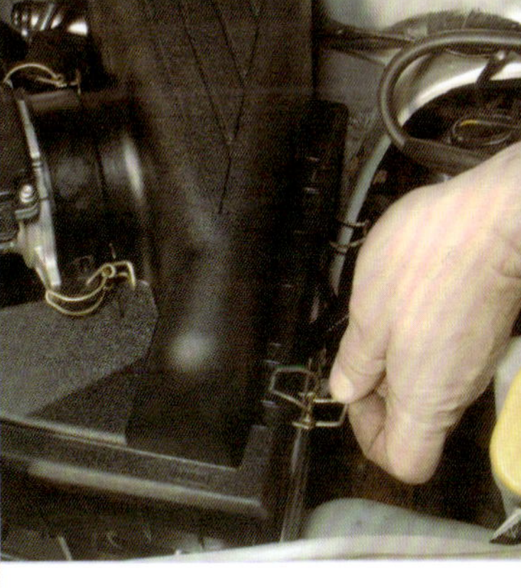

11 Lift the lid away, and take out the air filter.

12 Before we throw the top half away, there's the airflow meter to remove. Release two more of those wire clips . . .

13 . . . and take it off. This is a pretty delicate component, which is vital to the good running of the engine, so don't go chucking it on the floor - we'll be refitting it shortly.

14 The base of the air cleaner definitely isn't needed any more. It's now just pegged into two rubber grommets at the bottom, so give it a good pull to remove it.

Two Allen-headed bolts and nuts are provided in the kit, to mount the airflow meter to its new bracket. Remember what we said about this being a delicate component? We weren't lying, so make sure this can't fall off on the floor. 19

Before we fit our new rubber inlet hose, there's a minor 'adjustment' required to the top of the exhaust heat shield. Bend this flange out of the way, or it'll touch the hose, and could chop it through. 20

The only thing we had any trouble fitting was the inlet hose. In theory, you take the two Jubilee clips (different sizes - make sure you use the right ones) and slip the hose ends over your inlet manifold and airflow meter. Trouble is, our hose sat at an angle, instead of flat, and when the bonnet was shut down, the hose got a bit crushed. 21

15 The engine bay's looking a bit deserted now, so it's time for the induction kit to fill it. First step is to remove the top bolt from the thermostat housing . . .

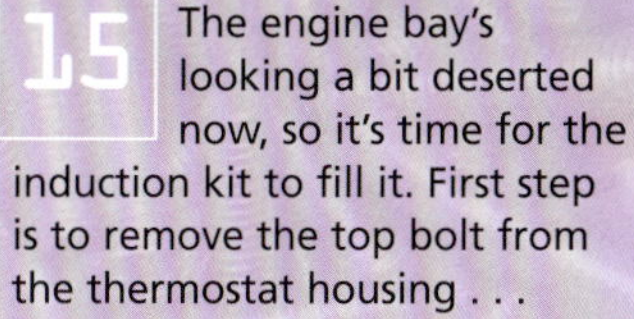

16 . . . then refit it, together with the horizontal part of the new mounting bracket for the airflow meter (told you we'd want that again).

17 Now there's a rubber spacer which fits to the new bracket (not much room to get the nut on here - if the Jubilee clip's in the way, loosen it slightly, and turn it so you can get the nut on) . . .

18 Lastly, the vertical part of the airflow meter mounting bracket slips onto the front of the rubber spacer. Do all the nuts up hand-tight for now - you might need a bit of movement to get everything fitting just right.

>>

22 The solution turned out to be that the hose was just a tad too long - chopping off about 10 mm from the airflow meter end gave us a better (but still not perfect) fit.

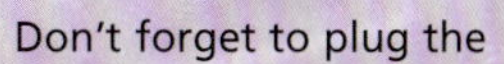

23 Don't forget to plug the airflow meter back in, otherwise it won't work. Obviously.

24 At last we get to see the familiar induction kit cone. Pop it onto the airflow meter . . .

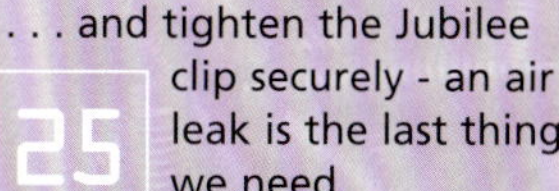

25 . . . and tighten the Jubilee clip securely - an air leak is the last thing we need.

26 Remember the breather hose we took off the base of the air cleaner? Of course you do. Now we have to refit it, or an eagle-eyed MOT man might fail your car on emissions (okay, so he'd have to be having a really bad day at the time, but he could...). Insert the joining tube into the hose end . . .

27 . . . and poke it into the hole provided on the rear side of the induction cone.

28 The only thing left is to feed the new filter with the coldest-possible air. The inlet end of the hose provided must be in the cold-air blast at the front of the engine - next to the radiator, not behind it. Once the inlet end's sorted, cable-tie the hose to any convenient spot, and aim the outlet end right at the cone - it's no good if that icy blast of power-giving air ends up pointing at the bulkhead, is it?

Finally...

Once you've fitted your new filter or induction kit, even if you don't take the car to a rolling road for setting up, at least take it to a garage and have the emissions checked - any minor adjustments should ensure that the engine will, if nothing else, still tick over okay, and should ensure an MOT emissions pass.

Carburettor? Single-point injection?

No need to feel left out of the induction kit action if your Escort happens to be a tad weedy in the engine department, or you're stuck with a carb. Our project Fiesta had the 1.3 HCS/CFi motor too, and we found an induction kit for that, which should fit all 1.3 injection Escorts, maybe the 1.4s as well (same CFi unit). Just make sure you can get your dosh back if it don't fit!

Carb models have actually got it best of all for extracting more go, and there's no power-sapping cat to worry about. Check your Yellow Pages for a carburettor specialist, and see what can be done by increasing the jet sizes first. In the end, you'll probably need a different carb (and maybe a different inlet manifold) for major oomph.

Other air filter-type mods

One old favourite, if you've got an injection Escort with a square filter box and haven't gone for an induction kit, is drilling holes in the air filter box. Only drill the air filter box below the level where the filter element sits, or the air going into the engine won't be filtered. Making your airbox look like a Swiss cheese won't make the car faster, but it does give you the nice throaty induction roar at full throttle.

Tricks 'n' tips

When fitting a bolt-on filter to a carb, don't leave the breather pipe hanging off (this is the large pipe which pulls off the base of the old air cleaner). Not only could this mean an MOT fail, it will make your Escort run like a Lada on two cylinders (lumpy tickover). Check with your filter supplier whether there's provision to connect the breather pipe into the new filter. The smaller vacuum pipes might have to be plugged to make the car run right, but don't plug the breather pipe!

Adjustable fuel pressure regulator (power boost valve)

Generally only available for cat-equipped Escorts with multi-point injection (all except the early 1.3 and 1.4 cat engines, which had single-point CFi systems), these valves allow the fuel system pressure to be increased over the standard regulator valve. Contrary to what you might think, they don't actually provide much more fuel (this is regulated separately by the injection ECU).

The effect of increasing the injection pressure is to improve the injector spray pattern, which helps the fuel to burn more efficiently, and has the effect of increasing engine power while actually reducing emission levels.

To see the true effect of these valves, they must be set up using emission test gear and ideally a rolling road - merely turning the pressure up to the maximum level might not produce the desired effect. Fitting one of these valves involves breaking into the high-pressure fuel line, which is potentially dangerous for the inexperienced - also, if the valve is poorly fitted (or the fuel lines are in poor condition), you could end up with fuel spraying out under pressure onto a hot engine. Make sure you know what you're doing - take great care when dealing with petrol, and watch carefully for any sign of fuel leakage after fitting, even if this is done by a professional.

No quicker but it looks nice

Looks are just as important as performance. No hot hatch is 'finished' without making it look sweet. Details to the engine bay as well as your interior and exterior mods are an important factor, especially if you were thinking about getting your motor featured in top magazines. Every one does it, and you're next.

First up - try cleaning the engine, for heaven sake! How do you expect to emulate the show-stopping cars if your gearbox is covered in grot? Get busy with the degreaser (Gunk's a good bet), then get the hosepipe out. You can take it down to the local jetwash if you like, but remember your mobile - if you get carried away with the high-power spray, you might find the car won't start afterwards!

When it's all dry (and running again), you can start in. Get the polish to all the painted surfaces you reasonably can, and don't be afraid to unbolt a few of the simpler items to gain better access. We're assuming you've already fitted your induction kit, but if not, these nicely do away with a load of ugly plastic airbox/air cleaner and trunking, and that rusted-out exhaust manifold cover, in favour of decent-looking product. Take off the rocker cover (or engine cover), and paint it to match your chosen scheme (heat-resistant paint is a must, really, such as brake caliper paint), set off with a funky oil filler cap. A strut brace is a tasty underbonnet feature, especially chromed. Braided hose covers (or coloured hose sets), ally battery covers and bottles, mirror panels - all give the underbonnet a touch of glamour.

01 Brighten up the underbonnet, and maybe (if you believe what it says on the tin) make your car go better too? Gotta be worth a punt, to find out. First, make sure the ignition's off - take out the key, to be certain. Work on one lead at a time here - pull this end off the spark plug . . .

02 . . . then unclip it from the rocker cover, and off the coil pack (squeeze the end fittings to release them). Might not be quite the same on your Escort (on many Escort engines, the coil pack's buried at the back of the engine - just follow the leads).

03 Lay the new leads out, and choose the lead closest in length to the one you've just pulled off. Always pays to check the leads look right, before you get too far in - and don't wreck the box they came in, when you open it up. Push the new lead home onto the spark plug, then clip it into the rocker cover, and finally, onto the coil. Worth spraying each end of the lead with some WD-40 (or similar stuff) to keep the damp out.

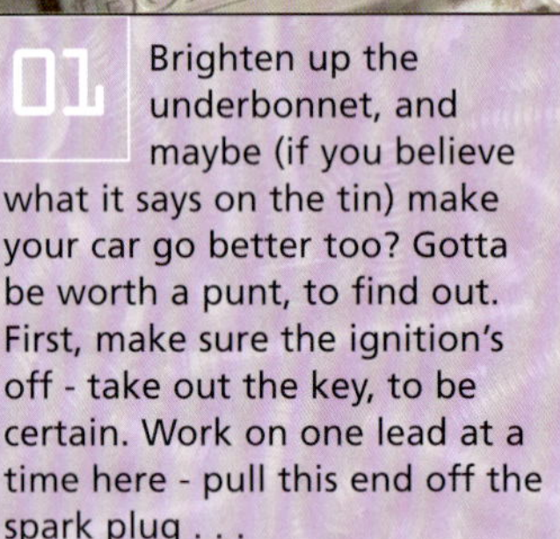

Coloured HT leads

Achtung!
Switch off the ignition and remove the key before starting this job. You don't want to be on the wrong end of 40,000 volts.

04 And here's some we did earlier. Don't like blue? Well, they also come in red, yellow...

05 Though it seems a shame to cover up your hard work, on the Zetec engines, there's a very tidy chrome HT lead cover you can get (from Mirage Stainless - see later in this Section). Just clips on, and would look really smart if you also painted/chromed the rocker cover.

You's a hose

There are many ways to add detail and colour to otherwise boring components. Spraying your hoses is just one of those ways. Only apply paint that is suitable for engine bay use, as temperatures get very high under the hood. The good folk from ABC Design supplied our paint.

01

The pipe must come off - so which ones will it be? The ones most visible seem the obvious choices - then how easy are the hoses to remove? Here, we've chosen a breather pipe. Coolant and fuel pipes can also be painted, but it does mean dumping some coolant, or losing fuel (dodgy). Unless you're very confident, the smaller the hose, the safer you are - undo the hose clips, and take it off.

02

Give the pipe a good clean to thoroughly degrease it. A preferred way of spraying, to ensure maximum coverage, is to hang the pipe from above. A stiff piece of wire inserted into the end of the hose (not poked through the hose) will do the trick.
Apply the paint in three or four light layers until the pipe is evenly covered. You'll also have to wait a while (ideally, leave overnight) before that hose can go back on.

03

Achtung!
The engine must be completely cold before you start. Even if you've only done a quick lap, it would be dangerous to attempt doing anything with a remotely warm engine, as the fluids inside the pipe are often a lot hotter than they appear. Be warned!

Braided hoses

Unroll your braiding, check the length against your freshly-removed hose, and trim it roughly to length - you might need something heftier than scissors for this.

01

Now expand the braiding to the right size using a suitable blunt object. Like a screwdriver handle, we mean - what were you thinking of? Once the braiding's roughly the right size, you can slip your pipe in (lovely). Smooth out the braiding round the bends, as it tends to gather up and look naff otherwise, then trim up the ends.

02

Slide a new Jubilee clip over the braiding at one end, then slip one of the coloured end fittings over the clip. Repeat this process at the other end of your chosen hose, and it'll be ready to fit back on. When you're sure the hose is fully onto its fitting, tighten the hose clip securely to avoid embarrassing leakage.

03

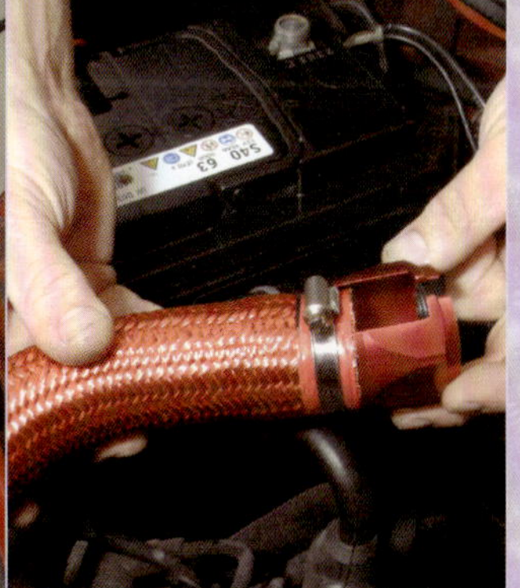

Silicon heaven

All Escorts with a cat (late 1992, roughly K-reg onwards) have fuel injection, as did all the sports models, 16-valve Zetec engines, and some early 1.6 Ghias. Fuel injection on all these Escorts is controlled by an engine management system with a 'computer' at its heart, known as the ECU, or Electronic Control Unit. The ECU contains several computer chips, at least one of which has programmed onto it the preferred fuel/air mixture and ignition advance setting for any given engine speed or load - this information is known as a computer 'map', and the system refers to it constantly while the car's being driven. Obviously, with the current trend towards fuel economy and reducing harmful exhaust emissions, the values in this 'map' are set, well, conservatively, let's say (read 'boring'). With a little tweaking - like richening-up the mixture, say - the engine can be made to produce more power, or response will be improved, or both. At the expense of the environment. Oh well.

Companies like Superchips offer replacement computer chips which feature a computer map where driveability and performance are given priority over outright economy (although the company claims that, under certain conditions, even fuel economy can be better, with their products). While a chip like this does offer proven power gains on its own, it's obviously best to combine a chip with other enhancements, and to have the whole lot set up at the same time. By the time you've fitted an induction kit, four-branch manifold, big-bore pipe, and maybe even a fast-road cam, adding a chip is the icing on the cake - chipping an already-modified motor will liberate even more horses, or at least combine it with majorly-improved response. Ford tuning specialists are best placed to advise you on the most effective tuning mods.

Another feature programmed into the ECU is a rev limiter, which cuts the ignition (or fuel) progressively when the pre-set rev limit is reached. Most replacement chips have the rev limiter reset higher, or removed altogether. Not totally sure this is a good thing - if the engine's not maintained properly (low oil level, cambelt changes neglected), removing the rev limiter and running beyond the red line would be a quick way to kill it. But a well-maintained engine with a rally cam fitted could rev off the clock, if the ECU would let it, so maybe not a bad thing after all...

Now the bad news

Chipping is often thought of as an easy, 'no-tell' route to increased performance and driveability - after all, the ECU is well-buried inside the car, not on show under the bonnet, so who's gonna know? Needless to say, the insurance companies have been wise to this trick for a long time. A sure way to tell whether a 'performance' product does what it says on the tin is to see what it'll do to your premium - telling them you're fitting a sports ROM chip will cost. Big-time. But, in the event of a claim, if they suspect your car's been 'chipped', rest assured, they will make efforts to find out, because if you haven't told them about it, it means they save on paying out. What's an insurance assessor's salary for one day, compared to the thousands you could be claiming in case of an accident or theft? Do it by all means, but at least be honest.

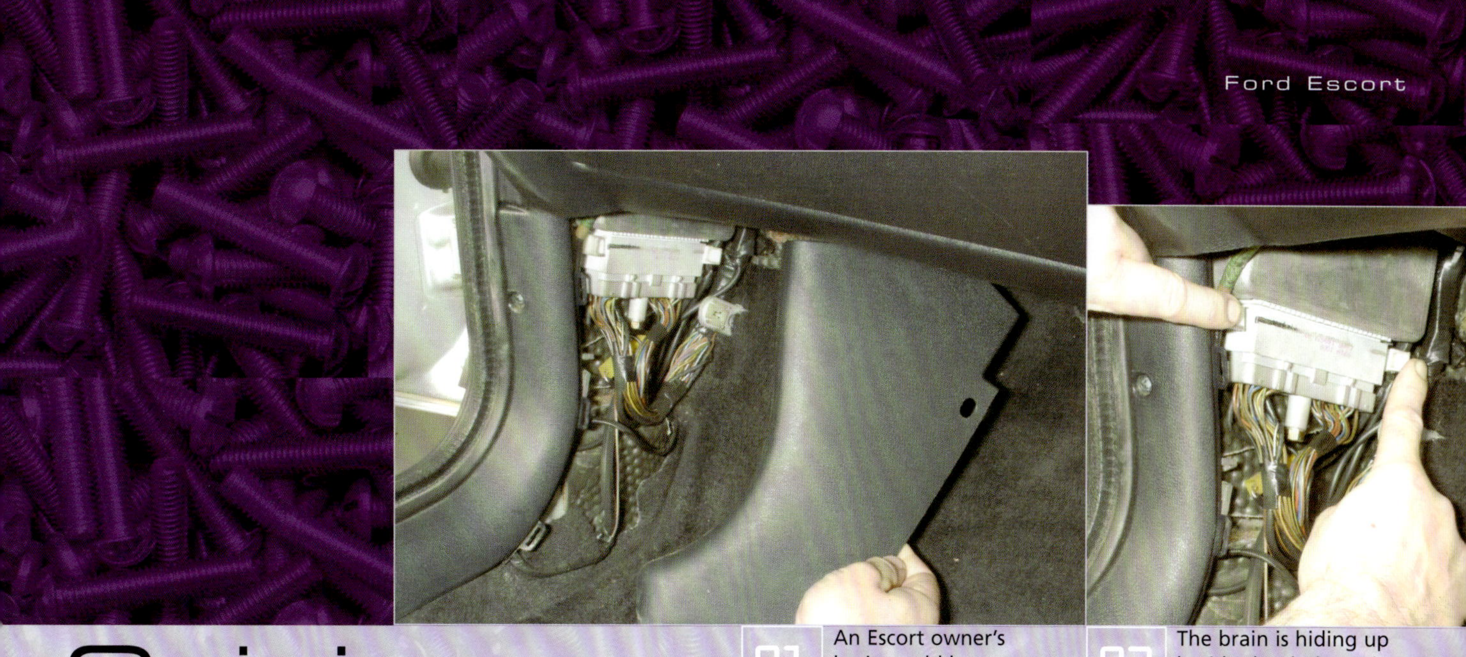

Gaining access **to the ECU**

01 An Escort owner's brain could be anywhere (at least if you listen to their girlfriends/partners). An Escort's brain, on the other hand, can only be hidden in one place - remove the passenger's footwell kick panel (one turn-screw, and three clips holding it to the sill trim panel) for a better look.

02 The brain is hiding up beside the dash, and we have to coax it down. By pressing these two clips apart, the whole thing should slide gracefully onto the carpet . . .

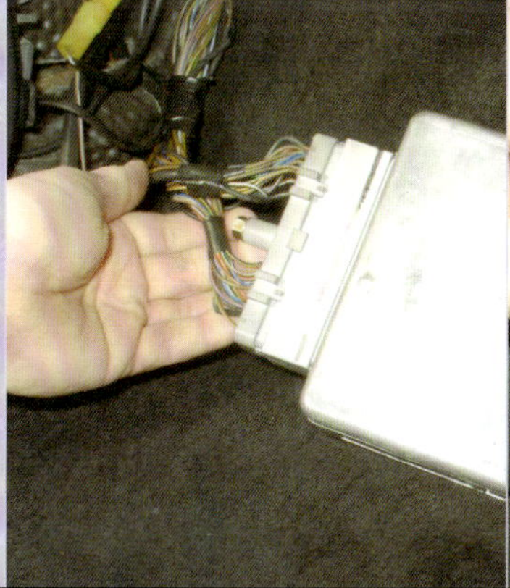

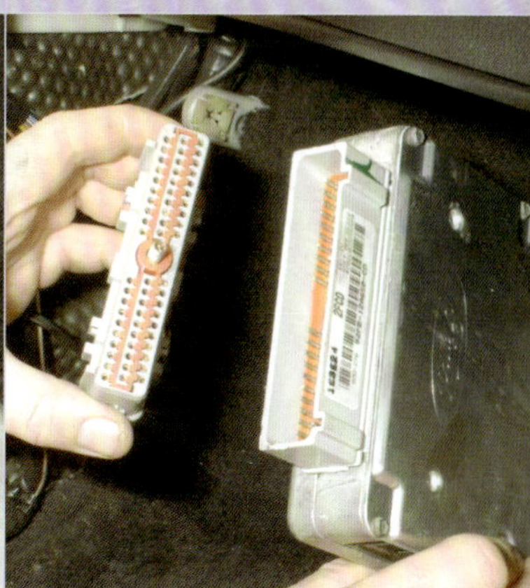

03 . . . so be ready to catch it - brains are pretty delicate objects, after all. Before you rush in and start disconnecting the wiring, make very sure the ignition's switched off. The best way to ensure this? Take out the key.

04 The ECU wiring plug doesn't just fall off - which is just as well - try driving without a brain if you don't believe us (or rather, don't). As the 10 mm bolt is undone, the plug should be pulled out of the socket. Ours was a bit stuck, but we didn't force it, for fairly obvious reasons.

05 A little gentle persuasion was all it needed. The ECU is now at your mercy. Treat it with some respec' once it's out (not dropping it on the floor is a good place to start, as is not 'having a go' yourself with a soldering iron). If you want it to work again, send it away for professional chippery.

Stainless caps and bottle covers

The cool mirror finish of stainless steel. It's one of those timeless classic looks, especially under the bonnet - it's never going out of style, and it'll never look out of place.

If it's a look you fancy, don't muck about with paint - it'll never look a patch on the real deal. Instead, talk to Mirage Stainless, for a top-quality, easily-fitted and good-value solution to all your stainless desires.

01 An obvious first choice, your oil filler cap - we were even supplied a strip of double-sided tape to help it stay on. Mind you, all the caps we had were an excellent tight fit, so tape isn't really necessary. But it's a nice touch. If you use the sticky stuff, clean the original cap first - tape and oily fingerprints don't mix.

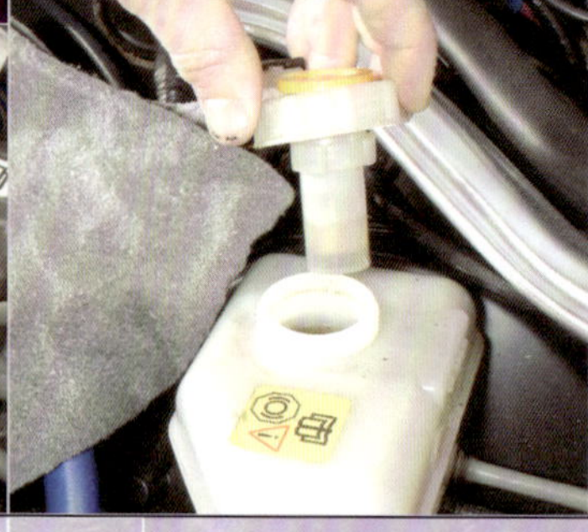

02 The stainless look doesn't stop with just caps - there's bottle and reservoir covers to drool over too. If you're thinking of tarting-up the brake fluid reservoir, take care when you unscrew the top - let the fluid drip into the reservoir, not on the paintwork. Have a cloth ready to sit the cap and float assembly on, while you give it the stainless treatment.

03 Another nicely-made item goes on over the reservoir body . . .

04 . . . and combined with the cap cover, the end result is so saucy, we know you want it. If it's got a cap under the bonnet, chances are someone has it covered - we also fitted caps to the power steering reservoir and washer bottle.

05 Okay, why are we showing you the less-shiny side of the battery cover? Because this is the first one we've seen to offer a sensible rubber insert on the inside. And why is this important? Without a non-conductive insert, your new battery cover would short out the battery terminals. And that's a fire. Like we said, there's plenty of covers on sale out there without this feature...

06 Engine detailing is all about giving your mates a feast of things to look at, so don't stop at caps and covers. Not when there's a stainless bonnet support strut . . .

07 . . . and suspension strut top caps available to catch their eye. You will need an extra nut to fit these strut caps, and it's a fine thread, but sourcing a couple of nuts is no effort.

Engine tuning

So you've done the induction kit, exhaust and chip - what's next, short of going for a complete engine swap? A new camshaft's a juicy way to pep up a standard motor, and all the Escort engines respond well to one of these. One small problem if you've got a 1.3 engine and fancy a cam swap - the engine will have to come out first (and you're not telling me you'd actually put a 1.3 lump back IN again afterwards?). Mind you, gains of up to 30 bhp can be had from cam swaps on the 1.3 - how wicked is that?

Extracting more go from one of the CVH (later known as PTE) engines is a much easier task. Besides a cam swap being far easier to do, there's more to come from having the head gas-flowed, ported, skimmed (to increase compression) and bigger valves fitted. If you've got the an early CVH with a carb, dump the original carb and get a Weber 34 DMTR (or the Weber 32 DFT fitted to the Mk 2 XR2 up to 1985, and a popular mod for the 1986-on ones). Most carburettor specialists have now "moved on" to fuel injection and engine management, but the knowledge is still out there. Get busy with the Yellow Pages.

The Zetecs are limited by their engine management systems, so specialist help will soon be needed for more than a mild tweak. However, if you've got a 105 bhp XR3i, you could get 130 bhp power by swapping the injection system throttle body from 47 mm diameter to 52 mm, together with the matching ECU. Zetecs were also fitted to Mondeos, remember - could be a rich source of engine bits from scrapyards, and the Mondy went up to 2.0 litre as well. Hmmm...

Engine swaps are, of course, dead easy on any Ford, with plenty of second-hand lumps lying around in scrapyards. One rather obvious engine swap to consider is the old RS Turbo unit from the Mk 4. One of the most tune-able engines of all - 130 bhp standard, with 200 a fairly easy target.

And finally tonight - the bad news. Any major engine mods means telling those nice suits who work for your insurance company, and it's likely they'll insist on a full engineer's report (these aren't especially expensive - look one up in the Yellow Pages, under *Garage Services* or *Vehicle Inspection*).

Exhausts

It's gotta be done, hasn't it? Your rusty old exhaust lacks the girth to impress, and doesn't so much growl as miaow. Don't be a wimp and fit an exhaust trim - they'll fool nobody who really knows, and they certainly won't add to your aural pleasure (oo-er). Sort yourself out a decent back box upgrade, and even a timid 1.3 Escort can begin to cut it at the cruise.

What a back box won't do on its own is increase engine power - although it'll certainly sound like it has, provided you choose the right one, and fit it properly. Check when you're buying that it can be fitted to a standard system - you'll probably need something called a reducing sleeve for a decent fit, which is a section of pipe designed to bridge the difference between your small-diameter pipe and the larger-diameter silencer. Try and measure your standard pipe as accurately as possible, or you'll have major problems trying to get a decent seal between the old and new bits - don't assume that exhaust paste will sort everything out, because it won't.

Fashion has even entered the aftermarket exhaust scene, with different rear pipe designs going in and out of style. Everyone's done the upswept twin-pipe "DTM" style pipes, while currently the trend in single pipes is "the bigger the better", or fat oval (or twin-oval) designs. If you must have the phattest Escort on the block, you can't beat a twin-exit system, even though it'll probably mean

Know your enemy - this is what your cat looks like inside. Is it any wonder they restrict gas flow?

losing your spare wheel in the fitting process. Well, when was the last time you had a puncture? And what are mobiles and breakdown cover for, anyway?

If you've got a capacity-challenged Escort, you might need to lightly modify even your standard rear bodywork/bumper to accommodate a bigger rear pipe; if you're going for a bodykit later, your back box will have to come off again, so it can be poked through your rear valance/mesh.

You'll see some useful power gains if you go for the complete performance exhaust system, rather than just the back box. Like the factory-fit system, the sports silencer again will only work at its best if combined with the front pipe and manifold it was designed for! Performance four-branch manifolds alone can give very useful power gains. Watch what you buy, though - cheap exhaust manifolds which crack for a pastime are not unknown, and many aftermarket systems need careful fitting and fettling before you'll stop it resonating or banging away underneath. A sports rear box alone shouldn't attract an increased insurance premium, but a full system probably will.

Most Escorts worth having have a catalytic converter (or "cat"), which acts like a restrictor in the exhaust, inhibiting the gas flow and sapping some engine power (maybe 5 to 10%). Companies such as Janspeed market replacement sections which do away with the cat (a "de-cat pipe"), and get you your power back. You could easily have one made up, if you know someone handy with the welder - all you need is the two flanges and some half-decent pipe (from a scrapyard or motor factors). Unfortunately, by taking off or disabling the cat, your car won't be able to pass the emissions test at MOT time, so you'll have to "re-convert" the car every 12 months. This fact, arguably, means that the car is illegal on the road with a de-cat pipe fitted - you'd have no defence for this, if questions were asked at the roadside, and potentially no insurance if the unthinkable happens. Sorry, but we have to say it...

One other point to consider, if your Escort's been slammed to the floor - will your big new sports system be leaving behind a trail of sparks as it scrapes along the deck? Shouldn't do, if it's been properly fitted, but will the local multi-storey be out-of-bounds for your Escort, from now on? And - pub trivia moment - you can actually be done for causing damage to the highway, if your exhaust's dragging. Well, great.

You probably couldn't give a stuff if your loud system's a very loud major public nuisance, but will that loud pipe start interfering with your sound system? If you rack up many motorway miles, you might find the constant drone of a loud pipe gets to be a real pain on a long trip, too...

Fitting a **sports back box**

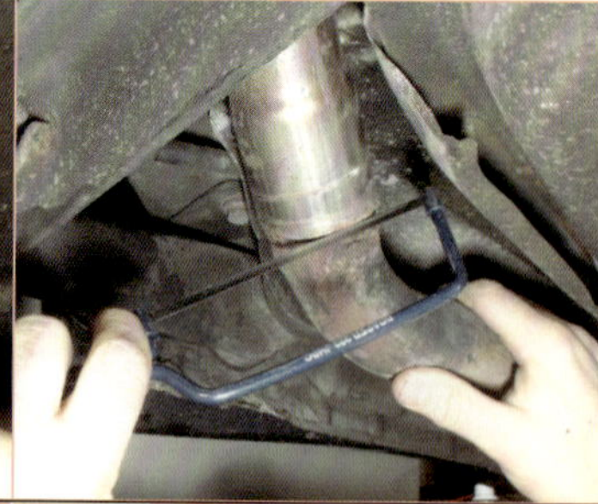

01 First we've got to survey the whole under-Escort situation. It helps to remove the nearside rear wheel for this, but it's not absolutely essential. Jack up the back end of the car - have a look in "Wheels & tyres" for more info on jacking up. Before we get undoing anything, the first job is to hold the new box up in place. Does it look like the right one for the job? Do the mounting points line up? How much swearing is going to be necessary?

02 Ah, the exhaust-fitter's friend. If you never need the likes of WD-40 on an exhaust job, you'll never need it.

03 So, we loosen the nuts on our exhaust clamp . . .

04 . . . and then we find some idiot's welded-on the exisiting backbox, so it's time for a spot of swearing. And hacksawing. A Dremel might make easier work of this - you certainly won't be getting a grinder in there. Working a stubborn (un-welded) joint apart usually entails trying to twist one section against the other (and more bad language).

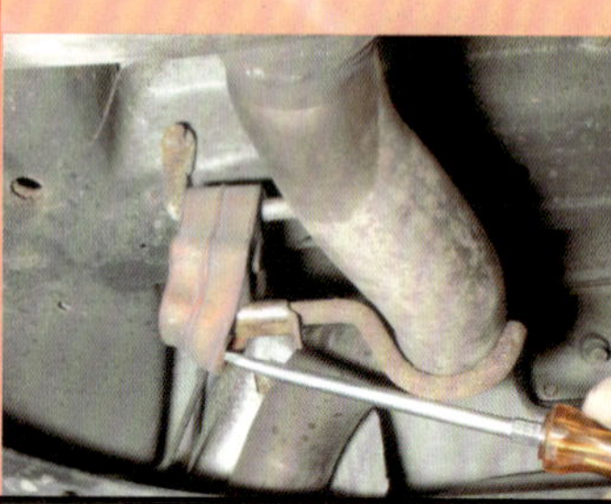

05 Even with the exhaust joint separated, your problems aren't entirely over - the exhaust mounting rubbers might take some persuading off, too.

06 At last - away with the rusty old metal, and in with the new - in this case, a splendid Peco Big Bore 4. Things are definitely looking up.

07 Clean up the rusty old mid-section of pipe you'll be fitting to, and treat it to a good coating of exhaust assembly paste, to get a gas-tight joint. There's loud, and then there's unnecessarily loud.

08 It's best to use a new exhaust clamp, but we have to admit we didn't have one the right size in stock. Tighten the clamp nuts evenly and firmly to seal in the nasties. Now stand back to admire the effect. Nice. You might want, or need, to modify the rear bumper slightly, to avoid melting plastic. Or to emphasise the phatness of your new pipe.

De-cat pipe

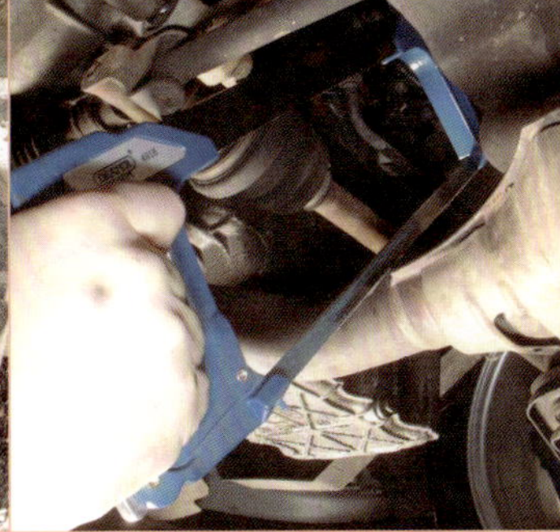

01 Don't even attempt this if the engine's still warm, 'cos the cat will be warmer still - like red-hot, if the car's been any distance. You have been warned. The first task here is to get the car in the air - jacking it up at the front is enough (see "Wheels & tyres" for jacking info). Offer the de-cat pipe up to the existing cat, and eye the pipe up for size. Looks good so far.

02 Out with the good old "magic spray" again, as these mounting flange nuts look well-rusty. Stripped or rounded-off nuts we can do without.

03 Leave the spray to soak in, and go to the front of the cat. We have to cut through here - do it as close to the cat body as you can, as this will leave you the maximum pipe at the front to join onto.

04 Now undo the flange bolts . . .

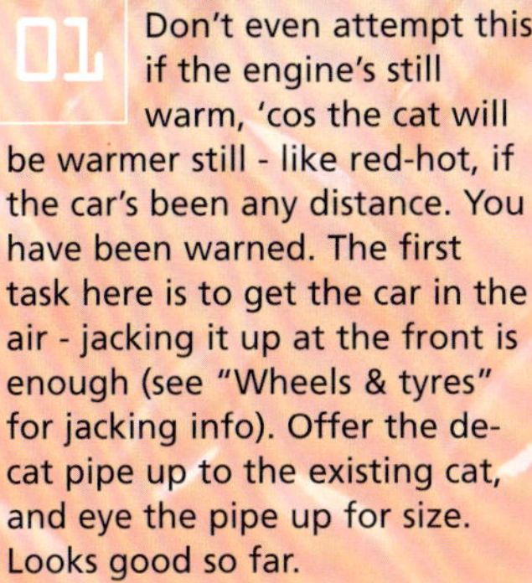

06 . . . and take that cat away for good - there's no going back now, so you'll have to resign yourself to being totally illegal from now on. Bad boy.

07 You wouldn't normally use exhaust paste on the joint in front of a cat, but - there is no cat now, so why not? Slip the new de-cat section on, and secure with an exhaust clamp.

07 At the rear flange, Janspeed thoughtfully provide a gasket . . .

08 . . . and it pays to fit new nuts, in place of those suspect-looking rusty old items you removed earlier. Don't be a skanker - get some shiny new nuts, or you'll never undo them a second time. And there it is - one de-catted Escort, with (in theory) a measurable and feel-able gain in horses. Strictly-speaking, completely and utterly illegal to use on the road, as it won't pass an MOT in this condition. But you don't want to hear that. Just remember we told you, that's all.

14

Reference

Safety and tools

Safety

We all know that working on your car can be dangerous - and we're not talking about the danger of losing your street cred by fitting naff alloys or furry dice! Okay, so you'd be hard-pushed to injure yourself fitting some cool floor mats or a tax disc holder, but tackle more-serious mods, and you could be treading dangerous ground. Let's be honest - we have to put this safety section in to cover ourselves, but now it's in, it would be nice if you read it...

Burning/scalding

The only way you'll really burn yourself is if your car's just been running - avoid this, and you won't get burned. Easy, eh? Otherwise, you risk burns from any hot parts of the engine (and especially the exhaust - if you've got one, the cat runs very hot), or from spilling hot coolant if you undo the radiator hoses or filler cap, as you might when you're braiding hoses.

Fire

Sadly, there's several ways your car could catch fire, when you think about it. You've got a big tank full of fuel (and other flammable liquids about, like brake fluid), together with electrics - some of which run to very high voltages. If you smoke too, this could be even worse for your health than you thought.

a Liquid fuel is flammable. Fuel vapour can explode - don't smoke, or create any kind of spark, if there's fuel vapour (fuel smell) about.

b Letting fuel spill onto a hot engine is dangerous, but brake fluid spills go up even more readily. Respect is due with brake fluid, which also attacks paintwork and plastics - wash off with water.

c Fires can also be started by careless modding involving the electrical system. It's possible to overload (and overheat) existing wiring by tapping off too many times for new live feeds. Not insulating bare wires or connections can lead to short-circuits, and the sparks or overheated wiring which results can start a fire. Always investigate any newly-wired-in kit which stops working, or which keeps blowing fuses - those wires could already be smouldering...

Crushing

Having your car land on top of you is no laughing matter, and it's a nasty accident waiting to happen if you risk using dodgy old jacks, bricks, and other means of lifting/supporting your car. Please don't.

Your standard vehicle jack is for emergency roadside use only - a proper trolley jack and a set of axle stands won't break the overdraft, and might save broken bones. Don't buy a cheap trolley jack, and don't expect a well-used secondhand one to be perfect, either - when the hydraulic seals start to fail, a trolley jack will drop very fast; this is why you should always have decent stands in place under the car as well.

Steering, suspension & brakes

Screwing up any one of these on your car, through badly-fitted mods, could land you and others in hospital or worse. Nuff said? It's always worth getting a mate, or a friendly garage, to check over what you've just fitted (or even what you've just had fitted, in some cases - not all "pro" fitters are perfect!). Pay attention to tightening vital nuts and bolts properly - buy or borrow a torque wrench.

To be absolutely sure, take your newly-modded machine to a friendly MOT tester (if there is such a thing) - this man's your ultimate authority on safety, after all. Even if he's normally a pain once a year, he could save your life. Think it over.

Even properly-fitted mods can radically alter the car's handling - and not always for the better. Take a few days getting used to how the car feels before showing off.

Wheels

Don't take liberties fitting wheels. Make sure the wheels have the right stud/bolt hole pattern for your car, and that the wheel nuts/bolts are doing their job. Bolts which are too long might catch on your brakes (especially rear drums) - too short, and, well, the wheels are just waiting to fall off. Not nice. Also pay attention to the bolt heads or wheel nuts - some are supposed to have large tapered washers fitted, to locate properly in the wheel. If the nuts/bolts "pull through" the wheel when tightened, the wheel's gonna fall off, isn't it?

Asbestos

Only likely to be a major worry when working on, or near, your brakes. That black dust that gets all over your alloys comes from your brake pads, and it may contain asbestos. Breathing in asbestos dust can lead to a disease called asbestosis (inflammation of the lungs - very nasty indeed), so try not to inhale brake dust when you're changing your pads or discs.

Airbags

Unless you run into something at high speed, the only time an airbag will enter your life is when you change your steering wheel for something more sexy, and have to disable the airbag in the process. Pay attention to all the precautionary advice given in our text, and you'll have no problems.

One more thing - don't tap into the airbag wiring to run any extra electrical kit. Any mods to the airbag circuit could set it off unexpectedly.

Exhaust gases

Even on cars with cats, exhaust fumes are still potentially lethal. Don't work in an unventilated garage with the engine running. When fitting new exhaust bits, be sure that there's no gas leakage from the joints. When modifying in the tailgate area, note that exhaust gas can get sucked into the car through badly-fitting tailgate seals/joints (or even through your rear arches, if they've been trimmed so much there's holes into the car).

Tools

In writing this book, we've assumed you already have a selection of basic tools - screwdrivers, socket set, spanners, hammer, sharp knife, power drill. Any unusual extra tools you might need are mentioned in the relevant text. Torx and Allen screws are often found on trim panels, so a set of keys of each type is a wise purchase.

From a safety angle, always buy the best tools you can afford - or if you must use cheap ones, remember that they can break under stress or unusual usage (and we've all got the busted screwdrivers to prove it!).

DO Wear goggles when using power tools.

DO Keep loose clothing/long hair away from moving engine parts.

DO Take off watches and jewellery when working on electrics.

DO Keep the work area tidy - stops accidents and losing parts.

DON'T Rush a job, or take stupid short-cuts.

DON'T Use the wrong tools for the job, or ones which don't fit.

DON'T Let kids or pets play around your car when you're working.

DON'T Work entirely alone under a car that's been jacked up.

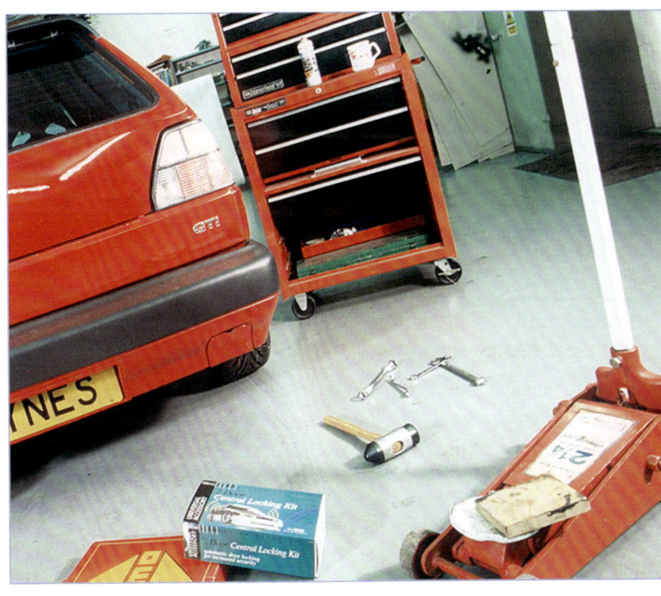

Legal modding? No such thing!!

The harsh & painful truth

The minute you start down the road to a modified motor, you stand a good chance of being in trouble with the Man. It seems like there's almost nothing worthwhile you can do to your car, without breaking some sort of law. So the answer's not to do it at all, then? Well, no, but let's keep it real.

There's this bunch of vehicle-related regulations called Construction & Use. It's a huge set of books, used by the car manufacturers and the Department of Transport among others, and it sets out in black and white all the legal issues that could land you in trouble. It's the ultimate authority for modifying, in theory. But few people (and even fewer policemen) know all of it inside-out, and it's forever being updated and revised, so it's not often enforced to the letter at the roadside - just in court. Despite the existence of C & U, in trying to put together any guide to the law and modifying, it quickly becomes clear that almost everything's a "grey area", with no-one prepared to go on record and say what is okay to modify and what's not. Well, brilliant. So if there's no fixed rules (in the real world), how are you meant to live by them? In the circumstances, all we can promise to do is help to make sense of nonsense...

Avoiding roadside interviews

Why do some people get pulled all the time, and others hardly ever? It's often all about attitude. We'd all like to be free to drive around "in yer face", windows down, system full up, loud exhaust bellowing, sparks striking, tyres squealing - but - nothing is a bigger "come-on" to the boys in blue than "irresponsible" driving like this. Rest assured, if your motor's anywhere near fully sorted, the coppers will find something they can nick you for, when they pull you over - it's a dead cert. Trying not to wind them up too much before this happens (and certainly not once you're stopped) will make for an easier life. There's showing off, and then there's taking the pee. Save it for the next cruise.

The worst thing from your point of view is that, once you've been stopped, it's down to that particular copper's judgement as to whether your car's illegal. If he/she's having a bad day anyway, smart-mouthing-off isn't gonna help your case at all. If you can persuade him/her that you're at least taking on board what's being said, you might be let off with a warning. If it goes further, you'll be reported for an offence - while this doesn't mean you'll end up being prosecuted for it, it ain't good. Some defects (like worn tyres) will result in a so-called "seven-day wonder", which usually means you have to fix whatever's deemed wrong, maybe get the car inspected, and present yourself with the proof at a police station, inside seven days, or face prosecution.

If you can manage to drive reasonably sensibly when the law's about, and can ideally show that you've tried to keep your car legal when you get questioned, you stand a much better chance of enjoying your relationship with your modded beast. This guide is intended to help you steer clear of the more obvious things you could get pulled for. By reading it, you might even be able to have an informed, well-mannered discussion about things legal with the next officer of the law you meet at the side of the road. As in: "Oh really, officer? I was not aware of that. Thank you for pointing it out." Just don't argue with them, that's all...

Documents

The first thing you'll be asked to produce. If you're driving around without tax, MOT or insurance, we might as well stop now, as you won't be doing much more driving of anything after just one pull.

Okay, so you don't normally carry all your car-related documents with you - for safety, you've got them stashed carefully at home, haven't you? But carrying photocopies of your licence, MOT and insurance certificate is a good idea. While they're not legally-binding absolute proof, producing these in a roadside check might mean you don't have to produce the real things at a copshop later in the week. Shows a certain responsibility, and confidence in your own legality on the road, too. In some parts of the country, it's even said to be a good idea to carry copies of any receipts for your stereo gear - if there's any suspicion about it being stolen (surely not), some coppers have been known to confiscate it (or the car it's in) on the spot!

Number plates

One of the simplest mods, and one of the easiest to spot (and prove) if you're a copper. Nowadays, any changes made to the standard approved character font (such as italics or fancy type), spacing, or size of the plate constitutes an offence. Remember too that if you've moved the rear plate from its original spot (like from the tailgate recess, during smoothing) it still has to be properly lit at night. You're unlikely to even buy an illegal plate now, as the companies making them are also liable for prosecution if you get stopped. It's all just something else to blame on speed cameras - plates have to be easy for them to shoot, and modding yours suggests you're trying to escape a speeding conviction (well, who isn't?).

Getting pulled for an illegal plate is for suckers - you're making it too easy for them. While this offence only entails a small fine and confiscation of the plates, you're drawing unwelcome police attention to the rest of your car. Not smart. At all.

Sunstrips and tints

The sunstrip is now an essential item for any modded motor, but telling Mr Plod you had to fit one is no defence if you've gone a bit too far. The sunstrip should not be so low down the screen that it interferes with your ability to see out. Is this obvious? Apparently not. As a guide, if the strip's so low your wiper(s) touch it, it's too low. Don't try fitting short wiper blades to get round this - the police aren't as stupid as that, and you could get done for wipers that don't clear a sufficient area of the screen. Push it so far, and no further!

Window tinting is a trickier area. It seems you can have up to a 25% tint on a windscreen, and up to 30% on all other glass - but how do you measure this? Er. And what do you do if your glass is tinted to start with? Er, probably nothing. Of course you can buy window film in various "darknesses", from not-very-dark to "ambulance-black", but being able to buy it does not make it legal for road use (most companies cover themselves by saying "for show use only"). Go for just a light smoke on the side and rear glass, and you'd have to be unlucky to get done for it. If you must fit really dark tints, you're safest doing the rear side windows only.

Some forces now have a light meter to test light transmission through glass at the roadside - fail this, and it's a big on-the-spot fine.

Single wiper conversion

Not usually a problem, and certainly not worth a pull on its own, but combine a big sunstrip with a short wiper blade, and you're just asking for trouble. Insufficient view of the road ahead. There's also the question of whether it's legal to have the arm parking vertically, in the centre of the screen, as it obscures your vision. Probably not legal, then - even if it looks cool. Unfortunately, the Man doesn't do cool.

Lights

Lights of all kinds have to be one of the single biggest problem areas in modifying, and the police are depressingly well-informed. Most people make light mods a priority, whether it's Morette conversions for headlights or Lexus-style rear clusters. If they fit alright, and work, what's the problem?

First off, don't bother with any lights which aren't fully UK-legal - it's just too much hassle. Being "E-marked" only makes them legal in Europe, and most of our Euro-chums drive on the right. One of our project cars ended up with left-hand-drive rear clusters, and as a result, had no rear reflectors and a rear foglight on the wrong side (should be on the right). Getting stopped for not having rear reflectors would be a bit harsh, but why risk it, even to save a few quid?

Once you've had any headlight mods done (other than light brows) always have the beam alignment checked - it's part of the MOT, after all. The same applies to any front fogs or spots you've fitted (the various points of law involved here are too many to mention - light colour, height, spacing, operation with main/dipped headlights - ask at an MOT centre before fitting, and have them checked out after fitting).

If Plod's really having a bad day, he might even question the legality of your new blue headlight bulbs - are they too powerful? Keeping the bulb packaging in the glovebox might be a neat solution here (60/55W max).

Many modders favour spraying rear light clusters to make them look trick, as opposed to replacing them - but there's trouble in store here, too. One of the greyest of grey areas is - how much light tinting is too much? The much-talked-about but not-often-seen "common sense" comes into play here. Making your lights so dim that they're reduced to a feeble red/orange glow is pretty dim itself. If you're spraying, only use proper light-tinting spray, and not too many coats of that. Colour-coding lights with ordinary spray paint is best left to a pro sprayer or bodyshop (it can be done by mixing lots of lacquer with not much paint, for instance). Tinted lights are actually more of a problem in daylight than at night, so check yours while the sun's out.

Lastly, two words about neons. Oh, dear. It seems that neons of all kinds have now been deemed illegal for road use (and that's

interior ones as well as exteriors, which have pretty much always been a no-no). If you fit neons inside, make sure you rig in a switch so you can easily turn them off when the law arrives - or don't drive around with them on (save it for when you're parked up). Distracts other road users, apparently.

ICE

Jungle massive, or massive public nuisance? The two sides of the ICE argument in a nutshell. If you've been around the modding scene for any length of time, you'll already know stories of people who've been done for playing car stereos too loud. Seems some local authorities now have by-laws concerning "music audible from outside a vehicle", and hefty fines if you're caught. Even where this isn't the case, and assuming a dB meter isn't on hand to prove the offence of "excessive noise", the police can still prosecute for "disturbing the peace" - on the basis of one officer's judgement of the noise level. If a case is proved, you could lose your gear. Whoops. Seems we're back to "do it - but don't over-do it" again. If you really want to demo your system, pick somewhere a bit less public (like a quiet trading estate, after dark) or go for safety in numbers (at a cruise).

Big alloys/tyres

One of the first things to go on any lad's car, sexy alloys are right at the heart of car modifying. So what'll interest the law?

Well, the first thing every copper's going to wonder is - are the wheels nicked? He'd need a good reason to accuse you, but this is another instance where having copies of receipts might prove useful.

Otherwise, the wheels mustn't rub on, or stick out from, the arches - either of these will prove to be a problem if you get stopped. And you don't need to drive a modded motor to get done for having bald tyres...

Lowered suspension

Of course you have to lower your car, to have any hope of street cred. But did you know it's actually an offence to cause damage to the road surface, if your car's so low (or your mates so lardy) that it grounds out? Apparently so! Never mind what damage it might be doing to your exhaust, or the brake/fuel lines under the car - you can actually get done for risking damage to the road. Well, great. What's the answer? Once you've lowered the car, load it up with your biggest mates, and test it over roads you normally use - or else find a route into town that avoids all speed bumps. If you've got coilovers, you'll have an easier time tuning out the scraping noises.

Remember that your new big-bore exhaust or backbox must be hung up well enough that it doesn't hit the deck, even if you haven't absolutely slammed your car on the floor. At night, leaving a trail of sparks behind is a bit of a giveaway...

Exhausts

One of the easiest-to-fit performance upgrades, and another essential item if you want to be taken seriously on the street. Unless your chosen pipe/system is just too damn loud, you'd be very unlucky to get stopped for it, but if you will draw attention this way, you could be kicking yourself later.

For instance - have you in fact fitted a home-made straight-through pipe, to a car which used to have a "cat"? By drawing Plod's attention with that extra-loud system, he could then ask you to get the car's emissions tested - worse, you could get pulled for a "random" roadside emissions check. Fail this (and you surely will), and you could be right in the brown stuff. Even if you re-convert the car back to stock for the MOT, you'll be illegal on the road (and therefore without insurance) whenever your loud pipe's on. Still sound like fun, or would you be happier with just a back box?

It's also worth mentioning that your tailpipe mustn't stick out beyond the very back of the car, or in any other way which might be dangerous to pedestrians. Come on - you were a ped once!

Bodykits

The popular bodykits for the UK market have all passed the relevant tests, and are fully-approved for use on the specific vehicles they're intended for. As long as you haven't messed up fitting a standard kit, you should be fine, legally-speaking. The trouble starts when you do your own little mods and tweaks, such as bodging on that huge whale-tail spoiler or front air dam/splitter - it can be argued in some cases that these aren't appropriate on safety grounds, and you can get prosecuted. If any bodywork is fitted so it obscured your lights, or so badly attached that a strong breeze might blow it off, you can see their point. At least there's no such thing as Style Police. Not yet, anyway.

Seats and harnesses

Have to meet the UK safety standards, and must be securely bolted in. That's about it. It should be possible to fasten and release any seat belt or harness with one hand. Given that seat belts are pretty important safety features, it's understandable then that the police don't like to see flimsy alloy rear strut braces used as seat harness mounting points. Any other signs of bodging will also spell trouble. It's unlikely they'd bother with a full safety inspection at the roadside, but they could insist on a full MOT test/engineer's report inside 7 days. It's your life.

While we're on the subject of crash safety, the police also don't like to see sub boxes and amps just lying on the carpet, where the back seat used to be - if it's not anchored down, where are these items gonna end up, in a big shunt? Embedded in you, possibly?

Other mods

We'll never cover everything else here, and the law's always changing anyway, so we're fighting a losing battle in a book like this, but here goes with some other legalistic points we've noted on the way:

a It's illegal to remove side repeaters from front wings, unless they're "replaced" with Merc-style side repeater mirrors. Nice.

b All except the most prehistoric cars must have at least one rear foglight. If there's only one, it must be fitted on the right. We've never heard of anyone getting stopped for it, but you must also have a pair of rear reflectors. If your rear clusters ain't got 'em, can you get trendy ones? Er, no.

c Fuel filler caps have to be fitted so there's no danger of fuel spillage, or of excess fumes leaking from the top of the filler neck. This means using an appropriate petrol-resistant sealer (should be supplied in the kit). Oh, and not bodging the job in general seems a good idea. Unlikely to attract a pull, though.

d Front doors have to retain a manual means of opening from outside, even if they've been de-locked for remote locking. This means you can't take off the front door handles, usually. It seems that rear door handles can be removed if you like.

e Tailgates have to have some means of opening, even if it's only from inside, once the lock/handle's been removed. We think it's another safety thing - means of escape in a crash, and all that.

f You have to have at least one exterior mirror, and it must be capable of being adjusted somehow.

g If you fit new fog and spotlights, they actually have to work. No-one fits new lights just for show (or do they?), but if they stop working later when a fuse blows, relay packs up, or the wiring connectors rust up, you'd better fix 'em or remove 'em.

h Pedal extensions must have rubbers fitted on the brake and clutch pedals, and must be spaced sufficiently so there's no chance of hitting two pedals at once. This last bit sounds obvious, but lots of extension sets out there are so hard to fit that achieving this can be rather difficult. Don't get caught out.

i On cars with airbags, if you fit a sports wheel and disconnect the airbag in the process, the airbag warning light will be on permanently. Apart from being annoying, this is also illegal.

j Pace-car strobe lights (or any other flashing lights, apart from indicators) are illegal for road use. Of course.

k Anything else we didn't think of - is probably illegal too. Sorry.

Any questions? Try the MOT Helpline (0845 6005977). Yes, really.

Thanks to Andrew Dare of the Vehicle Inspectorate, Exeter, for his help in steering us through this minefield!

Thanks to:

We gratefully acknowledge all the help and advice offered from the following suppliers, without whom, etc, etc. Many of those credited below went way beyond the call of duty to help us produce this book - you know who you are. Cheers, guys! Roll the credits...

ABC Design Autostyling Ltd (AutoArt & MHW)
www.abcdesignltd.com

Avo UK Ltd
(coil overs)
01604 708101
www.avouk.com

Brown & Geeson
(Momo)
01268 764411
www.brownandgeeson.com

Compomotive Wheels
01902 311499
www.comp.co.uk

Cooper Avon Tyres
01225 703101
www.coopertire.com

Corbeau Seats
01424 854499
www.corbeau-seats.co.uk

Dash Dynamics (dash kit)
0870 127 0003
www.dashdynamics.co.uk

Demon Tweeks
(accessories)
www.demon-tweeks.co.uk

ESP Design Ltd
0870 751 8000
www.espdesign.co.uk

Eurostyling (Folia Tec)
0870 162 4448
www.eurostyling.com

Halfords
www.halfords.com

Holden Engineering
(internal fuel tank)
01935 410615

Janspeed (de-cat pipe)
01722 321833
www.janspeed.com

K & N Filters
(induction kits)
01925 636950
www.knfilters.co.uk

Microscan Alarms
www.microscanalarms.co.uk

Mirage Stainless Styling
(engine styling)
01469 540427
www.miragestainless
styling.co.uk

A & I Peco
(exhaust box)
0151 647 6041
www.peco.co.uk

Quad Conversions
(afterburner rear lights)
01132 504527
www.quadconversions.com

Raid (accessories)
www/raid-rdi.com

Red Dot Racing
(brake discs & pads)
0870 300 2354
www.reddotracing.co.uk

Richbrook
(sport auto accessories)
01328 862 387
www.richbrook.co.uk

Ripspeed at Halfords
www.halfords.com

Safety Devices
(cage & fire extinguisher)
01638 560524
www.safetydevices.co.uk

A special thank you to:
Jon Hill (cover shots)
Bryn Musselwhite

Editorial Director	Matthew Minter
Designer	Simon Larkin
Page Build	James Robertson
Workshop	Paul Buckland Pete Trott
Editor	Ian Barnes
Project Co-ordinator	Carole Turk
Production Control	Charles Seaton

FREE AS THE WIND!

What's the best thing you can do on a hot summer's day? Get out on the open road in a sports car of course. Just a dream? Not any more!

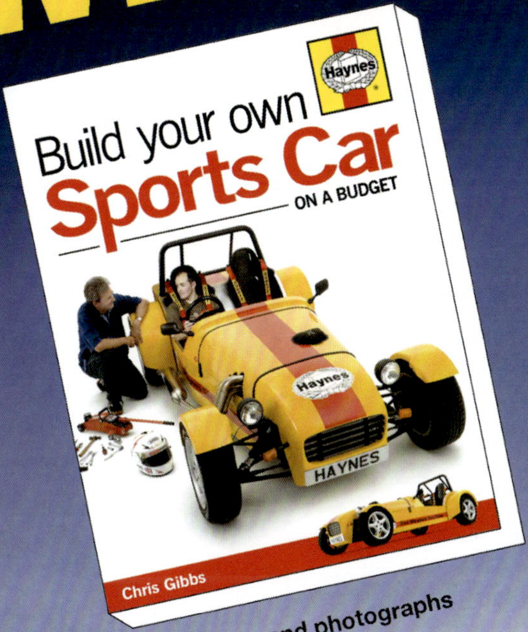

Build your own Sports Car ON A BUDGET

Haynes

HAYNES

Chris Gibbs

Colour working drawings, detailed descriptions and photographs • Step-by-step instructions • How to source the power unit, transmission, steering, brakes and other parts from donor vehicles • How to make the body panels • Fully illustrated assembly instructions • How to get the finished car on the road • Scaled drawings for all components.

ISBN: 978 1 84425 391 3

£17.99 RRP

HAYNES

Haynes

Haynes Publishing Sparkford, Yeovil, Somerset BA22 7JJ, UK
Tel: +44 (0)1963 442030 • Fax: +44 (0)1963 440001
E-mail: sales@haynes.co.uk
Website: www.haynes.co.uk

Stratospheric!

What the papers say about this great new book!

"WOW! Those brilliant people at Haynes... have done the same for the Fender Stratocaster!... it's essential reading for Strat owners... it's fan-strating-tastic" *Guitar Buyer Magazine*

"WOW! The full works... all in full colour... tons of tips and profiles... step by step and easy to follow... another connection I like and trust is Haynes!" *Musical Opinion Magazine*

Haynes
Fender Stratocaster Manual
Foreword by Hank Marvin
How to buy, maintain and set up the world's most popular electric guitar
Paul Balmer

This easy-to-use manual offers advice on how to get the best from your Strat, be it a budget Chinese Squier or the best Custom Shop special. With step-by-step guidance and clear colour photographs, this book explains how to buy, maintain and set up the world's most popular electric guitar.

ISBN: 978 1 84425 321 X

£17.99 RRP

Haynes Publishing
Sparkford, Yeovil, Somerset BA22 7JJ, UK
Tel: **+44 (0)1963 442030**
Fax: **+44 (0)1963 440001**
E-mail: **sales@haynes.co.uk**
Website: **www.haynes.co.uk**